D1203600

# LONG-RANGE PLANNING
# FOR MANAGEMENT

# LONG-RANGE
# PLANNING
# FOR MANAGEMENT

**EDITED BY  DAVID W. EWING**

Assistant Editor, *Harvard Business Review*

H|B

HARPER & BROTHERS, PUBLISHERS, NEW YORK

LONG-RANGE PLANNING FOR MANAGEMENT

*Copyright © 1958 by David W. Ewing*
*Printed in the United States of America*

*Library of Congress catalog card number: 58–7979*

# CONTENTS

## III.  STEPS IN MAKING A PLAN

## IV.  SPECIAL PROBLEMS

# V.  LIMITATIONS

# VI.  STRATEGY

# PREFACE

Long-range planning for business concerns the efforts of company executives to plan the firm's major moves five or more years in advance. It concerns what the company will try to do, how, and when. It is a job primarily for top management.

The contributors to this book analyze a series of long-range planning problems, suggest ways of coping with them, and seek to stimulate fresh thinking about management's approach. The materials come from a variety of sources—professional journals, papers delivered at professional associations, company manuals, and sections of other books dealing with management policy-making. Inevitably, there is some overlapping in the chapter material. In organizing the various papers, I have grouped them according to their *emphasis* on general principles, organization, steps and techniques, special problems, planning limitations, and basic strategy.

Oilmen say that every new refinery is at least partly obsolete the day it opens because of the speed with which new refining processes are developed. Much the same applies to this "refinery" of materials on long-range planning. In a literary sense, the subject has just begun to bloom. New articles are appearing every month in business magazines, although up to 1956 editors had given only spotty coverage to the subject. Accordingly, the reader should bear in mind that this book is limited to materials which had been published or were scheduled for publication by June, 1957.

Space has, of course, been limited, and I have not been able to include a number of papers that deserve attention. This collection, the first of its kind, is designed only as a start. In the introduction to the various sections I have tried to highlight some of the significant ideas that follow and do a little "reading between the lines." This business of long-range planning is a fascinating one and has many implications for business, education, and the economy.

At the end of these brief introductions the reader will find brief biographical notes about each of the contributors. These notes should be of some interest, for the assumptions an author makes about planning are necessarily based on a limited experience.

I wish to thank Miss Joan E. Foster for doing much of the work of preparing this book for publication, and also Miss Elizabeth H. Knox. I am indebted to Professors H. Edward Wrapp and Edward C. Bursk of the Harvard Business School for their helpful suggestions on the manuscript. Last but not least, my thanks to a patient and forbearing wife who helped in many ways to get this book ready for the publisher.

The Editor

# LONG-RANGE PLANNING
# FOR MANAGEMENT

# I

## NATURE AND PRINCIPLES

Make no little plans; they have no magic to stir men's blood and probably themselves will not be realized. Make big plans: aim high in hope and work, remembering that a noble, logical diagram once recorded will never die, but long after we are gone will be a living thing, asserting itself with ever-growing insistency. Remember that our sons and grandsons are going to do things that would stagger us.
—Daniel H. Burnham

# 1.

# *Introduction*

• By taking an aggressive approach to long-range planning, top executives can contribute more effectively to a dynamic economy.

• Long-range planning is in the trial-and-error stage. Yet its values for management are clear. It suppresses or reduces hesitancy, false steps, and unwarranted changes of course. It is a powerful management device for making things happen that would not otherwise occur.

• To implement a five- or ten-year "master plan," a number of short- and long-term programs are necessary. These programs tend to be interdependent, with objectives in one becoming premises for the planning of another. Effective well-coordinated planning therefore requires exacting managerial skill.

• Long-range planning is likely to be a lengthy and laborious task when done for the first time. But with every year that planning is repeated, it becomes simpler, more useful, and more interesting to executives.

These are just a few of the conclusions about long-range planning reached by the authors in this section. They bring to their subject widely differing viewpoints. They write from different kinds of backgrounds. Yet one cannot read the next three chapters without sensing a common conviction that this is no ordinary business we are discussing. Long-range planning is an unusual task involving executives in jobs they never used to do. Instead of looking at the company and its market and saying, "Let's do the best we can," they now ask, "What *is* the best we can do? How shall we do it? When?"

Long-range planning will come to mean many things to many people. Some will find it visionary and impractical. Some who latch on to it will find they have a "bear by the tail." Others will make a

3

fad out of it. But it should become for most companies—and for the economy—one of the really significant business developments of the century.

The concept of long-term profits has far-reaching implications. It should put an end, once and for all, to the old but slow-dying idea of nineteenth-century economists that the corporation seeks only to maximize short-term profits. For the more top management thinks of its job as building a *permanent* organization—an institution for generations of managers yet to come—the more willing it will be to sacrifice short-term profits when they come into conflict with long-term objectives. Long-range planning should also add to the growing sense of responsibility to the public that is held by businessmen today. And it should give impetus to many other current trends, such as management training, product diversification, and willingness to work with the government and the military on a continuing basis.

The reader of this and later sections of the book may sense a number of contradictions in long-range planning. A demanding task, it comes at a time when most executives seem already overtaxed for time. A job that requires considerable reading and introspection, it is being promoted by extroverts who are continually on the run. More interesting and inconsistent still, it calls on the management team to use, at the same time and in combination, different viewpoints toward its work.

For instance, it means looking at the company in a more analytical way. It puts a premium on the *conceptual* skills of the manager, as opposed to technical and human relations skills. Looked at diagramatically, the long-range plans of many of the companies mentioned in the following chapters would appear as a vast cobweb of short-term and long-term relations between marketing, production, finance, industrial relations, and the other functions of management. All of these plans are built on certain premises and assumptions; and the individual plans in turn become premises and assumptions for one another (a point which Messrs. Koontz and O'Donnell discuss at length in Chapter 3).

In fact, some of the more advanced planners have found that they can use not only a pencil and paper but also a computer. It is significant that in the literature of long-range planning these days one can find references to such things as probability, game, and queueing theory, Boolian algebra, input-output analysis, linear programing, and three-dimensional production-planning scale models.

Now, at the same time that long-range planning calls for skills of such a high analytical order, it requires a different and sometimes conflicting kind of ability. It asks the executive to use his "sixth sense." It asks that he go "visionary" now and then. He needs to look into the future, take calculated risks, imagine possibilities.

We hear a lot these days about how long-range planning is being forced on business because of changed technology, longer lead times, the demand for stable employment, and so forth; but actually the basic *appeal* of planning to top executives—particularly because of the imaginative aspects just mentioned—may account even more importantly for its popularity. After all, the men who guide business destinies today are on the whole an adventurous lot. They are risk-takers. They love challenge. They blaze trails rather than follow them. They create wealth where there was nothing. They are the present-day descendants of the nineteenth-century "captains of industry," the great merchants of the Renaissance, and the famous traders of ancient Phoenicia. Is it any wonder that they are seizing on long-range planning? It is one of the most potent tools for expansion ever developed.

Planning involves other contradictions, too. For instance, readers of the following chapters may wonder if it will not reduce the independence of managers. With more attention focused on the interrelationships of decisions, will executives feel less freedom of action? Maybe so. But how can an ambitious plan be realized without giving room to the genius and individualism of managers down the line? Some of the plans mentioned in this book require that top management give division and department heads *more* responsibility.

Such contradictions may be troublesome at times both to the scholar and the businessman. But this is as it should be. Business itself is full of contradictions. So are businessmen and their customers. Indeed, if we are to make long-range planning a true, living part of the business scene, we will probably have to let it keep its inconsistencies. At least it will be more interesting!

## CONTRIBUTORS TO THIS SECTION

*Edmund P. Learned* is Professor of Business Administration at the Harvard Business School. In addition to a distinguished career in teaching and research, he served with the Army Air Forces in World War II as Chief of the Office of Program Control, and since 1945 he has been Special Consultant to the Chief of Staff, United States Air Force. He is the author of a number of leading books and articles on business policy, marketing, and administration.

*Harold Koontz* is Professor of Business Policy and Transportation and *Cyril O'Donnell* is Associate Professor of Business Organization and Policy, both at the School of Business Administration, University of California at Los Angeles. They draw upon a good deal of original research data as well as personal experience in management. They are coauthors of an excellent textbook, *Principles of Management* (New York, McGraw-Hill Book Company, Inc., 1955), which explores the problems of planning in great detail.

*Henri Fayol* was a famous French industralist who lived from 1841 to 1925. The story of how he took a mining and metallurgical concern that was collapsing and turned it into a large strong combine is regarded as one of the romances of French industrial history. His book, *General and Industrial Management* (London, Sir Isaac Pitman & Sons, Ltd., 1949), has come to be something of a business classic.

# 2

# Emphasis Is on Long-Range Plan

## BY EDMUND P. LEARNED [1]

Long-range planning is a new dimension in our economy, according to Ralph J. Cordiner, president of the General Electric Company. In a talk to the Economic Club of New York last March, he said:

The prime requisite of management is vision. The hallmark of wisdom is the ability to foresee with at least some clarity and confidence the needs of tomorrow and beyond tomorrow. If we are to achieve in fact a glorious economic future, our leaders in business must free themselves of this year's plans and programs and look at least ten years ahead. The mounting problems and opportunities are making even a decade a short space of time for planning. More and more we should be planning fifteen or twenty years ahead—an entire business generation.

These are challenging, important, indeed prophetic words. The buoyant tone of this whole address leaves the impression that if businessmen will take an aggressive approach to long-range planning they can contribute more effectively to a dynamic economy. Skeptics, however, may be justified in suggesting that these words are merely the latest fad or fashion in business. Unless they are given form and substance in deeds, they will be meaningless.

### CONDITIONS

A number of conditions are stimulating the development of long-range planning. First, the population of the United States is growing at a more rapid rate than previously forecast. The social security system has had some effect on the spending habits of the people. In-

---

[1] *The Harbus News*, December 21, 1956. Reprinted by permission.

7

creases in real wages of former lower income groups, new concepts of living, decentralization of cities and factories, large highway and defense expenditures—all contribute to the need for reassessment of long-term plans. Hardheaded men of great vision, fully aware of the time aspects of their judgments, foresee possibilities for rebuilding some cities. The ever-increasing fruits of past research and development and the pronounced increase in the level of such expenditures affect not only near-term but longer-term plans.

Outside the United States there are increasing industrialization and commercial development in Canada, Mexico, and many South American countries. The forces at work in Asia and Africa may have real bearing on the long-range future of American business. A wise planner in many businesses must take account of developments in Europe, of their ideas capable of application here, of markets for products there, and of European suppliers as competitors for the American market.

There seems to be an acute shortage of certain skilled types of man power in the United States, and many seasoned observers believe that there is a prospective shortage of labor to produce the goods and services required by the expanding population. This is one of the reasons for increasing productivity per worker. Automation receives a part of its stimulus from this source.

Some industries find it easier to plan than others. For example, the electrical utility, oil, and telephone industries have experienced a relatively steady growth for many years and can foresee substantial continued growth. The aluminum industry has had phenomenal growth and is still planning for more.

## PROBLEMS

Even though all these industries appear to be in a long-time race, to have supply facilities equal to potential demand for specific products, they have major problems with respect to the timing of expenditures and the technical characteristics of future products, plants, and processes. The oil industry can hardly be independent of the automobile industry technology, and the electrical and oil industries must be aware of potential developments in atomic power. Long-range planning problems in these industries are also complicated by the degree of integration and by the size of various firms.

The chemical and electronic industries are faced with rapid change in their technology, and some say long-range planning is not possible. Instead, emphasis must be given to ability to adjust quickly to new developments. Others contend that while such near-term planning should be accomplished, it should be accompanied by longer-range planning, especially of research and development activities.

In many industries there is a long lag between the beginning of research and development and the perfection of a commercial product, as long as fifteen to twenty years and quite commonly seven to ten. World War II and later defense expenditures have clearly speeded up developments in many fields, but in defense industries long "lead times" are involved. Some executives feel that the shape of the next five to ten years is more or less fixed technologically, and what is of major concern to them is the next ten to twenty-five years. Answers to these questions may be important for decisions on capital investments. In addition, they may affect the form of organization and quality of individual people that should be developed to handle the jobs in sight. The rate of change is significant because it has much to do with the degree of risk incurred and the length of time in which a firm may turn around. Foresight on these matters often contributes to competitive advantage.

## SIZE

The long-time factors and the heavy investments in research and development are likely to favor corporations over individual enterprisers and large firms over small ones. But it is also well established that new ideas come from almost any source and that the small firm, if it concentrates its effort and spends its funds with special care, may have some chance to contribute to long-range developments. Firms of this size may call upon the new research institutes and development laboratories which have been expanding in the last ten years. Even large firms find these organizations of help. They have a wide range of scientists, engineers, market specialists, and economists on their staffs and use research skills, scientific techniques, and specialized physical facilities for studying both long- and short-range problems. The teaming up of experts is one of their strong assets.

Many companies are giving more emphasis to long-range planning inside their organizations. When top management farms out the job to the operators, whether functional or divisional, there is the danger that today's work will be considered more important than tomorrow's. Some companies have set up long-range planning departments; some designate one officer on a full-time basis to take charge of long-range planning. He is likely to have a small staff to support him and he may work through committees and the assignment of specific tasks on a time schedule to operating departments. Others set up special *ad hoc* committees or task forces to deal with specific problems.

The only safe conclusion about the present status of affairs is that firms that see the potential value of longer-range planning are in the trial-and-error stage. They are much concerned about more successful ways of accomplishing results. My own judgment is that the minimum safe policy for any firm involves assigning the responsibility for long-range planning to one ranking officer who has sufficient dedication to lead others to see that their future and the firm's well-being involve a careful, specific appraisal of what this company can do, who should participate, and when and how. Such men will avoid completely separating long-range planning from operation but will also find ways to organize so that the firm gets its planning job done.

# 3.

# *The Nature and Purpose of Planning*

## By Harold Koontz and Cyril O'Donnell [1]

Planning is one of the functions of the manager and, as such, involves the selection, from among alternatives, of enterprise objectives, policies, procedures, and programs. It is thus decision-making affecting the future course of an enterprise.

It is sometimes said that planning is the primary managerial function which logically precedes all other functions, since, without planning, a manager would not have activities to organize, would not require a staff, would have no one to direct, and would have no need to control. However, the managerial job is actually one in which all the managerial functions take place simultaneously rather than serially.

While no manager can successfully accomplish his task unless he does all the functions well, it is nonetheless true that control is peculiarly dependent upon planning. Since control is the function of making sure that events conform to plans, no manager can control who has not planned. No one can ascertain whether he is on the correct path unless he has determined where he wishes to go. . . .

### The Concept of Planning

Planning is, as Billy E. Goetz has so effectively said, "fundamentally choosing," and "a planning problem arises when an alternative course of action is discovered." [2] If there were no alternatives in objective,

[1] By permission from *Principles of Management* by Harold Koontz and Cyril O'Donnell. Copyright, 1955, McGraw-Hill Book Company, Inc.

[2] Billy E. Goetz, *Management Planning and Control* (New York, McGraw-Hill Book Company, Inc., 1949), p. 2.

policy, program, or procedure, planning would be so inflexible as hardly to exist. However, in practice there are probably few, if any, business problems for which some kind of alternative does not exist. Even in insolvent companies, which may seem to be doomed to bankruptcy, alternative courses of action are often still open. And should a company be forced into bankruptcy, there are usually legal alternatives available for accomplishing this unpleasant operation and, after bankruptcy, many alternatives for handling the bankrupt estate.

Planning is to a large extent the job of making things happen that would not otherwise occur. While seldom can the exact future of an enterprise be *made* to happen and while factors external to the firm or otherwise beyond its control may interfere with the actual operation of the best-laid plans, events, without planning, would be necessarily left to chance. Planning is thus an intellectual process, the conscious determination of courses of action, the basing of decision on purpose, facts, and considered estimates.

The pervasiveness of the planning function is not often fully appreciated. One often finds a tendency among middle and lower managers to regard planning as the exclusive activity of top managers. While it is true that more preoccupation with planning is found at higher levels, largely because the area of decision making is larger, it is nonetheless a fact that any person who manages has a planning function. Even the foreman of a road gang or a factory crew, operating under fairly strict orders and procedures, plans. It is practically impossible so to encircle any delegation of authority that no area of choice remains. Within this area of choice of each manager lies *his* area of planning. As a matter of fact, it is interesting that in some of the studies of work satisfactions that have been made, one of the principal factors accounting for the success of foremen at the lowest level has been their ability to plan.[3]

## The Nature and Variety of Plans

In order to appreciate the nature of plans and understand their variety in typical enterprise, one should note the major kinds of plans.

[3] D. Katz, *et al.*, *Productivity, Supervision and Morale among Railroad Workers* (Ann Arbor, Mich., Survey Research Center, Institute for Social Research, University of Michigan, 1951).

They may be classified as objectives, policies, procedures, budgets, and programs.

## Objectives

The basic plan is the enterprise objective or objectives. This is the goal of the firm. While these are ordinarily subject to simple state-ment [4] and are essential to the proper planning, organization, staffing, directing, and controlling of any enterprise or any part of it, one often finds that a business or other enterprise has not considered what its basic objectives are.

A good argument can be made that in the United States all business enterprises have one and the same objective—to make a profit. This purpose is often covered under a series of platitudinous statements having to do with service to the public and opportunity for em-ployees. Not that these objectives are improper: certainly the busi-ness enterprise that seeks to make a profit will tend to serve the public best by producing a good for which demand exists and at a price that will effectively meet the best efforts of others. A business that seeks to make a profit will likewise tend best to serve its employees. Good wages, security, and status for the employees are gained most effec-tively through a financially sound enterprise, efficiently operated and managed. The common element that identifies all business enterprise, from the newsboy and peanut vendor to the largest bank or insurance company, is thus the pursuit of profit.

And yet, it seems inadequate to speak of profit seeking as *the* objec-tive of business. It is almost as though one said business is business. Furthermore, there have been too many cases of business owners with incentives other than profit. They may be interested in empire build-ing and power, social prestige, security of position, public acclaim, or any of the other strong motivations of human conduct. The business may be dominated by the desire to develop new things and try new ideas, as was the case of the owners of an engineering company with which one of the authors has worked. It may be to keep the business small, simple, and friendly, as a sort of fraternal group. Or it could

[4] For example, the *Announcement of the School of Business Administration* of the University of California at Los Angeles states that its central objective is "to provide a professional type of education for positions of administrative responsibility."

be to beat their nearest, and larger, competitor, as was held to be one of the principal objectives of the Ford Motor Company in 1952. But even though enterprise purposes are stated in these or similar terms, none of them is realizable unless the firm in question actually makes a profit.

Sometimes the motive of profit maximization takes the form of enterprise-value maximization. In other words, many businesses are operated not for the maximization of profits immediately or even for the short period, but for the purpose of increasing the value of the business in the long run. Many businesses have been known to pass by profits and pursue policies that will increase the capital value of the enterprise. Unquestionably, the principal motivation for this kind of maximization for the individual is the tax structure, which places lesser taxes on capital gains than on profits or normal income. But there are many entrepreneurs who receive satisfaction from seeing a business grow large, even though profits are passed by in the process. This motivation may maximize profits in the long run, although there have been many cases where even in the long run profits are not greatest by so doing.

Another variant of the profit objective in business might be called maintenance of management security. Although evidence cannot easily be obtained on this point, since the controlling managers of a business would hesitate to admit that such is their objective, the fact is that managers sometimes follow a conservative path, which is not one that leads to maximum profits, in order to protect their position. This motive operates through an unwillingness to take even normal risks in order to gain a profit.

For example, the president of a large corporation told one of the authors that he would not approve embarking upon a certain expansion program, even though doing so promised great profits. He pointed out that, if he did not approve this expansion and the company continued to make its moderate profits, the stockholders would not feel dissatisfied and would not press for his replacement. If his conservative path led to reduction in profits, the very fact that *he* had not done anything unusual made it reasonable to blame the turn of events on external business or political conditions. On the other hand, if he took a moderate degree of risk for the promise of high profits and succeeded, stockholders would merely think that he was doing a normal job and, while being happy and content that things had turned out so well, would not especially reward him. But should he assume the risks of the expansion program and it did not turn out well, even through no fault of his own, stockholder reaction to losses might be quite adverse and he might lose his job. His reaction was, "Why take a chance? I like being president of this company!"

The motivation of management security is probably more widespread in business and more of an objective of planning than is generally realized. It is not surprising, either, when those responsible for the direction of an enterprise cannot often reap the advantages of profiting through the assumption of business risks. This motive, moreover, is not limited to persons at the top of businesses. Many department heads direct the energies of their departments toward the objective of maintaining their position as manager.

## Policies

Policies are likewise plans. They are general statements, or understandings,[5] which guide or channel the thinking and action of subordinates in an enterprise or one of its departments. While a distinction has been drawn, largely for purposes of emphasis and clarification, between objectives and policies, it can be readily seen that enterprise objectives are policies, since they furnish the basic guide to thinking and action. Policies ordinarily have at least as many levels as organization, ranking from major policies applicable to the company as a whole, to major departmental policies, and to minor or derivative policies applicable to the least segment of the organization structure.

The varieties of policies in practice are legion. It may be a company policy to promote from within, to conform strictly to a high standard of business ethics, to compete on a price basis, to insist on

---

[5] One can hardly refer to policies as simply "statements," since they are often implied from the actions of managers. While many policies are stated verbally, others grow like Topsy from one or more assorted decisions. The president of a company, for example, may strictly follow, perhaps for convenience rather than as policy, the practice of promoting from within: the practice may then be interpreted as policy and be rigorously followed by his subordinates. In fact, one of the problems of the manager is to make sure that subordinates will not interpret as policy a decision or a line of decisions made by him but which he does not intend to serve as a guide to their thinking.

pricing at fixed prices, to forsake civilian business for military, or to shun publicity. It may be a department policy to hire only persons with an engineering background, to require strict adherence to lunch-hour schedules, or to encourage subordinates in the department freely to offer suggestions for improvement.

Policies, being guides to thinking and action, are seldom specific. It is the task of subordinates, therefore, to interpret policy though the exercise of initiative, discretion, and judgment. The amount of freedom will naturally depend upon the policy, which in turn tends to be a reflection of position in the organization structure. The president of a company with a policy of aggressive price competition has a broad area of discretion in which to interpret and apply this policy. The district sales manager of the company abides by the same basic policy, but the interpretations made by the president, the vice-president for sales, and the regional sales manager become derivative policies and tend thereby to narrow the scope of policy-making of the district manager.

Policies must, however, be consistent and must be integrated in such a way as to contribute to the realization of enterprise objectives. This goal is difficult to attain for many reasons. First, policies are too seldom written, and their exact interpretations too little known. Secondly, the very delegation of authority that policy-making is intended to implement leads through its decentralizing influence to widespread participation in policy-making, with almost certain variations among individuals. Thirdly, it is not always easy to control policy, in the sense of comparing actual policy against intended policy, largely because actual policy may be difficult to ascertain and intended policy not always clear.

## Procedures

Procedures are also plans, for they involve the selection of a course of action and apply to future activities. They detail the exact manner in which a certain activity must be accomplished. Their essence is chronological sequence. Their pervasiveness in the organization is readily apparent. The board of directors may follow procedures quite different from those of the foreman. The expense account of the vice-president may go through quite different approval processes than that of the minor salesman. The vacation and sick-leave provisions and the procedures under which they are effected may vary considerably at various levels of organization. But the important fact is that procedures exist throughout an organization, even though, as one might expect, they become more exacting and numerous in the lower levels, largely because of the necessity for more careful control, the lesser need for discretion in action or decision-making, and the fact that the things done lend themselves to obtaining greater efficiency through prescription of the one best way.

Just as policies have a hierarchy of importance, so do procedures. Thus, in a typical large corporation, one may find a manual of "Corporation Standard Practice," outlining those procedures that apply to a corporation as a whole, and a manual of "Division Standard Practice," covering those procedures designed especially for division operations. There might also be special sets of procedures for a department, a branch, a section, or a unit of a business.

Procedures often cut across departmental lines. For example, the procedure for accomplishing the order handling of a product in a large manufacturing company will almost certainly encompass the sales department (for the original order), the finance department (for proper acknowledgment of receipt of funds or for credit determination of the customer), the accounting department (for recording the transaction), the production department (for order to produce or authority to release from stock), and the traffic department (for proper determination of the shipping means and route).

In comparing procedures and policies, Billy E. Goetz has said:

Policies are relatively general, reasonably permanent managerial plans. Procedures are less general but comparably permanent. A policy maps out a field of action. It determines objectives and limits the area of action. Procedures are stipulated sequences of definite acts. Procedures mark a path through the area of policy. They may fork, generally with adequate clues to determine clerical choice of the path; they may contain trivial gaps to be filled in at the discretion of a clerk; but there is little that resembles the extension of a policy. Procedures are not multidimensional; they do not cover areas of behavior; they have only chronological sequence. . . .

Policy always sets an objective or delimits an area of action while procedures fix a path toward the objective or through the area. Sequence is the *sine qua non* of procedure.[6]

[6] Goetz, *op. cit.*, p. 84. For an excellent study of procedures, see Richard F.

The relationship of procedures and policies may perhaps be indicated by a few examples. A company may have a policy of granting two weeks per year to each employee for a vacation. Procedures will be established to implement this policy, providing for scheduling of vacations to avoid disruption of work, methods and rates of pay, the maintenance of records to assure employees a vacation, and means by which an employee may apply for the vacation. Or a company may have a policy of shipping orders the day received; this policy will, of course, necessitate, particularly in a large company, careful procedures to assure that the order is handled expeditiously. A company may have a policy of requiring clearance by the public relations department of all public utterances by its employees. Naturally, to implement this policy, procedures must be established to make sure that clearance is obtained with a minimum of inconvenience and delay.

## Budgets

A budget is essentially a plan, a statement of expected results expressed in numerical terms. It may be entirely expressed in financial terms, or it may be a statement of results anticipated in terms of man-hours, units of product, machine-hours, or any other measurement that can be reduced to numerical expression. A budget may be designed to deal with operations, such as the budget of expense and revenue; it may be designed to reflect expected capital outlays, such as the capital expenditures budget; or it may be formulated to show expected flow of cash, such as the cash budget.

Budgets are usually conceived as control devices, as indeed they are, and the principal discussion of them will be reserved for the chapters on control. However, the *making* of a budget is clearly planning. In fact, it is often the fundamental planning instrument in many companies. By being forced to establish for a period in advance a numerical compilation of expected cash receipts and expenditures, or anticipated expenses and revenues, or capital outlays, or man-hour and machine-hour utilization, whether the advance period is for one week or five years, a company is forced to plan. The budget cannot

Neuschel, *Streamlining Business Procedures* (New York, McGraw-Hill Book Company, Inc., 1950).

be used for control until it is in existence, and it cannot be in existence as a sensible standard of control unless it reflects plans.

## Programs

Programs are a complex of policies and procedures, ordinarily supported by necessary capital and operating budgets and designed to put into effect a course of action. Programs may be as major as that decided upon in 1952 by the General Petroleum Company to put a $35-million refinery in the Pacific Northwest, or the five-year program embarked upon by the Ford Motor Company in 1946 to improve the status and quality of their thousands of foremen. Or they may be as minor as a program formulated by a single foreman in a parts manufacturing department of a farm machinery company to improve the morale of his workers.

While a budget of one kind or another is usually an instrument to implement a program, it may actually serve as a program. One of the authors recalls a company in difficult financial straits, which installed an elaborate budgetary-control program, designed not only to control expenditures but to instill a singular cost consciousness in the management of the firm. Furthermore, a budget may also encompass the entire program, with all other programs contained in it.

Programs may be basic, or they may be derivative, in the sense that they are required by the primary program. For example, in 1948, Trans World Airlines acquired twelve new Constellation aircraft along with necessary spare equipment, an order amounting to approximately $15 million, at a time when the company's entire assets were scarcely five times as much, its cash position extremely weak, and the company itself operating at a large loss, partly because of lack of equipment. This major program required many derivative programs. A program for provisioning the airline with adequate spare parts and equipment had to be developed. Pilots and flight engineers to man the new aircraft had to be hired and trained. It was necessary to prepare and expand maintenance facilities and hire and train new maintenance personnel. Ground personnel had to be hired and trained as the new kind of aircraft was scheduled to additional cities. A revised program of schedules was developed, along with an advertising campaign to notify prospective travelers of the new service. A program for financing the purchase of the aircraft and the spares was required. New insurance commitments were necessary. These and other programs had to be devised and effected before any of the new aircraft could be received and placed in revenue service. Furthermore, all these programs necessitated coordination and timing, so that all would be accomplished at the right time, since the failure of any part of the vast network of derivative programs would delay the major program with consequent unnecessary costs. It is also worth noting that some of the programs, such as the hiring and training of new personnel, could be accomplished *too soon* as well as too late, since needless expense would have been encountered if employees had been available and trained before their services were required.

Thus, one seldom finds that a program of any importance in business planning stands by itself. It is usually a part of a complex structure of programs, depending upon some programs and affecting others. Indeed, it is this interdependence of plans which causes so much difficulty and complexity in business planning. The results of poor or inadequate planning are seldom isolated, for planning is only as effective as its weakest link. Coordinated, and hence effective, planning requires extraordinarily exacting managerial skill.

## THE IMPORTANCE OF PLANNING

The essential importance of planning has already been indicated. An enterprise, and every part of it, must plan if it would gain its objective or objectives. Without planning, business becomes random in nature and decisions meaningless *ad hoc* choices. It is as though an airplane pilot set out over the ocean blindfolded. Because business operates in an environment of uncertainty and change and requires the attainment of goals at the least possible costs, planning becomes a highly important function.

Planning may be likened to navigation. The navigator lays out a plan and sets a course toward an objective. But his job is not completed by so doing. Instead, he constantly rechecks his position as he proceeds toward his goal,[7] modifying his plan as errors or unforeseen circumstances prove that his course is leading to some point other than the goal sought.

[7] As the reader will readily understand, this constant rechecking is similar to the management function of control.

## Planning a Necessity Because of Uncertainty and Change

In view of the fact that the future is characterized by uncertainty and change, planning is a necessity. Just as the navigator cannot set a course once and forget about it, so the business manager cannot establish his goal as profit and let the matter rest at that. It is true that certainty may lead to the elimination of all alternative courses of action but one and thus reduce planning to the minor function of confirming an obvious course of action. But future events are seldom very certain, and the farther in the future the results of a decision must be considered, the less the certainty. Thus a business executive may feel quite certain that within the next month orders, costs, productive capacity, scheduled output, cash availability, and other factors of the business environment will be at a given level. Perhaps a fire, an unforeseen strike, or an order cancellation by a major customer may affect the actuality of these events, but in the short period this is unlikely. However, as the period for which this manager plans in advance becomes larger, the certainty of the internal and external business environment diminishes rapidly. With increased uncertainty, the possible alternatives of action become greater, and the rightness of any decision necessarily becomes less sure.

However, even where the future bears a high degree of certainty, some planning is necessary. In the first place, there are many ways to consider accomplishing an objective, and there is the necessity of selecting from among these the best way. With conditions of certainty, this kind of planning becomes primarily a mathematical problem, one of calculating which alternative course on the basis of the known facts will yield the desired results at the least costs. In the second place, when the decision as to a course of action is made, it is necessary to lay out plans or blueprints so that each segment of the business will contribute toward the job to be done.

Even though trends indicating change are easily discernible, difficult planning problems arise. The manufacture of stoves for family cooking purposes may be cited as a case in point. The change away from the use of coal and wood burners was distinct, but the change did not take place overnight. It was essential for the manufacturer of a half century ago to determine what percentage of his production should be assigned to the new burners and what to the old; it was also important to produce new burners in such a way as to retain efficient production of both lines. But there came a time when the small declining business of old burners became uneconomical. This was an obvious cutoff point. However, the manufacturer could have chosen an entirely different plan. Having satisfied himself with the certainty of change, he might have deliberately sacrificed some old-burner business in order to concentrate on the design and development of new burners, with the hope of becoming the leader among gas- and electric-stove manufacturers.

Where trends are not discernible, uncertainty is greatest. Many businessmen missed the significance of heavy government expenditures, pent-up demand, extensive savings, and rapid population growth, with their effect on the course of business following World War II. The recession expected by many did not occur, with the result that many firms missed opportunities for profit through underexpansion of capital facilities and lack of readiness for new markets.

It has sometimes been objected that planning in the face of great uncertainty is wasteful because plans must be changed continually and the margin of error is likely to be great. But, just as the navigator must premise some kind of winds in order to make a start toward his goal and must make corrections as necessary, the businessman must make his decisions against some kind of assumption as to the future. The existence of uncertainty implies, not only that the manager must be alert to necessary changes in his plans as changes become discernible, but also that he would prefer to avoid making decisions that tie him irretrievably for a long period of time to a given course of action.

*Planning Focuses Attention on the Enterprise Objective*

Because the enterprise objectives serve as the goal of all activity and the end of all planning, the very act of planning tends to focus attention on these objectives. By continually measuring decisions against this kind of standard and acting in a manner to attain it, the various managers in an enterprise become consciously alert to the objectives of the firm.

This focus is especially important in that most policies, procedures, and programs are interdepartmental in scope. Without central goals, there is a very real danger that departmental goals will be established that may or may not be consistent with the objectives of the entire enterprise. Well-considered planning tends to direct the stream of interdepartmental activities toward one objective and consequently restricts the area of freedom in the development of purely departmental plans. It also has the collateral advantage of bringing attention to the need for possible revisions and extensions of plans. Managers, being typically inclined to concern themselves with immediate problems, tend to overlook the future and its effect. But if those who plan are forced to keep the attainment of purpose clearly in mind, they are far more likely to see the need for revisions.

Again, as Goetz has stated the problem, plans "focus action on purposes. They can forecast actions which tend toward the ultimate objective of economic efficiency, which tend away, which will likely offset one another, and which are merely irrelevant. Managerial planning attempts to achieve a consistent, coordinated structure of operations focused on desired ends. Without plans, action must become merely random activity producing nothing but chaos." [8]

## Planning Is Economic

Because of the concentration on achieving the best way and because of the attempt to secure consistency, planning tends to minimize costs. It results in joint directed effort in the place of individual and piecemeal activity. It can replace uneven flow of work with even flow. It can result in studied decisiveness and designed action, as against recurring crises and snap judgments. In short, plans give rise to efficient and coordinated effort.

To guide subordinates requires careful planning at the top, as well as dissemination of adequate planning information to those who must exercise their authority to fill in the chinks of the major programs at the departmental level. It requires also an insistence that each manager recognize his duty to plan. Much of this endeavor can be accomplished through example, some through adequate clarity and information of top-management plans. Some can be effected through recognizing the ability to plan as a basic requirement for promotion or pay increases. And other results can be obtained by a thorough system of control to make sure that planning is done throughout the range of management.

[8] Goetz, op. cit., p. 63.

Effective planning requires a careful understanding of plans and an agreement upon certain basic factors. If the production manager of a company is by nature a pessimist and figures that the company would not sell more than a certain volume of output, while the sales manager is an optimist and has hired salesmen to sell twice that volume, when, as a matter of fact, the market will most profitably absorb an intermediate amount, the loss in profits would be obvious. Individual managers are likely to differ in their outlook and appraisal of situations, and planning must be designed so as to channel their decision-making toward a unified objective if profits are to be maximized.

The economy of planning is easily understood at the production level. No one who has watched the assembly of automobiles in one of the nation's large factories can fail to be impressed with the way that the parts and subassemblies come together. From one overhead conveyer system comes a yellow body, and from another the various appurtenances of the same color scheme. For another car, exactly the right engine or transmission or accessories fall into place at the exact appointed time. These events do not occur without extensive and detailed planning, and if such planning were not undertaken, the manufacture of automobiles would be chaotic and impossibly costly. While any manager sees the imperative necessity and economy of planning at the production level, it is surprising that other planning of equal and sometimes greater importance is occasionally left to chance and individual discretion.

Even where uncertainty causes plans to go awry, there is better chance for bringing about economy of effort by planning than by not doing so. Random, inconsistent, and uncoordinated activity is sure to give rise to unnecessary and high costs. With planning, these costs are avoided, even though the business may fail because of unforeseen changes. But to the extent that the unforeseen can be anticipated or circumvented and plans be tolerably accurate, it is certain that the goals striven for will be attained at the least cost through adequate planning. Even a poor plan is better than no plan at all. As a successful business manager said to one of the authors, "To make poor decisions is understandable, but not to realize why a person made them or where he intended to go by making them is unforgivable."

## Planning Essential to Control

The basic importance of planning for purposes of control has already been mentioned. A manager cannot determine whether his subordinates are accomplishing what he had hoped unless he has projected a future course of action. The navigator cannot check his route unless he has had a plan against which to measure it. As another top business executive told one of the authors, "After I leave my office at five o'clock this evening, I do not care what happened today, for I cannot do anything about it; I only care about what will happen tomorrow or the next day or next year, for they are the things I can do something about." Perhaps this is an extreme position, but it does serve to emphasize the point that the most effective control is one that looks to the future.

### THE MULTIPLE HORIZON OF PLANNING

Shall plans be for a short period or a long one? How shall short-range plans be coordinated with long-range plans? These questions suggest that there exists a multiple horizon of planning, that, in some cases, planning a week in advance may be ample and that, in others, the desirable period may be that of years. Even within the same firm at the same time, various planning periods may exist for various matters.

## The Planning Period

The National Industrial Conference Board, reporting on a survey of business planning in 1952,[9] disclosed, as might be expected, that businesses varied considerably in the period for which they planned. In some instances long-range plans were confined to two years in advance, while in others they were measured in terms of decades. But three to five years appeared to be the most common term for long-range planning, and few companies planned less than a year in advance. Moreover, the study disclosed a tendency toward lengthening the planning term, a tendency many companies attributed to tax policies and government actions.[10] On the other hand, certain busi-

[9] "Industry Plans for the Future," *Conference Board Business Record,* August, 1952, pp. 324-328.

[10] As one company executive stated, "One reason why our long-range planning is getting to have a longer range is that, with taxes the way they are,

ness executives saw in the same factors influences limiting the length of their planning period.[11]

Observation of business planning leads to the belief that the long-run period tends to be picked on the basis of a period of years in which the management has some confidence that predictions bear a permissible degree of validity. The company that bases its long-run plans on a three- or five-year period may have picked this length arbitrarily or from the fact that other businesses do otherwise. But it is more likely that the period is selected because such a length of time is believed to be predictable.

Yet there must be some logic in selecting the right time-range for planning. In principle, this seems to lie in the nature of investment of resources of the enterprise. Capital is the lifeblood of enterprise. It is normally extremely limited in supply, relative to a firm's needs, and, when expended, there must be a reasonable possibility of recovering it through operations. When expended for various things, it represents a sunk cost that can only be recovered over time. For example, when Lever Brothers sank $25 million into a new soap factory on the West Coast, they were, in effect, making the decision based upon the belief that the soap business would justify the recovery of this investment over a period of time. If this period were twenty years, then logically the plan should have been based upon a projection of business for such a time. Of course, the company might reduce the risk (as the company did) by spending extra funds to give the plant possible usefulness for other production than soap manufacture.

Investments other than for plant and equipment should likewise be based upon a planning period that will anticipate the recovery of investment. If a company, for example, embarks upon a project that

we cannot afford to spend so much as we would like to in a year. Therefore, many things have to be held over." *Ibid.*, p. 325.

[11] For example, one manufacturer stated: "We are finding it more difficult to make long-range company plans because of the many uncertain factors which are ever-increasingly interrupting the normal thinking of today's businessman. I believe that every business should, as nearly as possible, be conducted on a long-range program, but find that it is necessary to inject so many 'ifs' into one's thinking that in the end what would normally be a long-range program has boiled down to six months or a year, on the average. We hope that before too long things will be established so that longer planning can be made a reality without too much interference from governmental activity." *Ibid.*

requires unusual training or if it spends funds to improve the quality of its management, these costs are in the nature of sunk costs.[12] In some cases they can be recovered in a short time; in others the recovery may require a fairly long period.

In fact this recovery-of-cost principle as one determining the planning period may be applied to short-range as well as long-range planning. Such planning is ordinarily for periods ranging from three months to one year. It usually emphasizes that portion of planning which has to do with revenues and expenses and, as such, tends to reflect the cycle of raw materials, production, inventorying, sales, and collection. The company offering a product with little raw material, no need for much equipment or a long labor commitment, and immediate collection of accounts can operate on a short-range planning period. For example, the gardener who tends lawns and collects his pay from his customers weekly has little need to plan further in advance than recovery of investment in his limited tools. On the other hand, a company manufacturing airplanes, which may require from four to six years from inception to final collection of funds, may literally be required to regard the short range as a four- to six-year period.

Despite the principle underlying determination of the proper planning period, there is a tendency for companies arbitrarily to limit the short range to six months or one year and the long range to three to five years. These periods are often compromises. The short range is selected to conform to fiscal quarters or years, because of the practical needs for conforming plans to accounting periods. And the somewhat arbitrary limitation of the long range to three to five years is usually based, as has been indicated, on the prevailing belief that the degree of uncertainty over longer periods makes planning of questionable value.

In any case, even with the application of the recovery-of-cost principle, it is abundantly clear that various appropriate periods will exist for various portions of the planning program. The planning period for the acquisition of a multipurpose machine will be shorter, because of its ready liquidity, than that required for a special-purpose machine. The planning period for almost any piece of machinery will

---

[12] Even though these costs are expensed, they are nonetheless sunk in the enterprise at least to the extent that these are not tax offsets.

tend to be shorter than that for a large capital investment with special applications, such as a new refinery.

## Coordination of Short-Range Plans with Long-Range

Often short-range plans are made without reference to their relationship to long-range planning. This is plainly a serious error. The importance of attaining integration between the two can hardly be overemphasized, and no short-run plan should be made unless it contributes to the achievement of the relevant long-range plan. Many of the wastes of planning arise from decisions relating to immediate situations that fail to consider the effect of the action on more remote objectives.

The difficulty is that sometimes these short-run decisions not only fail to contribute to the long-range plan but may actually have effects which impede or require changes in the long-range plan. For example, if a small company accepts a large order for its goods without reckoning with the effect on productive capacity or cash position, it may so hamper its future ability to finance an orderly expansion as to require a complete reorientation of its long-range program. Or in another company, the urgency of obtaining needed small additions to plant may utilize vacant property so as to thwart its longer-range use as the site for a large new plant. In other instances the decision of a plant superintendent to discharge workers without adequate cause may interfere with the company's longer-range objective of developing a fair and effective personnel program. The short-range decision of Sewell Avery, chairman of Montgomery Ward, to curtail expansion of the business after World War II, because of his belief that a serious recession was at hand, has probably interfered with what must be his long-range program of enhancing the profitability of the company.

What is desired is that short-range planning contribute positively toward long-range plans or objectives. The company must, therefore, have long-range plans. Responsible managers, too, must understand them and provide continual scrutiny of the most immediate decisions to ascertain whether they contribute to the long-range programs. It is far easier to assure that short-range planning is consistent with long-range plans than it is to correct inconsistencies after they are made.

Short-term commitments tend to set precedents for further commitments along the same line.

## ECONOMIC THEORY AND PLANNING

It is in connection with the managerial function of planning that economic theory has much to offer. Holding that the profit motive is the mainspring of a capitalistic economy, economists have done much to develop principles applicable to decision-making. With the tool of marginal analysis, many of the aspects of choosing between alternatives yield to solution. This tool is simply one of finding the results of incremental changes. Thus, marginal cost refers to the *additional* cost incurred by producing an additional unit, and marginal revenue is the additional increment of revenue received by the sale of an additional unit. These increments are spoken of as the margins of the subject matter under consideration, and an entrepreneur producing and selling a good is thought of as operating at the margin when his additional costs are just compensated by the additional revenue received. As can be shown by analysis, this point is the one of most profitable output, for it is the point beyond which any additional costs incurred would not be recovered through additional revenues and below which the spread between marginal costs and marginal revenues would decrease profits.[13]

### Planning and the Static Theory of the Firm

The static theory of the firm is postulated on the assumption that a kind of snapshot is taken of the firm at a given instant of time in order to rule out variations caused by uncertainty due to time. Under this kind of condition, that of "everything else being equal," planning becomes a matter of selecting from available alternatives based upon known market factors and input-output relationships. These variables are "timeless," and planning becomes a problem of finding the optimum plan, that which will maximize net receipts of the firm.[14]

[13] A pioneer work in the application of economic theory to business planning is that published by Albert G. Hart in 1940. See his *Anticipations, Uncertainty, and Dynamic Planning* (New York, Augustus M. Kelley, Inc., 1951). This work, as well as that of other economists, is drawn upon here.

[14] *Ibid.*, p. 14. Hart refers to this as the maximization of "present discounted value of scheduled net receipts," in order to take into account the fact that future returns must be corrected for interest on a discounted basis.

In marginal terms, the optimum plan will be the one in which additional inputs (or costs) will just equal (but not exceed) *additional* receipts (revenues). Obviously, in a complex business plan, such as the location and construction of a new refinery, the number of factors bearing on costs and revenues are innumerable, and the determination of margins very complex. But the marginal analysis is a useful tool for the planner, for it highlights the importance of determining profit maximums by considering incremental costs and revenues.

Thus, a firm may already have a certain-sized plant and an overhead (service and supervisory) organization to operate it. If capacity for more production is available, the desirability of accepting a new contract should logically be decided upon the basis of the additional costs to be incurred and the additional revenue to be obtained. This kind of analysis implies that the customary system of using average costs, with a prorate of all burden and overhead costs, may not always lead to the most profitable course of action, for it may lead the manager to turn down a contract that would more than pay for additional costs.

The marginal analysis also emphasizes the importance of fixed costs, whether these are in the nature of sunk capital investment or of an established minimum of service and supervisory personnel. Depending upon the range of output considered (obviously, if an increase in output would require a larger plant or a larger overhead organization, these new fixed costs become marginal to the problem under consideration), costs that are fixed in nature do not enter the planning problem, except in the sense of getting increased utilization of these facilities and personnel.

The fact that marginal analysis does not normally reflect all costs, but only additional ones, also serves to show the importance of flexibility in business planning. Flexibility is the quality of operations (facilities or personnel) that permits changes in kind and volume of output without undue costs. If machines or people can be utilized

While this is indubitably an adjustment for the sake of strict accuracy, it is an adjustment that is seldom made in practice because of the margins of error unavoidably existing in planning. It is, in a sense, refining the unrefinable, and, in any case, the businessman enters interest as an offset against the revenues to be expected from a plan of action.

for different products or different volumes of production, without loss in investment already incurred, the firm may be regarded as having perfect flexibility, so far as production is concerned. But it may have other inflexibilities. If, for example, it could not obtain additional working capital for expansion of operations, the flexibility of production machinery and personnel would allow changes in output only at a level permitted by the working capital.

Problems of flexibility in business planning arise generally under conditions of dynamic planning, primarily because of the factor of uncertainty. However, even under static conditions, some question of flexibility exists. Where it is known that varying quantities of varying products will be produced, the manager plans for the flexibility needed for these changes, but he does so with complete certainty.

## Planning Under Dynamic Conditions

The analysis of economic forces under static conditions is useful only to isolate the effects of uncertainty [15] and thereby develop tools for analysis. Static conditions do not exist in practice, and business planning is, therefore, undertaken under conditions of change and uncertainty. It is this dynamic character of the business environment that makes planning difficult and the utilization of many economic principles of questionable value.

The central problem under dynamic conditions is the accuracy of a planner's estimate of the future. Obviously, the future is uncertain, although the degree of uncertainty may vary widely as between products, markets, geographical and political areas, and times. If a business manager makes an estimate of a future situation, he necessarily makes certain assumptions as to what will happen. As he weights his contingencies in one way or another, he obtains different results. Sup-

[15] *Ibid.*, pp. 25, 27. Hart adds capital-market imperfections and other market discontinuities to uncertainty as major factors that distinguish the dynamic from the static. These are important factors, since the firm cannot practically add or subtract extremely small quantities of capital and since orders are often for minimum quantities. It is a fact that in most real business situations the schedule of supply of capital or the schedule of demand for a product do not represent smooth connected lines. While these discontinuities have a significant bearing on planning and while other frictions exist (such as the desire of an owner of a small business not to use outside capital because of danger of loss of control), in this discussion simplification of the issues is obtained by dealing with the primary cause of dynamic conditions—uncertainty.

pose, for example, that a manager were planning a new plant for the manufacture of a product and felt that he needed a ten-year span to be sure of recovering his costs. He might estimate the future with respect to markets, prices, labor costs, material costs, utilization of plant, labor efficiency, taxes, and other factors. Suppose further that he estimated six possible situations that he regarded as being most likely to occur, created out of different sets of assumptions as to what the future would bring. These might bring completely separate estimates of net profits to be obtained from the operation and could be charted, as follows:

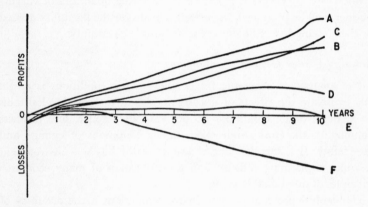

Fig. 1. Accumulated profits from new plant on basis of six estimates of future

As might be expected, all estimates for the first year or two are fairly close together, since the manager may feel more certain of near-term than of long-term results. But as the planning period is extended, the fact that this or that contingency may occur tends to make the estimate of accumulated profits vary from one of high profits, as in forecast A, to one of bare break-even (E), to one of projected loss (F).

Several observations may be made concerning this simplified model of planning under conditions of change and uncertainty. In the first place, the tools of marginal analysis are still useful in arriving at these various estimates of the expected situations. In each set of contingencies assumed, the planner would attempt to maximize profits by assuring himself that additional costs are compensated by additional revenues and that, within the limits of divisibility of units of production, no opportunity exists for maximizing profits by increasing or reducing costs or revenues.

In the second place, this example may be utilized to emphasize the fact that the uncertainties over time, plus the alternatives available to accomplish results under each set of uncertainties, give alternative possibilities astronomical in number. While only six possible forecasts are included here, the actual number may be infinite. In order for a manager to plan, therefore, especially where the subject is complex and the time period long, he must have some means of limiting his analysis to the most probable. In most cases, this is done by judgment and test. An experienced business analyst tends to have a feeling for problems, which grows out of his familiarity with the underlying factors. If he can consider the basic estimates from which his profit calculation is made and decide which are most likely to occur, he can soon limit the alternative projections to a few most probable ones. At this point, the adoption of a plan is likely to be based upon a weighing of the risks and benefits expected from these few probabilities in the light of the character of underlying uncertainties, the resources of the firm, and the ability and willingness to assume the risks involved.

As can be seen, the difficult problem in planning is the determination of underlying factors, such as future markets, prices, and costs. This is a matter of the forecasting and the calculation of probabilities. For those companies that can afford the work of specialists in this field, with their utilization of mathematical, statistical, and market-research techniques, a fairly high degree of accuracy in forecasting can be attained. A forecaster may not be able to anticipate with any degree of accuracy such things as war, revolutionary invention, or cataclysmic economic changes, but within the framework of an assumption that one or the other major happenings will occur, forecasting can be undertaken with a workable degree of accuracy for periods of at least five years in advance.[16]

[16] In 1945 forecasters of three major airlines estimated that 1951 domestic airline traffic would reach approximately 10.5 billion passenger-miles. The actual figure for 1951 was 10.2 billion for the trunk lines and 10.5 billion for the combined trunk and feeder lines.

## STEPS INVOLVED IN PLANNING

The nature and techniques of planning may be clarified by outlining the steps involved in major planning. Although they are presented here as dealing with a major program, such as the acquisition of a new plant or a new fleet of airplanes or the development of a new product, they are still steps that in their essential nature must be followed in any kind of thorough and logical planning. Minor plans may not be as complex, and certain of the steps may be more easily accomplished, but these differences should not obscure the fact that the planning process has a logical and practical set of techniques and principles of general application.

### *Establishment of Objectives*

The first step in the planning process is the establishment of planning objectives. This must be first at the level of the entire enterprise, but the necessity for having an objective or objectives for each derivative or subordinate plan likewise becomes evident. Planning must be for or toward some goal to be meaningful, because the objective gives the key as to what basically to do, where to place the primary emphasis, and what to accomplish by the network of policies, procedures, budgets, and programs.

Regardless of the nature of objectives, they must be understood if plans of any meaning are to be pursued in the enterprise. Thus, the objective of the entire enterprise should control the direction of major plans affecting the enterprise as a whole. These plans, then, in their reflection of this objective, define the objectives of the major departments. Major department objectives and plans give a key to the objectives of the derivative departments, and so down the line through the organization structure. Moreover, the lesser subdivisions will do their planning more effectively if they understand the over-all objectives of the enterprise.

But even this may not be enough. A group of research engineers in a military laboratory once remarked that, while they understood the objectives of the Defense Department and those of the military service for which they worked and while the detailed project plans of the laboratory were well understood, they did not always understand the objective of the project on which they worked. Their feeling was that, if they knew for what purpose their project was to be utilized, they might better be able to formulate plans for accomplishing more efficiently the principal objective. It is, therefore, of great importance that the entire hierarchy of objectives applicable to a department's planning be understood.

## Establishment of Planning Premises

A second logical step in the planning process is the establishment of, agreement upon, and dissemination of, planning premises. These are forecast data of a factual nature and basic policies expected to be applicable for the future. Premises, then, are planning assumptions. They are the future setting against which all planning takes place.

The establishment of planning premises necessarily involves forecasts of the future. What kind of markets will there be? What quantity of sales? What prices? What products? What costs? What wage rates? What tax rates and policies? What new plants? What policies with respect to dividends? How will expansion be financed? It is important to realize that planning premises include far more than basic forecasts of population, prices, costs, production, markets, and similar matters.

Some premises are forecast policies that have not yet been made. If, for example, a company does not have a pension plan and if no policy with respect to having one has been made, those who would develop planning premises must forecast whether such a policy decision will be made and what it will contain. Other premises naturally grow out of policy decisions or plans already made. If, for example, a company has a policy of paying out 5 per cent of its profits before taxes for contributions and if there is no reason to believe that this policy will be changed, this policy becomes a planning premise for the future. Or, if a company has made large investments in special-purpose fixed plant and machinery, the very fact that this has been done becomes a planning premise of some importance for the future.

As one moves down the organizational hierarchy into divisional, departmental, branch, or section plans, the composition of planning premises tends to change somewhat. The basic outlook will be the same, but the existence of major plans and the development of new major plans will materially affect the future picture against which the managers of these lesser organizational units must plan. Plans affecting a manager's area of authority become premises for *his* planning.

Planning premises may be divided into three groups. There are those planning premises that are noncontrollable, in the sense that the individual firm doing the planning cannot do anything about them. These include such premises as population growth, future price levels, political environment, tax rates and policies, and business cycles. Then there are those planning premises that may be regarded as semicontrollable, in the sense that the individual firm cannot control them but can influence their happening to a greater or lesser degree. In this category may be assumptions as to the share of the market, the character of labor turnover, labor efficiency, company price policy, and even industry legislative policy. And finally, a group of typical planning premises may be characterized as controllable by the firm. Among these are those policy matters and programs that the company management can decide largely for itself. They may include such policies as expansion into new markets, the adoption of an aggressive development or research program, or the selection of a site for headquarters offices.

One of the difficulties with establishing a complete set of planning premises and keeping them up to date is the fact that every major plan, and many minor ones, tend to become planning premises for the future. The decision to establish a major factory in Kansas City, for example, will become an important premise for making other plans where this plant location will be important. Or a railroad, for instance, would find little sense in premising its future plans on reaching markets in Florida if its line were in the Pacific Northwest, and there could be no reasonable expectation of expanding to the Southeast. And when an airline equips its long-haul routes with one type of aircraft and builds maintenance and overhaul facilities for this purpose, this very act tends to become a premise for other plans.

It would be a matter of some surprise if all members of a company's management at all levels would agree independently as to the kind of future a company faces. One manager might expect world peace to last for ten years; another, world war for the same period. One manager might expect prices to go up 10 per cent in five years; another, 50 per cent; and another expect that prices would drop.

The lack of planning coordination through use by managers of different sets of premises can be extremely costly to a company. Planning premises should, therefore, be agreed upon. A single standard for the future is a necessary step in good planning, even though this standard includes several sets of premises, with the instruction that different sets of plans be developed on each. In many companies, for example, it is customary to develop plans in prospects of both peace and war, so that, regardless of what occurs, the company will be ready. Obviously, however, a course of action taken for any future period can follow only one set of premises for that period.

Since agreement upon planning premises is important to coordinated planning, it becomes a major responsibility of managers, starting with those at the top of the company, to make sure that their subordinates understand the premises upon which they are expected to plan. In well-managed companies the top managers obtain unanimity with respect to premises for planning purposes, even if the chief executive must force a selection of the future outlook upon subordinates with differing views. In most cases, these major premises are the subject of careful study, including often extensive economic and other research, and of considered deliberation, so that the best thinking available in the company can be brought to bear upon them. It is not unusual for chief executives to force the top managers to come to some conclusion on the future that the company faces and, through group deliberation, arrive at a set of major premises that all can accept. But whether they are accepted by all or not, no chief executive can afford to chance a situation where his lieutenants are planning their portions of the company's future on substantially different sets of premises.

Established and accepted planning premises are only useful to those managers who are aware of them. As in other phases of the managerial job, it is important that planning premises be appropriately disseminated throughout the organization. This does not necessarily mean that all planning premises be communicated to all managers, but it does imply that all managers will have knowledge of those premises necessary for him to do an intelligent and coordinated job of planning.

### Search and Examination of Alternative Courses of Action

A third step in the planning process is to search for and examine alternative courses of action. There is seldom a business plan for which reasonable alternatives do not exist. Moreover, before weighing alternatives and reaching a decision, one is wise to search for alternatives that may not be immediately apparent. Quite often an alternative not immediately seen proves to be the •most profitable way of undertaking a plan.

Having searched for the alternative courses of action and having reduced the available alternatives to those few that seem to offer the best possibilities for fruitful action, the planner must next examine these alternatives. In the case of a major plan, this examination may be very complicated, leading to the preparation of detailed forecasts of costs and revenues, effects on cash position, and other considerations of a tangible nature, as well as to the consideration of many intangible factors. In deciding to build a new aluminum plant in 1950, the American Aluminum Company not only made a careful study of the costs of electricity at various locations in the country, the availability of suitable sites, the costs of transportation of raw and finished materials, costs of transmission of power, and other items that could be reduced to figures but also made a careful analysis of such intangible factors as the effect of the plant on local opinion and the question of taking the capital risk of building its own power-generating facilities.

## Evaluation of Alternative Courses of Action

Having sought out the available alternatives and having made an examination of their strong and weak points, the planner must evaluate the alternatives. This evaluation involves the weighing of the various factors entailed. One alternative may appear to be the most profitable course of action but may require a large outlay of cash and a slow payback. Another course may be less profitable but involve less risk. Still another course of action may better suit the company's long-range objectives.

If objectives were simply to maximize profits immediately, if the future were not fraught with uncertainty, if a company did not have to worry about cash position and capital availability, and if there were not so many factors that could not be reduced to definite data, this evaluation would be easy. But the typical planning problem is so replete with uncertainties, problems of capital shortages, and intangible factors that the evaluation is usually very difficult. Even with relatively simple problems, the evaluation may not be easy. A company may wish to enter a new product line primarily for purposes of prestige. The forecast of expected results may show a clear loss. But the question is still open as to whether the loss, which is believed to be forecast within a narrow margin of error, is worth the gain in prestige.

## Selection of a Course or Courses of Action

The fifth planning step is that of selecting the course or courses of action to be undertaken. This is the point at which the plan is adopted. Often an analysis and evaluation of available alternatives will disclose that two or more courses are advisable and the manager concerned may decide to do several things rather than the one best thing.

## Formulation of Necessary Derivative Plans

But the planning process is not complete. Once a plan is adopted, there are almost invariably necessary derivative plans to be constructed to give effect to and support the basic plan. A derivative program may be necessary, as was the case mentioned above where the airline decided to acquire a new fleet of airplanes and, in turn, required plans for the hiring and training of ground and flying personnel, the acquisition and placing of spare parts, and other programs. In addition, it may be necessary to develop new policies and procedures for effecting the plan. And in most instances these plans will be accompanied by various cash, capital expenditure, and expense and revenue budgets to make sure that individual managers, in exercising their authority, will be contained within the framework of the plan contemplated.

In other words, plans do not accomplish themselves. They require a breakdown into further plans, with each segment of the company and each manager concerned executing the subsidiary plans necessary for making a basic plan a reality.

### PLANNING WITHIN THE ORGANIZATION STRUCTURE

The type of planning in which a manager engages depends upon his position in the organization structure. Top-management planning has to do with broad over-all programs and policies important to the company as a whole. Planning within each department will, of course, be related to the departmental function and to the scope of authority delegation of the manager. In production or factory planning, for example, the programs devised and undertaken will be primarily concerned with scheduling machines, with utilization of manpower, and with procurement and use of materials.

The essential point is that the planning process is basically the same, wherever planning is undertaken. It may vary in complexity and breadth as the problem area and the kind of authority differ. As a matter of fact, planning at the lower levels of the organization structure, particularly in the production department, tends to be better and more thorough than that at upper levels. Among the more important reasons for this is that at the lower levels planning tends to be less a problem of dealing with the uncertainties of human reactions and more a problem of dealing with the definiteness of materials and machines. In addition, the emphasis on production management during more than four decades of scientific management development following the work of Frederick Taylor has resulted in more attention to planning at this level than on any other. Another factor is that at this level mistakes in planning show up more quickly because the results of poor planning are soon disclosed by missed production schedules, confused operations, and high costs. While the quality of planning at top levels of an enterprise is of the greatest importance to management, sometimes the results of poor planning are not apparent until a company has lost an important market, has declined in financial strength or competitive position, or has become grossly inefficient.

What is often forgotten is that participation in planning is important at all levels in organization. It is even wise to have participation in *major* planning by all the managers in an enterprise. Every manager should be currently informed of all major plans affecting his area of authority. The informed manager is better able to develop suitable plans for his own department and to understand the part he is required to play. Furthermore, it is desirable for managers to be encouraged to contribute suggestions to top managers. Not only may these be of value to those making plans, but loyalty toward major plans can be nurtured from a feeling of participation. A third important element of participation is the desirability of managers' being consulted in advance as to those plans they are expected to execute within their own department. Clearly, also, each manager must be required to make those plans necessary if his department is to carry out the objectives, policies, procedures, and programs of the enterprise, and he must be held responsible for checking continually upon the effectiveness with which his subordinates carry out the plans.

Participation in all planning affecting a manager's area of authority, through his being informed, contributing suggestions, and being consulted, contributes to good planning, loyalty, and managerial effectiveness. Yet one may ask how in a large plant the hundreds of foremen and superintendents, sales managers, and other managers *can* be consulted. One cannot imagine the top managerial team of the Ford Motor Company, for instance, consulting with their thousands of subordinate managers on the plans for a new line of cars.

Unfortunately, in large companies it is frequently not possible for this kind of planning communication to take place. Even so, there are devices available to management that can lead to wider participation of subordinate managers in the making of programs affecting their areas of operations. One is the use of a planning staff, which can spend time with key subordinate managers in developing plans and which will encourage these managers to discuss such matters with their subordinates. In some companies, this practice has produced valuable suggestions and greater understanding of what the top managers were trying to do.

Another valuable device is the establishment of suitable planning committees. While committees have limited administrative use, one of their most important values is improvement in communication. If appropriate committees are established at various levels and points of the organization structure, they can be effective in transmitting planning information, in eliciting suggestions, and in serving as a consultative device. They must be skillfully handled to avoid the expenditure of too much time, but, if properly used, they can pay handsome dividends in terms of helpful advice, understanding of objectives and programs, and in loyalty.

Still another helpful means employed successfully in some companies is the management club. This is an organization of all members of management, from the president to the foreman, and in a large company may be broken up into a number of divisional or territorial clubs. At a specified number of meetings during the year the president of the company or a team of top managers should conduct a meeting at which the planning and thinking of this top echelon are candidly reported to the management group and questions on these matters answered. The authors have noted that in several companies where this device has been tried the lower-management group has responded avidly and gained a strong feeling of unity of objective with the top management of the company. Even the dullest financial matters thus become vital, and the most complicated plan interesting. What many managers overlook is the simple fact that the rank and file of managers have a strong interest in these matters because, after their church and family, there is no more significant force in their lives than the enterprise for which they work.

But no device of encouraging participation in planning and the development of effective planning throughout an organization will replace managerial deficiencies in other directions. The strength of top leadership and the example given to lower managers, clear delegations of authority and careful descriptions of job duties, the development of managerial skills through proper training, and effective techniques of direction and control are among the priceless ingredients of good management that no system of communication and participation can replace.

# 4.

# *Planning*

## By Henri Fayol [1]

The maxim "managing means looking ahead" gives some idea of the importance attached to planning in the business world, and it is true that if foresight is not the whole of management, at least it is an essential part of it. To foresee, in this context, means both to assess the future and make provision for it; that is, foreseeing is itself action already.

Planning is manifested on a variety of occasions and in a variety of ways, its chief manifestation, apparent sign, and most effective instrument being the plan of action. The plan of action is, at one and the same time, the result envisaged, the line of action to be followed, the stages to go through, and methods to use. It is a kind of future picture wherein proximate events are outlined with some distinctness, whilst remote events appear progressively less distinct, and it entails the running of the business as foreseen and provided against over a definite period.

The plan of action rests: (1) on the firm's resources (buildings, tools, raw materials, personnel, productive capacity, sales outlets, public relations, etc.); (2) on the nature and importance of work in progress; (3) on future trends which depend partly on technical, commercial, financial, and other conditions, all subject to change, whose importance and occurrence cannot be predetermined. The preparation of the plan of action is one of the most difficult and most important matters of every business and brings into play all depart-

[1] From Henri Fayol, *General and Industrial Management* (New York, Pitman Publishing Corporation, 1949), pp. 43–52. Reprinted by permission.

43

ments and all functions, especially the management function. It is, in effect, in order to carry out his managerial function that the manager takes the initiative for the plan of action, that he indicates its objective and scope, fixes the share of each department in the communal task, coordinates the parts, and harmonizes the whole; that he decides, in fine, the line of conduct to be followed.

In this line of conduct it is not only imperative that nothing should clash with principles and rules of good management, but also that the management adopted should facilitate application of these principles and rules. Therefore, to the divers technical, commercial, financial, and other abilities necessary on the part of a business head and his assistants, there must be added considerable managerial ability.

## GENERAL FEATURES OF A GOOD PLAN OF ACTION

No one disputes the usefulness of a plan of action. Before taking action it is most necessary to know what is possible and what is wanted. It is known that absence of plan entails hesitation, false steps, untimely changes of direction, which are so many causes of weakness, if not of disaster, in business. The question of and necessity for a plan of action, then, does not arise; and I think that I am voicing the general opinion in saying that a plan of action is indispensable. But there are plans and plans; there are simple ones, complex ones, concise ones, detailed ones, long- or short-term ones; there are those studied with meticulous attention, those treated lightly; there are good, bad, and indifferent ones. How are the good ones to be singled out from among the others? Experience is the only thing that finally determines the true value of a plan, i.e., of the services it can render to the firm, and even then the manner of its application must be taken into account. There is both instrument and player. Nevertheless, there are certain broad characteristics on which general agreement may be reached beforehand without waiting for the verdict of experience.

Unity of plan is an instance. Only one plan can be put into operation at a time; two different plans would mean duality, confusion, disorder. But a plan may be divided into several parts. In large concerns, there is found alongside the general plan a technical, commercial, and a financial one, or else an over-all one with a specific one for each department. But all these plans are linked, welded, so as to make up one only, and every modification brought to bear on any one of them is given expression in the whole plan. The guiding action of the plan must be continuous.

Now the limitations of human foresight necessarily set bounds to the duration of plans, so, in order to have no break in the guiding action, a second plan must follow immediately upon the first, a third upon the second, and so on. In large businesses the annual plan is more or less in current use. Other plans of shorter or longer term, always in close accord with the annual plan, operate simultaneously with this latter. The plan should be flexible enough to bend before such adjustments as it is considered well to introduce [changes], whether from pressure of circumstances or from any other reason. First as last, it is the law to which one bows.

Another good point about a plan is to have as much accuracy as is compatible with the unknown factors bearing on the fate of the concern. Usually it is possible to mark out the line of proximate action fairly accurately, while a simple general indication does for remote activities, for before the moment for their execution has arrived sufficient enlightenment will have been forthcoming to settle the line of action more precisely. When the unknown factor occupies a relatively very large place there can be no preciseness in the plan, and then the concern takes on the name of venture.

Unity, continuity, flexibility, precision: such are the broad features of a good plan of action.

As for other specific points which it should have, and which turn on the nature, importance, and condition of the business for which the plan is drawn up, there could be no possibility of settling them beforehand save by comparison with other plans already recognized as effective in similar businesses. In each case, then, comparable elements and models must be sought in business practice, after the fashion of the architect with a building to construct. But the architect, better served than the manager, can call upon books, courses in architecture, whereas there are no books on plans of action, no lessons in foresight, for management theory has yet to be formulated.

There is no lack of good plans; they can be guessed at from the externals of a business but not seen at sufficiently close quarters to be known and judged. Nevertheless, it would be most useful for those whose concern is management to know how experienced managers go about drawing up their plans. By way of information or sample, I am going to set out the method which has long been followed in a great mining and metallurgical concern with which I am well acquainted.

## Method of Drawing up the Plan of Action in a Large Mining and Metallurgical Firm

This company includes several separate establishments and employs about ten thousand personnel. The entire plan is made up of a series of separate plans called forecasts; and there are yearly forecasts, ten-yearly forecasts, monthly, weekly, daily forecasts, long-term forecasts, special forecasts, and all merge into a single program which operates as a guide for the whole concern.

*Yearly Forecasts.* Each year, two months after the end of the budgetary period, a general report is drawn up of the work and results of this period. The report deals especially with production, sales, technical, commercial, financial position, personnel, economic consequences, etc. The report is accompanied by forecasts dealing with those same matters, the forecasts being a kind of anticipatory summary of the activities and results of the new budgetary period.

The two months of the new plan which have elapsed are not left without plan, because of provisional forecasts drawn up fifteen days before the end of the previous period. In a large mining and metallurgical firm not many activities are quite completed during the course of one year. Cooperative projects of a technical, commercial, and financial nature, which provide the business with its activities, need more time for their preparation and execution. From another aspect, account must be taken of the repercussions which proximate activities must have on ultimate ones and of the obligation to prepare far ahead sometimes for a requisite state of affairs.

### YEARLY AND TEN-YEARLY FORECASTS

#### CONTENTS

*Technical Section*

Mining rights. Premises. Plant.
Extraction. Manufacture. Output.
New workings. Improvements.

Maintenance of plant and buildings.
Production costs.

## Commercial Section

Sales outlets.
Marketable goods.
Agencies. Contracts.
Customers. Importance. Credit standing.
Selling price.

## Financial Section

Capital. Loans. Deposits.

Circulating assets
$$\begin{cases} \text{Supplies in hand.} \\ \text{Finished goods.} \\ \text{Debtors.} \\ \text{Liquid assets.} \end{cases}$$

Available assets.
Reserves and sundry appropriations.

Creditors
$$\begin{cases} \text{Wages.} \\ \text{Suppliers.} \\ \text{Sundry.} \end{cases}$$

Sinking funds. Dividends. Bankers.

## Accounting

Balance sheet. Profit and loss account. Statistics.

## Security

Accident precautions.
Works police. Claims. Health service.
Insurance.

## Management

Plan of action.
Organization of personnel. Selection.
Command.
Coordination. Conferences.
Control.

Finally, thought must be given to constant modifications operating on the technical, commercial, financial, and social condition of the industrial world in general and of the business in particular, to avoid being overtaken by circumstances. These various considerations come outside the framework of yearly forecasts and lead on to longer-term ones.

*Ten-Yearly Forecasts.* Ten-yearly forecasts deal with the same matters as yearly ones. At the outset these two types of forecast are identical, the yearly forecast merging into the first year of the ten-yearly one, but from the second year onward notable divergences make their appearance. To maintain unity of plan each year the ten-yearly forecasts must be reconciled with annual ones so that at the end of some years the ten-yearly forecasts are generally so modified and transformed as to be no longer clear and need redrafting. In effect the custom of redrafting every five years has become established. It is the rule that ten-yearly forecasts always embrace a decade, and that they are revised every five years. Thus there is always a line of action marked out in advance for five years at least.

*Special Forecasts.* There are some activities whose full cycle exceeds one or even several ten-yearly periods; there are others which, occurring suddenly, must sensibly affect the conditions of the business. Both the one and the other are the object of special forecasts whose findings necessarily have a place in the yearly and ten-yearly forecasts. But it must never be lost sight of that there is one plan only.

These three sorts of forecast, yearly, ten-yearly, and special, merged and harmonized, constitute the firm's general plan.

So, having been prepared with meticulous care by each regional management, with the help of departmental management, and then revised, modified, and completed by general management and then submitted for scrutiny and approval to the board of directors, these forecasts become the plan which, so long as no other has been put in its place, shall serve as guide, directive, and law for the whole staff.

Fifty years ago I began to use this system of forecasts, when I was engaged in managing a colliery, and it rendered me such good service that I had no hesitation in subsequently applying it to various industries whose running was entrusted to me. I look upon it as a precious managerial instrument and have no hesitation in recommending its use to those who have no better instrument available. It has necessarily some shortcomings, but its shortcomings are very slight compared with the advantages it offers. Let us glance at these advantages and shortcomings.

## Advantages and Shortcomings of Forecasts

The study of resources, future possibilities, and means to be used for attaining the objective call for contributions from all departmental heads within the framework of their mandate; each one brings to this study the contribution of his experience together with recognition of the responsibility which will fall upon him in executing the plan.

Those are excellent conditions for ensuring that no resource shall be neglected and that future possibilities shall be prudently and courageously assessed and that means shall be appropriate to ends. Knowing what are its capabilities and its intentions, the concern goes boldly on, confidently tackles current problems, and is prepared to align all its forces against accidents and surprises of all kinds which may occur.

Compiling the annual plan is always a delicate operation and especially lengthy and laborious when done for the first time, but each repetition brings some simplification and when the plan has become a habit the toil and difficulties are largely reduced. Conversely, the interest it offers increases. The attention demanded for executing the plan, the indispensable comparison between predicted and actual facts, the recognition of mistakes made and successes attained, the search for means of repeating the one and avoiding the other—all go to make the new plan a work of increasing interest and increasing usefulness.

Also, by doing this work the personnel increases in usefulness from year to year, and at the end is considerably superior to what it was in the beginning. In truth, this result is not due solely to the use of planning but everything goes together; a well-thought-out plan is rarely found apart from sound organizational, command, coordination, and control practices. This management element exerts an influence on all the rest.

Lack of sequence in activity and unwarranted changes of course are dangers constantly threatening businesses without a plan. The slightest contrary wind can turn from its course a boat which is unfitted to resist. When serious happenings occur, regrettable changes of course may be decided upon under the influence of profound but transitory disturbance. Only a program carefully pondered at an undisturbed time permits of maintaining a clear view of the future and of concentrating maximum possible intellectual ability and material resources upon the danger.

It is in difficult moments above all that a plan is necessary. The best of plans cannot anticipate all unexpected occurrences which may arise, but it does include a place for these events and prepare the weapons which may be needed at the moment of being surprised. The plan protects the business not only against undesirable changes of course which may be produced by grave events, but also against those arising simply from changes on the part of higher authority. Also, it protects against deviations, imperceptible at first, which end by deflecting it from its objective.

### Conditions and Qualities Essential for Drawing Up a Good Plan of Action

To sum up: the plan of action facilitates the utilization of the firm's resources and the choice of best methods to use for attaining the objective. It suppresses or reduces hesitancy, false steps, unwarranted changes of course, and helps to improve personnel. It is a precious managerial instrument.

The question may be asked as to why such an instrument is not in general use and everywhere developed to the farthest extent. The reason is that its compilation demands of managerial personnel a certain number of qualities and conditions rarely to be found in combination. The compilation of a good plan demands for the personnel in charge—

1. The art of handling men.
2. Considerable energy.
3. A measure of moral courage.
4. Some continuity of tenure.
5. A given degree of competence in the specialized requirements of the business.
6. A certain general business experience.

### The Art of Handling Men

In a large firm the majority of departmental managers take part in the compiling of the working arrangements. The execution of this task from time to time is in addition to ordinary everyday work and includes a certain responsibility and does not normally carry any special remuneration. So, to have in such conditions loyal and active cooperation from departmental heads, an able manager of men is needed who fears neither trouble nor responsibility. The art of handling men is apparent from keenness of subordinates and confidence of superiors.

## Energy

Yearly and ten-yearly forecasts and special forecasts demand constant vigilance on the part of management.

## Moral Courage

It is well known that the best-thought-out plan is never exactly carried out. Forecasts are not prophecies; their function is to minimize the unknown factor. Nevertheless, the public generally, and even shareholders best informed about the running of a business, are not kindly disposed toward a manager who has raised unfulfilled hopes, or allowed them to be raised. Whence the need for a certain prudence which has to be reconciled with the obligation of making every preparation and seeking out optimum possible results.

The timid are tempted to suppress the plan or else whittle it down to nothing in order not to expose themselves to criticism, but it is a bad policy even from the point of view of self-interest. Lack of plan, which compromises smooth running, also exposes the manager to infinitely graver charges than that of having to explain away imperfectly executed forecasts.

## Continuity of Tenure

Some time goes by before a new manager is able to take sufficient cognizance of the course of affairs, the usefulness of employees, the resources of the business, its general set-up and future possibilities, so as usefully to undertake the compiling of the plan. If, at such a moment, he feels that he will not have enough time to complete the work or only enough to start putting it into execution, or if, on the other hand, he is convinced that such work, condemned to bear no fruit, will only draw criticism upon him, is it to be thought that he will carry it out enthusiastically or even undertake it unless obliged? Human nature must be reckoned with. Without continuity of tenure on the part of management personnel there can be no good plan of action.

## Professional Competence and General Business Knowledge

These are abilities just as necessary for drawing up a plan as for carrying it out.

Such are the conditions essential for compiling a good plan. They presuppose intelligent and experienced management. Lack of plan or a bad plan is a sign of managerial incompetence. To safeguard business against such incompetence—

1. A plan must be compulsory.

2. Good specimen plans must be made generally available. (Successful businesses could be asked to furnish such specimens. Experience and general discussion would single out the best.)

3. Planning (as a subject) must be introduced into education.

Thus could general opinion be better informed and react upon management personnel so that the latter's inefficiency would be less to be feared—a state of affairs which would in no wise detract from the importance of men of proven worth.

I shall not here go into detail about monthly, weekly, or daily forecasts which are in use in most businesses and which, like long-term forecasts, aim at marking out beforehand the line of action judged to be most conducive to success. All these forecasts must be made available early enough to allow time to prepare for their execution.

# II

## ORGANIZATION

No matter how much wisdom may go into planning, whether it be an insurance program, an armed invasion of a continent, or a campaign to reduce the inroads of disease, the measure of its success always will be the spirit and mettle of the individuals engaged in its execution. No matter how much treasure may support a project, or how elaborate its organization, or how detailed and farsighted its operational scheme, the human element is always the central one.

—Dwight D. Eisenhower

# 5.

# *Introduction*

• For starting the work of the planning group, management should pick a project which poses some operating questions, has long-term implications, and involves the operating experiences of several members of the group.

• It is dangerous to divorce planning from doing. Line officers should be given the responsibility for developing a plan. Then they will be more ready to support it when the time comes for action.

• Management should charge a specific executive or group with the responsibility for getting the plans in writing and revising them as necessary when new facts or conditions come into play.

• Lawyers and economists are helpful on some planning jobs. But because of their intellectual incompatibility, they should be organized as *ad hoc* groups, assembled for specific assignments, and disbanded on completion of their missions.

These are some of the propositions advanced in this section. They are not necessarily the most important ones, but they will serve to emphasize an important point. Top executives cannot have long-range planning unless they organize for it, and they cannot organize for it effectively unless they recognize some essential differences between this and other management jobs. It will be helpful to keep a few of these contrasts in mind as we read the chapters in this section.

In the first place, the long-range planner needs to be better than average at the art of problem solving. It is not enough merely to apply his past experience as he might do, say, in working out next year's budget. If he were to do that, he would miss half the point of long-range planning.

Let me illustrate. Let us suppose that a division's sales goal calls for volume to increase from $10 million to $20 million during the next seven years. Now, if this problem is looked at in the usual way, the marketing man will say that the increase calls for so much in the way of new salesmen, the procurement man will estimate that so many new resources are required, the production man will figure out the plant expansion that is needed, and so forth. To each of these managers, in other words, the planning goal means *adding on* so much in the way of new people and facilities in his department. He is going at long-range planning in the same way as he has always gone at short-range planning, even though they are quite different.

If the long-range planner really wants to give the company its money's worth, however, he will take quite a different approach. He will think of that company with $20-million sales in seven years as a good engineer might think of a new model. He may decide, for instance, that $20-million sales will require a good deal more speed in management decision-making, a considerably higher level of customer service, and a better system of control. He will analyze the implications of these changes for data processing, inventory, production programming, market analysis, and so forth. He will pay particular attention to how one chain reaction affects another chain reaction and how the second, when changed, affects the first. He will come up with a master plan that is far different from—and far more effective than—that produced by the "adding-on" approach. This is because he thinks of the company as a whole, as a system.

I do not want to belabor the value of the systems approach as opposed to the "adding-on" approach; it has been described in detail before.[1] But I do think it is important to ask whether management can afford to put long-range planning in the hands of "just another committee." Planners need to develop and use a skill in problem solving that is rarely needed in our usual day-to-day routines. How much chance would they get to do this if they were organized in the way most committees are organized? It is one thing for experienced managers to agree, on the basis of past experience, how much new plant is needed to produce twice as much volume; it is quite another

[1] See, for example, Melvin E. Salveson, "High-Speed Operations Research," *Harvard Business Review*, July–August, 1957.

to visualize a company-wide operation with the kind of logical detachment that the engineer uses in making a new model.

A second important difference between planning and other jobs stems from the fact that planners must work not only in close association but also in unfamiliar association. Inevitably, therefore, problems of working together will arise. There is the danger that these problems will pile up on top of the problem originally assigned by management. In fact, there is even the possibility that the planners will never really *get* to the conceptual problems underlying the creation of a master plan. Of course, this can happen with any committee, as all of us well know. But in forward planning, because of its strangeness, it is particularly important to allow time for good teamwork to develop.

In the third place, it is not enough merely to set up a long-range planning group and let it go. The senior executives must keep with it. As Mr. Wrapp says in his article, the most serious obstacle "is the subtle, but occasionally open, opposition of some executives which appears in the early stages of the development." In a sense, we are working against human nature in long-range planning. It is the unusual executive who really relishes the look forward, who is tantalized by what remains to be done. Most of us are afraid of change. We attempt to find security in a changing world by trying to fix things. And the more we try to fix them, the more rigid we get, and the more insecure and inept we become in dealing with the day's problems. We don't go seeking possibilities. We don't voluntarily go out in search of adventure. We shy away from it like cold water.

Unfortunately, the modern office makes it easy to retreat from forward thinking. The day is an unending series of interruptions— conferences, visits, telephone calls, coffee breaks. Professor Sune Carlsson clocked twelve top Swedish industrialists for several days and found that not one was ever able to work uninterruptedly for more than twenty minutes at a time in his office.[2] Businessmen in this country seem to work under the same conditions—if anything, worse. So when an executive has to make a long-range decision, it is tempting to make it "off the cuff" without really going into its ramifications. Later in this book, Peter Drucker cites the example of a railroad

[2] Sune Carlsson, *Executive Behavior* (Stockholm, Strombergs, 1951).

company that spent much time on traffic forecasts but decided on a
$10-million investment quickly in a board meeting.

Against these disadvantages in long-range planning, there are several basic advantages which management can work for all they are
worth. First, planning is somewhat removed, because of its nature,
from the time pressures of the usual operating job. Secondly, most
businessmen like to have goals to shoot for. Planning gives them not
only that but a dash of optimism as well. It gives them a picture of
expansion to identify with—one of the reasons, perhaps, for the popularity of planning among younger men. Finally, as the psychologist
Robert N. McMurry once observed, "Planning sessions are 'future'
oriented" and "don't degenerate into the recrimination sessions so
common in executive committee meetings."

## CONTRIBUTORS TO THIS SECTION

*H. Edward Wrapp* is Associate Professor of Business Administration
at the Harvard Business School. He was formerly a member of the
University of Chicago faculty and served as Director of the Executive
Program there. His conclusions are based on a series of studies of
medium-sized and large companies.

*Peter Drucker* is the well-known author of *America's Next Twenty
Years, The Practice of Management,* and other books published by
Harper & Brothers. He is Professor of Management at the Graduate
School of Business at New York University and a consultant on busi-
ness policy and management organization to several of the largest
companies in the country.

*Robert F. Dick* writes from his experience as Vice-President and
Assistant to the President of Illinois Tool Works. It is interesting to
note that businessmen and writers have said that long-range planning
is impossible for an industry such as Mr. Dick's. His practical, down-
to-earth article should refute their claim.

*Melvin Anshen* is Professor of Industrial Administration at the
Graduate School of Industrial Administration, Carnegie Institute of
Technology. Over the years he has been active as a management con-
sultant and writer in professional journals. He was formerly asso-
ciated with the faculties of the Harvard Business School, Indiana
University, Stanford University, the University of Georgia, and the
University of Wisconsin.

# 6.

# Organization for Long-Range Planning

## BY H. EDWARD WRAPP [1]

Long-range planning has been high on the hit parade at management meetings and conferences in recent months, and as a technique it promises to be the next addition to the formula for "progressive" management. Moreover, the fact that consultants are much interested in it is a reliable harbinger that, ready or not, top executives are going to be hearing a lot about why they should embrace it. In fact the interest is so great—particularly as compared with accomplishment to date—that there is real danger of the whole thing rapidly becoming a fad.

But just because a fad sometimes turns into a fiasco when introduced in a company, it does not follow that management can ignore the long-range planning task. Fad or not, here is something management must look at seriously—cautiously, perhaps, but nonetheless purposefully—that is, unless the company wants to undergo deliberate or unconscious liquidation.

Unfortunately, as pointed out in a recent issue of this magazine,[2] it is difficult to find plans to study and learn from. In the few companies where real projects of this kind have been undertaken there is reluctance to disclose the conclusions drawn by the planners, for

[1] Reprinted by permission from *Harvard Business Review*, January–February, 1957, pp. 37–47.
[2] David W. Ewing, "Looking Around: Long-Range Business Planning," *Harvard Business Review*, July–August, 1956, p. 135.

fear that this might reveal to competitors the company's most closely guarded secrets on strategy and tactics. However, there is less hesitation to discuss *how* the planners went about getting the answers, and any executives who are considering the establishment of long-range planning in their firms can learn a great deal from a study of the ways in which other companies have approached the problem.

For this reason, and also because I think the administrative problem of introducing the planning activity and nursing it through the early stages is critical, I will concentrate on various organizational devices, on the approaches used to develop plans, and on some words of advice gathered from talking to executives who made a few mistakes along the way.

## TRENDS AND COUNTERTRENDS

Long-range planning is that activity in a company which sets long-term goals for the firm and then proceeds to formulate specific plans for attaining these goals. There seems to be some indication that five years is the appropriate time span.[3] A shorter period hews too closely to operating problems and discourages the consideration of planning problems, whereas a longer period becomes too nebulous as a basis for developing "supporting" plans, i.e., detailed statements of what must be done in order to meet the long-term goals.

Up to now, not many companies other than the giants have done very much about such long-range planning on any formal basis. Typically, managements in small and medium-sized companies are too busy trying to make a profit for the current months to find time to think about what the company will be doing five years from now. Yet these same managements are making frequent decisions with long-term implications—decisions which, in many cases, are even more critical for them than for their bigger competitors—simply because they cannot as easily afford a costly error on a new product or a new plant.

Of course, no successful company is able to get along without some kind of forward planning. In the past, however, this has usually taken the form of one or two top executives setting the general direction of

[3] See Mark W. Cresap, Jr., "Long-Term Planning," *Advanced Management,* January, 1953, p. 34.

growth. It may have been no more explicit than a strong urge to expand sales. Even where companies have joined the rush to diversification, the purpose has often been expressed in terms of adding volume rather than in terms of making effective use of company resources or reinforcing particular weak spots. Only in isolated instances has a wide group of company executives been involved in laying out detailed plans for the growth of the enterprise which they manage.

What accounts, then, for the sudden flurry of attention to planning? In particular, why is so much interest being given to the committee type of organization for planning?

Certainly a part of the explanation lies in the fact that the financial analysts in search of growth companies have reacted favorably to those situations where management has attempted to forecast the specific shape and scope of potential growth and then taken positive action in anticipation of future demands. With this stimulus, a strong "follow-the-leader" influence has developed. More and more top managements, trying to get something started, have looked around at what others have done. And they have seized on the organizational devices used by the very big companies which, because of their size and complexity, have almost inevitably had to set up some kind of formal group effort.

## Support and Opposition

However, the habits and traditions of the past are not easily overcome. Down the line, the feeling still persists that planning is the main function of the chairman and the president, and vice-presidents and lower echelons should concentrate on running the company. So it is not enough for top management itself to *awaken* to the need for more formal planning. Someone very near the top must also take the initiative in *pushing* long-range planning of the company-wide kind; otherwise the chances are remote that it will ever be started.

Even in an organization conditioned to welcoming new developments and improvements in techniques, the long-range-planning function will probably not be self-generating. The trouble is that in most companies the rules of the game are such that the managers concentrate on short-term objectives. Budgets, performance ratings, and bonuses almost always are focused on the near term; accomplishments toward long-term objectives, by contrast, are more difficult to measure, and in most instances no attempt at measurement is even made. It is not surprising, therefore, that after years of conditioning under these circumstances managers are less than enthusiastic about the "obvious" advantages of long-range planning. For example:

The president of a company with five divisions, each of which was headed by a general manager who had complete responsibility for sales and production, was disappointed because his general managers were not taking a "long-term view." But as one of the general managers commented to an outsider: "I'm too damn busy with day-to-day problems to even think beyond the current year's operations. We have to submit budgets, and this takes us twelve months ahead, but that's as far as we go. I'm judged on profit performance year by year."

Another kind of resistance stems from the fact that, in order to be effective, long-range planning must be comprehensive and in the process "look under all corners of the rug." Often the initial reaction is to regard the development of a master plan as a meddlesome, unnecessary intrusion. Many vice-president and highly placed executives look upon it as a direct reflection on the caliber of the management in their respective departments; and, no matter how careful the precautions, the planners will find it difficult to avoid such an interpretation.

Indeed, I would venture the hypothesis that the most serious obstacle to long-range planning is not so much the drain on management time, the actual problems of doing good planning, or the danger of revealing company strategy, as it is the subtle, but occasionally open, opposition of some executives which appears in the early stages of the development.

Hence top-management support is absolutely essential. I am aware that if you add up all the speakers and writers who stipulate top-management support in the area of their particular interests, each and every activity in the company appears to need such backing— and that is a physical impossibility. But the argument in the case of long-range planning is overriding, if only because the activity has always been thought of as so distinctly top-level.

## COMPANY APPROACH

Once the board of directors or the chief executive has committed the company to undertake long-range planning, the most critical decision to be made is how to approach the organizational problem—particularly the question of who is to be responsible for carrying the work through.

To get down to specifics, let me describe how one company approached this part of the long-range planning task, and then evaluate its efforts in comparison with those of several other companies.

## Operating Managers

The president of Company A appointed a senior vice-president with a background in sales as chairman of a planning committee. With the advice of the president, the chairman selected for the committee six managers from among the immediate subordinates of the vice-presidents: one each from product development, purchasing, staff engineering, research, production, and personnel. The chairman of the committee asked a junior executive from the market research department to serve as secretary of the committee, with the understanding that the task would require only about one-third of his time.

The chairman preferred not to assemble a special staff for the planning committee, and he suggested that the members of the committee draw upon existing staff personnel in their various departments for the studies required by the committee. An outside consultant was retained to meet with the committee, with the explicit understanding that he would act only as an adviser. Here is how the group functioned:

*Sales Forecasts.* The president had charged the planning committee with formulating a plan which would achieve a doubling of the company's sales within five years, without specifying how this goal was to be met. The committee decided to begin its work with an examination of the growth potential of the company's existing products. Considering such factors as population trends, a rising standard of living, and a high level of personal income, the planners estimated the total market for each of the products for the next five years.

They now attempted to estimate what share of the total market Company A could expect to get with each of its products. At this stage, the committee reckoned with expected improvements which the research group predicted for existing products, as well as with the best guess on the efforts of competitors in the various markets. The forecast assumed that expenditures for advertising, sales promotion, and sales salaries would rise proportionately with sales.

After surveying the domestic markets, the committee turned to the foreign markets and estimated the possible five-year growth in various countries over the world.

The total potential growth in existing products fell short of the total sales goal set by the president. To fill this gap the committee turned to new products. A detailed appraisal of the sales potential year by year was made for each of the four most promising new products then in various stages of development by the research department. Incidentally, the committee was the first to see that since one of the products had a large potential market yet was still in the early stages of research for large-scale production, there was both need and opportunity for making a closer study of possible acquisition of an existing company as an alternative to new plant.

At this point, the sales forecasts for existing products and new products were presented to the top executives. In their judgment, the estimates served as a reasonable basis for proceeding with more detailed studies of sales, production, manpower, and finances.

*Subcommittees for Special Studies.* With this general outline for company growth established, the members of the committee were able to break up into subcommittees to make more comprehensive studies in each area. For instance, the assumption previously made, that the dollars spent for advertising, sales promotion, and sales salaries would have to be increased proportionately as sales increased, had to be examined by a subcommittee of marketing specialists. The committee felt that as sales volume increased, perhaps a smaller percentage of the sales dollar would be needed for these purposes. On the other hand, as competitors intensified their efforts and as Company A sought an increasingly larger share of the total market, there was some reason to believe that a bigger share of the sales dollar would be needed to generate the expected volume of sales.

Before each subcommittee began any extensive studies, it was asked to prepare a description of how it proposed to collect the data needed for its final report. This proposed approach was presented to the entire committee for discussion, and many time-saving and money-saving suggestions were offered. For instance, the need for one expensive study was eliminated by the consolidation of two completed studies made by separate departments but not previously circulated outside the departments.

Concurrent with the sales study, a group of production representatives worked out a year-by-year schedule for existing production facilities. As shortages of facilities became apparent, they planned the type and location of new facilities needed over the five-year period. They also investigated the company's sources of raw materials and forecasted the pattern of price movements which might be expected. Finally, this group estimated the year-by-year capital requirements for the new facilities and predicted the manufacturing, freight, and warehousing costs for each product. A specialist on linear programing was called in to assist with this phase of the study.

A personnel group was also active. By keeping in touch with the deliberations in the sales and production subcommittees, it was able to draw plans for organizational changes, training needs, and recruitment requirements which would fulfill the expectations of the sales and production subcommittees.

*Future Steps.* The first five-year plan is not yet finished. The final stage is to compute the total capital requirements for new facilities and for working capital purposes. By projecting the budgeting procedure five years ahead, pro-forma profit and loss statements can be prepared for each of the years. Crude calculations of return on investment made at many stages to test the feasibility of certain individual projects will then be refined in the light of data available on all phases of the master plan.

Two years of the five-year planning period will have transpired before the committee is able to present a detailed master plan which the chairman believes is reliable as a basis for management action. The next task of the committee will be to project the plan for an additional two years. Each year thereafter the committee will review the four years of plans remaining and add a fifth year, so that a five-year plan will always be available for management guidance. The methods developed and the evidence gathered during the preparation of the first five-year plan will greatly simplify future projections, and the committee will concentrate on refining the projections and making detailed studies of proposals which have long-term implications for the company.

## Solid Accomplishments

During the months of staff work and meetings, the committee members constantly found it difficult to avoid being sidetracked on studies of urgent operating problems; but under the subtle prodding of the chairman, who tolerated occasional detours, the group has made steady progress in assembling a mass of data, interpreting it, and drawing conclusions in terms of specific plans for future expansion. The president is enthusiastic about the committee's work; he sees a blueprint emerging that can serve as a general framework within which management can make specific decisions on sales, production facilities, new products, man-power needs, and capital requirements.

In addition, the planning committee has been a valuable training ground for developing future top executives. The members of the committee, who were already key operating managers, have been introduced to the difficult task of planning before being moved into positions where they have a major responsibility for thinking ahead. And having prepared and understood the plans, the members of the committee are ready to make the moves which will put those plans into effect when the "go-ahead" is given. In several instances, departmental projects have been initiated as a result of committee discussions without waiting for completion and approval of the over-all plans. The company enjoys the further advantage of having a real "team" of managers at the second level who have learned to work together.

Finally, the committee chairman has been able to sharpen his evaluation of each committee member's ability to put aside operating pressures and to devote a portion of his energies to the broader tasks of management. By combining executives who are especially imaginative and "creative" with men who tend to be more analytical and "scientific," and by mixing a great range of company experience, the chairman has been able to achieve a happy blend of bold, expansionist-oriented thinking and rigorously logical planning based on factual data.

## Difficulties Experienced

Despite some solid accomplishments during its tenure, the planning committee's work has not always gone smoothly. The members of the committee, as well as the vice-presidents they report to, are extremely busy with operating problems; and while they recognize the value of the committee's work, both they and their bosses put top priority on immediate problems. In a way, this situation has been advantageous in that it has forced the committee member to delegate much of the spadework to subordinates, but without any question the committee's progress has been slowed by the continual preoccupation with immediate problems.

Also, the vice-presidents of the company are not charged directly with responsibility for planning, and this probably accounts for a certain amount of indifference toward the aims of the committee.

Another difficulty growing out of such an approach, which centers the planning function below the vice-presidential level, is that at certain stages the committee members may not be fully informed about proposals under consideration by the president and vice-presidents. Although most committee members have welcomed the opportunity to deal with broad company policies and problems, nevertheless they have experienced real frustration when, after weeks of study and discussion, a planning proposal has been rendered obsolete by top management's announcement of a move which the members of the committee did not know was under consideration.

Up to now, no workable line of communication has been set up for keeping the planning committee posted on the disposition of its proposals. As one committee member put it, following a two-hour presentation to the executive staff (composed of the president, executive vice-president, and vice-presidents): "There goes another four months' work down the well. We'll probably never hear from it again." Top-policy decisions are made by the executive staff; and since the committee members do not participate in these deliberations, they cannot appreciate the part that their studies may have played in the final decisions.

Another problem has been the sharing of information. As the subcommittees got set to work on various aspects of the master plan, some tended to hold off beginning their jobs until they had received the conclusions of other groups. Of course, it was to be expected that operating men would be inclined to plan within the specifications set by others; yet, to make the most effective progress, each group needed to be working with the others so that ideas could flow back and forth. For instance:

During the production subcommittee's study of the possibilities of expanding plant facilities, such factors as comparative costs, ease of distribution to markets, and availability of raw materials were considered. The group assumed that the management organization could adjust to whatever proposal it devised, and only after it had settled on a plan was a personnel subcommittee invited to prepare supporting programs for a management staff and a work force.

If, from the start, a personnel subcommittee had been studying the ideal expansion plan, considered from the standpoint of organization and personnel, it might have added an additional dimension to the production group's deliberations and thus have helped it to come up with a more practical proposal. As it was, the personnel subcommittee simply "planned" within the limits set down by the other subcommittee.

## ALTERNATIVE APPROACHES

Top executives who anticipate or have experienced the shortcomings of Company A's approach may want to consider different systems. A company that began with a planning committee similar to Company A's, but was discouraged by the difficulty of combining planning and operating responsibilities in the same persons, abandoned this approach in favor of a group whose members were assigned full-time to the planning activity. As before, the members of the committee were selected from the various departments of the company, but under the new arrangement they were completely relieved of operating responsibilities.

There is a noteworthy advantage in such an approach in that a more detailed master plan could be developed sooner. But most chief executives would be horrified at the prospect of having a group of operating managers—at least, if they were good men—taken away from their jobs completely for a very long period of time. Almost immediately these operating managers would be tagged as *staff* men and, as a result, lose their preferred positions for influencing the line managers. This raises the question of what kinds of variations from Company A's approach are possible and practical.

### Top-Level Vice-Presidents

Company B, which, like Company A, had a centralized management consisting of functional departments reporting to vice-presidents, decided in favor of the following kind of committee organization:

The president of Company B gave his highest-ranking assistant additional duties as vice-president for planning and administration. This vice-president became chairman of a fifteen-man planning committee composed of all the other vice-presidents. A subcommittee was appointed for each project which the planning committee decided to investigate. (Note how much less comprehensive the aims of this group were than the aims of Company A's planning committee.) A vice-president was always selected as chairman of the subcommittee, which might include other vice-presidents as well as company officials who were not members of the planning committee.

An assistant vice-president for planning was appointed. He became an ex-officio member of each subcommittee and coordinated their activities. The chairman of the subcommittee was responsible for the writing of the report to the planning committee, although he was free to call upon anyone to assist him in collecting and organizing data.

The planning committee did not attempt to formulate an over-all five-year plan, but studied a variety of individual projects, some of which were initiated by the president, some by members of the planning committee, and others by executives at various levels in the company. All of the projects had long-term implications.

Originally, a subcommittee was dissolved when its recommendations on a project had been accepted by the planning committee; but over a period of time, as the proposals began to fall into a definite pattern, the chairman of the planning committee decided to appoint standing subcommittees. For instance, the subcommittee on facilities came to be in continual operation and reviewed all projects which concerned the company's physical plant and equipment.

As the organization evolved, the top-planning committee became a review committee, while the real spadework of collecting and interpreting facts and judgments went on in the subcommittees. The chairman convened the fifteen-man planning committee only to consider a report by one of its subcommittees. This happened on an average of four times per year.

The prompt and serious attention given to recommendations emanating from the planning activity created an extremely favorable atmosphere. There was never a delay in setting a meeting once the subcommittee was ready to report, and members gave top priority to attendance at these meetings. The president and board of directors responded similarly in taking up recommendations submitted to them. Because of this favorable top-management attitude, the subcommittees encountered little resistance in persuading various members of the company to undertake staff work, some of which was quite extensive.

At the same time, Company B's planning was not, obviously, as ambitious as Company A's. There was no master plan systematically accounting for the activities of all major company functions for a prescribed period of future years. It might be said, therefore, that in the short term Company B sacrificed the potentials of Company A's over-all planning for a thorough study of projects stemming from immediate problems. I do not mean to imply, however, that this is a case of "either-or," that there is no middle ground between the approaches of Companies A and B. Indeed, as we shall see, other alternatives have already been proved practical—at least in the case of divisionalized companies.

## Divisional Heads

Ordinarily, a company which is decentralized into divisions, each with a general manager responsible for sales, production, man power, and profits, presents a simpler long-range-planning problem than that of either Company A or B. Within a division, the general manager and his staff are trained to work together on over-all divisional problems. Thus in effect each division becomes a separate planning center concentrating on a single product or line of related products. Such a setup can be advantageous in long-range planning, as the following example illustrates:

The president of Company C asked each of his eight division managers to prepare a five-year plan for his division. Each plan was to be presented at an all-day meeting at the home office attended by the president and all the vice-presidents. The home-office meetings were primarily intended to keep the top staff informed. The president and vice-presidents were free to comment on the plans, but any modifications had to be made by the general manager of the division.

Members of the home-office staff were available to assist the general manager in preparing his plan, but for the most part the division personnel did the work. For instance, all the plant managers in a division were active in drawing up production plans. The division controller also played an important role in assembling quantitative data.

The caliber of the initial presentations varied greatly. Moreover, they were so disparate as to organization, content, and criteria that comparisons among divisions were difficult. But by coordinating subsequent reports through a member of the home-office staff who was assigned the task, greater uniformity was attained.

At first there was resistance to Company C's planning attempt. Some managers argued that their divisions were doing very well profitwise and that they should not be dictated to on the question of whether or not to prepare a long-term plan. But since the first round of presentations, when several skeptics became convinced by what they saw come out of the other divisions, the opposition has dwindled, and almost without exception the managers have accepted the planning job with a high level of enthusiasm. They have discovered that a well-documented plan provides the best evidence they can muster to persuade the home office to allocate additional funds to their divisions.

At the same time, the presentation of long-range plans has put top executives at headquarters in a better position to judge the performance of the division managers. In a few instances the early presentations disclosed a lack of staff work even for day-to-day operations, much less for the more difficult task of forward planning. Those divisions with the most refined cost systems, budgets, and market research were able to produce more comprehensive plans from the outset. The emphasis on long-term planning in the meetings highlighted the efforts of those managers who were planning for long-term return on investment concomitantly with good profits from current operations.

It is interesting to note, in passing, that while top management effectively delegated the planning for the divisions to the general managers, it called on a consulting firm to help in drawing up an over-all plan for the company. The consulting firm was asked to study such problems as further diversification, the growth potential in existing divisions, and the prospects of competition from products and processes which might be introduced by other companies.

## Specialists and Consultants

When the long-range-planning task is added to the already crowded schedules of a company's executives, progress on the plans may be painfully slow. To alleviate this problem, several companies have set up a special staff, usually reporting at a high level in the company, or have retained a management consulting firm to prepare the plans. For instance:

The chairman of the board of Company D hired an economist to develop a five-year plan. The economist brought three assistants with him. This group conducted extensive interviews and investigations in the company and drew upon sources close to the industry, such as the trade association, investment bankers, and government agencies. Within about eighteen months, the economist made a four-hour presentation outlining a master plan to the board of directors, which is composed mainly of the top officers in the company. The meeting broke up after a brief discussion, and the chairman asked that each member of the board study the 450-page report written by the economist and his staff. At the time this article was written, six months had elapsed since the initial presentation, but discussion of the report had not been resumed.

The lesson of this case is clear. The master plan was supported by a mass of evidence and had been carefully reasoned. As a starter, it was more complete and embodied a greater range of ramifications than most plans developed in companies that have relied on existing line and staff personnel. Yet I suspect that nothing will come of it. The understanding and confidence in a plan that can come only from months of painstaking development by the managers concerned are missing. Unless the chairman of the board presses hard, none of the major propositions in the plan will ever be acted upon. And the chairman probably has a bad case of indigestion as he looks at his untouched copy of the big report and thinks of the equally sizable bill.

I do not deny that at certain stages a special staff or a management consultant may be indispensable to a company planning group. Rather, someone with technical knowledge or broad experience in a market or industry quite often can assist tremendously by bringing a fresh and objective point of view to bear. But specialists lose their advantage when complete responsibility·for the planning is turned over to them, and, unfortunately, many companies have foundered on this "easy" course of action. Part of the gain to be secured in long-range planning is the thinking-through that the company itself must do, without regard for whether it ends up as pieces of paper with words and graphs on them.

## The Starting Point

The type of management organization, the diversity of products, and the extent of previous budget and research activity are probably the most important factors in deciding how to pick a starting point for the planners.

For instance, a company organized into divisions with a relatively autonomous general manager responsible for a single product or related group of products may be able to begin, as did Company C, by asking each division to prepare a five-year plan. Implicit in such a request is the assumption that the division will continue to expand so long as a satisfactory return on investment can be earned. Home-office management may even leave to the division manager the burden of presenting arguments as to what rate of return should be expected in his organization, although it will probably reserve the right of final decision.

Some home-office coordination may be required if comparisons are to be made of one division with another or if uniform yardsticks are to be applied. One company, for instance, developed a "standard" outline for each division's presentation:

| | |
|---|---|
| The industry | Return on investment |
|     Our position | Location of new facilities |
|     Competitors' activities | Man-power requirements |
| Sales forecasts | Management controls |
|     Present products | Pricing policies |
|     New products | Appraisal of strengths |
| Capital investment requirements |     and weaknesses |
| Working capital | |

Special problem areas

If a company has had considerable experience with market research and budgeting procedures, the planning group may be able to start by setting five-year sales goals as did Company A. The point, however, is that sales and cost forecasting techniques are indispensable to this phase of planning. Unless the members of the planning group are familiar with such techniques—and certainly many operating managers are—they will probably be skeptical of the "crystal gazing" when first introduced to it. Because it is foreign to their own experience, the planning may seem to them like so much "guesswork."

## Selection of Projects

For starting the work of the planning group, the most desirable kind of project is one which poses some operating questions, has long-term implications, and involves the operating experiences of several members of the committee. For instance:

If the committee sets out to formulate a plan for taking a new product from the research laboratory through the various stages of introducing it in a national market, the members can learn how to function effectively as a group; and at an early point they may derive a sense of accomplishment which will give them more "steam" for the forays ahead.

Also, since the time span for the introduction of a new product may be two or three years or even longer, the committee will get some practice in setting up timetables and in stating explicitly the action which needs to be taken at various stages. As an illustration, training assignments may be needed immediately if management personnel with proper qualifications are to be available three years hence, when the product reaches the market.

After working with one or two limited projects of this type, committee members should be more ready to tackle a more comprehensive planning assignment, if it happens to be called for. Interestingly enough, in this connection, one planning committee which has functioned successfully for several years has never in fact attempted to draw up a master long-term plan for the company's future. But look at some of the projects which have been undertaken:

Optimum size of main manufacturing facility (a major expansion is now under way as a result of the planning committee report).

Building versus renting home office space (a large office building has now been started).

Employee housing adjacent to main plant (this was undertaken as a company project and subsequently developed into a major rehabilitation project by the community).

Scholarships (a policy on contributing to educational institutions was formulated).

Employee stock purchases (a plan for acquisition of company stock by employees at all levels evolved).

Reappraisal of an existing product (production and sale of this product were discontinued as a result of the planning committee's recommendation).

Note that the decisions reached in each of these projects represent *long-term* commitments. Moreover, the chairman's insistence that the committee produce definite recommendations and put them in writing has resulted in a series of carefully documented statements; and as these seemingly unrelated recommendations are accumulated, a very useful background of sales, production, and financial data is being built for a possible over-all company plan.

Perhaps more important, these studies have forced the planners to make more explicit the criteria which will guide the company's growth. For instance, in making a recommendation to expand its main plant, the committee found itself involved in long-term market forecasts for certain geographical areas. Once the commitment for expansion was made, the company was tied irrevocably to concentrating its marketing efforts in those areas.

The significant thing to keep in mind is that such "piecemeal" efforts would not be making a contribution to real planning if they focused on projects oriented toward operations. Unless such a focus is avoided, the committee may find itself falling into the role of supervising a sort of top-drawer suggestion box and never pushing on to the task of tackling long-range problems.

### Within Real Limits

One good way to start, it seems to me, would be for the planners to make a study of the factors which will limit the company's growth in the future. This approach has the advantage of permitting a number of subgroups to begin simultaneous exploration of questions vital to the planning activity, and in addition it encourages realism.

Take the sales forecast, for instance. Management falls too frequently into the trap of planning how the company will increase its share of the market with only slight recognition of what its competitors are doing. It is certainly understandable that this happens when the sales outlook is worked out by a committee of enthusiastic marketing men. But a planning group composed only partly of salesmen is more likely to be realistic on this point.

Again, shortage of capital may put a limitation on a company's growth, and so it is a good question to study. Even when management can plan for a liberal return on additional capital, other conditions may prevent the attraction of funds to the company. Shortages of production facilities place still another limitation upon growth, albeit a short-term one; and also raw-materials supplies may present a problem.

An important limitation to examine is management personnel. Planners seem to have a tendency to assume that an existing management organization can undergo unlimited upgrading and that the lack of capable, trained managers need never hamper a company's growth. The almost universal experience of managers when they come face to face with expansion, however, is that this is not true.

## GENERAL OBSERVATIONS

As I review the experience of several different companies that have organized for long-range planning, a number of general points and suggestions stand out in my mind. I shall set them forth briefly by way of conclusion.

### By-Products

Several valuable by-products can be derived from a long-range planning effort:

"Crystallization" of executive thinking is more likely to take place if planners are expected to produce recommendations, and especially if these recommendations are to be put in writing.

Committee investigations and deliberations are an excellent means of keeping the top executives informed about different parts of the business. Such a channel may be particularly needed in a company which has been growing rapidly, for oftentimes there is no systematic means for top executives to learn of developments in a new division, especially if its managers come to the corporation as a part of a smaller company. (Incidentally, new executives in a company might be appointed to a planning group as a part of their indoctrination in over-all company problems.)

A planning group may find blind spots and potential problem areas which the regular management group might easily miss in a rapidly expanding firm. When given an over-all responsibility rather than a limited assignment, the planners should become skillful in catching up loose ends which are either being overlooked or perhaps even deliberately ignored.

The planning group may provide a company-wide sounding board for appraising the potential of new techniques. Linear programing, for example, may be introduced as a valuable planning tool for making decisions on plant location, production scheduling, and shipping patterns. However, the use of the technique requires the massing and interpretation of data from many parts of a company. A planning group composed of managers with diversified backgrounds is better equipped to judge the usefulness of such a complex device.

### Common Blind Spots

The planners may find it difficult to persuade sales managers to disassociate sales estimates for planning purposes from the estimates they set as goals for the sales force. The practice of setting sales goals higher than those which are reasonably attainable is so habitual for the sales executive that he unconsciously carries over his heady optimism into planning work. Moreover, the objective of expanding sales volume can become such an obsession that the costs of expansion are ignored. For example:

In one company, the sales representative on a planning committee insisted that a certain volume of sales was attainable, in the face of opposition from every other committee member. Only when he was confronted with the costs of production facilities needed to back up his goal, and asked to vote on a recommendation that this expenditure be made, did he finally suggest that the sales estimates be scaled downward.

As previously noted, planners tend too easily to assume that enough management talent will be available no matter how ambitious the expansion plans may be. If their record is marred by one mistake, it is their failure to recognize that the "lead time" needed for building the management organization may be longer than that needed to adjust any other single factor to higher profit goals. Rather than the afterthought that it oftentimes is, man-power planning should figure prominently in the conception of a master plan.

Moreover, top management must not expect immediate results from long-range planning. It requires a type of thinking which is strange and difficult for most line executives, whose training and experience have prepared them to deal with operating problems but not to probe too far into the future. Unlike some new undertakings where the cream can be skimmed at the start, effective long-range planning will start slowly and gain momentum as more and more data are gathered to throw light on the future.

Any problem which is so complex as to require that it be analyzed piecemeal, and the analyses regrouped for an over-all appraisal, is particularly difficult in the early stages. The long-range planners usually have so few facts about other phases of the business that they must rely on wholesale assumptions in order to make progress; forward thinking based on such assumptions is alien to most practical operating men. However, once they can point to a tangible recommendation which sparked a line of action that otherwise would not have been taken, interest in long-range planning is sure to grow.

## "Inside Job" Needed

If line officers are given the responsibility for developing the plans, they will be more ready to support them once they are translated into the action stage. The planning function strikes so close to the heart of the management task that line managers are almost certain to become defensive and resist intrusion if the board or the chief executive hires a consultant or an economist to master-mind the planning.

In working and talking with executives about long-range planning, I have been surprised, but agreeably so, that so many have resisted the temptation to begin by hiring a staff of specialists to do the job, and instead have taken the more difficult course of depending on the existing management staff to do the spadework.

If given the primary responsibility, specialists have a way of introducing new techniques and ways of thinking strange to a company, and such a start on long-range planning may saddle it with a handicap which can never be overcome. By dependence on the people already in the company, management gains another advantage in discovering the strengths and weaknesses of existing departments. As indicated earlier, however, the consultant can often serve usefully by giving *assistance* to the executives in charge of planning—for instance, by providing new leads or by making special studies.

## Conditions of Success

Good long-range planning is expensive in more ways than one. The plans are inevitably complex, and many risks must be assessed. A comprehensive plan in which everyone can exhibit confidence will require hours of discussion even after the time-consuming collection of data has taken place. Management should not be led to believe that long-range planning can be added to the list of executives' tasks without making noticeable demands on their time. To have a set of plans based on less-than-thorough discussions and superficial investigations by the managers who design them is probably worse than to have none. Such plans are a dangerously shaky foundation for commitments of company capital.

At the start top management must give strong support to the planning activity. Not only is it time-consuming, but the kind of thinking needed is foreign to most executives, and the returns are difficult to predict. However, there is a brighter side of the picture. Unlike other activities calling for strong top-management support, the long-range-planning function need not be *perpetually* parasitic. If the top company officer and the board of directors show by their interest and action that they value planning, and if the planners can make one or two solid contributions, the activity should become self-sustaining.

The development of a master plan for growth probably must be entrusted to executives very near the top of the organization. In today's competitive scene, so many factors must be considered that only men with real management breadth are capable of assigning proper weights to the many different considerations involved in charting a future course of action. The specialist with a departmental point of view can make only limited contributions to an over-all plan for the company. Another argument in favor of placing the planning at the top level is the fact that the planners must have access to confidential information, and broad dissemination of such material in a company may provide dangerous leaks to competitors.

Finally, the planners should be near enough to the top to see their efforts as an influence on company policy. Planning has many frustrations, but the worst is to see top management making major commitments while failing to recognize or ignoring the long-term implications which the planning group could help to clarify.

These are some of the real difficulties involved in inaugurating a comprehensive and reliable long-range planning program. If management will face these difficulties, the rewards will be equally real.

# 7.

# Long-Range Planning

## BY ROBERT F. DICK [1]

The actual planning consists of two ingredients: (1) the determination of long-term goals; and (2) the establishment of specific programs to achieve the goals.

My company's long-term objectives are reasonably clear—though, as each future year comes into sharper focus, we may revise our goals if the acid of reality eats away earlier wishful thinking. Here's what is done:

Five-year sales goals, established by product lines, are expressed in units and dollars.

Five-year sales goals also are set for new product lines currently in the engineering stage, the pilot-plant stage, or early commercialization.

Gross and net profit margins are predicted by product lines. Return on investment is computed by years for each product division.

Capital availability is estimated after dividends and taxes for working capital and fixed capital additions.

Machinery and equipment expenditures are estimated in detail by product division for three years, and in total for the fourth and fifth years. These estimates are not always very meaningful, since, under our equipment replacement policy, requests for equipment replacement are refused unless economically justified.

Building and plant expansion plans are forecast on a three-year basis. Under a current assignment from the president, this period is being extended by two more years.

[1] From Robert F. Dick, "Long-Range Planning," in *Management Planning and Manpower Development* (American Management Association, General Management Series, Number 173, 1954), pp. 8–12. Reprinted by permission.

These steps are typical of the action taken to determine our long-term objectives. In addition, we still badly need to improve our thinking ahead on new products, product sales emphasis, and percentage of desired market penetration.

The second ingredient of planning consists of long-term program development that will aid in attaining the objectives laid down. The problem here is to see that the follow-through is as good as the intentions. Four of our programs which are rather typical are concerned with organization, management development and attitudes, product lines, and physical facilities and equipment.

## ORGANIZATIONAL PLANNING

We are in the process of decentralizing our organization along the lines of both products and plants for the purpose of promoting growth. Decentralization primarily means one thing—decentralization of decision-making. Two years ago the Shakeproof Division had functional heads over sales, engineering, production, and industrial relations. Today we have three general managers and our marketing manager reporting to a division vice-president.

In my opinion, it will take three additional years before both organizational and supervisory requirements have been fully met. Decentralization has been difficult and has been further complicated by the fact that management control is being passed to a younger group of men. The following are typical of the problems raised:

1. To decentralize is one thing; to get the new general managers to "reach out" and make their own decisions is another. Conversely, getting the old guard to "let go" is not always easy.

2. How should the general managers participate in over-all planning?

3. Duties and responsibilities under decentralization have to be exceedingly precise.

4. How should controls be established that will coordinate the different decentralized divisions?

5. Cash needs, inventory levels, capital expenditures, and levels of employment, for example, all follow centralized planning but affect the decentralized unit's operations.

We have made considerable progress, and we feel that the direction trends are right. However, good communication, prompt decision-making, and intelligent planning are a coresponsibility of central staff and decentralized operating executives. Failure here can result in decentralization neurosis.

## MANAGEMENT DEVELOPMENT AND ATTITUDES

The most priceless ingredient a company has is its supervision—from the group leader up to the president. Therefore, in my opinion, there is no more important high-command responsibility than that of developing able younger men. How frequently all of us fumble this ball by:

Poor selection or failure to use modern selection techniques.

Failure to delegate authority.

Lack of courage to clean out the incompetents who act as roadblocks to stronger men on the management pyramid.

Letting too many potentially strong executives slip through the fence to greener pastures.

Adopting training programs that create more specialists when we need generalists or men with a broad over-all management background.

Failing to realize that developing men of management caliber requires an individual, not a mass, approach.

At the Illinois Tool Works we have quietly asked ourselves: What will the business need in the next five to ten years in the way of executive competence? Shall we have the potential timber available? Five plans were set up and followed for the development of the management group:

1. Every supervisor in the company has been given psychological tests in order to ascertain individual strengths and weaknesses. We believe in aptitude testing as a tool to supplement judgment in promoting, transferring, downgrading, and eliminating men.

2. Under our management inventory process, each supervisor is rated on current job performance, as well as on future potentiality. Merit ratings, coupled with counseling interviews, are made semiannually. Management replacement and promotion tables are established, and selected "comers" are isolated for special attention.

3. Training requirements have been established in cooperation with immediate supervisors for all team members. Job rotation is consistently practiced. Through plant visitations, job training, counseling, supervisory training, and attendance at AMA seminars and workshop clinics, we have tried to get the feeling of training needs.

4. We are evolving our own criteria to choose the right men for areas of enlarged management responsibility. These relate to present job performance, as well as to performance on special assignments tossed out as "bait" to see what happens. It frequently takes hours of informal counseling before the "bait" is taken—and many times it is never taken. This kind of fishing requires patience, and it needs more than the slim-reed support of presidential edict if results are to be continuously acceptable.

5. While formal development techniques have been useful, they don't actually develop leaders. The leaders seem to develop themselves. We can encourage them by removing restrictions, by creating a favorable atmosphere, and by working with them on an individual basis through listening and asking questions on the problems they have to solve. I am convinced that our development program will become productive in proportion to the opportunity provided to these "comers" to utilize their talents in applying the principles of sound management. However, they must forge themselves in the fires of their own decisions.

A significant part of training generally overlooked is that of engendering the right attitudes. You can call it communication, open-mindedness, or freedom of speech—the label is unimportant. In brief, our young "comers" are encouraged to think out loud and present ideas regardless of how stupid they sound. They verbally bounce around thoughts on problems and plans without any fear of "blotching" their record. They know that beaten paths are for beaten men. They are also encouraged to "reach out"—to take the ball and run with it, so to speak, and to try their ideas for size. We have a president who accepts the principle of "reaching out" and accepts the consequences. The obstacle that has to be overcome is not to get more men to talk—but to get more of the right men to listen.

## Product Lines

The introduction of new products is the lifeblood of most businesses. Our minimum goal has been a major new product every five years. As research and development effort is stepped up, this time period must be reduced. We depend upon engineering skill and patent protection to build our lines.

In our new-product planning, a prescription is followed. This is really a screening device that the product must go through. The yardsticks include requirements relating to sales, profit margins, equipment utilization, patentability, fixed and working capital, and return on investment. Through a centralized new-product research function reporting to the president—and through customer application engineering at the decentralized division levels—a vehicle is provided for adding to the line products of both long- and short-term life. On completely new products, Centralized Research carries the ball from the inception of an idea through engineering, market evaluation, pilot-plant operations, and preliminary commercialization. At this point, an operating division takes over.

In product planning, there are three ingredients essential to success —in addition, of course, to the required technical know-how and organization:

1. An open-minded and enthusiastic top management that is willing to explore new ideas, provide the funds, write off its failures, and continue to gamble.

2. A top management that, through cooperation, interest, and teamwork, has integrated itself into new product development effort.

3. A top management that is constructively dissatisfied with research results.

## PHYSICAL FACILITIES AND EQUIPMENT

In collaboration with key operating executives, capital expenditures for plants and equipment are planned for a minimum of three and a maximum of five years. These determinations are based on long-term sales predictions.

All men have perfect vision when it comes to hindsight. Looking ahead, on the other hand, is more difficult. Our five-year unit or piece-part forecasts are utilized in determining equipment types, capacities and speeds, and tooling investment. Briefly cited, here are the factors that we use in our long-term equipment planning:

1. We know from an actual inventory how many machine units are either obsolete or practically obsolete, and what the dollar replacement values are. Present equipment evaluations are based on competitiveness and operating costs rather than on age.

2. We know what equipment will be needed for expansion and what the space and dollar investment requirements are going to be.

3. In spite of fads and fallacies, we follow an equipment replacement policy based on economic values. Within a given year, certain equipment and building decisions are controlled by profit performance.

4. We estimate costs, savings, investment, and profitability of all expansion programs.

5. While operating managers follow their equipment budget, each individual machine proposal amounting to more than $2,500 is subjected to a replacement analysis.

We are rapidly getting away from equipment replacement based on an exercise of intuition in favor of a factual and objective approach that is related to such formalized factors as the cost of not replacing, interest charges, original capital cost and capital addition, salvage value, cost savings, and service life. We all recognize that today's capital expenditures make the corporate bed that we must lie in tomorrow. It is necessary to make today's decisions on assumptions of what tomorrow will be like. Therefore, we must continue to project equipment and facility plans into the future to the best of our abilities.

## EVALUATION OF THE PLANNING EFFORT

The effectiveness of the planning effort is related to the growth of the business, the addition of new products, the development of people, the profit result on sales, and the profit return on investment. These are realistic criteria for evaluating the entire planning function. However, in order to evaluate the planning effort on a short-term basis—say, every three to six months—let's ask ourselves these questions:

1. Is some individual or some group within the company specifically charged with the responsibility for thinking out the plans, getting them in writing, and revising them as necessary when new facts or conditions come into play?

2. Is the thinking of key operating personnel included in the plans? Are they informed of final plans? Do they agree with the plans?

3. Is a postaudit made frequently enough to satisfy the requirement of integrating short-term plans into the over-all long-term goals?

4. Are roadblocks to successful completion of the plans being removed fast enough to permit eventual reaching of the goals?

5. Do we have sufficient courage to stick to our plans in spite of temporary squalls? Conversely, are the "misfires" written off soon enough to avoid sending good money after bad?

6. Do we have adequate financial, production, market, operating, and timing yardsticks to evaluate performance so that we really know whether the objectives are being reached?

If we can answer yes to these questions, then our planning ingredients are being properly mixed. Through their skillful short- and long-term blending companies grow and prosper.

Along with our planning, we should never forget that each business has a personality and a heart of its own. It is more than money, machines, markets, and methods. It is also people, and the character, wisdom, skill, and courage of those people, in the final analysis, reflect the success of the business. What better equation than *planning plus people equals profits!*

# 8.

# The Divorce of Planning from Doing

## By Peter F. Drucker [1]

The second blind spot of Scientific Management is the "divorce of planning from doing"—one of its cardinal tenets. Again a sound analytical principle is being mistaken for a principle of action. But in addition the divorce of planning from doing reflects a dubious and dangerous philosophical concept of an elite which has a monopoly on esoteric knowledge entitling it to manipulate the unwashed peasantry.

To have discovered that planning is different from doing was one of [Frederick W.] Taylor's most valuable insights. To emphasize that the work will become the easier, more effective, more productive, the more we plan before we do, was a greater contribution to America's industrial rise than stopwatch or time-and-motion study. On it rests the entire structure of modern management. That we are able today to speak seriously and with meaning of management by objectives is a direct result of Taylor's discovery of planning as a separate part of the job, and of his emphasis on its importance.

But it does not follow from the separation of planning and doing in the analysis of work that the planner and the doer should be two different people. It does not follow that the industrial world should be divided into two classes of people: a few who decide what is to be done, design the job, set the pace, rhythm and motions, and order others about; and the many who do what and as they are being told.

[1] From Peter F. Drucker, *The Practice of Management* (New York, Harper & Brothers, 1954), pp. 284–285.

Planning and doing are separate parts of the same job; they are not separate jobs. There is no work that can be performed effectively unless it contains elements of both. One cannot plan exclusively all the time. There must be at least a trace of doing in one's job. Otherwise one dreams rather than performs. One cannot, above all, do only; without a trace of planning his job, the worker does not have the control he needs even for the most mechanical and repetitive routine chore. Advocating the divorce of the two is like demanding that swallowing food and digesting it be carried on in separate bodies. To be understood, the two processes have to be studied separately. They require different organs, are subject to different ailments, and are carried out in different parts of the body. But to be nourished at all, the same body needs both, just as a job must contain planning as well as doing.

Taylor's divorce of planning from doing was both specifically American and specifically late nineteenth century. It is a descendant of our eldest tradition: the New England theocracy of the early Puritans. It puts the priestly-elite concept of Increase and Cotton Mather into modern dress, but leaves it otherwise almost unchanged; and like the Puritan divines Taylor deduced a God-given right of the planning elite to rule. It is no accident that we hear this right to rule described today as the "prerogative of management"—the term has always been applied to right by divine or priestly anointment.

But the divorce of planning and doing was also part of the elite philosophy that swept the Western world in the generation between Nietzsche and World War I—the philosophy that has produced such monster offspring in our time. Taylor belongs with Sorel, Lenin, and Pareto. This movement is usually considered to have been antidemocratic. It was—in intent and direction—fully as much antiaristocratic. For the assertion that power is grounded in technical competence—be it for revolutionary conspiracy or for management— is as hostile to aristocracy as to democracy. Both oppose to it the same absolute principle: power must be grounded in moral responsibility; anything else is tyranny and usurpation.

The divorce of planning from doing deprives us of the full benefit of the insights of Scientific Management. It sharply cuts down the yield to be obtained from the analysis of work, and especially the yield to be obtained from planning. We saw in the IBM story that productivity greatly increased when the workers were given responsibility for planning their work. The same increase in productivity (not to mention the improvement in worker attitude and pride) has been obtained wherever we have combined the divorce of planning from doing with the marriage of planner to doer.

# 9.

# Businessmen, Lawyers, and Economists

## By Melvin Anshen [1]

In recent years a number of changes have occurred in the internal dynamics of business which have affected the relative importance of fixed and variable costs, the scale on which operations are conducted, and the time in which decisions are made and their results realized. There have also been changes in the economic, social, and political world in which business functions. These developments are challenging established decision-making procedures.

One way management has tried to meet the challenge has been by appointing policy-formulating teams that assemble new combinations of skill and experience. Large organizations, faced with far-reaching decisions in allocation of resources, are turning with increasing frequency to working parties made up of businessmen, lawyers, and economists charged with responsibility for assessing the potential gains and risks of alternate policies, recommending action programs, and planning the strategy and tactics of their execution.

The effective use of this new combination of knowledge and experience raises several interesting administrative problems which I shall discuss in this article:

How can diverse abilities, attitudes, and intellectual personalities be assembled into valuable analytical and decision-making teams?

How should problems be selected for assignment to such teams?

How should the team be led, and what role should management play?

[1] Reprinted by permission from *Harvard Business Review*, March–April, 1957, pp. 107–114.

## The Modern Triumvirate

The questions involved in the use of teams arise because of the varied abilities, attitudes, and value systems that make up the characteristic intellectual personalities of the team members. The kinds of problems men recognize, the ways in which they weigh these problems and the elements in problem complexes, and their assessment of alternative policies and the means for their execution are the products of special aptitudes developed by education and experience.

Businessmen, lawyers, and economists start from markedly different foundations. These differences are significant. So, too, are the ways in which the differences are adapted to the problems assigned to such mixed teams.

### The Lawyer

We are not, of course, contemplating combinations of talent assembled for the first time. The lawyer is an old associate of the businessman. But until recently his classic assignment has been almost wholly of the attorney-client character: to get a company out of the trouble it has stumbled into inadvertently, and to tell management how best to avoid difficulties with its competitors, suppliers, customers, and the government.

Except when he himself became an operating executive (a professional transfer that appears to have been uncommon until the current management generation), the lawyer did not make policy decisions or participate in their formulation. The businessman decided what he wanted to do. He then informed his lawyer of his plan, and the lawyer advised him of the legal safety or risks of the proposed course of action, perhaps suggesting ways of accomplishing the announced program with minimal risks.

The lawyer's role is now changing from one of pointing out pitfalls and ways around them to one of recommending policy objectives and ways to achieve them. The transition is not difficult in an economy increasingly subjected to public regulation and administration.

As the lawyer takes an increasingly large part in formulating policy and in devising the strategy and tactics of its execution, he is likely to think and behave in a manner that reflects not only the special intellectual personality resulting from his legal education and professional experience, but also the philosophy and mental "set" often found in a young man who selects a career in the practice of law. With prompt acknowledgment of the many individuals to whom these observations do not apply (see my postscript to the article), I want to suggest that *in the main* the lawyer's characteristic intellectual personality is likely to be marked by the following dispositions:

To respect and to be guided by antecedent thought and action, and hence to prefer conservation to innovation.

To practice precision and avoid discontinuities in thought, word, and action.

To accept logic and reject emotion; to distrust impulse.

To value surface appearance above inner concept when they are in conflict.

To prefer qualitative to quantitative techniques.

To minimize technology as a social force.

To favor conciliation and compromise over authoritarian dissolution of differences.

Armed with these dispositions, and with the combative view of problem-solving that may well be an inevitable by-product of his education and experience, the lawyer often is disposed to study a complex management situation as if the essential assignment were to discover an issue on which the "case can be won." When he finds this issue, he may be masterly in his organization of precedent and current evidence to prove the rightness of his choice. He is likely to be impatient with those who want to consider alternate or supplementary courses of action. And he may not be interested in problems of administration and operation, including those growing out of organizational inertia and the many management headaches involved in "getting people to do things."

Like the business executive, the lawyer wants to distinguish between the important and the trivial. But in any given policy-making situation he is not likely to distinguish by the same criteria as the executive. Furthermore, his verbal facility, when added to his inclination to seek grounds for compromising differences, often leads him to mask fundamental disagreement in a seductive cloak of impressive language that has a high potential for misleading unwary associates.

Finally, he is likely to reveal his precedent-oriented cast of thought in a preference for small changes as against big jumps, for evolution rather than revolution. He is suspicious of sharp turns in policy that represent adventures in the selection of ends or means. He is a bloodhound in searching for booby traps, to an extent that may handicap rapid progress in a dynamic environment.

## The Economist

Now, in contrast, consider the economist. He comes to the business scene from his so-called ivory tower as a comparative stranger. Even in the capacity of observer, only a fraction of all economists are familiar with the structure and behavior of business organizations. Many assumptions with respect to the motivation and reasoning of business executives, which are fundamental to the great bulk of economic theorizing, have only recently been challenged as bearing little resemblance to the facts.[2]

Insofar as economics is concerned with studying, understanding, and explaining the decision-making process in business organizations (it is, of course, concerned with many other matters as well), economists have much to learn. But the rising rate of their employment by business organizations suggests that many managements suspect that they have something to contribute too. What this contribution may be, particularly in the area of policy formulation as distinct from forecasting, is suggested by their training and experience.

Like the lawyer, the economist is disposed to think and behave in a special manner. His intellectual personality is not an accident. Again acknowledging the many exceptions to these observations, I suggest that *in the main* economists characteristically reveal the following dispositions:

To be skeptical of all traditionally accepted theories.

To be willing to make bold experiments with new ideas, and to be equally ready to withdraw from commitments if the results prove unfavorable.

To accept both logic and emotion as valid components in the process of understanding and predicting human and organizational behavior.

To value inner concept above surface appearance when they are in conflict.

To have confidence in the possibility of devising methods for bringing

[2] See, for example, Leland Hazard, "What Economists Don't Know About Wages," *Harvard Business Review,* January–February, 1957, p. 48.

within the scope of quantitative techniques many phenomena hitherto handled only in qualitative terms.

To be interested in the process of manipulating people, and to believe that successful manipulation to achieve desired objectives is attainable in the foreseeable future.

To place a high value on technological development and innovation.

To welcome the resultant economic and social dynamics; to be unintimidated by change.

To suspect conciliation and compromise as potentially evasive in nature.

Armed with this risk-oriented set of dispositions, less restricted by precedent than the lawyer, and generally innocent of experience in the complexities of administration in large organizations, the economist is brassy in his approach to policy issues. He sees many possibilities in each situation, and he sees them with fresh vision. To the lawyer he often appears radical in his willingness to abandon the past. To the businessman, on the other hand, he may appear naïve in his ignorance of the extent to which people and organizations determine the feasibility of policies. And if he often undervalues the record of experience as a guide to current action, he may with equal frequency undervalue future risks as a constraint on the scope of decision-making and policy execution.

When successfully engaged in maximizing his assets and minimizing his liabilities, the economist is probably a better strategist than the lawyer, but a poorer tactician. At the same time, the potential contribution of his venturesome approach to policy formation is frequently weakened by his impatience with the lawyer's concern for a solid foundation for every construction, on the one hand, and with the businessman's concern for getting practical results fast, on the other.

## The Businessman

It is considerably harder to characterize the businessman, in his policy-making function, because he is not ordinarily the product of a systematic education. However, his unique administrative experience makes an indelible mark on the quality of his decision.

The businessman is characterized, above all else, by a kind of controlled pragmatism in his approach to new ideas. He has a disposition to experiment, but within limits defined in advance. He may be impatient with abstract reasoning and technical detail. He has great respect for organization as a tool for action. He knows from hard experience that turn-around time is always longer than anticipated, and that both the time and the costs of change usually exceed standard forecasts.

He tends to believe that successful management—which requires a high batting average in making sound policy decisions, devising sound plans for putting these decisions into effect, and getting organizations to execute action programs—is an art rather than a science. As an art, it is best learned by doing; education, diversified experience, exercise of authority under observation, and coaching by superiors may help to improve skill in performance, but only as supplements to responsible action.

He sees the decision-making job growing increasingly complex and even technical in nature, and he recognizes the economic and social influences that are combining to bring about this change—influences stemming from a society that has come to be strongly marked by public administration of the conditions within which private business operates, an external economic environment in which the most prominent characteristic is dynamic change, and an internal organizational necessity for making planning horizons distant as levels of fixed costs rise.

He may resent and resist the introduction of considerations with which he feels some lack of competence to deal; but with or without this resentment he finds himself increasingly compelled to solicit and ponder the advice of specialists. He has acquired some familiarity with the problems of working with and utilizing experts in the areas of engineering and research, and at least with the former group he is likely to have considerable confidence in the relationship.

When the businessman deals with lawyers and economists, he often senses himself at grips with minds, attitudes, and vocabularies that are foreign and even hostile to his own natural way of thought and expression, which can be characterized as follows:

To be pragmatic; to be skeptical of precedent and unafraid of, even eager for, change.

To be deeply conscious, in assaying change, that it rarely occurs quickly or by jumps, and that while it can be planned and guided, it cannot be absolutely controlled.

To recognize that organizations are complex associations of people resistant to change and not easily enlisted in common tasks, with the result that the accomplishment of innovation is always slower than anticipated.

To prefer concrete to abstract reasoning, quantitative to qualitative calculation.

To regard professionals and technicians with a mixture of respect and contempt, as being the possessors of essential special knowledge which they often cannot put to use.

To consider the body of legislative and administrative law as being probably essential but frustrating and unreasonably arbitrary, and therefore as something to be outwitted, circumvented, and, if necessary, evaded.

To approve technological innovation in principle, but often to deplore its speed in practice.

To acknowledge the necessity for long-range planning, while retaining an uneasy sensitivity and responsiveness to short-term fluctuations in economic indexes.

To profess a belief in the rationality of managerial decision-making, but to remain the servant of emotional judgments and hunches.

To respect and work for unanimity of staff opinion; to be disturbed by firm disagreement; and to accept group recommendations unmarked by dissent as evidence of thorough analysis and sound judgment.

The businessman has some of the lawyer's concern with the legislative and administrative framework within which he must function, and some of the economist's risk orientation. But he differs from both in his intense respect for and preoccupation with the operational aspects of management. He wants to know not only what to do but how to do it.

Moreover, he is well aware that business organizations are not simple tools for accomplishing assigned tasks. Organizations can also be quicksands in which executive purpose becomes mired and devitalized. They can delay schedules, they can blunt management's attack on critical problems, they can shift objectives. Under skilled leadership and with favorable external factors they can be manipulated. But on occasion they escape control and can compel management to accept decisions fashioned deep within the organization structure.

The businessman also differs from the lawyer and the economist in his overwhelming concern with the here and now. Before Lord Keynes reminded us of the hollowness of long-range thinking, the businessman knew, because the circumstances of his survival taught him to know, that in the long run we are all dead. Although he accepts and even supports long-range planning, he knows that the health and the survival of his organization depend on short-range success; and when, in a policy matter, he must choose between the two time horizons, he has no doubt how he should make the decision.

Finally, probably because he has not been the victim of the more rigid aspects of a professional education, the businessman brings to analysis and decision-making a more flexible mind than does the lawyer or the economist. This flexibility is evident in his willingness to cut his losses and move in a new direction when policies work out badly. It is evident, too, in the ease with which he lays the past aside, whether as precedent or as lesson. In short, he respects experience without being its prisoner.

## ORGANIZING TEAMS

What can be made of these diverse, often contradictory, skills? Obviously we do not want to keep lawyers, economists, and businessmen segregated and working in independent groups. A team composed of individuals with totally overlapping knowledge and skill is likely to contribute little more than could one of the members working individually, although there may be comfort in noisy unanimity. On the other hand, a team made up of polar opposites can turn out to be little more than a generator of mental static. What is the way out of the dilemma?

### Goals and Means

Perhaps the most important question to consider in building teams composed of diversely talented individuals is this: How specifically can the objectives and methods of the company be prescribed in advance?

Where higher authority can lay down concrete goals and can define means for their achievement—where it can define the fundamental working agreement—it can concentrate on finding the requisite combination of talent and experience without being seriously concerned about how the group will function as a social organism. But where a large degree of freedom must be left to the team to develop its own fundamental working agreement, one of top management's principal concerns must be the social aspects of the "product-mix" of talent and experience to which the assignment is entrusted.

To illustrate, let us consider some typical problems:

*Long-Range Planning.* The facts of life in a dynamic society compel management to make provision for long-range planning as a continuing function. But long-range planning can be directed or unguided, can have real targets or function without specific goals, can be concerned with defined problem areas (such as market potential or product requirements ten years ahead) or embrace all potential problem areas. If performance of the long-term planning function is made a group responsibility, who is to establish the group's fundamental working agreement? What are appropriate terms for such definition of mission?

It is top management that initially must recognize and accept the importance of getting effective long-range planning accomplished, and must allocate responsibility for the function within the organization structure.[3] But what can it know about the goals, the content, and the method of planning? Common experience suggests that in the usual situation it can define some targets for the planners, while others must be left undesignated. If top management tries to set all objectives, it assumes an omniscience it cannot possibly possess.

Where the planning team is given a range of freedom to determine operating goals, the composition of the group becomes a critical top-management decision. Unable to define in advance the full content of planning, management must choose planners who can themselves, from time to time as needed, make the necessary definitions.

*A Legal Problem.* Consider the radically different problem that is posed by government action against a firm under the Sherman or Robinson-Patman acts. The organization of defensive response has a specific ultimate objective. However, the operational complexities—starting in the legal area but quickly spreading to business practices and procedures and economic performance—are not predictable in advance and call for a high degree of intellectual flexibility under acute pressure of time.

A fundamental working agreement on the total mission of the team responsible for preparing the firm's defense can be laid down by top management. The task is, in effect, defined by the need for it. But beyond this point the assignment becomes immersed in detail in which only technicians can claim competence. In normal practice and by any rule of reason, the lawyers call the shots. But the records of court trials and proceedings before the Federal Trade Commission offer ample proof of the frequency with which evidence bearing on business practice and economic performance is unimaginatively projected or ineptly presented. An economist may be in a

[3] See H. Edward Wrapp, "Organization for Long-Range Planning," *Harvard Business Review,* January–February, 1957, p. 37.

position to make a powerful and strategic contribution if he is encouraged to approach the assignment imaginatively and if the team is so organized and led that his role is more than that of research assistant for the lawyer.

Much more than in the case of long-range planning, the working party in this situation needs a range of freedom beyond management's capacity to define the mission. The members' ability to determine efficiently the content of their own performance can be, in these circumstances, an important influence on their success or failure. The composition of the group, therefore, becomes a prime management responsibility. Where management cannot define in detail what is to be done, it must be unusually concerned about who is to do it and how they interact.

*A Diversification Program.* A third example is product diversification. Ordinarily, serious diversification studies are preceded by top management's tentative decision that the firm's competitive position and earnings performance would be strengthened by some type of branching out into new products and services, although little thought may have been given to specific diversification possibilities or to criteria bearing on the choice of alternatives.

Again, as in the earlier illustrations, a considerable area must be left undefined within which the group responsible for developing a specific program is to reach agreement on ends and means. Any accomplishment will depend on the placement of leadership and on the mixture of training and experience in the group. In the course of establishing a working party for an assignment of this type, top management may, without knowing it, go far toward determining the results of the team effort.

## Mixing Talents

Lawyers and economists with the characteristic intellectual personalities sketched earlier in this article are not ordinarily well equipped to work together without rather specific ends-and-means assignments laid down by higher authority or strong business-oriented leadership within the group. They look at policy problems from sharply differentiated viewpoints. While the lawyer is likely to regard the economist as naïvely, even recklessly, innovative, the economist often finds the typical legal mind bound over to the status quo, distrustful, even resentful, of change. The one attribute they share is a disposition to minimize practical problems of putting policies into effect—of getting work done in a large organization.

The inherent intellectual incompatibility of these men may be confounded by semantic difficulties. It is quite possible for a lawyer and an economist not only to hold a long conversation without common understanding but also to finish it without awareness that common understanding has been lacking.

So management's job is cut out for it. There are a mounting number of policy problems which both legal and economic skills can help solve. Not only in the examples cited above, but in other areas of prime concern to top management, policy formulation may be hamstrung without close legal and economic participation.

This is obviously true in the wide range of cases dealing with price policy and customer relations, and in the areas of labor relations and wage policy. Moreover, economic and legal skills are often indispensable in defense contracting, an area of growing significance to company policy-makers. Additional examples can be found in matters related to the direction, method, and speed of expansion (not necessarily connected with diversification); in community and (more broadly) public relations; and in that field of policy formulation in which depreciation accounting, taxation, and financial planning come into focus.

In these circumstances, it is extremely important for management to discover how to employ efficiently these pools of knowledge and skill that are at once so contradictory and so complementary.

## Effective Direction

The businessman who organizes a working party of lawyers and economists confronts an interesting problem. Passive administration is likely to encourage intellectual friction, to waste effort, and to generate a high proportion of ideas not readily adapted to operating realities. On the other hand, aggressive direction may inhibit professional capabilities and diminish the unique potential of their joint contribution. I cannot offer a definitive set of administrative principles, but, having observed the performance of several mixed professional teams, I can suggest some rough working rules for administrators.

### Assigning Problems

*Lawyer-economist teams should be organized as ad hoc groups, assembled for specific assignments and disbanded on completion of their missions.* On the positive side, this practice takes the critical job of selecting work assignments away from the professional technicians, who are not well equipped either to recognize problems of prime concern to management or to appraise their own ability to perform specific tasks. On the negative side, the practice makes it difficult for administrators to avoid their responsibility for defining a team's fundamental working agreement or for organizing a team that is capable of devising its own working rules wisely and harmoniously.

Permanent lawyer-economist teams—that is, those functioning without fixed assignments and terms—are likely to waste their energies on tasks which seem important to them but not to management. Their greatest common deficiency—unawareness of and indifference to operating problems in business organizations—leads them to ends-and-means explorations that are administratively impractical.

Moreover, experience in undirected work is likely to diminish their future usefulness either (a) because the conflict between their sharply contrasting intellectual personalities results in common frustration or (b) because each converts the other, with the result that over the duration of a prolonged association without specific guidance they learn to merge their differences and think alike. Here is an example of a permanently organized team that "ran down":

One company with broadly diversified interests in several industries organized a mixed working party composed of its assistant general counsel, a retained outside attorney, and a retained outside economic consultant, with the mission of examining a proposed corporation acquisition in the light of possible government attack under the Sherman Act and recommending a "safe" course of action. The specific assignment was completed within six months.

Pleased with the results, management gave the same group a "blue sky" charter to explore other ill-defined expansion projects then in conversation status at several points in the organization. During the following two years, the team selected several such projects for examination and conducted extended studies. However, these projects turned out to be of little value because management found ample reason in independent pay-back analyses for discarding the projects. Somehow or other, the team had developed "blind spots" from continuous association.

The value of lawyers and economists in administered team efforts grows precisely out of their contrasting and complementary technical knowledge and attitudes toward problems. Management does not need economists who think like lawyers or lawyers who think like economists. It needs the sharp uniqueness of each professional group.

It needs, also, to learn how to harness these qualities in a common effort to reach a common goal.

*Every team should have a prescribed assignment but should not be limited strictly to it.* This working rule has several advantages and contains one important safeguard: it gives direction to the team effort. The basis which it provides for appraising performance is useful not only as a tool for management but also in stimulating the professional participants and building their confidence that constructive work will be recognized.

Furthermore, adherence to the rule prevents management from attempting the one judgment that it is not equipped to make: the advance selection of an optimum goal, such as the specific amount of desirable product diversification or a pricing strategy.

The rule suggests, for example, that if management organizes a mixed professional team to develop a "package" proposal as a basis for collective bargaining, it should specify the general dimensions of the group's objective and at the same time encourage the team to think beyond these dimensions if it finds good reason to do so. In carrying out such a mission, the group cannot fail to work toward management objectives. It may modify and improve the original goals, and it may discover novel ways of attaining them, as in the following case:

A small company manufacturing a widely used consumer product found itself in trouble when the Internal Revenue Service challenged certain expense charges in several of its annual tax returns. The president directed the controller to work with retained outside legal counsel and an outside economic adviser to develop an effective defense.

In the course of its work, the team discovered that the company had failed to set up as an appropriate expense charge a reasonable reserve for the contingent liability created by the company's unconditional guarantee, without time limit, to repair its product without charge after any malfunction or failure in use. This provided the basis for action to amend prior tax returns in amounts substantially in excess of the sums involved in the government's original complaint.

*The choice of problems should not be limited by predetermined judgments as to what is practical for operations.* The preceding discussion has pointed to the inherent blindness of most lawyers and economists to management's difficulties in effectively translating policies into action programs. In appraising the product of team effort, management must fulfill its critical function of measuring every proposal by the yardstick of what is practical and feasible (including investment and pay-back, of course). But this is not the equivalent of saying that management should inhibit professional thinking in advance by stipulating the limits of feasibility. Doing this may ease management's job, but only at the price of shrinking the potential contribution of the professional team.

## Management Participation

*Management should be a participant in every professional team.* Adherence to this working rule has both short- and long-range benefits. As to the immediate assignment, management can guide the work of the group by steering from within; it can also supplement, extend, and modify the initial guidance that accompanies the organization of a team and the definition of its mission. Over the longer term, management can develop an understanding of professional abilities and deficiencies that will help it to organize teams more efficiently.

*Management should not assume complete leadership within the group.* There are good reasons why the businessman participating in a professional group should not permit himself to be an authoritarian leader. First, the problems which constitute the group's field of interest, assuming that they have been appropriately selected, are not his forte. Secondly, he runs the risk of inhibiting his associates and thereby reducing the value of their contributions.

The businessman's proper function in the group is that of a catalyst. He should stimulate his associates, direct their thinking toward the principal objectives of the common undertaking, compose or set aside differences that are unproductive, and at the appropriate time bring up for consideration operational problems related to specific policy proposals. In this last area, of course, the businessman can contribute his own unique experience.

This is a difficult assignment. Anyone undertaking it must acquire sufficient familiarity with legal and economic ways of thought and expression to meet his associates on their own terms and while their work is still in the formative stage. His counsel must be of such a quality that both lawyer and economist will respect it for its relevance and value, yet so offered that they will not feel compelled to yield to it as management fiat.

## SUMMARY

To sum up, much of what has been said in this article is a description of problems and difficulties for which only tentative and rough working solutions are now visible. After more experience with lawyer-economist teams, management can doubtless refine and improve on the rules suggested here. An intensive effort should be made to discover how to use the new aggregations of professional ability efficiently and effectively. They have important contributions to make, and the return in the improved quality of decision-making can be substantial.

P.S. Some businessmen, lawyers, and economists have discovered how to work well in teams. They do not misunderstand one another. They respect their individual disciplines and merge them harmoniously and profitably in joint assignments. Needless to say, this description fits all my friends.

# III

## STEPS IN MAKING A PLAN

If you have built castles in the air, your work need not be lost; that is where they should be. Now put the foundations under them.

—Henry David Thoreau

# 10.

# *Introduction*

• Long-term planning, properly conceived, answers the question: "How fast should we grow?" It points up the obstacles to growth and prepares management to overcome them.

• Do not view the master plan as a blueprint of future action which can be pulled out of a bottom desk drawer from time to time to answer managers' problems. The true purpose of a master plan is to lay out feasible, rational, and desirable *patterns of future growth*.

• The question of how far ahead to plan varies from company to company. The planning period should not exceed the maximum period which will influence decisions to be made, say, in the current year.

• Planners should gear the corporation's long-term development to broad trends rather than to forecasts of short-term swings.

• Top management should give departments and divisions the opportunity to submit their own plans for growth. "Bottom-up" planning helps assure that much of the important work will be done where the most specific knowledge exists.

• The unique advantage of operations research is that it gives the planner an objective basis for making decisions that best serve the company *as a whole* rather than just one of its parts. It has been used profitably in planning product lines, power plant expansion, departmental objectives, and other tasks.

• In most businesses not one but seven distinct marketing goals are necessary.

Underneath these and many other ideas outlined in the following section lies an important assumption. This assumption is that company growth is a good thing. It is made on almost every page. Yet it is never stated in so many words.

*Is* company growth a good thing? If so, why? Is it a good thing because it increases profits? Because it satisfies an urge for power and command? Because it is necessary for survival? Because the population and gross national product are growing?

Profits does not seem to be the answer because expansion does *not* necessarily mean more profits. In fact, as many firms have found out in the last decade, expansion often leads to a *reduced* profit rate. But even if growth did mean more profits, it is doubtful that this alone would make it such a good thing as assumed. Some of the most aggressive long-range planning today comes from senior executives who will not be around to cash in when the profits are made. No, it does not seem to be the profit motive that drives them. But it does make a good postrationalization.

Is power the reason? Here again the answer seems to be no. As a practical matter, expansion often leads to the diffusion of command, not greater concentration of it. Executives know this if they think about it. But the truth is that they hardly ever think about it this way. The urge for power has little to do with their assumptions.

Is growth good because it is necessary for survival? It is true that a company can get in real trouble when its share of the market falls too low. However, most of the companies that lead in forward planning, including many of those mentioned in this book, would seem to have fairly healthy shares of the market already. Their growth could be stunted for quite a while before they became too small for the competition.

The growing "GNP" argument makes little more sense. In fact, it might conceivably serve the needs of a larger economy to have more companies instead of larger ones.

Why is growth assumed to be such a good thing, then? Perhaps the answer has nothing at all to do with economics. It may simply be that management is basically a creative process, and growth is both a means to and a result of creativity. Just as a tree grows when it is alive, so a company grows when it is alive. A company may lack any conscious "reason" for expanding. But it needs to grow in order for the executives in it to function creatively. It needs to grow in order to make room for men who are "reaching out" for more influence and authority.

Don't many managers realize this in one way or another? May they not be driven to plan for growth because of the realization, conscious or unconscious, that they cannot otherwise make a real success out of current operations? As Keith Powlison, Vice-President and Secretary of Armstrong Cork Company, says in a later section: "A company cannot stand still. If it stops growing, it starts going downhill; there is no in-between." Similarly with nature. If the tree isn't adding more rings, the cells in it—the life force—are dying.

It is significant, for instance, that long-range planning for growth is typically a company-wide operation. As different authors in these pages point out, the planner is always seeking a balance among the steps taken for marketing, production, finance, personnel, and other functions; he is always seeking to keep the actions of one department in phase with the actions of another. Here he is applying nature's law of growth—the cells working together, the different parts and functions serving a mutual purpose. Growth is a good company policy because it is a governing objective for *all* managers. It is a discipline enabling one to serve all and all to serve one.

Moreover, it is interesting to note how many of the steps and techniques outlined in this section call for agreement among managers on certain basic assumptions. What business do they want to be in? How much of the market do they want? And so forth. A common viewpoint toward such questions gives each manager a legacy of understanding that enables him to operate independently yet in concert with other departments and divisions. The plan tends to create something of a "superintelligence" in the company (although this analogy should not be carried so far as to suggest that the plan itself solves anybody's problems).

There are other basic values of growth, but the point should now be clear. Planning for growth is a good thing because it stimulates the creative working of the other two management processes—current operations and control. It gives a sense and direction to operating decisions; it provides bench marks for control. (At the same time, it is ineffective without helpful information from current operations, and operations in turn is ineffective without good control data.) Perhaps even more significant still, a long-term plan for growth helps managers in different departments to get away from functional thinking and to take instead a company-wide viewpoint toward their work. Thus they broaden their horizons, become more effective as managers, and find fulfillment as individuals.

## CONTRIBUTORS TO THIS SECTION

*Bruce Payne* is President of Bruce Payne & Associates, Inc., a management consulting firm with long-range planning experience in a wide variety of companies and industries. The author of articles in many professional business journals, he is also a Director-at-Large and former President of the Society for Advancement of Management, and a former President of the Harvard Business School Association.

*L. Eugene Root* is Vice-President of Lockheed Aircraft Corporation and General Manager of the Missile Systems Division. Formerly Chief of the Aircraft Division, The Rand Corporation, he is a member of various military and government committees and a Fellow of the Institute of Aeronautical Sciences.

*George A. Steiner* is Professor of Business Administration and Director of the Division of Research at the Graduate School of Business Administration, University of California, Los Angeles. He is also Senior Economic Advisor to Lockheed Aircraft Corporation and the author of books and articles on business management, economics, and government regulation.

*George L. Parkhurst* is Chairman of the Board of Oronite Chemical Company and Vice-President of Standard Oil Company of California. Both a chemist and attorney by profession, he was formerly associated with Standard Oil Company of Indiana.

*Mark W. Cresap, Jr.,* is President of Westinghouse Electric Corp. He was formerly with the consulting firm of Cresap, McCormick and Paget, of which he was cofounder, and Merchandise Manager of John B. Stetson Co., Philadelphia. He is a Director of Westinghouse Radio Stations, Inc., and a Trustee of Williams College.

*J. B. Misenhimer* is with American Can Company as Assistant Comptroller in charge of a newly created Planning & Methods Division which coordinates sales and plant-operation planning with financial budgeting and profit planning. With American Can Company since 1925, he has held various positions in the past in the accounting, manufacturing, and sales departments.

*American Brake Shoe Company,* which kindly gave permission to reproduce part of its *Profit Planning Guide* in these pages, has become increasingly active in long-range planning in recent years. Planning is undertaken under the personal supervision of Kempton Dunn, President.

*Sherman Maisel* is Associate Professor of Business Administration at the University of California, Berkeley. He was formerly an economist with the Board of Governors of the Federal Reserve System and also directed several large-scale research projects concerned with the economics of the construction industry.

*Manley Howe Jones* is Associate Professor of Business Management, Illinois Institute of Technology. His main areas of interest have been executive decision-making (the subject of his recent book published at Homewood, Ill., by Richard D. Irwin, Inc.), sales management, and agricultural economics. From 1950 to 1954 he served as a consulting economist for Armour & Co.

*Robert C. Tait* is President of Stromberg-Carlson Company, a division of General Dynamics Corporation. He is also a Senior Vice-President and a member of the Board of Directors of General Dynamics Corporation. Prior to his present affiliation he was a vice-president of three banks.

*E. Leonard Arnoff* is Associate Professor and Assistant Director of the Operations Research Group at Case Institute of Technology. The author of numerous articles in his field and a coauthor of *Introduction to Operations Research* (New York, John Wiley & Sons, Inc., 1957), he is a member of the Operations Research Society of America and of the American Mathematical Society.

*Melvin E. Salveson* is President of the Center for Advanced Management, New York. He was formerly with General Electric Company as Consultant, Operations Research & Synthesis, in the Management Consultation Services Division.

*Wendel W. Burton* is Employment Manager of Minnesota Mining and Manufacturing Company. The unique program described here illustrates how a company can go about forecasting employment. In Minnesota Mining, manpower forecasts are now made a part of the budget plan for each operating division.

*Peter F. Drucker* is the author of *America's Next Twenty Years* and other well-known books published by Harper & Brothers. (For further details, see Part II.)

*Clinton F. Robinson* is President of The Carborundum Company. During World War II he served with the War Production Board and was active in theater logistic operations in Europe and the Pacific. He retired from the Army in 1948 as a major general. He has been active as a Director of the American Metallic Corporation and the Fansteel Metallurgical Corporation.

# 11.

# Steps in Long-Range Planning

## By Bruce Payne [1]

Long-range planning is the one really new technique left to management that can give a company a major competitive advantage. Looking back, we have seen how industrial engineering, market research, control, and other techniques have given progressive companies an important edge over competitors. Looking ahead, I see long-range planning as another concept that will spell the difference between success and mediocrity in business.

One of the advantages of the new technique is that it enables a company to go farther than it would otherwise dare to in taking advantage of its strengths. Management can safely extend itself more, get more mileage out of its assets, flex its muscles more. There is less holding back because of needless fears about how far and how fast the firm can go. We live in an expanding economy. Some companies need to expand at unprecedented rates just to stay in competition. Long-term planning, properly conceived, answers the question, "How fast should we grow?" It points up the obstacles to growth and prepares management to overcome them.

Among successful companies such planning is often supervised only in a broad, general way by the chief executive, even though it is one of his main responsibilities. This is natural, for many presidents are temperamentally unsuited to the kind of work that is involved. They are too impatient to guide the plodding, thorough fact-finding which is necessary. But they do, of course, make the key decisions affecting

[1] Reprinted by permission from *Harvard Business Review*, March–April, 1957, pp. 95–106.

the organization, scope, methods, and aims of planning. Here are some of the questions and propositions facing these chief executives which I shall discuss in the pages to follow:

What is a true long-term plan? Here we will need to look at some concrete examples of the work of successful companies.

How should the work be set up? The essential proposition here is that the development of a five- or ten-year plan is not an "ivory tower" job for one or two gifted individualists to do, but a very practical, factual, down-to-earth assignment which makes a team approach absolutely necessary.

How should the planning team go about setting objectives? A new method, *marketing variables analysis*, has proved extremely valuable in making projections. However, the really basic problems are to decide what kinds of products, selling, expansion, and organization the firm should have, and to keep company activities in balance during a period of expansion.

What about the timing of a company's future moves? Several lessons from experience will be discussed in regard to the scheduling of early and later steps in the plan of action.

How should modifications in the plan be handled? One of the most important concepts is that the planning team should *expect* gyrations in the market. The possibility of future reverses makes a long-term program more important, not less important.

How can top executives tell whether or not a plan submitted for their approval is a good one? I shall outline six criteria which have been found especially helpful.

## True Planning

Much of the work that goes on under the name of "long-range planning" today does not deserve the title at all. True long-range planning is still rare, and it involves a unique set of activities. Let us look at the kinds of things executives do when they work out a really effective program.

### Activities Involved

Such executives are likely to begin with present products, appraising future sales potentials and the hurdles to be taken. Next they may look at possible future products and ideas for service; in so doing, they consider the direction of future growth. Then they analyze company strengths and weaknesses—man power, finance, production know-

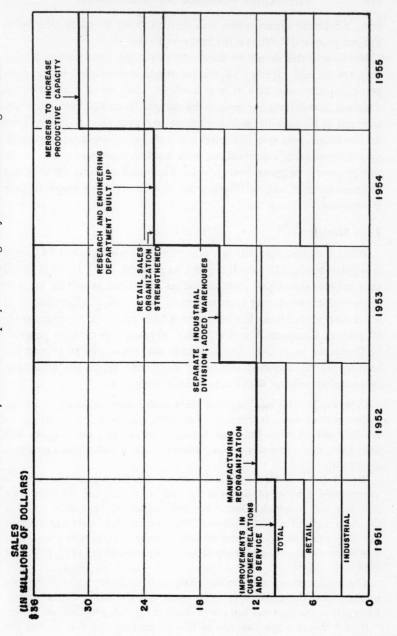

EXHIBIT I. Five-Year Summary Plan of Company A Showing Major Moves Plotted Against Sales

how, marketing organization, and the rest. They go on to ask: What are our potentials? What is the best we can do?

Next—and this should be done only at the top management level—they try to pull together all the information developed in the foregoing inquiries and look at it as a whole. They try to summarize the different possibilities for growth by merger, research, better marketing, and so forth, with special attention to *return on investment*. They decide to promote one line harder, cut down on another; to consolidate the company's position, or push hard to expand; to turn to the merger route, or grow from within. They look at every facet of the business for five, ten, or fifteen years ahead, whatever length of time is necessary.

## Two Models

What they end up with is a plan that tells management (1) *what* it is going to do, (2) *how* it is going to proceed, and (3) *when* it will take action—developed in broad terms first, then in specific steps to be accomplished during each month of each year. As illustrations of what such a plan looks like on paper, I have taken the summary over-all plan of Company A and a portion of one year's detailed program of Company B. (Other disguises have also been used to protect the identity of the concerns involved.) Each case represents an actual, successful experience with long-term planning:

*Company A.* This company is a fairly autonomous subsidiary of a large eastern manufacturer. Its product is hardware, some lines being marketed to retailers and others to industrial buyers. Prior to 1951, the company had been losing ground steadily to competitors and was showing a poor return on investment.

Exhibit I sets forth the plan. Drawn up for the president in 1951, it incorporated a series of decisions reached after analyzing the company's problems and potentials. One of the most important conclusions was that the retail and industrial businesses of the company had become so different that they could not now be run efficiently by one management group. This conclusion was the basis of many of the moves planned for 1952, 1953, and 1954.

The exhibit shows the steadily rising sales goals for each of the two product lines, the major steps to be taken, and the timing of these steps. Each part of the plan was laid out in detail in separate programs not shown. Here I should emphasize that no five- or ten-year plan runs as such for more than a year. With the passage of each year, another year must be added to the plan, with all recent changes taken into account. In other words, in 1952, the Company A management would have extended its plan to cover 1957, and the continuing impact of the Korean War might very well have changed its thinking about the immediate future.

*Company B.* This company manufactures home appliances in the Midwest. Several different lines are produced, each priced for a different consumer market. Long-range planning was started in 1952 as a result of a disagreement among senior executives over policy and of growing concern about the firm's falling profit margins.

Exhibit II reproduces part of the detailed program for the first of several years covered by the over-all plan (not shown) which called for a large increase in volume and profits. The executives agreed that this growth was possible if certain steps were taken to reduce costs, merchandise more aggressively, and meet other needs. The exhibit reproduces the program for only five management functions, which are enough for illustration; but similar plans were made for other company areas. The three major product lines are designated as X, Y, and Z; the latter two came in for the most attention since they were believed to have the largest unrealized sales potentials.

Just because a plan is on paper does not mean, of course, that it is a good one, although a written statement gives the program definiteness and makes it harder for management to ignore. Rather, the crucial questions are whether the goals are sound; whether the moves and timing are realistic; and, perhaps of first importance, whether management is ready to implement the plan. Let us examine these questions carefully.

## Team Approach

A concept of planning such as the one described means that the program cannot be the brain child of any one man, even a genius. In the first place, he cannot possibly know enough or be objective enough. In the second place, other executives will inevitably react with some such comment as, "What ax is he grinding now?"

Often the burden of long-range planning has been carried by a controller or some financial executive. But neither officer has the expert knowledge of marketing or production required to develop a plan in which marketing or production executives will have real con-

EXHIBIT II. PORTIONS OF DETAILED FIRST-YEAR PLAN OF COMPANY B

| Time | Marketing Organization | Sales effort | Advertising | New Products and styles | Production control |
|---|---|---|---|---|---|
| November 1952 | Formulate sales organization plan, sales policies, pricing plan, forecasting program. | | Plan catalogues, national advertising, and cooperative advertising. | | Construct factory fixed budget for 1953; make sure historical cost system is accurate and accepted by all personnel. |
| December 1952 | Complete new sales plans. | | Consult with advertising agency. | Select industrial designers. | Determine IBM requirements; manually schedule production of products X, Y, and Z. |
| January 1953 | | Outline new policies and programs to personnel. | Analyze media for X, Y, and Z product lines. | | Begin work on over-all production control plan; as departments go on new standards, construct variable budgets for each department. |
| February 1953 | Select assistant sales manager; select southern, southwestern, and Canadian sales directors. | | Select media; complete cooperative program. | Consult with designers on Y and Z product lines. | Complete production control plan; begin experimental run of plan. |
| March 1953 | Begin recruiting new salesmen. | Introduce new selling procedures; lay out routes. | | Z Mock-up construction product line. | Hire production control and scheduling supervisor. |
| April 1953 | | Continue sales training with films, role playing, etc. | Begin planning outdoor advertising campaign; announce cooperative advertising program; distribute catalogues and dealer aids. | Y Mock-up construction product line. | |
| May 1953 | | Start new salesmen. | Begin national advertising program. | | |
| June 1953 | | | Begin regional advertising Y and Z product lines. | Z Market tests for all new Z product line styles. | Review all production schedules; prepare progress reports and continue expediting. |
| July 1953 | Recruit new salesmen for South and Southwest. | Assess new sales plan at sales meeting; hold meetings with new dealers. | | Y Market tests for all new Y product line styles. | Hire industrial engineering assistant. |
| August 1953 | | | | | Meetings on quality control and inspection standards. |
| September 1953 | | | Outdoor advertising campaign Chicago, Detroit, Milwaukee, and other cities. | Show selected new Z product line styles at fall trade shows. | Inventory modernization program to reduce in-process inventories. |
| October 1953 | Appoint new midwest district managers. | Special consultations and meetings with managers of Y and Z product lines. | | Show selected new Y product line styles at trade shows and conventions. | Fixed and variable budgets for 1954 with tighter operating budgets. |

fidence. This was the case not too long ago in one of the country's larger corporations:

The president gave the job to an extremely able executive in the financial department. Although the executive went to the production and sales managers for his facts, the plan was primarily an individualistic one. He did not work with those men every day; and after his fact-finding interviews he did not keep in touch with them out of habit. Also, as frequently happens, the long-range planning job was just a springboard for him—a temporary proposition. Nobody was surprised when he was promoted to a higher management position. Nobody should have been overly surprised, either, when his work was quietly filed away.

The trouble with handing the task of planning to such a man is not just that he is likely to have difficulty gaining the confidence of his associates. More important, he cannot "crank in" to the plan he draws up any real depth of experience and know-how. The ideas will seem biased or impractical to others, even if they like him. A frequent comment is: "The facts are hazy." When this is the situation, the management team as a whole tends to be skeptical of the program.

Here, in a nutshell, is one of the main causes of failure in long-range planning today. Controller, sales executive, economist, production manager—it makes no difference. No one man can carry the burden alone of getting the broad factual background "in depth" (particularly the company's competitive strengths and weaknesses) which will make other managers willing to *commit themselves* to what is written out on paper.

## *Specifications*

Reviewing successes and failures in setting up the job of long-term planning, it appears to me that three important lessons have been learned:

1. The work should be directed by someone who is in more or less *continuous* contact with the different managers concerned, so that the results reflect a team approach. (And if a consulting firm is called in, it should be one which can make available a parallel *team* of specialists as needed.) In this sense, the planning head must have the same continuing relationship with all top executives as the president has.

Incidentally, there seems to be an illusion that planning can be done by getting a bunch of executives together and "going off into the hills" for a couple of days, away from telephones and other interruptions. This is useful for "brain-storming" purposes, but it is no way to get the factual work done —the groundwork which is the basis of a good plan.

2. A long-range plan is so confidential—its contents may be worth many hundreds of thousands of dollars to competitors, and this is only a partial measure of the cost—that it is risky to bring anybody in to the final stages of it who might resign and join a competitor. The man in charge should therefore be a trusted officer of the firm. Equally important, he should be a man who has *shown ability to take normal calculated business risks*. Often the "elder statesman" does not qualify, therefore, although he may be ideal in other respects.

3. The planning head needs a particular kind of temperament. He should be one who is not afraid to say that this is right and that is wrong. Something of a "let the chips fall where they may" attitude is ideal—an indifference to the personal implications of fact-finding and analyzing in the most objective way possible.

If the planner tackles his work in the way described, he may run into resistance from other executives when he is drawing up the plan; but, once it is down on paper, much of this resistance usually disappears. And he has one real advantage. There is a kind of impersonalness about long-range planning which, when combined with objective, realistic preparation of a program, makes it less controversial. It does not center around individuals as much as short-range planning does, simply because it is hard to say who will be sales manager or manufacturing vice-president four or five years hence.

These comments on the question of organization are far from comprehensive and have dealt primarily with the problem of getting facts. For other aspects of this question readers should refer to H. Edward Wrapp's article, "Organization for Long-Range Planning." [2]

## SETTING GOALS

The problem of setting goals is one of the most fascinating and fundamental ones in long-range planning. And it is not easy. Goals should be not hopes but realistic, attainable objectives. Moreover, setting goals is far more complex than forecasting. You can get a pretty good forecast, if you manufacture for a few large customers, by asking

[2] *Harvard Business Review,* January–February, 1957, p. 37.

them what their needs will be; or if you sell color television, by doing a good market research study; or if you make building supplies, by having a good economic analysis made. But much more than this is involved in setting targets in forward planning.

## What Should We Be?

Management's first step in setting goals is to answer the question: What kind of business should we be in? (By "kind of business" I mean type of product sold, type of selling, kind of expansion needed, and so forth.) Getting executives to think inquiringly about this question is probably as challenging a job as any the president and planning heads have. To illustrate the possibilities:

A midwestern firm has always specialized in the manufacture of the founder's basic invention, It has always conceived of its business as doing the best it could with that one product. Changing conditions now force it to consider merging with another company making a related but quite different product. By merging it can make more money—but management will have to divide its attention among several different lines of manufacture. Does its strength lie in manufacturing one kind of product—or what? Will its business security be enhanced by merger? Is a larger return on its investment a true measure of its business success?

A large eastern manufacturer of a staple product finds that it cannot expand and keep its share of the fast-growing national market with the simple management organization it has traditionally had. To keep its market share, it must completely reorganize its sales organization, production system, and management assignments. Does management conceive of the company as a well-known national producer, or is its business to operate its present plan as profitably as possible?

The management of a prosperous lumber yard business in the West anticipates that in a couple of years the demand for housing, the main prop in its market, will fall off for a period. Should it sell its lumber yards and go into the booming prefabrication business, or should it get into commercial construction?

A materials producer, undertaking for the first time to make an end product, begins to worry about the implications of moving into a market where the company will be competing with some of its present customers. Will they look at the firm as a less desirable source of supply and turn to some other supplier? Should the company back out of the retail market as soon as possible?

How can questions such as the foregoing be answered by anyone except top management itself? No one else can tell management what kind of business it should be in because so much depends on what management *wants* to achieve. At the same time, it is important to realize that the question cannot be answered realistically and constructively just by sitting back and reflecting, at however high a level in the organization. Down-to-earth analysis is called for; and the most important things to study, as I shall indicate later, are: (1) the key influences in the growth of the industry and (2) the strengths and weaknesses of the company as compared to those of its present or potential competitors.

## What Rate of Growth?

One of the most decisive factors to consider in making goals realistic is the desirable rate of expansion. As every executive knows, all companies have their limitations. In the early stages of a new industry, these limiting factors are most likely to be internal. But as competitors come into the market and the company loses its quasi-monopolistic position, the major limiting factors become external. Often the external limitations become so severe after a time that the firm must get a new product or process.

Of the different factors to watch in planning the growth rate, personnel is certainly as important as any. For instance, one nationally famous concern purposely holds back the rate of launching new products so that volume will increase no more than a certain percentage every year, because the board feels that the executive organization simply cannot "take" a faster rate of expansion.

Finance as a growth factor is probably overemphasized by businessmen. The tendency in long-range planning has been to focus attention on capital expenditures, other cash requirements, profits, working capital, and similar considerations.[3] Once a comprehensive plan is completed, however, finance is likely to appear as a relatively small and obvious part of the program.

If anything, marketing is the key to a long-term plan. But even this statement must be qualified. The program of Company A, a good

[3] See, for example, "Industry Plans for the Future," *Conference Board Business Record,* August, 1952, p. 324; and Wrapp, *op. cit.*

case in point, took into account marketing, manufacturing, organization, and finance. Although marketing underlay and formed the basis for the other three, each was planned for and integrated into a course of action that would provide a step-by-step attainment of objectives. The planners realized that it was of the greatest importance to keep each basic activity in phase with all the others, and to guard against opportunistic moves which might endanger other parts of the organization.

What I am arguing for, in other words, is a concept of *balanced* expansion. It is tempting to consider one problem or area the "key" to the speed of growth. Such a temptation should be guarded against. It may be harder and more painstaking to plan the rate of growth so that the different company activities are continually reinforcing each other, but it is certainly the most successful approach.

## Making Projections

Now I wish to outline a method of projecting growth and volume which has proved helpful in a number of situations where long-range planning has been done. This method should *not* be confused with forecasting. Forecasting is a part of it, but only a small part.

The unique value of this method, which I call *marketing variables analysis*, is that it begins with the market and ties sales objectives to the steps in finance, production, and so forth that are necessary to accomplish them. In other words, planners using the approach come up not only with sound, realistic targets but also with the elements of a plan of action. (Incidentally, the basic procedures can be used in setting production goals too, if desired.)

In principle this method is similar to an approach used by chemical engineers to analyze the effect of change on a system. When a system has a series of known inputs, the engineer can postulate on paper what will happen if one input is changed and the others are held constant; with this data he can design changes in the system or diagnose trouble where it has occurred if the output or performance varies a certain amount from standard.

Similarly, in setting marketing objectives, the planners agree that sales volume is a function, let us say, of brand management, territorial sales, dealer effectiveness, advertising, promotion, and sales effort. Next they ask how much the management of these functions could improve in, say, two years if certain changes in staff, policy, and budget are made. Then they ask what will happen to sales in two years if performance is improved in *one* of these functions (e.g., a 30 per cent increase in advertising effectiveness) but not in any of the others. They record this change, ask the same question about each of the other functions, and on the basis of all of the changes estimate a realistic over-all goal in sales volume.

Each projection should be made by two or three men, not one, in order to reduce the margin of error. Also, the projections should be made first for the functions which can be analyzed in the most factual way, and last for the functions where the most assumptions and guess-work are involved.

In making these last estimates, the planning team should adjust the *assumptions* used in the light of the first few estimates. For example, it might be tempting to assume a highly elastic demand for a product and estimate that a very great increase in volume would result from heavier promotion and advertising. This temptation might be resisted if it had earlier been predicted that great improvements in brand management and sales territorial work would produce only moderate sales increases. Taking the earlier, more factual estimates into account means that errors in them may be compounded, of course; but this risk is more than offset by the value of these estimates in "anchoring" the assumptions used in the later, more speculative predictions.

## *Example of Analysis*

Let us take a hypothetical example which, although oversimplified, is in principle similar to other cases where *marketing variables analysis* has been applied:

*Projections Made.* Let us suppose that Company C manufactures small boats in twelve branded models priced from $350 to $1,000. The main plants are located in Wisconsin, and the sales territories include the Great Lakes and the inland lake areas of Wisconsin, Minnesota, Michigan, Illinois, Ohio, and Ontario.

Beginning with a sales territory analysis (fairly good factual estimates can be made here), the planning team figures for each territory the percentage of actual sales to potential sales (computed on the basis of population, income, competitors' sales, etc.) of the lower-price models. They find that the highest percentage is in the northwest Michigan territory—65 per cent of the total potential.

Some unusually favorable circumstances are at work here, however, and so 65 per cent is not considered a good target for other territories. The planners agree that a more realistic target would be the 50 per cent figure for the Green Bay territory. If all territories could reach or surpass this target, the planners estimate, actual sales of the lower-price models would increase 35 per cent. A similar analysis for the higher-price models indicates that their sales can increase 45 per cent and that *total sales volume of all models could reasonably be expected to increase 40 per cent with improved territorial management alone.*

Next the planners predict how much sales can be increased with better brand management, if no changes in other phases of the marketing effort are made. They choose this function because here again a good deal of reliable factual evidence is available. They examine the total sales of each of the leading brands as a percentage of total potential sales. They ask: Do these sales figures look right? What should they be? Are we doing a good enough job on the best selling brand to use it as a goal for the others? They conclude that *with better brand management total dollar sales volume could be increased 35 per cent.*

The planners go on to make similar analyses for all other functions, estimating what would happen if the number of dealers in the different territories were increased, advertising stepped up, the selling effort improved, and so forth. Estimates for these latter functions vary from 10 per cent to 80 per cent, with greater margins of error being allowed for because more unknowns and intangibles are involved.

*Plan of Action.* Many of these projections assume that certain steps are taken in other areas of the company as well as in marketing. For instance, an increase in the number of dealers and better average sales performance from them may require establishment of a more efficient inventory system to cut down backlogs; improved brand management may call for better quality control, because customer dissatisfaction with quality has been a factor in the lagging sales of certain brands; and an increase in total units sold may mean that funds must be raised for new plant and equipment.

In addition, the projections help in scheduling activities because the different sales-increase estimates are made for specific units of time, i.e., two-year periods.

*Growth Line.* Theoretically, management could concentrate on improving one function at a time, in which case estimating total sales goals in the future would be easy. Actually, of course, this will not be the case; progress in all the areas will be going on concurrently, and management will be

dividing its attention and resources among all of them. A judgment will
have to be made, therefore, as to what is a reasonable five-year sales goal.
When this is done, the results of the analysis can be summarized in some
such form as Exhibit III.

EXHIBIT III.   Five-Year Sales Growth of Company C

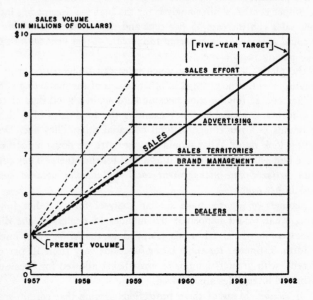

On the vertical line above 1959 (two years hence) the planning team
plots the five independent estimates of the increases in sales volume possible.
Horizontal lines are drawn through these points to indicate the continuing
benefit of improvement in the function.

The diagonal line begins with current sales and represents a conservative
estimate of the growth of volume over the five-year period. Actually, of
course, the growth will probably not be linear, but the line serves as a rough
estimate. In drawing it, the targets for territorial sales and for brand
management, which were computed with a minimum of guesswork and
checked out closely, are especially important. However, the line is based
mainly on management judgment using the five estimates only as bench
marks. Usually management will be inclined to make its five-year goal conservative. The goal of $9,500,000 in Exhibit III is a very conservative one
in the light of the two-year estimates.

*Notes on Application*

The sales goal obtained by the method described is not necessarily the sales goal which will appear in the master plan for the company as a whole. For instance, it may develop that too much expenditure on new plant and equipment is called for in view of the company's limited financial resources, with the result that the sales goal will have to be lowered. (Any such revisions would necessarily have to be downward, because the sales goals represent the *maximum* possible growth of the company.)

The number and kinds of projections made will, of course, vary from company to company; it is up to the planners to pick out the pertinent factors in the market. For instance, public relations would be a major factor in some companies' sales, although not for Company C. Also, the facts and forecasts used in making the projections will vary. In Company C's situation, obsolescence (of small boats in use) would be an unimportant factor; but in the machine tool industry it would be a very important one indeed, and the annual obsolescence data collected and published by the industry each year should be studied carefully.

Finally, it should be noted that the projections for each function depend not only on its present efficiency but also on the company's position in the market. To illustrate, a greater effort in advertising and promotion ought to result in a fairly substantial increase in sales in the case of Company C if it has only 15 per cent or so of the total market; but a similar increase in the advertising effort of a competitor with a larger share of the market would be expected to produce a smaller increase in volume because sales resistance would develop more sharply. In this respect a company like E. I. du Pont de Nemours & Company, for example, which is often selling in new markets, enjoys an advantage over companies like Ford Motor Company and General Motors Corporation, which have large shares of long-established markets.

## PROBLEM OF TIMING

The problem of timing a company's major moves is especially intriguing to the top two or three executives working on a long-range plan. Certainly no other aspect of the work calls more for native good judgment, experience, intuition, and imagination.

If any one lesson stands out in practical experience with forward planning, it is that the senior planners must *set a date* for the completion of projects scheduled or else they will not get done. A case in point is that of a Midwestern manufacturer of industrial equipment:

> The executives visualized a $36-million operation for their company some day, and they had a pretty good idea of where the added volume would come from and of some of the steps that would be necessary to attain it. But whether that volume should be attained in five years, seven years, or ten years was a question they had not decided. Their sales objective was, therefore, meaningless. Until they put that $36 million down with a date on it, they could not think of it in terms of the organizational, production, financial, promotional, and other steps that were essential if their planning was to become *real*.

In other words, it is not enough to set objectives, however carefully thought out, and say, "That's our goal." There must be a timetable.

## Flexible Timetable

It is a good idea to keep the timetable flexible, especially where financing is an important factor. Planners must often make a very careful forecast of the funds that will be required to support the major moves, and estimate the extent to which retained profits and depreciation reserves can provide these funds. In such cases flexibility becomes a much-needed safeguard against the forecasted results being obtained either ahead of or behind schedule. The fewer the commitments to a precise timetable in production, marketing, and organization, therefore, the better.

How much flexibility is needed? This can be judged in the light of the alternative courses of action planned to meet possible company reverses or dips in sales (to be discussed in a later section). But the planning group may find it more practical to switch to substitute plans (in case of certain contingencies, such as war, for example) than to try to build a great deal of flexibility into the basic plan itself.

Sometimes it is wise to make timing conditional upon certain other things happening, with a clear understanding that any dates put down are tentative only. For example, management may have, as at least one large corporation has, a concept of what is an ideal economic unit—a figure of so many thousand people per plant, arrived at on the basis of such factors as management effectiveness, recreational facilities needed, schools, and past operating experience. It will not commit itself to building a new plant until it has to, but it will state in the plan that the company *will* build when sales volume gets to a certain point, and estimate as well as possible when that time will be.

## Quick vs. Slow Start

The timing of the first major moves is strictly dependent on the degree to which the company house is in order. To put long-range planning in high gear on top of unsolved current problems is obviously foolish. In Company A's case, for instance (Exhibit I), major moves to increase sales were postponed because the company was saddled with a bad delivery problem; until that was straightened out and better customer liaison established, it would have been premature to launch into large-scale promotion, salesmen recruitment, and so forth.

Another factor that may make a slow start advisable is overhead; it may need to be either cut or *increased* before the organization is ready to take on new responsibilities.

The time needed to prepare the organization for increases in volume or for a change-over to a different type of production can be used often to very great advantage, particularly in this day of increasingly complex marketing strategy. For example, take the problem of a materials producer who wants to promote a product utilizing a new material he has developed:

If he begins by trying to sell to the manufacturers who would normally manufacture and sell the new product to retailers (or use it in other products they sell), he may run into considerable resistance. These manufacturers tend to favor the products they are already set up to produce, and if they hesitate to adopt the new idea, reports discrediting it have an opportunity to circulate. But if the product can first be publicized quickly and effectively to the ultimate consumer, the materials producer can go on and in a short time build up pressure on manufacturers to buy his idea. The consumer is *their* market.[4]

[4] For a fuller discussion of this problem, see E. Raymond Corey, *The Development of Markets for New Products* (Cambridge, Division of Research, Harvard Business School, 1956), p. 81.

In cases of this kind where an indirect approach, while taking more time at the start, succeeds in creating sales faster in the end, the strategy can be doubly helpful by allowing the manufacturing organization extra time to straighten out any problems it has. The possible value of delaying the sales "burst" is therefore well worth looking into.

In terms of the *number* of steps planned in the annual schedules, the foregoing may mean considerably more activity in the fourth or fifth years of a five-year plan than in the early years. To refer to Company A again:

> During the first three years a lot of hard work was planned in developing present customers of the firm. On paper this "groundwork" would not have looked particularly impressive. But a detailed plan for the fourth year, when the new business was to start coming in, would have shown new salesmen and supervisors going out on new routes, catalogues being issued to acquaint new customers with the business, preparations for mergers being made, plant space added, research additions, and many other activities coinciding with a marked rise in volume. It took several years, in other words, before forward planning could really "look good" on paper.

## MAKING A PLAN WORK

The biggest danger of long-range planning, according to many men who have had experience with it, is atrophy. Company managers must understand the *why* of the steps and timing planned, or they will give up the plan when they are under pressure. Earlier in this article I outlined a special method of setting objectives. It is a good case in point. It works beautifully *if* executives keep in mind how the objectives were set. And that means some pretty strong leadership at the top. One of the best planners I know put it this way:

> Modifications will be necessary even in the best plan. But from time to time managers down the line will *think* that more changes should be made than really are needed. The chief executive needs to be the kind who can say, "Al, that's a good idea, but it isn't our policy."

Usually there are five or ten key decisions that lead to the final conclusions in a plan about market share, volume, and so forth. In one company these conclusions may be drawn from such things as projections of population increase and trends in consumer use; in another, from such things as the probability of new technological applications of a product and projections of the needs of a few large industrial buyers. Whatever these conclusions are, the top planners must "watch them like a hawk," reviewing them carefully from year to year and keeping them before the men who run the company.

I think that one of the most important concepts of forward planning is that it does *not* assume there will be ideal business conditions or "smooth sailing." Unexpected things will happen—gyrations in the market or the loss of a key man—but they in no way affect the practicality of planning. As a matter of fact, one of the values of a good long-term program is that it helps to keep executives from panicking when reverses happen or dips occur. Let me illustrate the kind of top-management perspective that often spells the difference between success and failure:

A southwestern manufacturer of plumbing equipment had a plan predicated on a series of rising sales levels. One year house construction slowed unexpectedly, and naturally the company's sales fell off. The pressure was on to abandon the plan. But the planners checked their original assumptions and projections and found that the same number of homes still had to be built as first thought. So top management stuck with the plan—and before too long a 22 per cent spurt in sales occurred which the company was ready to take advantage of, thanks to its having gone on with the steps in the program. But competitors, plugging along on a day-to-day basis, were caught unprepared by the rise in demand.

The same sort of crisis confronted a large firm manufacturing appliances when sales took a serious slump. Reviewing the economics of demand, it decided not to cut back, although one of its leading competitors did. Some months later sales shot up again. The company was ready for the increase while its competitor was not, and as a result it got back its No. 1 sales position.

## Modifications

As a rough guess, I think that management more often finds it necessary to revise *timing,* when modification is necessary, than to change the steps or actions that were planned.

What often happens is something like this. The planners find that there is a lot of room for expansion, and in their five-year plan they map out steps to increase production, suppliers, dealers, and so forth. But the sales manager who was supposed to turn the reins over to a younger man delays doing so, with the result that nothing happens to sales despite the fast-rising levels drawn on paper. Obviously, in such a case, management needs to suspend (but not shelve) the plan. Once it can find a way to take care of that sales management problem, however, it can go back and use much of the thinking that went into the original plan, including not only the actions recommended but also some of the time relationships.

As those who have had experience with modifications realize, although the different steps in a plan are dependent upon each other in a great many ways, there are also many divisible parts. When a plan is laid out, one can usually predict right at the outset which parts, if any, will not have to be changed and which ones will most likely have to be revised because they are contingent on forecasts of supply or sales. For instance, product development and engineering schedules can be followed even though it is still far from certain when and in what plants the products should be produced. Again, the product restyling program of Company B (Exhibit II) might have been followed with only minor changes even if major revisions had become necessary in other parts of the plan.

## SIX CRITERIA

By way of conclusion, let us suppose that a true long-range plan is submitted to the president or board of directors. How can they tell whether or not the program—one along the lines of those shown in Exhibits I and II, for instance—is a good one? In short, what are the earmarks of a good plan?

It seems to me that top management ought to keep in mind six criteria, which can best be stated in the form of questions:

1. *Has the planning team determined the key influences in the growth of the industry and evaluated the influence of each?* These influences vary from industry to industry. In the case of a hosiery or sugar company, sales potentials are obviously tied to per capita consumption, and management can project the market fairly accurately, barring any revolutionary changes. By contrast, in the case of the atomic energy industry, the key influences are likely to be research and technological developments. Most companies, however, have to take both types of influences into account. To illustrate:

A manufacturer of an improved, more heat-resistant bearing may find that the key influences are not only the rising number of bearing users and projected expenditures on heavy machinery using bearings, but also developments in the use of faster machinery which would increase the incidence of bearings freezing.

2. *Have the strengths and weaknesses of the company been accurately evaluated?* This is without doubt one of the most important questions in forward planning; an incorrect answer here has probably caused more failures than inadequate research on any other topic.

To add dimension to their appraisal, the planner should look at the strengths and weaknesses of *competitors* as well as of their own firm. Why has one rival been able to get a larger share of the market than others? Maybe its costs are not the lowest in the industry by a long shot, but that does not matter if selling effort is the key. The implications of this question for planning are tremendous:

A holding company's strengths may be money and large tax carrybacks; its weakness may be that most of its subsidiaries are in a declining industry. The question arises, then, whether it should not plan to buy and sell its way out of the industry.

A company with an excellent distributor organization might well plan to move into other industries where jobbers are important; but a firm with a weak distributor organization would not be in a position to make such a move.

In his article on "Conditions of Marketing Leadership," [5] Arthur Felton cited the case of a large eastern manufacturer of a staple product considering the building of a large new plant 1,500 miles away, where the greatest *future* sales potentials were believed to exist. Here one of the company's strengths was an almost certain boom in national consumption of its product, while one of its weaknesses was that the center of the market was gradually moving westward, with all that meant for higher warehousing and freight costs if production continued to be centered in the East.

3. *Have the capacities of different company functions to support the plan been projected far enough ahead?* This is not a hard question in the case of, say, industrial relations, personnel, or advertising; if the main plan covers four or five years, that is as far ahead as these functions need to be carried. But the question can be a subtle one where financing and research are important factors. For instance:

I know of one company considering a large plant-expansion program which wisely carried its *pro forma* balance sheets ahead fifteen years. If it

[5] *Harvard Business Review*, March–April, 1956, p. 117.

had not, the planners would never have recommended the program which they did, because nine years were needed to reach the break-even point on the planned investment. The prospect of a very high return on investment after nine years was so good that the long look ahead was completely justified.

4. *Is there a practical timetable?* It needs to be detailed for the forthcoming year (as in Exhibit II) but progressively less detailed for later years. The timetable should not be rigid. Thus, if mergers are planned, it does not conflict with the principles of good long-range planning to make an opportune purchase a few years in advance of the time scheduled. It *is* inconsistent, however, to make such a move without considering the effects it may have on the rest of the plan by diverting limited financial or executive resources.

5. *Have alternatives been considered?* To put this in terms of a specific situation, did the planners of Company A decide to increase productive capacity after first looking at the make-or-buy question? Did they consider the possibilities of cooperative research with one of the institutes organized for that purpose before deciding to expand the company's R and D program as much as they did? And perhaps most important of all, how seriously did they explore, with top management, the question of what kind of business the company should be in?

6. *What provisions have been made for future reverses?* A number of companies have found it possible to include safeguards in their plans in case future expectations do not materialize. For example:

One company's policy is to manufacture not more than 50 per cent of its requirements, so that if sales fall off unexpectedly, it can cut back purchases from suppliers rather than its own production.

A large company has a reserve of products that have gone through the research-and-development stage but have not yet been put on the market. If sales fail to meet expectations, new products can be put on the market faster than planned.

The best built-in form of protection that a plan can have, however, is good planning—not only good execution of the program but also steps to keep the company effort in *balance*. In Company A's case, management could expect a measure of protection to come after the fourth year from the increasing research and development effort.

Again, for a company dominated by engineering thinking, the best long-run protection may be to strengthen the marketing effort.

To the extent that the planners can anticipate future reverses against which there is no protection, management should have a pretty good idea of what it is going to do if these reverses occur. With such steps spelled out, operating managers will be in a better position to foresee in what direction the company will move when and if the reverses come. Also, they will tend to "think together" better when crises approach.

## Profit Insurance

So much for the criteria of a good plan. In addition to any practical value they may have, I hope they serve to indicate the dynamic nature of long-range planning. Here is where it differs from certain other management functions which also deal with the future and are therefore sometimes confused with planning. While the aim of forecasting is to show what future trends will be, forward planning aims to *take advantage of them.* And while budgeting involves forecasts, coordination, and control of future management actions, planning goes into the what, how, and when of these actions—and for a longer period of time.

Long-range planning is certainly one of the most creative aspects of management, and it is easy to see why it gives management such a tremendous advantage in competition. No wonder many executives are so excited about it that they are referring to long-range planning as their "profit insurance."

# 12.

# The Lockheed Aircraft Corporation Master Plan

## BY L. EUGENE ROOT AND GEORGE A. STEINER [1]

This analysis is divided into three parts. The first concerns the origins and basic objectives of the Lockheed Master Plan. The second treats the principal methods used in constructing the plan. The third deals with the underlying philosophy and uses of master planning.

### THE ORIGIN AND OBJECTIVES OF THE LOCKHEED MASTER PLAN

In speaking of the beginning of a program as broad and complex as the master plan it is well to get behind the surface record of who asked who to do what and when. Basically, the plan developed because management recognized the need for an organized, cohesive, and balanced evaluation of future growth patterns and alternative profitable courses of action upon which current decisions could be made. Many problems in and characteristics of the airframe industry explain why management felt the need for such a tool. We would like to highlight just a few of these.

Two important characteristics of the airframe industry necessitate not only long-range planning, but long-range planning in considerable detail. They are the extended production lead-time (up to ten years

[1] From a presentation given by George A. Steiner to the Controllers Institute of America, Los Angeles, September 20, 1956. Reprinted by permission of the authors. The first half of this article is based on "Development Planning for Management Decision" by L. Eugene Root and George A. Steiner, American Management Association Special Report No. 12, *Organizing for Executive Systems Planning and Control* (1956).

from concept to flight for complicated airborne weapons) and an extremely dynamic technological rate of advance (one which has been greater in the past few years than in the entire history of man's efforts to conquer the air).

The development of a turbine transport illustrates the type of long-range planning problems these considerations create. Actual production of such planes is some time ahead in the future. In the meantime, Lockheed, or any company interested in such airplanes, must answer such questions as these: What specific research and production facilities will be needed? What type of people will be required for research? For production? Where should the facilities be located? How much will they cost? These matters, it will be recognized, must be resolved at least tentatively and some decisions made a long time before the production of one single airplane.

This states a problem, but it fails to portray the magnitude and complexity of such questions. The scope of these problems when coupled with the nature of the business is such that a very large part of the company's resources—engineering, scientific, and management brains, as well as money—could easily and inevitably become firmly committed long before income was generated from the venture, assuming the outcome was successful. Add to such problems the fact that a large part of the demand for the company's products depends upon a cloudy foreign political situation, or that the product mix can easily change rapidly with substantial leverage on profits, and the urgency to get an informed look at the future becomes even more understandable. In this light, there is not much margin left for off-the-cuff vague decisions, or for decision-making on the principle of Donnybrook Fair —"Hit a head when you see it."

Like all major planning efforts the Lockheed Master Plan (LMP) has multiple objectives. Mr. Courtlandt Gross, Lockheed's President, established the superior objectives for the Plan when he launched LMP (II) in December of 1955. He said: "Our primary objective is to develop solid bases for important management decisions at all levels in the corporation. These decisions, of course, are those necessary to insure that Lockheed will meet major technological challenges which lie ahead, maintain and improve its market position, and make an ever effective contribution to the national security posture of the United States."

These broad corporate goals were reduced to more concrete objectives for Lockheed's master planning work, as follows:

To indicate:      Future product characteristics and demand, both military and commercial.

To analyze:       Development and manufacturing needs to meet new product requirements, including investigations into facilities, organization, financing, and man-power needs.

To present:       Desirable growth patterns for a long period of time, at least one decade, for each division and subsidiary and for the entire corporation.

To recommend:     Preferred policies over a broad range of specific management actions to guide the corporation toward preferred patterns.

Although these objectives suggest a pattern of approach, many different methods could be used to meet them. We think that Lockheed's methodology is uniquely suited for achievement of these objectives. In this light, a summary account of the basic methods used by Lockheed in preparing its master plans may be of general interest. Although the basic patterns have been established, future plans will certainly modify methods used in the past. What we are about to describe relates to the plan prepared in the summer of 1956.

## THE BASIC METHODS USED IN PREPARING LMP (II)

By way of introduction to this section the four main structural members of the plan are given in capsule form.

First, is a detailed forecast of probable sales. By detailed we mean projections of specific models of airplanes, missiles, and other products in units, time, and dollars. Injected into these data are the manifold considerations which are associated not only with the levels of output but with the technical characteristics of production.

Second, is a detailed projection of the fixed capital investment required to meet the probable sales level, as well as research and development facilities necessary to maintain a desired technical competence. Individual buildings and major pieces of equipment are specified. Dates for their construction or acquisition, as well as dollar costs, are determined.

Third, is a detailed projection of balance sheets and profit and loss statements.

Fourth, is an analysis of emerging problems and suggestions for solving them. Ample opportunity is provided for setting forth and examining alternatives. Different patterns and projections are developed, based upon selected possibilities in such areas as sales, new models, financial capability, organization, plant location, technical and executive man-power availability, general industry competitive conditions, and product diversification.

The nature of the problems considered in the plan dictates coverage of a long span of years in the analysis. Sales, capital investment, financial, and most other areas of analysis are made for a ten-year period. It is recognized, however, that some "feel" for the decade succeeding the one analyzed is essential for long-range planning. For example, it is clear that any effort to determine the nature of research and development needs, or of production facilities, required in the years 1960–65 will depend much upon products to be made and the demands for them in the decade 1965–75. Hence, some parts of the plan cover two decades.

## Organization for LMP (II)

Something should be said about the organization for completing LMP (II). LMP (I) taught Lockheed that organization into a team effort is required for such a large undertaking. A great many people have been and will continue to be involved in master planning. The successful completion of a task of such magnitude and importance requires sound organization.

Mr. Courtlandt Gross' letter of December 8, 1955, to top corporation officials not only launched LMP (II) but set the basic patterns for organization and methodology. At the very beginning of his letter, Mr. Gross observed: "We all realize that preparing a revised Master Plan is a formidable undertaking. It is one that will require the energies of our best talent over an extended period of time. . . . As we proceed in our periodic revisions of the Master Plan we must develop as effective a team operation as possible."

In conformance with this team spirit, and with the need for central guidance, an *ad hoc* organization was erected to complete the plan. Exhibit I shows the basic outlines of this organization. At the very top stands the Administrative Committee (now called the Policy Committee). Directly underneath is the Director of Development

Planning and the Controller. These executives work as a team in guiding the effort. They head a Steering Committee, the general functions of which are, as noted to the left of the chart (Exhibit IV), providing guidance and planning assumptions; coordination; evaluation; and recommendations.

Executives throughout the corporation, of course, help the Committee in discharging its functions. One type of help is made available by working groups. Three were established. They are indicated to the right of the chart. The Corporate Sales Directors spearheaded the work of the Working Group for Sales Assumptions. It was the function of this group to develop the basic guidelines and assumptions upon which the divisions prepared detailed sales estimates, and to make appropriate evaluations of the work done by the divisions.

The next Committee, called Working Group for Investment and Finance, was headed by the corporate manager of Budget and Financial Forecasts. This group had the job of preparing the instructions for division reporting of fixed capital investment programs and the financial forecast. In addition, the Committee set forth some broad guides to be used in evaluating submitted data.

The next group, called the Technical Group for Research and Development Investment Program, was headed by the Assistant Director of the Development Planning Department. This group was responsible for guiding and evaluating the research and development programs submitted by the divisions.

The work of all these groups was reviewed and approved by the Steering Committee before being sent to the divisions. The divisions had an opportunity to see and criticize instructions prepared for their guidance before officially sent.

In the middle of the chart are shown various central corporate offices. These are permanent offices which, in their fields of responsibility, act on behalf of the Steering Committee. As noted to the left of the chart, they supervise the work of the divisions, serve as channels of communication between the Steering Committee and the divisions, and make preliminary analyses of work done by the divisions in their respective areas of responsibility.

Finally, of course, one always finds on a chart—usually at the bottom—the people who do most of the work. In this case it is the operating divisions and subsidiaries of the corporation. In our arrangement

Exhibit IV. Organization for Lockheed Master Planning

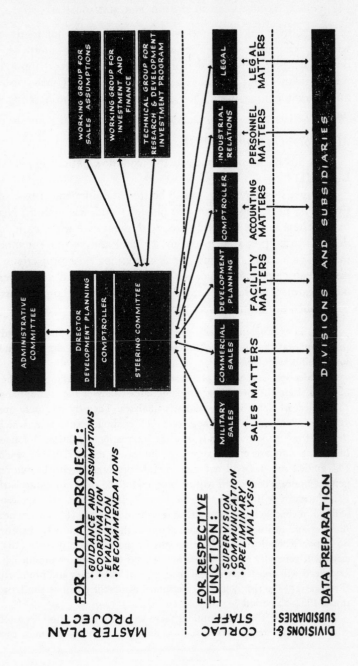

of things, to maul Tennyson somewhat, "theirs is not to do or die without reasoning why." They are partners in the enterprise. They do in fact prepare detailed working data under broad top-management guidance. But they have a chance—which they take—to review any work touching upon their interests done by the Steering Committee.

## Major Steps in Completing the Master Plan

With this backdrop, what was the work flow pattern in completing LMP (II)?

The first step obviously had to be the establishment of basic objectives. The next step was to fix guidelines and assumptions. Needless to say, these should be formulated with great care if the basic factual detail is to be prepared in the most useful and accurate manner. Of major significance are assumptions concerning sales projections, fixed asset requirements, and balance sheet and profit and loss statements. The treatment of sales assumptions illustrates the thoroughness with which such assumptions were prepared.

Three sales projections were prepared for LMP (II). The first and most important was the "probable" sales level. The other two were the high and low possible sales levels.

The Steering Committee prepared detailed assumptions to guide the work of the divisions in forecasting probable sales. Many of the assumptions were the subject of detailed and scholarly analyses. They covered only one ten-year period of the plan. They were (1) continued cold war, which was derived from a thorough analysis of the international political situation; (2) increasing emphasis on air power; (3) increasing total defense expenditures; (4) guided missiles will cut into aircraft procurement in the future; (5) general business conditions will be prosperous; (6) present military airframe manufacturers will continue to compete; (7) missiles systems responsibilities will go increasingly to non-airframe manufacturers; (8) government influences and attitudes will remain about as they now are; (9) there will be no major technological break-throughs in the planning period; (10) divisions will generally stick to types of products they are now producing; (11) Lockheed will constantly endeavor to expand when sales and profit expectations warrant the risk; and (12) personnel availability will be similar to that in the 1952–55 period.

In addition to these assumptions there were a number of others associated with the commercial market, such as airline availability of funds, competition, and market potentials. Wherever appropriate, assumptions (e.g., gross national product and defense expenditure forecasts) were quantified.

The high and low possible sales calculations were made by the corporate staff with some division help. A great deal of work went into the examination of various possible events which could lead to sales much higher or substantially lower than the probable levels. Care had to be exercised in appraising the probability of many assumptions and possible events.

On the *low* side, possible events such as the following had to be appraised in terms of their likelihood and the resulting impact on Lockheed: disarmament and the level of military spending in general and for airborne weapons in particular, economic depression, competitive conditions in the aircraft industry, and possible technological advances. On the *high* side, the following types of possibilities had to be judged: small wars, technological developments among major competitors, and unusual Lockheed sales successes. Once the assumptions were laid down, detailed dollar and unit sales projections were made.

*Division Investment Programs.* There is no need to get into deep detail about the instructions to the divisions for calculating the fixed capital investment program associated with the probable sales level. But to understand how the divisions prepared and reported their fixed investment programs some of the pages from principal facility reporting forms are given in accompanying Exhibits.

As Exhibit V shows, the first page provided space for the usual type of facility information. There were blanks for the name of the reporting division; name of the facility; its function; and physical description, including land, installations, and machinery.

The next page (Exhibit VI) provided for cost data relating to land, land improvements, buildings, building installations, and machinery and equipment. Two basic estimates were required. The upper group of boxes were for desired specifications and the desired time schedule of construction. The lower boxes provided space for yearly costs for minimum specifications and maximum deferral. Also note the provision for estimating the extent to which the federal government might be expected to help finance facilities.

The next page (Exhibit VII) provided space for division responses to specific questions about their facility program. Brief answers were requested to questions concerning the difference between cost and timing variations in the two programs presented, the existence and location of available facilities similar to those requested, the floor space to be vacated if the facility were built, what the division will do if the facility were not built, and so on.

Exhibit VIII shows the type of questions asked about research and development facilities. Divisions were requested to report for all such facilities technical data on dimensions or capacity, quantities and characteristics of elements to be controlled, special technical features, abnormal hazards, the exact nature of work to be done in the facility, what the company would do if the facility were not constructed, and whether experienced people would be available to operate the facility.

Detailed instructions to the reporting forms were prepared. These, of course, provided liberal illustrations of the precise type of information to be given.

Another set of complementary assumptions was prepared for the financial forecasts.

This by no means completes the guidelines for or the information requested on facilities. It merely illustrates the degree of detail, the general scope of requested response, and the methodology for reporting fixed capital requirements.

*Future Projections.* With the basic guidelines earlier discussed, the operating divisions, along with the central corporate offices, were in a position to begin the third step in the planning process. This was to produce the detailed analyses, data, and related information concerning future projections and growth patterns. The divisions prepared basic information in three main areas: (1) probable sales; (2) plant and equipment requirements; and (3) balance sheet and profit and loss statements. While this work was moving along the corporate staff studied, from an over-all corporate point of view, various problems and policies associated with these growth patterns.

The process of evaluation then followed. It is not hard to list the major steps in evaluation. They were validation of data inputs, aggregation of all relevant factors bearing upon a problem, application of judgments to facts, and examination of and choice among alternatives.

The final step was that of preparing results for presentation, first to the Administrative Committee and then to others in the corporation.

No fixed patterns have been established for either the drafting or the presentation of the results of the planning process. In the case of LMP (II) a short-range problem triggered the official presentation

Fixed Asset Requirements 1956-1965

I. FACILITY
   TITLE _____

II. ORIGINATING DIVISION (CHECK ONE)
   CALAC ___ GELAC ___ MSD ___ LAS ___ LAT ___ CORLAC ___

III. FACILITY
    NUMBER _____

IV. FACILITY FUNCTION _____
    RESEARCH ___ DEVEL.___ MFG. ___ ADMIN.___ SERV.___ OTHER ___

V. PHYSICAL DESCRIPTION

A. LAND     AREA IN ACRES _____ NOW LAC-OWNED? YES ___ NO ___

B. LAND IMPROVEMENTS

C. BUILDINGS

| BUILDING NO. (1) (PRIMARY) | BUILDING NO. (2) | BUILDING NO. (3) |
|---|---|---|
| FLOOR AREA _____ AVERAGE NO. OF EMPL. _____ | | |

D. BUILDING INSTALLATIONS

E. MACHINERY & EQUIPMENT

## EXHIBIT VI. Individual Facility Report—Lockheed Master Plan II Fixed Asset Requirements 1956-1965

FACILITY NO. _____

### VI. DESIRED SPECIFICATIONS

| DESIRED SCHEDULE (a) | (a) COMPLETION DATE DESIRED | (c) TOTAL FACILITY COST (OMIT 000) | (b) AMOUNT GOV'T. FINANCED (OMIT 000) | 1956 | 1957 | 1958 | 1959 | 1960 | 1961 | 1962 | 1963 | 1964 | 1965 | TOTAL |
|---|---|---|---|---|---|---|---|---|---|---|---|---|---|---|
| | | | | LAC SCHEDULE OF EXPENDITURES (OMIT LAST THREE 000) (e) | | | | | | | | | | |
| (A) LAND: | | | | | | | | | | | | | | |
| (B) LAND IMPROVEMENTS: | | | | | | | | | | | | | | |
| (C) BUILDINGS: | | | | | | | | | | | | | | |
| 1. | | | | | | | | | | | | | | |
| 2. | | | | | | | | | | | | | | |
| 3. | | | | | | | | | | | | | | |
| (D) BUILDING INSTALLATIONS: | | | | | | | | | | | | | | |
| 1. | | | | | | | | | | | | | | |
| 2. | | | | | | | | | | | | | | |
| 3. | | | | | | | | | | | | | | |
| (E) MACHINERY & EQUIPMENT: | | | | | | | | | | | | | | |
| 1. | | | | | | | | | | | | | | |
| 2. | | | | | | | | | | | | | | |
| 3. | | | | | | | | | | | | | | |
| TOTALS | | | | | | | | | | | | | | |

### VII. MINIMUM SPECIFICATIONS

| MAXIMUM DEFERRAL (a) | (a) COMPLETION DATE DESIRED | (c) TOTAL FACILITY COST (OMIT 000) | (b) AMOUNT GOV'T. FINANCED (OMIT 000) | 1956 | 1957 | 1958 | 1959 | 1960 | 1961 | 1962 | 1963 | 1964 | 1965 | TOTAL |
|---|---|---|---|---|---|---|---|---|---|---|---|---|---|---|---|
| | | | | LAC SCHEDULE OF EXPENDITURES (OMIT LAST THREE 000) (e) | | | | | | | | | | |
| (A) LAND: | | | | | | | | | | | | | | |
| (B) LAND IMPROVEMENTS: | | | | | | | | | | | | | | |
| (C) BUILDINGS: | | | | | | | | | | | | | | |
| 1. | | | | | | | | | | | | | | |
| 2. | | | | | | | | | | | | | | |
| 3. | | | | | | | | | | | | | | |
| (D) BUILDING INSTALLATIONS: | | | | | | | | | | | | | | |
| 1. | | | | | | | | | | | | | | |
| 2. | | | | | | | | | | | | | | |
| 3. | | | | | | | | | | | | | | |
| (E) MACHINERY & EQUIPMENT: | | | | | | | | | | | | | | |
| 1. | | | | | | | | | | | | | | |
| 2. | | | | | | | | | | | | | | |
| 3. | | | | | | | | | | | | | | |
| TOTALS | | | | | | | | | | | | | | |

Exhibit VII. Individual Facility Report—Lockheed Master Plan II

Fixed Asset Requirements 1956–1965

(PLEASE ANSWER THE FOLLOWING
QUESTIONS IN THE SPACE PROVIDED)    APPENDIX A – FACILITY QUESTIONNAIRE – GENERAL EXPLANATION AND REMARKS    FACILITY NO. _____

I. PLEASE EXPLAIN PRINCIPAL CONSTRUCTION VARIATIONS THAT ACCOUNT FOR THE COST DIFFERENCES IN SCHEDULES VI AND VII.

II. DOES THE DIVISION CONSIDER THE STATED AMOUNT OF GOVERNMENT FINANCING TO BE:

1. IN SCHEDULE VI    OPTIMISTIC ☐    PESSIMISTIC ☐

2. IN SCHEDULE VII    OPTIMISTIC ☐    PESSIMISTIC ☐

III. A. IS THE REQUESTED FACILITY REQUIRED BY AND TIED DIRECTLY TO A SPECIFIC ANTICIPATED CONTRACT(S)? MILITARY OR COMMERCIAL?
YES ☐    NO ☐

B. WHICH CONTRACT(S)?

IV. A. DOES AN AVAILABLE FACILITY SIMILAR TO THE ONE REQUESTED EXIST NEAR THE DESIRED FACILITY LOCATION? YES ☐ NO ☐

B. IF "YES", PLEASE EXPLAIN WHY THE EXISTING FACILITY CAN NOT FILL THE DIVISION'S NEEDS.

V. A. IF THIS REQUESTED FACILITY IS PROVIDED, WILL EXISTING FLOOR SPACE BE VACATED? YES ☐ NO ☐

B. IF "YES", PLEASE ESTIMATE
(A) VACATED SPACE _____ SQ. FT. (TOTAL)
(B) VACATED HIGH BAY SPACE _____ SQ. FT.

C. WHAT DOES DIVISION SUGGEST BE DONE WITH VACATED SPACE?

VI. IF THE FACILITY BEING REQUESTED CANNOT BE PROVIDED, WHAT WILL THE DIVISION DO?

VII. REMARKS. (ENTER ANY COMMENTS THE DIVISION FEELS SHOULD BE A PART OF THIS REPORT.)

Exhibit VIII.  Individual Facility Report—Lockheed Master Plan II
Fixed Asset Requirements 1956–1965

FACILITY NO. _____
LAB/UNIT NO. _____

ORIGINATING DIVISION:
__ CMJC   __ CBJC   __ MSD
__ LAS    __ LAT    __ CDLJC

INDIVIDUAL LABORATORY
OR TEST UNIT TITLE: _____

APPENDIX B - TECHNICAL EXPLANATION AND REMARKS
(SPECIAL FORM FOR EXPERIMENTAL RESEARCH & DEVELOPMENT UNITS ONLY)

I.   FACILITY PURPOSE

II.  MAJOR ITEMS OF EQUIPMENT

III. PERTINENT DIMENSIONS AND/OR CAPACITY

IV.  QUANTITIES TO BE CONTROLLED

V.   SUPPLY REQUIREMENTS

REMARKS BELOW APPLICABLE TO DESIRED [ ] OR MINIMUM [ ] SPECIFICATIONS

VI.   SPECIAL FEATURES

VII.  GROWTH POTENTIAL

VIII. ABNORMAL HAZARDS

IX.   NOISE AND/OR VIBRATION PROBLEMS

X.    UTILIZATION ANTICIPATED

XI.   BY WHAT MEANS COULD THE NECESSARY DATA BE OBTAINED
      IF LOCKHEED DID NOT HAVE SUCH A FACILITY?

XII.  AVAILABILITY OF EXPERIENCED PEOPLE

      DESIGN:
      CONSTRUCTION:
      OPERATION:

XIII. REMARKS

to the Administrative Committee. As a result the presentation took place in steps. The initial report, tailored to fit the immediate problem, summarized basic results about future sales, capital investment, and the financial result of operations. In each of these areas such matters as the following were treated: major trends and growth patterns, major current and future problems, and suggested corporate actions to correct some problems. Analyses of the master plan not given to the Administrative Committee in the initial presentation were presented later.

In the meantime, of course, the divisions utilized their part of the master plan as guides to operations. Their decision-making process reflected the larger patterns for the entire corporation set by the Administrative Committee following the initial presentation of the plan.

So long as the data of LMP (II) can serve management in the decision-making process it is a living program modified, of course, by decisions made upon the basis of it and other information at the disposal of management. When major decisions are made which affect importantly the future, or when external factors alter enough to make the existing plan relatively obsolete, a new plan is formulated.

## PHILOSOPHY AND USES OF THE LOCKHEED MASTER PLAN

This concluding section treats some of the ideas with which master planning is approached at Lockheed and some of the many uses this work has in the development of the corporation. These two matters can appropriately be considered together.

Concepts underlying the methodology of the master plan have much to do with approaches to the work, the value of the information contained in any plan, and how the corporation may and will use the information to maximum advantage. To speak of the master plan without dealing with philosophies and concepts associated with it would be like describing a man in terms of his flesh and bones and omitting his personality characteristics.

There are eight major uses of the master planning process at Lockheed. They follow:

*First,* the master plan is a basis for management decision at all levels in the corporation and over a broad range of policy and operations. The use of the materials in the plan for this purpose covers a rather wide field of activity. Hence, we shall touch upon only a few major points.

To begin with, the plan identifies major problems ahead before they arise or become acute. It seeks to find out the *right questions* to which management must give attention. The toughest problem in management is not to find the answer to a problem. It is rather to find the right question to be answered at the right time. LMP (II) seeks to place the right question before management for solution.

The company has benefited considerably by the fact that the master plan has clearly delineated some important future problems. Being forewarned is to be forearmed. Because of action today, many of the problems detected will not assume the proportions they otherwise might have, or will not arise at all. Master planning therefore *highlights important future problems and gives the corporation time to solve them.*

The planning operation also provides a *long-range perspective,* as well as a basic policy frame of reference, for all sorts of current decisions. Many decisions made at lower echelons in the corporation reflect the guidelines which the decision-maker found in the master plan as well as top policy formulated by the Administrative Committee. The proclivity of the human animal to seek support for his actions in some ground, as well as a genuine need for the larger perspective as a basic frame of reference to better decisions, makes this understandable.

The plan, and subsequent revisions of it, provides not only a base for current decisions but is also a model by means of which the impact of current decisions on future operations can be measured. Mr. Robert E. Gross (now Chairman of the Board and Chief Executive Officer of the company) pointed out in a management memorandum on the subject of the master plan: "Our plan suggests appropriate management policies and decisions to be taken to achieve desirable growth patterns for at least the next ten years. . . . The plan influences decisions that we must make today for the course of our production operations through the next five to ten years. It does not commit us, however, to irrevocable courses of action beyond the implication of immediate and near-term decisions."

The corporation recognizes that data collected today about the long-range future cannot be considered to have unchanging validity.

There are many events that will alter "the best-laid plans of mice and men," to take plenty of license with Robert Burns. It is also recognized that the further out in time the planning, the less certain one can be about the precision of numbers. As a basic principle in planning it is understood that in the longer range details merge into trends and patterns. For these and other reasons, the master plan drafted today cannot stand like the Tablet of Moses for years to come as the one and only oracle for a dynamic corporation like Lockheed.

The master plan is considered to be very flexible. Everyone recognizes the need for continuous adjustment and improvement in it. There is an understanding of the need for periodic review of the entire plan, re-examination of basic assumptions, restudy of market estimates and trends, and a fresh appraisal of strategic judgments and alternative choices.

One other important aspect of the plan and the decision-making process is that the plan does not present alternative courses of action or suggested solutions for *all* major problems. This is done only for some questions. Nor does the plan presume to make top policy decisions. The master plan is a basis for decision. It incorporates past decisions. But it does not make new decisions to meet new major problems. That is the prerogative of top management.

The master plan is not, therefore, a blueprint of fixed action steps over time which the Administrative Committee can pull out of a bottom desk drawer in the coming years to find the answers to a particular problem. Rather, the plan periodically seeks to lay out feasible, rational, and desirable patterns of future growth. It is a basis for clarifying fundamental objectives of the corporation and the divisions. It is a basis for determining the major problems which must be met and faced in achieving objectives. It also provides a framework for working out the best alternative courses of action by means of which corporate and divisional objectives can be met and problems in their achievement solved in an acceptable way.

You will recognize these things as ingredients needed by top management before it makes an important decision. Good decision-making is not simple. Elementally the process requires finding the right problem, defining the problem, analyzing the problem, developing alternative solutions, and choosing the best solution. Our master plan is an organized effort to do these things.

Rather than a blueprint, the plan is a malleable model which alters and changes over time. Clarification of objectives, problems, and policies in any master plan will constitute important guides in the development of the next one. New environmental forces operating on the corporation must also be reflected in ensuing plans. Thus, each plan is a link in a chain of analyses supporting management decisions over the broad range of actions importantly affecting the company's future.

This point deserves elaboration. The materials in each master plan are organized facts and judgments based upon past decisions, future desires, and rational expectations inside and outside the corporation. Matters in the plan concerned with new policy decision problems and alternative solutions are proposals. They are not prophecies of new decisions to be made. It is the Administrative Committee that solely is the maker of major decisions for the corporation. To a lesser degree—within their areas of responsibility and in light of Administrative Committee decisions or knowledge of top management attitudes —the divisions also make decisions during and after the compilation of the plan.

When the Administrative Committee receives the plan, in whole or in part, it does not bless the plan in its entirety. Rather it deals with problems presented in the plan. It weighs the risks of different solutions to problems and determines the solution that achieves the maximum result with the minimum effort, establishes right timing, and relates the decision to the organizational structure. These are tasks of the highest difficulty and responsibility. When a decision is made it is transmitted to the appropriate divisions in the corporation through regular line organizations. It is not transmitted as a part of the master plan.

Such a plan supports major decision. It reflects past decision. It is not the vehicle or instrument for either transmission or control of decision and resulting actions.

In a sense, most of the other uses which are here ascribed to the master plan can be subsumed under this one subject of aid to management decision-making. There is, however, a case for segregating them.

*Second,* the plan establishes a basis for getting at the major determinants of Lockheed's future. Not everything that goes on in the corporation or outside it carries equal weight as a determinant of Lockheed's future. Hence, some trends and forces will have more importance than others. The master planning technique provides a mechanism for segregating such strategic forces and giving them the analysis and weight they deserve within a unified and understood framework.

*Third,* the plan establishes a framework for organizing value judgments. No one should suppose that a master plan such as described here is completely unbiased, purely scientific, and always probable. The data in the plan are derived from or importantly reflect personal value judgments. But the methodology of the plan provides a focal point for measuring one judgment against another. It provides a central frame of reference for testing individual judgments, weighing them, and getting a reading. It does not, of course, force conformance to one collective judgment. By this process, however, not only does there tend to be registered consensus of judgment about important matters by people most competent to judge, but the possibility of an extreme position held by a forceful individual getting too much attention is reduced.

*Fourth,* this type of plan opens up new horizons for further profitable exploration. The mere fact that it brings to light important problems which otherwise would be dim or not perceived means that analysis is merited if the solution is not readily discernible. Master plans have launched a number of important study programs which ultimately will result in major policy decisions. Some of these undoubtedly would have been undertaken without the master plan. One wonders, however, whether they would have been made at the same time, in the same general context of corporate expectations, and with the same strength of support for top policy decision.

*Fifth,* the master plan stimulates thought about and information concerning basic company policy, strategy, and future developments to all who should be aware of such matters.

New ideas, suggestions, self-appraisal, and criticisms are more freely generated when they have a chance of being heard and properly evaluated at appropriate management levels. One good way to choke initiative, silence self-criticisms, and formalize the outdated, the outworn, the outmoded, the wrong, and the costly is to insist on formal conventional channels of communication or to have no such community of thought between the top management and lower line and staff personnel.

We do not mean to imply that the company has now or had prior to the master plan a poor method of communication. We wish merely to point out that in our judgment, the plan, for matters within its purview, provides a new, fresh, and adaptable channel of communication to the highest management level in the corporation. Because the plan is reviewed at the top-management level, because everyone knows this, and because everyone knows that the Administrative Committee considers the plan and its associated analyses highly important, it becomes a fresh channel of communications. It broadens the opportunity for more and more people at all levels of line management and staff to contribute information and suggestions that ultimately promote soundness in final decisions.

The plan also has served a useful function in disseminating important information downward. The mere organization in the plan of basic corporate objectives, premises, policies, reflections of top-management points of view, and evolving problems gives the corporate organization the same unified body of facts and operating plans at the disposal of top management.

One other aspect of this subject of communications deserves mention here. All groups have semantic problems in communication. Words mean different things to different people. Confucius said that the first thing he would do if he were to become Emperor of China would be to fix the meaning of words, for actions follow words. Lack of understanding of the meaning of words is a serious baffle in any system of communications. The master plan has served to fix the meaning of many words. There is more agreement than before in the company about such words as corporate objectives, planning, forecast, major problems, probable sales, corporate technical competence, research and development, rate of return on investment, and master planning. The substantive elements of such words have also been more clearly delineated. In addition, the meaning of words and concepts important to Lockheed has become, as a result of master planning, part of the mental equipment of more and more people. In mind are such terms as gross national product, alternative costs, acid-test ratio, elasticity of demand, constant versus price-inflated forecasts, net worth, and return on investment.

*Sixth,* the master plan is an important integrating force. To begin with, it has served as a catalytic agent in fusing line and staff, in both the corporate offices and the divisions, in a team effort to tackle important problems affecting each other and the entire corporation. The mere fact that the plan provides a common meeting ground for exchanging ideas and testing them against the judgment of others is healthy. Beyond this, however, the plan serves as a framework within which the many areas of knowledge and expert talents in the corporation can be welded together to support management decision. We refer to areas of importance in management decision such as the technical, military, personnel, production, organizational, financial, administrative, accounting, and economic. Top corporate policy reflects elements of all these disciplines. To ignore any one or give any one too much weight can be costly. Hence, any means to integrate and balance them has great value.

It is not suggested that the master plan forces unanimity of opinion in all these areas on a given problem. No comprehensive plan can do that. It has served, however, to produce a surprising degree of concurrence on matters which, without it, would probably stimulate strong, entrenched, diverse points of view. When there are diverse points of view, the plan serves as a mechanism for organizing the differences and insuring that they receive an appropriate hearing and weight.

*Seventh,* the master plan helps to prevent piecemeal solutions to problems. There is a natural tendency in most operating organizations to concentrate on immediate problems. In the absence of long-range planning, current decisions often are made within the context of short-range considerations. In addition, each problem tends to become isolated from other problems. The result may well be that operating decisions not only conflict in the short term, but run quite contrary to the long-range interests of the enterprise. The existence of such a management tool as the master plan not only reduces the number of piecemeal *ad hoc* solutions, particularly in the capital investment and financial areas, but helps to insure that decisions made currently do not jeopardize the desirable long-range growth patterns of the corporation.

*Eighth,* and closely associated with the foregoing point, the master plan brings a comprehensive, coordinated, and uniform picture of the present and future business of the corporation as a whole to those who must operate the business. Without this sort of framework, pieces of strategic information—on sales, capital investment, profits, and so on—would come before top management individually and would not be so well related with other important elements in the operation of the business.

In sum, the master plan has multiple objectives and uses. Topping all is its use as a tool for management decision. Abraham Lincoln once observed that "If we could first know where we are, and whither we are tending, we could then better judge what to do, and how to do it." The master plan translates this keen observation into action at Lockheed.

# 13.

# Long-Range Planning in the Chemical Industry

## By George L. Parkhurst [1]

It is apparent that long-range plans can and should be of many types, pervading all branches and functions of the enterprise. Long-range planning, for instance, often involves the planning of raw material supplies, the planning of processing changes, marketing plans, pricing plans, man-power plans, financial plans, public relations plans, and many others. All of these functions can be accomplished more readily and more intelligently if goals are established well ahead and yet kept sufficiently flexible to avoid having policy decisions become "sacred cows" which are adhered to long after they have outlived their usefulness and which are applied automatically in circumstances not visualized when the plans and policies were adopted.

One question which immediately arises when one begins to discuss the matter of long-range planning is "how long is long?" The question is no more answerable in terms of long-range planning generally than is the proverbial question "how long is a piece of string?" The answer with regard to planning varies not only with every different organization but within an organization varies from time to time, and from type of plan to type of plan.

There are, it seems to me, two criteria which determine how far ahead one should endeavor to plan. The first criterion is most readily

[1] Reprinted by permission from *Proceedings, Industrial Economics Conference* (Menlo Park, California, Stanford Research Institute, 1956), pp. 45–50.

stated in negative form: a plan should not extend so far into the future that it can have no influence on near-term decisions. If a ten-year goal would have no influence on decisions made in the near future, the establishment of the ten-year goal becomes an intellectual exercise of no pragmatic value and the planning period could well be reduced to the maximum period which will influence decisions to be made, say, in the current year. The proper planning period judged by this criterion may be two or three years or as much as two or three decades depending on circumstances.

The second criterion, also pragmatic, is that the maximum effective length of plan is that period for which the correct assumptions can be made with a sufficient degree of certainty so that the establishment of goals and methods of achieving them is substantially more likely to lead to the desired results than to mislead into undesired results. Here again the answer may be months, years, or decades depending on circumstances and type of plan.

Having established these two criteria, the proper thing to do, in theory, is to base the length of the plan on the shorter of the two periods. To say the same thing more simply and more practically, one should plan ahead as far as it is useful to plan, but no farther than it is possible to plan with a reasonable degree of reliability.

The chemical industry is perhaps the most complex of our industries and should not properly be thought of as a single industry at all but as a congeries of many different industries. The manufacture of sulfuric acid has little in common with the manufacture of antibiotics. The marketing and other problems in the two cases are equally diverse. Accordingly, it would be folly for me to attempt to generalize in terms either of what type of planning should be done in the chemical industry or on the proper duration of such plans. One can, however, make the observation that in most parts of the chemical industry technological advances are so rapid and have so many interactions that planning more than about five years ahead is not usually feasible or profitable. There is at least one exception to this unreliable generalization and it is an exception which I will discuss later, namely, the matter of executive development planning.

Whatever period is selected for a given plan, the result inevitably will be a plan in which the near-future periods have a relatively high degree of certainty and reliability, whereas the plans for subsequent periods fade into lesser and lesser degrees of reliability and usefulness. Such plans should be periodically reviewed and, in most cases, the review should be no less frequent than annual. As each succeeding year fades into history, the second year of the preceding plan should be reviewed and then form the current basis for action. The plans for each successive year should also be revised in an open-minded manner with no reluctance to reverse the decisions previously made either as to the goals to be reached or the means to be used to reach those goals.

## TYPES OF LONG-RANGE PLANS

While there are, as has been pointed out, a great many types of long-range plans which have been or are used by various companies to plot the course in almost every function with which industry is concerned, I think that in terms of the chemical industry there are three types of long-range plans which are of such dominant importance that further discussion can be confined to them. These are the planning of how capital money should be expended, the planning of how that capital money will be obtained, and the planning of the development of the organization necessary to utilize the facilities thus provided most effectively and efficiently.

Implicit in this oversimplified summary of the three principal areas of long-range planning is the assumption that the company doing the planning is not one which is content merely with the maintenance and small-scale expansion of an established type of business but rather one which is interested in dynamic growth of the kind which is so typical of our chemical industry.

Under our free-enterprise system, the ultimate objective is profit; however, I cannot resist stating that this is no sordid motive. Dollars are our best and only effective common denominator for such diverse elements as raw materials, manufacturing plants, and human effort. Profits are the result of the efficient use of those physical and human elements in the service of our over-all economy. So long as the consumer has the ultimate control, that company or industry making the greatest economic contributions is the one which is able to do the job most efficiently and thus produce the greatest margin of profit. This profit is, in turn, available, directly or indirectly, either for consumption expenditures or reinvestment in the further service of our expanding economy.

The planning of capital expenditures is usually the focal point of the planning done in an expanding organization. It has two closely interrelated elements, as has previously been indicated. One of these is the planning of what capital expenditures are most attractive from the standpoint of ultimate profits. The other is the financial planning necessary to achieve a proper balance between the needs for capital expenditures and other needs, including the needs for financial stability, the need for a proper level of operating expenditures, the need for an appropriate dividend policy, and many others. It would be equally wrong to allow decisions as to capital expenditures to be controlled solely by the apparent profitability of the available projects, without reference to financial policy considerations; or to determine the proper level of capital expenditures within an unduly rigid framework of financial policy, without thorough assessment of the virtues of the individual capital expenditure projects which are available or can be devised. The ultimate adjustment and accommodation of these two considerations to each other is one of the most important, and probably the very most important, single activity of top management. It is an activity which cannot be delegated to any staff organization or planning group, although such organizations and groups can be of great assistance to top management.

Taking first the matter of developing and addressing the available types of optional capital expenditures, we come immediately to the conclusion, particularly in the chemical industry, that the key to the situation is research. It is almost a truism to say that there are very few major new projects of a high degree of potential profitability which can be developed without a substantial research contribution.

On the other hand, long-range planning of the growth of a company is one which cannot be left solely to the research organization. If such an organization is to operate at maximum effectiveness, a large part of its efforts should have clear guidance from the operating and other staff parts of the organization. I do not mean in stating this to minimize the importance of unguided fundamental research. In fact, I believe that such research is of potentially great long-range value. However, by the very nature of its being unplanned and unguided it cannot be relied upon for the development of a company within those future periods which are susceptible to specific long-range planning. Hence, the chemical industry has come, quite uniformly I believe, to the conclusion that the greater portion of its research effort should be directed to reasonably specific goals which are short-range in a sense, even though those goals may extend, in some cases, at least ten years ahead.

In planning research programs, the guidance of such operating departments as manufacturing and marketing is needed for two reasons. The first and most obvious is to assure that the research effort is directed toward goals which would, if attained, have a reasonable degree of likelihood of resulting in successful commercial operations. Research, like every other industrial operation, should be aimed at the maximization of profits. In planning to this end, close correlation between technical research and market research is also obviously necessary.

The second reason why technical research needs to be done in active collaboration with operating organizations is that if research is to have commercial value it must be readily and enthusiastically accepted by the operating organizations in order to be put to use. If the operating people think of a research idea as something of an impractical or "long-haired" nature, there will be a serious road-block in putting it into operation. If, on the other hand, the operating people are not only closely familiar with the research program but have a sense of participation and responsibility in connection with it, they will have a feeling of proprietorship which is of very great value.

Accordingly it is my belief that there should be very intimate cooperation between manufacturing people, marketing people, market research people, and technical research people in the planning of a research program. There are many devices for accomplishing this and it is not possible to say which of them is the best. One of the commonest devices in the chemical industry is to break down research into departmental organizations under a general manager who is concerned with all the functions of his part of the business, including the research function, thereby assuring their interlocking.

A type of organization which has been very effective in the company with which I am connected is to have the research program planned and "audited" by committees which represent both the operating organizations and the research organization, with the operating organizations actually paying the research bill, thereby assuring an attitude of proprietorship.

It is also necessary in planning a research program that there be some reasonable degree of top management participation so that research which leads to new types of capital expenditures will be sympathetically accepted not only by the operating organizations but by top management as well. A further reason why this is essential is that long-range plans for capital expenditures necessarily interlock very intimately with long-range financial planning and the ultimate integration must, as has been previously pointed out, be achieved at the top-management level.

This interlocking of research with capital expenditure planning and the interlocking of capital expenditure and financial planning have led in at least one company to putting these three functions under a single vice president. Perhaps no one would urge this as a general pattern, but, given the right man, it certainly has virtues. In any event, it illustrates the close relations between these superficially distinct planning processes.

## Obtaining Capital

It would be outside my competence for me to expound in detail on the financial planning process. That process is a delicate mixture of cold-blooded mathematical logic and highly imaginative thinking. There is no set right and wrong to guide a decision as to what proportion of a company's earnings should be paid out in dividends, what proportion should be reserved to insure financial stability and to take advantage of future opportunities, and what proportion should be put into expansion of the business. In my own mind, the decision as to the proportion of profits reserved for new and optional types of capital expenditures should, within broad limits, be determined primarily on the attractiveness of the available capital expenditure projects. Similarly, given an excess of attractive capital expenditure opportunities as compared with available funds, there is no right and wrong guide to the decision as to the extent and nature of borrowings, if any, and the decision as to the raising of new equity capital. Here, again, company policies vary widely and it is in the best interest of our economy that varied approaches to the problem should be used.

While I suggest no tenets to guide this type of long-range planning, it is apparent that its importance is very great indeed.

In the foregoing discussion I have pointed out that two of the most important kinds of long-range planning are those related to optional types of capital expenditures and those related to finances. The two together include the most important type of budget planning.

## MAN-POWER PLANNING

There is a third type of long-range planning which likewise constitutes a most significant function of top management and which is represented in many companies by staff organizations set up to guide top management. I refer, of course, to organization and man-power planning and to that most important facet of man-power planning known as executive development.

Given ample funds, a fine research organization, and the resulting healthy flow of prime investment opportunities, it is still not possible to build a highly efficient, successful, and profitable expanding company without good organization and an adequate flow of managerial talent at all levels.

As our economy has grown in recent decades, industry, and notably the chemical industry, has come more and more to recognize the supreme importance of these twin matters of organization planning and executive development planning. In our own case, both of these have received a great deal of attention for many years.

Much has been written and said on this subject and I shall confine myself to a few high spots. Organization planning is obviously far more than the determination of proper organization charts. It involves not only the determination of the most effective organization structure but also a clear and precise determination of authority and responsibility. While these must be defined clearly and precisely, it is important, as in any type of planning, to avoid excessive rigidity and to provide for gradual adaptation of organization structure to the changing needs of a company.

We have all seen examples of companies which have followed one of three extreme courses and have suffered by so doing. One extreme is the situation typical of small companies. It is one which can be highly effective in the case of very small companies but which must not be retained by growing organizations, namely, the use of a very loose organization or of a so-called "one-man" organization. The second undesirable extreme is an organization pattern which is so inflexible and so long retained that it stifles initiative and prevents evolutionary growth. The third extreme is one of recurring drastic organization changes of a "shake-up" nature. A major shake-up is a confession of failure and while such failures do occur and can, perhaps, be remedied by such shake-ups, the recurrence of drastic, sudden organization changes is fatal to morale and efficiency. The ideal is an organization pattern which is susceptible to gradual evolutionary growth with very frequent but minor changes made as soon as the need therefor becomes clearly apparent and instituted in a way which maximizes rather than disturbs morale.

Organization structure, however, is obviously no better than the people who fill the spots on the organization chart. Without good management at all levels, an organization is obviously bound to suffer. We have all seen a great many companies, including large and prosperous ones, whose executive development programs have been so deficient that when the chief executive officer dies or retires they must bring in a man from outside the organization to replace him. While it is true that any organization may at times profit by some modest infusion of new blood, I believe it is now almost universally recognized that a predominant practice of promotion from within is most effective. In order to insure an adequate reservoir of management and executive talent, planning is imperative. Moreover, this field of long-range planning is one in which the plan must be long-range indeed. Fifteen or twenty years is certainly none too much to use in the training of a promising young man for a top executive position. I do not mean, of course, that one should select the next president fifteen or twenty years ahead. I do mean, however, that one should locate, fifteen or twenty years ahead, an ample reservoir of people who show promise of having the potentiality for rising to a high level in the organization and that one should give these people a sufficient variety of training and experience in order to ascertain and develop their full potentialities.

Many companies, including that with which I am connected, now practice executive development planning involving the careful evaluation of people many steps below the top so as to determine, as best they can, which of those people have high potentials. Every promotion and every new job at any level of a managerial or submanagerial nature should be filled with a view to the needs of executive development. In fact, in most cases, this should be the prime consideration.

Perhaps the commonest tool for accomplishing good executive development is that of preparing replacement charts in which the incumbent of each job is noted with regard to probable date of retirement. Potential candidates for that job are listed, including those who could be immediately promoted into the job and those who would, or might, be promotable with some period of future training. Such a chart, carried down through many levels of management in the case of a large company, makes it possible to spot candidates who have high growth potential. It also permits a ready recognition of the potential trouble spots in an organization represented by the instances in which no available candidate for replacement exists. Such planning constitutes a vast improvement over the situation of only a few years ago in which most organizations gave no systematic advance thought to the replacement problem and in which promotions were sometimes blocked because the man who would otherwise be promoted was considered irreplaceable in his existing assignment. I believe it is now quite general to recognize that there is no such thing as an indispensable man and that if a man appears to be indispensable it indicates a lack of adequate executive development planning.

Such planning must necessarily be done on a top-level basis. If for no other reason, this is necessary because the development of maximum potentials involves transfers between different parts of the organization. Not only are such transfers essential to executive development but they are essential to good morale as well. Every man should feel that his advancement opportunities are company-wide and not limited to waiting for his boss to die or retire.

It is too much to ask of human nature to expect that a manager will always voluntarily suggest that one of his most effective people be transferred or promoted into another part of the organization. To accomplish this free flow of people, two things are necessary. One is a staff organization which will bring promising people in all parts of the organization to the attention of the executive concerned with filling a given vacancy. The other is a gradual development of a company-wide philosophy that no man's progress must be blocked.

To summarize, there are many types of long-range plans applicable to the chemical industry, but the three which I believe to be of greatest importance relate to the development and assessment of new optional capital expenditures, the planning of the financial structure and policies which will achieve the desired goals, and organizational and man-power planning with particular reference to executive development in order to provide the human team effort necessary to the achievement of the desired goals.

Such planning, undertaken with proper humility and with a recognition that plans need constant adaptation, can lead to the accomplishment of the over-all objective of maximizing profits and to the minimization of the applicability of Robert Burns' observation that "the best laid schemes o' mice an' men gang aft agley."

# 14.

# Some Guides to Long-Term Planning

## By Mark W. Cresap, Jr. [1]

Some planning, in spite of the best underlying intentions, is wrecked or badly damaged by techniques which have not been thoughtfully and carefully crystallized.

The length of the future period for which long-term plans should be made is a technical factor of the first magnitude. It seems to me that, as a general rule, future planning is most soundly approached on the basis of a five-year projection. Less than five years provides too short a period of time for accomplishing the underlying groundwork to achieve the planned objectives. A longer period may result in a serious case of eye strain for those who are charged with contemplating the crystal ball.

Plans without a high degree of flexibility run a great risk of subsequent abandonment. It is a practical impossibility to design even a five-year pattern and then resolve to stick by it through hell and high water (both of which occurrences will probably be experienced in the course of the period). Of course, you *can* do it but you may look a little foolish trying. How would you like to be operating today, in your business, on a plan that was set up in January, 1947, without revision in the meantime? Figuratively, long-term plans should be written in pencil rather than in ink. Specifically, plans should be reg-

[1] From Mark W. Cresap, Jr., "Some Guides to Long-Term Planning," *N.A.C.A. Bulletin,* January, 1953, pp. 601–606 (published by the National Association of Cost Accountants). Reprinted by permission.

ularly revised every year, with each revision embracing the five subsequent years and reflecting new circumstances and conditions, thus providing a rolling five-year plan based on up-to-date information and estimates.

Another technical question is whether to project goals and other elements of plans on a trend or a cyclical basis. I favor the former, i.e., projections following normal trends without regard to cyclical fluctuations. In the first place, the prognostication of yearly economic fluctuations is a function of the most hazardous species. Trend forecasting is difficult but I am convinced that trend projections, on the whole, have been vastly more accurate than guesses as to cyclical swings. *Fortune* magazine recently displayed a mortality table of the cyclical predictions of professional economists. It revealed a high correlation between forecast and prediction—but in reverse. And yet, if you examine the more soundly based long-term forecasts in recent years, taking for examples national product, electrical energy, and steel production, the correlation, while by no means perfect, is not of the reciprocal type.

My second reason for favoring the trend basis of planning is that the long-term development of a business should be geared to long-term movements and should not be governed by guesses as to short-term swings. Employment of the latter procedure involves a company in the risk of being strategically whipsawed and of losing its position in growing markets. The "trend" approach to planning accepts the fact that there will be periods (of a reasonably short duration, it is hoped) when some plant capacity will be temporarily idle. But such an approach recognizes that, if the alternative is to delay action in the face of reliable indicators of future market growth—to delay for "more favorable circumstances"—action should be taken.

In fact, it is more speculative to attempt to time long-term strategical development by cyclical guesswork as to the "right moment" than to move ahead sure-footedly when the distant signal is clearly "green," at the same time assessing the extent of the risks involved and reflecting this assessment in the long-term plan by appropriate provisions for periods of retrenchment. Reasonable periods of idle plant capacity are far less costly than the loss of basic competitive and market status, the recapture of which may prove a crippling effort.

## The Use of Ratios in Business Planning

A great deal of attention has been devoted to the question of what are the most pertinent bases for expressing objectives and measuring performance as regards the profitability of a company's operation. While the choice of such a basis is again dependent, to a large extent, upon the nature of an individual business, the most accepted and appropriate performance ratios for most manufacturing companies appear to be these:

1. Net income to net sales billed.
2. Return on gross fixed assets.
3. Return on current assets.
4. Return on total assets, representing the sum of gross fixed assets and current assets.

Some explanation of these ratios is relevant, since the manner of computing each is highly important, particularly if comparisons are to be made of operations within a company, and between a company and others in the same line of business. In computing these ratios, net income after taxes is employed instead of a before-tax figure, for two reasons: (1) the only effective result of a company's operations is the net amount remaining for reinvestment and dividends; and (2) it is past experience and the future expectation that, on a long-term basis, the effect of changing tax rates on net income margins is not permanent. This statement would not apply to short-term projections or annual budgets, in which cases sudden changes in tax rates have a direct and substantial effect on profits, as in 1951 and 1952. But a fifteen-year comparison of tax rate trends and after-tax corporation income ratios will quickly and convincingly confirm the fact that taxes do not necessarily affect net income margins over the long pull.

The ratio of net income to plant investment is based on the gross fixed assets figure, instead of the net amount remaining after depreciation, as a means of injecting a rough adjustment factor to provide some equalization of facility values of various divisions of a company or of comparable companies—between those with old plants built at relatively low cost and those with new plants built at high cost. By dealing with all plant values at their gross book value, the distortion of respective ratios of return on plant investment is minimized and it is felt that the relative inefficiency of the older plants is compensated adequately by their relatively lower gross value, without deduction of accrued depreciation. The use of gross plant figures does not result in truly reliable comparisons, but, unless a realistic basis for evaluation of plants on an appraisal basis is feasible, it is the most practical approach available.

The key performance standard and measure is the ratio of return on total assets. Some argue that return on net worth is preferable. The "total asset" basis is preferred because it measures management in terms of profits returned on total capital employed, without injecting consideration as to the sources of capital. A "net worth" basis of measuring profit return is pertinent to a financial evaluation, but the "total asset" basis is the best for appraising management's basic responsibility for earnings. I was interested to note that, in a recent survey of practices in this regard among a representative group of large companies, the measurement of return against total assets, with the fixed assets included at gross value, was the predominant approach.

The four profit performance ratios which have been mentioned serve not only to establish objectives and to measure performance but also to provide standards for evaluating the desirability and value of a new or existing product line.

Application of these standards must reflect the fact that, because of inherent characteristics, product lines will vary in their profitability ratios as between (1) "margin" of profit and (2) return on investment. Some lines with high margins produce a low return on investment because "turnover" is low—that is, the volume of sales in relation to capital employed. Other lines with moderate margins are able to produce a good return on investment because of high turnover. Often heavy special-purpose machinery is in the first classification and standardized mass production items (automobiles, refrigerators) in the second. Nevertheless, the more significant of the two measures of profitability is return on investment (rather than per cent profit to sales), since it evaluates a proposition in terms of the earnings generated by stockholders' investment, which in turn influences the rate of dividends and the market price of the company's shares.

The key criterion as to a product line, therefore, should usually be the return which it produces on its investment, expressed in terms of the ratio of profit on total assets. The component ratios of return on fixed assets and on current assets, while helpful in analysis, are useful only in an auxiliary manner. Some situations involve high fixed investments and low current assets, while others are of the reverse type. The real measure is the return on total assets. From the standpoint of risk, of course, situations requiring relatively greater current investment than fixed investments are more attractive, but only from the standpoint of risks. Funds permanently required for working capital represent the employment of capital as truly as investment in plant and equipment, and a true gauge of management's ability to return profits on investment must reflect all capital employed, both fixed and current.

The use of existing price levels as a basis for projections is advocated because of the difficulty of forecasting movements in the price level and because of the complications and dangers inherent in attempting to make all of the various adjustments required in the relationships between price realization and costs incident to fluctuations in the value of the dollar. The use of current price levels provides a stable basis for making projections. The goals can be understood and interpreted more readily by hinging them to current price levels than otherwise. Furthermore, with regular and frequent revisions of objectives, projections can be adjusted to new price levels when these revisions are made. Then, too, if major emphasis is placed on performance objectives in terms of ratios (per cent market, per cent margin to sales, per cent return on investment), the problem of varying price levels is not as acute as would be the case if the dollar objectives were stressed.

### Preserving Initiative and Maintaining Direction

The direction of the planning process should be upward, not downward. Planning cannot soundly be centralized. Specific plans should be developed by those responsible for carrying them out within the framework of over-all company objectives, policies, and capabilities. In the description of the planning program to our organization, for instance, we have announced the following:

The Westinghouse Planning Program is conducted under the ultimate control of the headquarters Management Committee, and with all basic objectives, policies, programs and decisions subject to its concurrence and the approval of the President. Division managements, assisted by their Planning Boards, develop divisional objectives and plans. The headquarters Planning Committee formulates over-all objectives, programs, and policies with respect to the Company's development and assures company-wide coordination with them.

The principal purpose in providing for Planning Boards for each division is to implement a fundamental company management policy to further extend the delegation of business decisions to the divisional level. This policy has been generated by the growing complexity and size of the company, and by recognition of the fact that the flexibility, agility, and profitability of the corporation will benefit from the maximum practicable degree of decentralization of management policy-making, planning, and action.

One of the primary intentions influencing the design of the Westinghouse Planning Program has been to create a framework of basic company objectives and policies, within which division managements can plan and work, with broader independence of action than is otherwise possible. Without such a framework, greater centralized control of division activities is necessitated.

The thought expressed in the final sentences of the foregoing quotation is worthy of stress. The relationship between adequate long-term planning and certain organizational characteristics now receiving a widespread and intensive emphasis—delegation and decentralization —is of greatest importance. The benefits of attempting to spread initiative throughout the company cannot be soundly realized without the proper framework of plans which serve as the guiding instrument to assist all concerned in the direction of their own efforts. A sound and thorough program is an essential preparation to delegation and decentralization. Attempting to achieve these organizational ends without the availability of detailed and well-understood plans will inevitably result in confusion, conflicting efforts, and working at cross purposes internally.

## Good Planning Is Required of Good Management

Many contend that the difficulty of predicting the future obviates all opportunity for laying long-term plans for the future. In fact, a recent study reflects this quite prevalent point of view among companies. It is true that we live in uncertain times—the most uncertain that any generation of businessmen has ever experienced—but to ignore planning for this reason is, in effect, to decide to quit the race. Not to plan is not to look ahead, and not to look ahead is retirement. The uncertainty of tomorrow is no license to management to forget about tomorrow. It would be like saying that rising labor rates justify ignoring manufacturing costs. One of the principal functions of management is to plan ahead. Simply because the clouded horizon makes this a difficult process is no excuse for complete default.

The answer lies in flexibility of the same type that military plans must possess, so that incorrect assumptions and unpredicted developments do not destroy the eventual execution of a planned operation. Flexibility in planning is achieved by frequent revision of plans and by a knowledge of what alternative courses of action must be taken to meet the requirements of temporary interim developments, without abandoning the basic long-term program. In other words, there is required employment of quick tactical footwork within the structure of the broader strategical plan.

# 15.

# Long-Range Sales Planning

## By J. B. Misenhimer [1]

All industries have their production and sales planning problems. We in the American Can Company are not unique in that sense, but I do believe that some of the special problems we have are unusual—and certainly they are difficult to solve with a reasonable degree of accuracy.

Can production in many of our plants must be closely geared to agricultural production, and the best-laid plans can be suddenly upset by adverse weather conditions, insects, blights, and so forth. Nevertheless, it has long been a company practice—and, I might add, a necessity—to plan sales and manufacturing operations at least one year ahead. There are a number of reasons for this.

In the first place, many of our plants, especially those making food cans, are called upon to deliver up to 60 per cent of their annual production within a six- to eight-week period. Secondly, the long lead time required in the production of tin plate makes it necessary to anticipate our raw material requirements many months in advance. Consequently, inventory and production plans must be carefully worked out well ahead of the peak season.

For these reasons, among others, we have found it necessary no later than September of each year to forecast the annual volume and project monthly sales for each of our sixty plants for the next year. That, however, is just the beginning.

[1] From an address to the Marketing Conference of the National Industrial Conference Board, September 22, 1955. Reprinted by permission of the author.

Although forecasting and planning even one year in advance are fraught with unpredictables, we came to the conclusion soon after World War II that planning one year ahead was not enough. In fact, we became convinced that much of our increasing expense for cross-shipping raw materials and containers, overtime charges, and costs of relocating manufacturing facilities could be traced directly to inadequate long-range planning.

During the war, many of our operating flexibilities had disappeared, and shortly after the close of the conflict we found ourselves faced with enormous pent-up demands for containers that had been under various wartime restrictions. We could meet these demands only through a great deal of juggling between plants. This "robbing Peter to pay Paul" kind of operation set up a chain reaction that spread from plant to plant as the seasons progressed, with the result that the techniques each plant had developed for planning its own year-to-year operations gradually broke down.

Furthermore, shifts in population and consumer demands, as well as in the introduction of new products (such as frozen citrus concentrates), presented many new postwar problems.

## ANALYTICAL PLANNING GROUPS

These and other factors led to an exhaustive study of our planning problems and the eventual formation of analytical planning groups in our General and Division Offices. There is a continual interchange of information between these groups, whose responsibility is to analyze general, as well as specific, situations related to our manufacturing and sales activities.

The group in our General Office makes appraisals of the over-all economic atmosphere for the various forecast periods being studied. We have learned that such appraisals are a useful step as a framework for analyzing and forecasting the demands for individual product lines which have a bearing on our business.

Better planning was necessary because we simply had to bring plant production into better balance with future sales of containers, area by area, to establish individual plant control of production planning and regain operating efficiencies disrupted by the peculiar urgencies of a wartime economy.

In short, it had become apparent that longer-range sales forecasts and more effective longer-range planning had to be undertaken. After considering the time needed to plan and economically build plant facilities, we concluded that we must forecast container potentials and develop related sales and operating plans at least five years ahead.

In our short-range planning we had always relied a great deal on the close contacts our salesmen in the field had with their customers and the intimate knowledge they obviously had of each customer's container requirements. However, we soon learned that this knowledge did not extend five years into the future and the estimates we were getting from the field were just not reliable, through no fault of the salesmen concerned.

It was obvious to us after the war that the sum total of these field forecasts was not a reliable enough barometer on which to base the spending of millions of dollars for new or improved plant facilities. This was shown when five-year sales estimates were received from salesmen all over the country prior to the formation of the long-range planning staffs. When these nation-wide estimates were totaled, the figures were astounding. It was evident that this over-all estimate bore no relation whatever to the total annual consumption of each product. What had happened was that each salesman had reflected in his estimates the optimism of individual container users who were predicting hopefully that in the next five years they would capture an increased share of the total market for an individual product.

## Further Study Needed

We concluded that intelligent long-range sales planning required a deeper analysis of the underlying economic factors that influence the demand for containers. We had to study the factors that influence consumption of products and where those products would be produced and packed.

Geographical considerations had to be studied. Many products are distributed nationally but are only produced in certain areas. These include the vast vegetable crops, the seafood packs from coastal areas, and the citrus crops in Florida and California. Other products—such as motor oil, paints, and insecticides, to name a few—are turned out in many areas. The production of many of these tends to increase or move to certain areas as growth and shifts of population to those areas result in increased consumption. Since the demand for containers usually arises in the area where the product is produced, regional analysis of production in relation to the over-all national consumption of the product was essential, so that we could better judge the proper location of manufacturing facilities and establish sales plans in line with the container potentials of each area.

The consumer demand in total for a certain product was not the only trend we had to watch. We had to analyze the various forms in which a product was being marketed and sold. For example, we needed to know not only the trend in total per capita consumption of fruits and vegetables but whether canned, fresh, or frozen varieties were losing or gaining popularity. Consumer preference for either ground or soluble coffee was another example of the many situations requiring study.

This meant we had to analyze changes in the consumption and production of many products, as the form of the product has a decided bearing on the type and size of the package used. Such analyses help us foresee the impact of such shifts on the demand for the containers we produce. They supply our Research Department with valuable guides as to what directions their work should take to keep pace with technological advancements and provide the stimulus for development of longer-range sales plans to combat unfavorable trends.

The further we went into the problems of long-range sales planning, the more we realized that it was a job for an independent, unbiased, analytical staff able to sort out and evaluate the underlying economic influences that affect the consumption and production of the many products in which we are interested. Thus, we adapted the concept of setting up small analytical planning groups in our General and Division Offices. In a sense, these groups, in addition to their analytical and forecasting activities, function in a coordinating capacity in assisting the company's various operating departments to formulate their long- and short-range plans.

The planning group in the General Office handles basic commercial research and analyses of product lines common to all American Can Company Divisions. Guidance forecasts of total national consumption of products are furnished to Division planning groups and, through exchange of information and views, forecasts are projected for each Division. When added together, these forecasts provide an acceptable over-all national forecast.

The Division staffs have primary responsibility for regional analyses of production and the development of forecasts by plant area. These regional and plant area forecasts must reconcile with the accepted over-all forecasts of each Division. Thus, we are able to better correlate the anticipated regional production of a product with the forecasted total national consumption of that product.

Our experience indicates that this mutual responsibility and exchange of views between the General and Division planning groups produces a much more realistic long-range forecast of sales potentials than that obtained either by combining individual estimates of salesmen in the field or by relying wholly on the opinions of top management in the General Office. This system, we believe, provides a sounder base for developing long-range sales plans and directs sales efforts along lines offering the greatest possibilities for success.

# 16.

# Determining and Reporting
# Division Objectives [1]

The purpose of objectives or targets is to set a level of performance toward which divisional plans of action will be directed. Objectives are redetermined each year for each of the next succeeding three years. They are determined for each product line or plant and for the division as a whole. Once formulated together with their supporting programs they become an integrated plan for the control of operations.

Objectives are determined for each product line or plant for:

(a) share of the market
(b) sales volume
(c) earnings from operations

and for the entire division for these factors plus:

(a) necessary investment
(b) turnover
(c) return on investment

What constitutes a product line is largely one of division determination. However . . . the important thing is that all concerned know what is included or excluded in the product line and the industry or market.

. . . The objectives to be reported should be determined within the framework of the following:

1. In August each division will be furnished a forecast of the out-

[1] From American Brake Shoe Company, *Profit Planning Guide*, pp. 20–21 and 32–34. Reprinted by permission.

179

look for general business. This forecast can be used as a guide for the general direction of business during the period for which objectives will be determined.

2. Objectives are to be determined for each of the next three succeeding years. Data with respect to the current year should be actual up to the time of determining objectives plus forecast for the balance of the year.

3. No attempt should be made to predict inflationary or deflationary movements in general wage levels and prices. Thus objectives set in 1955 for 1956, 1957, and 1958 should be in terms of 1955 wage and price levels. However, known or reasonably anticipated changes in selling prices, wages, and purchased materials for the next year ahead should be reflected. The General Purchasing Department will advise division of anticipated changes in material prices.

4. Objectives for cost, earnings, and assets should be established on the basis of sales volume objectives. They should reflect not only the improvement in the rate of earnings to sales and investment turnover which can be expected from higher volume, but other operating improvements flowing from better control of costs, expenses, and investment.

In order to assure reasonable consistency in reporting practices the following forms (obtainable upon requisition from the General Purchasing Department) are to be used:

Form 1  —Product line or Plant Objectives
Form 1A—Product line or Plant Objectives, by Quarters
Form 2  —Division Earnings Objective
Form 2A—Division Earnings Objective, by Quarters
Form 3  —Investment Objectives
Form 4  —Summary of Division Objectives [2]

In addition to such copies as are needed within the division five (5) copies of each form should be submitted.

Instructions as to the use of each form are given on an explanation sheet accompanying a sample of the form.

On all forms data shown on lines styled "target" or "present estimate" for years prior to the current year should be actual figures.

[2] This form, which is similar in format to the others, is reproduced, with the accompanying instructions for its use, on pages 181–182.—ED.

## Form No. 4

### Summary of Division Objectives

This form is used for the determination and recording of objectives for the division as a whole. It provides, on one piece of paper, in summary form a picture of division objectives expressed in dollar amounts.

The explanations which follow are numbered to correspond with the arrow overlays on each of the six areas of the accompanying sample of the form.

1. *Sales Value of 40 Hour Capacity.* The sales value of the 40 hour capacity is reported here. The amount so reported should be equal to the sum of that shown on line 1 of individual Forms No. 1. Provision is also made for recording previously reported 40 hour capacity targets.

2. *Markets.* Entries for the dollar volume of market or industry should only be made here if the division is in only one market or industry. If such is the case then the amount entered should be equal to the total reported on line 3 of Form No. 1 for each plant. Comparisons where applicable should be made with previous market estimates.

3. *Net Sales.* The net sales objective for the division is entered here. This amount should agree with line 1 of Form No. 2. Comparisons with previous targets should be made where applicable.

4. *Earnings Before Taxes.* The earnings objective is shown here as well as its percentage relation to net sales. The amount entered for each year should agree with line of Form No. 2. Comparisons with previous targets, where applicable, should be made.

5. *Facilities Program.* Reference should be made to Form No. 5 (described in Section VII on developing the facilities program) for the amounts to be entered here.

6. *Investment Average.* The division investment objective as well as investment turnover and return on investment are reported here. The amounts shown for average investment for each year are found by reference to line 14 of Form No. 3.

Division _____

| | | 1 | 2 | 3 | 4 | 5 | 6 | 7 |
|---|---|---|---|---|---|---|---|---|
| | | 1958 | 1957 | 1956 | 1955 | 1954 | 1953 | 1952 |
| | **SALES VALUE OF 40 HOUR CAPACITY** | | | | | | | |
| 1 | TARGET | — | | | | — | — | — |
| 2 | PREVIOUS TARGET | | | | | | | |
| | **MARKET** | | | | | | | |
| 3 | PRESENT ESTIMATE | — | | | | — | — | — |
| 4 | PREVIOUS ESTIMATE | | | | | | | |
| | **NET SALES** | | | | | | | |
| 5 | TARGET | | | | | | | |
| 6 | % of 40 Hour Capacity | — | | | | — | — | — |
| 7 | % of Market | — | | | | — | — | — |
| 8 | PREVIOUS TARGET | | | | | | | |
| 9 | % of 40 Hour Capacity | | | | | | | |
| 10 | % of Market | | | | | | | |
| | **EARNINGS BEFORE TAXES** | | | | | | | |
| 11 | TARGET | — | | | | — | — | — |
| 12 | % of Net Sales | — | | | | — | — | — |
| 13 | PREVIOUS TARGET | | | | | | | |
| 14 | % of Net Sales | | | | | | | |
| | **FACILITIES PROGRAM** | | | | | | | |
| 15 | CAPITAL | | | | | | | |
| 16 | AUTHORITY EXPENSE | | | | | | | |
| 17 | TOTAL | | | | | | | |
| | **INVESTMENT - AVERAGE** | | | | | | | |
| 18 | TARGET | | | | | | | |
| 19 | TURNOVER | | | | | | | |
| 20 | % Return before Taxes | | | | | | | |

Division President _____    Date _____

Form No. 4.  Summary of Division Objectives
(Thousands of dollars)

# 17.

# *Forecasts and Structural Change*

## By Sherman J. Maisel [1]

Planning is touched off by the knowledge that change is inevitable. Some current products will disappear. Production techniques will develop. People's tastes and their ability to indulge them will alter. Periods of low income will alternate with those of high demand. These potential shifts in demand must enter into business calculations.

A well-run enterprise will map out several lines of defense and attack. One defense will be an attempt to develop automatic stabilizers. A business, like the economy, can be organized so that certain adjustments will occur as demand shifts. Well-planned diversification may mean that some products and operations are expanding while others contract either seasonally, cyclically, or secularly. Another form of diversification may be achieved by firms which sell in many markets and are not, therefore, dependent on the vagaries of sectors in distress. These are aids to stability.

A structure can be devised in which vital spots are not exposed, one designed to absorb shifts without critical losses so that adaptations can be made smoothly to new conditions. Fluctuations in total output or in production of individual products will do the least damage if flexibility is built into plants, products, selling, and financing procedures. Even though it may result in somewhat reduced efficiency and profitability at optimum sales, flexibility insures greater average profits and fewer risks.

Another line of defense is improving knowledge of the future

[1] From Sherman J. Maisel, *Fluctuations, Growth, and Forecasting* (New York, John Wiley & Sons, Inc., 1957), pp. 490–492. Reprinted by permission.

through better forecasts. However, since no forecast is perfect, businesses must protect themselves against being misled, by contriving a rapid communications system to warn when forecasts are wrong and enable them to make new adjustments with all possible speed.

Plans are not expected to be carried out to the letter, just as forecasts are not expected to be exact. They must remain pliant and subject to adjustment. The very fact that a firm has thought through its strategies and methods of implementing them makes it easier to cope with unexpected situations.

Although the triggering of plans depends initially on the projections for the future, if something goes wrong the business should be able to shift positions rapidly. Adapting the firm to take dynamic movements in stride has sometimes been likened to the design of efficient servomechanisms. These are devices in which departures from desired patterns are measured and action is brought about to reduce the divergence. A frequently cited example is the thermostat, which measures the difference between desired temperature and actual temperature and sets in motion prior arrangements (in this case, the furnace) designed to narrow the margin. The amount of divergence and the efficiency with which a goal is attained depend on how well the system is constructed.

In the average enterprise, management policies or decisions are frequently not carried out because implementing techniques are deficient. Decisions to change the levels of inventories, of investments, of financing get watered down or percolate too late to the operations level. In planning for adjustments, it is essential both that information move back to the control center and that new policies be transmitted forward without delay.

Modern management is accelerating the development of both forecasting procedures and adjustment mechanisms. They may be joined in a good budgeting operation. The budget sets the initial goals of the organization in accordance with the best prior estimates. Reporting procedures show divergences between the goal and the results. The reason for the differences can then be examined and corrective action taken.

# 18.

# Raising Capital to Finance the New Program

## By Manley Howe Jones [1]

Regardless of the size of the sum required and the sources of the funds, the executive must be in a position to demonstrate just what makes his company "tick"—how and why it has been able to compete in the past and, even more important, how and why it will be able to compete in the future. The underwriter requires detailed information which will provide him with the premises for deciding whether to float the issue, how much money should be (and can be) raised, and what kind of security would be most appropriate. His reputation among his clients and customers depends on how well his decisions stand up. This same kind of information, though perhaps less of it, will have to be prepared when the company intends to sell directly to individuals. Some of the more discriminating investors may want rather complete data, so that they can make their own decisions— they may want proof rather than some expert's recommendations which they must take on faith—so that they themselves can determine whether the investment is the best alternative for their purposes. . . .

The executives of the brokerage firm (and the individual investors?) first want a history of the company and copies of its operating statements, balance sheets, and the details of the surplus account for the past ten years or so. They will also ask about the background and

[1] From Manley Howe Jones, *Executive Decision Making* (Homewood, Illinois, Richard D. Irwin, Inc. 1957), pp. 439–441. Reprinted by permission.

the strong points and weaknesses of the company's executives, as well as the character and ability of the young management coming up. The young men are the ones on whom the investors will eventually have to depend for their returns.

But *most of all*, they will want a diagnosis of the company's departments—answers to most of those questions . . . which the company executives pondered when they were appraising the company and comparing it with its competitors. The premises derived from these are the ones that will be given greatest weight. Incidentally, the tendency of investment houses is to stress information that can be cast in numerical form.

Having secured information on the company's history and its executives, and on trends in the financial statements and the competitive position of the company's product development, sales, and manufacturing departments, the broker (and the investor?) next wants to examine the purpose of the new financing. What is desired here is a description of the niche the company is planning to fill, the premises underlying this choice, the executive's plan for improving the departments, and the expected costs of introducing the various changes versus the contributions these will make to overhead and profits.

Finally, it is necessary to show how the company expects to meet these obligations. A projection of earning power over the next few years provides the foundation for this—estimates of probable sales in units and dollars; the expected out-of-pocket costs of manufacturing as a percentage of selling price; the probable overhead in salaries and other fixed contractual obligations, including interest on the new loan, if any; and, out of this, an estimate of profits. They will also want to know what collateral the firm can offer as security if the loan is to be in the form of mortgage notes, and how the company plans to use the profits for paying off the loans. If stock is to be issued, estimates of the dollar earnings per share on the outstanding stock will be needed, even though the estimates of dividends must of necessity be conjectural; and they would hope for some inkling of when the dividends could be expected.

Not all the companies seeking investors will need to supply equally complete information on all the questions dealing with the company's competitive position. . . . Depending on the company, some of them can be covered in a sentence or two, while other facets will need to be discussed in considerable detail. The information described above would constitute the maximum demanded by a broker who is investigating a company with a view to issuing securities to the public. If the company is planning to raise the funds itself by offering securities directly to prospective investors, less elaborate information will ordinarily be required. But in such a case an attorney familiar with the issuance of securities should be consulted to ensure compliance with the rather complicated state and federal statutes and regulations relating to new security offerings.

Normally, a company will not require all the new money immediately, because the plan cannot be put into effect all at once. This is fortunate, for it takes time to sell securities such as these. If an underwriter is used, the executive's time schedule for introducing the changes in the departments provides a basis for scheduling the transfer of the new funds.

# 19.

# Long-Range Planning

## By Robert C. Tait [1]

Long-range planning for business is being talked and written about more in this country today than ever in history. Some types of business, such as the electric and communications utilities, have always had to do a great deal of long-range planning because they must foresee well in advance the extent of increased need for electric power or telephone service. It takes a long time to construct new facilities in the steel industry and many others, and, incidentally, the steel people have pretty consistently missed the mark on the underside with respect to the need for additional tonnage facilities. Of course, having a lot of excess steel capacity at present costs of construction would be a pretty intolerable load to carry, but on the other hand producing at capacity or in excess of capacity is also an expensive proposition.

It is only since the end of World War II that the ordinary manufacturing industry has really gotten very far with long-range planning, and one of the principal reasons for this, in my judgment, is the fact that any industrial planning must be developed against a background of a reasonably sound projection of the entire economy. And it has really been only recently that we have developed sufficient indices and statistical data on various phases of our economy to make such reasonably sound projections. There are still a lot of gaps and inadequacies in the data available, and especially there is far too long a time lag in getting these data; but still we have made a lot of progress in the right direction since World War II.

---

[1] From *The Controller,* July 1956, p. 307. Reprinted by permission.

## Annual Rate of Savings

One of the most important areas in our national statistics that has been quite inadequate is data on the savings of our people. The national dollar figure on savings and the percentage it bears to personal disposable income are most important figures. What we have had until most recently is wholly inadequate and inaccurate, and even if the figures were accurate they have not been available soon enough. Sometimes almost unaccountable changes in the savings habits take place quickly with changes in the general confidence with which our people face the future.

Back in the spring of 1951, for instance, the annual rate of savings, as then quite erroneously calculated, practically doubled in a few weeks, and nobody really expected this or knew why it took place—but it had a terrific effect on our economy. A lot of good reasons were apparent a considerable time after the fact, but they were not apparent soon enough to be of any value in taking protective measures to cushion the impact. One of the reasons for this sudden change was undoubtedly the fact that the Korean War had induced all kinds of purchases of semidurable goods in the fear that they would not be available later on, and these were bought for cash, out of savings, or on installment purchases.

By the late spring of '51 the average maturity of much of this installment paper was behind us, and more importantly, the public suddenly began to realize that we were going to be able to produce both guns and butter. All ordinary consumer goods were still available and apparently likely to continue to be—so quite without warnings or predictions a significant change in savings habits took place, and the rate of savings as then measured practically doubled overnight.

One of the great weaknesses in the whole savings figure was that the statistics for personal savings had traditionally been derived by deducting personal taxes and personal consumption expenditures from total personal income. The resultant figure, however, in no way represented unspent cash income since it included such durable or semidurable goods as houses and even automobiles, as well as payments of insurance premiums. And while it is intriguing to think one could save $7,500 by buying an Eldorado convertible, that amount of money once spent was certainly no longer available for other purchases.

## "FLOW-OF-FUNDS" FIGURES

A couple of months ago the Federal Reserve Board brought out a new series of figures with most interesting potentialities. For want of a better term this is referred to as a "Flow-of-Funds" system of national accounts. The structure of the Flow-of-Funds accounts is intended to reflect the functional and institutional features of importance in analyzing the role of financial factors in economic fluctuation and growth. Back in my days in the banking business we used to construct what we called a "Where Got—Where Gone" statement in analyzing certain companies. Your conventional balance sheet and income statements do not give the whole story that a Source and Application of Funds report over a period of time reveals, this being merely a fancier term for what we called the Where Got—Where Gone statement.

The new Federal Reserve Flow-of-Funds figures are more like this type of Where Got—Where Gone statement for our entire economy. For example, in 1953 consumers purchased goods and services in the amount of $237 billion; paid $23 billion for insurance, retirement benefits, and gifts; $41 billion in taxes; and added $13 billion to their cash and other financial assets—all of which adds up to $314 billion. Approximately 60 per cent of this sum came from wages and salaries, another 20 per cent from investment income of one kind or another, but the remaining 20 per cent, or around $60 billion, could not be accurately accounted for. The Flow-of-Funds accounts reveal that approximately $20 billion of this was covered by receipts from the sale of tangible assets, such as real estate, automobiles, etc.; that somewhat more than this came from insurance benefits, pension receipts, gifts, and public and private aid. Tax refunds accounted for $3 billion, and the remaining $11 billion came from borrowings, the mortgage debt rising by $6 billion and other consumer indebtedness by about $5 billion. Thus there is a full accounting of consumer receipts, expenditures, and finances in a single statement.

This system not only provides some missing links, but also develops far more accurate figures in respect to the elusive savings that I have been talking about. The old Department of Commerce figures on personal savings showed them as 7.2 per cent of disposable income in 1954, while net liquid savings according to the Flow-of-Funds system, that is, the amount that could have been spent additionally without any further borrowing, were only $3 billion, or 1.2 per cent of disposable income.

## USE OF STATISTICS

I seem to have gotten off the track here a bit on this subject, but I feel that the introduction of the Federal Reserve's Flow-of-Funds figures will do much to increase our knowledge of what is happening in our economy, and if we can step up the speed with which this information is made available, we can perhaps more nearly approach the point where corrective measures can be taken early enough to be increasingly effective. So, despite the fact that we need more and better statistics more rapidly and more accurately, we still have by far the best statistics available with respect to our amazingly complex economy of any country in the world. Furthermore, we are making better use of them since World War II. We have the President's Council of Economic Advisors; the greatly improved statistics of our powerful Federal Reserve Board that I have already mentioned; the CED; the National Planning Association; the U.S. Chamber of Commerce; Brookings Institution; the so-called "Paley Commission," officially known as the President's Materials Policy Commission, which reported to the President in June 1952 with five volumes of data projecting our economy into 1975; the Twentieth Century Fund, which has turned out such monumental works as *America's Needs and Resources* and has just brought out a new revision of this study entitled *America's Needs and Resources: A New Survey;* and so on and so on.

## BASIS FOR ECONOMIC PROJECTIONS

When you add to such organizations the consensus of opinion of our many able public and private economists, we are really approaching a basis for sound economic projections which take into account all the major factors affecting our economy. Take just one example of an important factor—the tremendous impact of the rapid increase in our population that is on its way. Population growth estimates in the past have generally been quite a bit on the low side. If the present projections still prove to be on the low side we are really going to have an onrushing increase in our population that will affect every phase of our lives. So I repeat, any long-range planning for industry must be conceived against a background of the general economy, and we are now in better position than ever to evaluate the probable course of the general economy.

Now, in the average industry, how far should long-range planning attempt to reach? In an industry such as ours, which deals in communications and the rapidly developing field of electronics, anything less than five years seems too short a time. Five years is an awfully short time these days—or maybe it's my age. Actually it frequently takes longer than that to dream up a new product, perhaps uncovered in our Research Department, and then refine it for commercial application, redesign it for production, subject it to field and market tests, eliminate the bugs and get it into quantity production, and then successfully gain public or commercial acceptance for volume sales. This cycle, I think, runs longer than most people, even businessmen, realize. In addition to this, it takes time to plan and build the new facilities that may be required, to plan the type and timing of new financing that may be needed, to train the required supervisory personnel, etc.

Five years, therefore, appears to be the minimum round number of years for which we should attempt to plan ahead. To reach out to ten, on the other hand, in most businesses would appear to me to involve too much crystal-balling, again except the utilities, transportation, and other segments of our economy that depend largely upon the general population trend and growth of the economy as a whole. The aircraft industry, with which we are now affiliated in General Dynamics Corporation, is another longer-range industry. It takes between five and ten years from the drawing-board stage of a new airplane to quantity production of the finished product. As you know, there are about one-half billion dollars' worth of commercial jet aircraft now on order for delivery some years hence. This is good, but in passing, I might add that if we had them now our airport, communications, and navigational facilities would be completely inadequate to handle them.

## Long-Range Planning Techniques

Let's assume, therefore, that for our purposes we want to develop long-range planning techniques for at least a five-year period, in order to obtain the most efficient and profitable use of our facilities, funds, and man power during the next few years. If intelligently and honestly conceived, such plans should assist top management in making decisions with respect to:

1. Stabilizing profits and improving return on investment.
2. A long-range capital program.
3. Development and training of supervisory and management personnel.
4. A more effective long-range *sales* program.
5. Improvement in the procurement of purchased parts and materials.
6. A more effective means of smoothing out the production peaks and valleys, which should also lead to
7. Improved labor relations.
8. A sounder basis for divisional and departmental budgeting.

The scope of such planning should cover all major phases of the business: types and quantities of products, methods of distribution, use of productive facilities, financial requirements, personnel requirements, procurement schedules, the timing and effect of automation and where it can best be applied, the extent and direction of research and development, profit margins and return on investment by product and division, etc.—all, of course, weighed against that backdrop of the general economy which we have been talking about.

It seems to me there are two general approaches to this type of long-range planning: one is to set up desirable goals by products, departments and divisions, and then try to figure out how to reach these goals; and the other is to have each department and division of your company calculate its own future growth as accurately as it can without regard to other segments of the business or any particular emphasis on the most desirable goals.

Neither of these is right in and of itself, in my judgment, but rather the more nearly correct answer is likely to come from a combination of both; that is, you try to calculate the future growth pattern of a given product or series of products in a division of your company, then weigh that against what would appear to be the most desirable growth pattern, and then see how closely you can reconcile the two within the realm of practical limitations and fit them into an over-all pattern for your company.

## BOTTOM-UP PLANNING

Thus the roots of our long-range planning are decentralized to the individual departments and divisions of the business on what might be called a philosophy of "bottom-up planning." In passing, I might add that I think it is a sound tenet of good management that decisions should be made at the lowest practicable level. We could spend considerable time on this one point but I don't think it is particularly relevant here. By giving the departments and the divisions the opportunity to submit their plans we are fairly well assured that no aspect of the business will be overlooked, and we also get much of the important work done at the level where the greatest degree of specific knowledge exists. From there on it becomes a matter of relative evaluation.

We decided to place the over-all responsibility for our long-range planning with our corporate treasurer, if for no other reason than the fact that this man had already done a great deal of effective work along these lines. He is a student and analyst by nature. But also this is a staff department with no axe to grind, and it is in an ideal position to weigh, analyze, and evaluate equitably the growth patterns set up by each department and division, which, as I have said, are set up without any particular respect to other divisions or the over-all welfare of the company.

The central planning department is responsible for:

1. Study of business conditions and forecasting with respect to the general economy.
2. Market analysis and research, performing services available to all divisions.
3. Determination of capital budgets and long-range appropriations on the basis of return on gross investment.
4. Redetermination of product line goals that will fit into the over-all company pattern of availability of capital facilities, engineering, and technical man power.

## CRITERIA

Certain criteria are needed to measure or evaluate long-range plans, especially when it comes to establishing a priority of one specific plan over another, or approving or disapproving a plan. Such criteria vary with the nature of each particular project. From the over-all standpoint, one of the most important yardsticks is return on gross assets employed. For us this is the real acid test. It is not always easy to apply this measurement to an individual project under consideration, but it is possible to apply the test to a divisional forecast once that particular project, along with others, has been incorporated into a division's long-range program.

Another criterion which is of importance to us in passing general judgment is the relative stability of the project in question. For example, projects within our telephone equipment division are generally predicated on long-range requirements within the telephone utilities market. Hence they carry considerable weight in our thinking as compared with a project that would be in for a short period only, and then out again.

Another criterion which is important to us is the extent to which a given project supplements our present product or market lines. A new market for an existing product or a new product for an existing market gains more weight in our judgment than projects which are brand new in both respects. I might add that in my judgment it is much harder to sell a product than to make it, and more weight should be given this in the determination of a new product or a new line than I feel is sometimes the case.

Weighing these factors in the evaluation of a long-range objective is difficult at best. The important thing is that the facts be available to management so that it can make as intelligent a decision as possible. While we are on this subject I might mention that there is a tendency to establish standards for some of these criteria. For example, we have come to feel that a return on gross assets employed of about 20 per cent before income tax (or about 10 per cent after tax) is a reasonable goal on the average in our business. Some projects we feel should return a greater percentage if they are relatively short-term and unstable in nature. Others might be checked in at somewhat less than that return if they show promise of a long and successful life. There is always danger in allowing certain standards of performance to become the rule, and each project should be carefully evaluated in terms of the existing circumstances, rather than determined by rigid preconceived minimums or maximums.

## CAPITAL REQUIREMENTS

I have purposely deferred consideration of the determination of capital required to provide the fixed assets and working capital necessary to operate at the levels established by our objectives until last because, prior to our merger with General Dynamics Corporation on June 30 of last year, this was quite a different problem from what it is today. We formerly had to take into consideration the availability of funds for our business; the extent to which we could obtain credit, long-term and short-term, and the relative costs thereof; the extent to which we should resort to equity issues, and the proper timing of these.

Now we have access to considerably more capital, so our concern is not with how to raise it but how to justify our needs as against other divisions of the corporation, and here is where return on investment becomes more and more important. Incidentally, I am convinced that this is one of the major reasons why large corporations have a better over-all return on investment than the smaller ones; namely, that, generally speaking, the larger the corporation the more places there are to put funds to work and the wider the choice.

It is only natural, therefore, that, on the average, the corporation's money is going to be put to work where it will bring the best return, whereas many smaller companies are confined to the fields in which they now operate, relatively locked in or limited in choice with respect to where they can put their money to work—if they have it—to best advantage.

I doubt if this could be classified as a scientific discussion of the problems and techniques of long-range industrial planning, but I hope I have been able to suggest a few ideas and lend some emphasis to the increasing importance of long-range industrial planning in doing business under today's—and tomorrow's—conditions.

# 20.

# Operations Research and Long-Range Company Planning

## By E. Leonard Arnoff [1]

The words "Observe always that everything is the result of change" were spoken some 1,900 years ago by the Roman emperor, Marcus Aurelius.

The timeliness of these words is evident when one examines the change in product mix of many of our American companies over the past ten years. Even in rather stable industries, one observes a great amount of change. For example, J. Irwin Miller, Chairman of the Board, Cummins Engine Company, recently reported that for a certain month of the preceding year, 45 per cent of the engines shipped by Cummins were of models which the company was not producing three years previously, and that the engine models which, seven years before, had accounted for 70 per cent of the company's business constituted less than 5 per cent of the shipments for that month. Other companies have reported on even more striking changes.

Today, business and industry recognize that they must be able to adapt themselves readily to change if they are to survive, let alone grow and prosper. As a result, business and industry are exhibiting an ever-increasing interest in long-range planning—long-range planning which takes into account economic, political, and social changes as well as scientific and technological developments.

[1] Reprinted by permission of the author from *Implementing Long-Range Company Planning* (Menlo Park, California, Stanford Research Institute, 1957).

## How Operations Research Works

Although there are obviously many viewpoints as to what constitutes long-range planning, I should like to consider one particular approach, namely, the application of operations research methods, techniques, and tools to the solution of long-range planning problems. In particular, I should like to illustrate this use of operations research in long-range company planning by means of specific case histories.

Operations research may be defined as the application of scientific methods to problems of the executive, that is, problems of the manager responsible for integrating the operations of functionally distinct organizational components.[2] Teams of scientists and engineers of diverse backgrounds examine all aspects of a problem and draw from a wide range of scientific concepts, methods, techniques, and tools those which are most applicable to the problem at hand. Out of this integrated and synthesizing research procedure, the executive is provided with an objective basis for making decisions and establishing policies which best serve the organization as a whole, rather than any one—or combination of less than all—of its individual parts.

The method of operations research may be described in the following terms: By analysis of the objectives and operations of the organization, a particular problem is formulated in its broadest possible terms. Then, a scheme is developed to express the "effectiveness" of the organization. The manner in which the organization's effectiveness is dependent on the constant and variable aspects of the system is then usually described in a mathematical way. This functional relationship is called a "model," and is essentially an expression of the assumptions upon which analysis is based. Values of those variables which are subject to control are then determined so as to yield maximum effectiveness. These results are then tested, both for validity and practicability. Once validated and shown feasible, these results are applied in plans and procedures in a form which provides for their continual re-evaluation as conditions change.

Most of the applications of operations research reported on to date

[2] A complete and detailed discussion of operations research and its definition; history and development; methods, techniques and tools; areas of application; and of the administration, selection, and training of personnel for operations research can be found in Reference 7, page 223.

have occurred in areas which might be classified as short-range planning, both strategic and tactical. There are relatively few published operations research studies primarily concerned with long-range planning. This lack, however, is readily explained. In the first place, operations research is a new science, and management has not as yet had sufficient opportunity to develop confidence in the merit of utilizing an operations research approach. Consequently, operations research teams are often initially obliged to consider problem areas where the results of their efforts can be evaluated in a rather short time. This has resulted in a concentration on the solution of short-range problems, such as in the area of production and inventory control, where data are readily available, where many of the problems are of easily manageable size and of high potential pay-off, and where this pay-off is readily measurable.

In the second place, even when management confidence is present and when the Operations Research team is permitted to consider long-range planning problems, short-range planning is still a necessary prelude. Only after a company has established its day-to-day and short-term operations on a sound basis can it fruitfully enter into long-range planning. Stated in another manner, in any long-range planning problem, one must, of necessity, consider the short-range problems as the first phase.

## DEVELOPMENT OF CRITERIA FOR LONG-RANGE PLANNING

In business and industry, long-range planning manifests itself in one or more of several ways. These include new product development, market development, expansion and acquisition, and other areas . . . Fundamental to each of these major paths of company growth is the development of criteria, measures, and standards for accurately and realistically guiding the research and, in turn, gauging the effectiveness of the team's efforts and plans. The importance and value of establishing such criteria can be illustrated by referring briefly to a particular company of which the executive committee wished to evaluate certain plans of action that pertained to the company's operations over a forthcoming five-year period.

Management agreed upon a list of five-year objectives. These objectives were:

1. Continuation of existing management
2. Guaranteed 6 per cent return to the owners of their original investment
3. Ability of the company to make up to 15 per cent return on investment if market for the product stayed in the range of 100 per cent or 200 per cent of current demand
4. No layoffs, and reasonable promotion of key company personnel
5. Stable labor relations (as evidenced, for example, by the absence of strike threats and a minimum of hiring and layoffs)
6. Technological leadership
7. Community service over and above legal requirements

The objectives were then weighed by management to determine their relative importance.[3] The final distribution of relative weights was as follows:

| Objective | Relative Weight |
|---|---|
| 1. Security of existing management | 0.25 |
| 2. Financial security | 0.30 |
| 3. Financial opportunity | 0.10 |
| 4. Key personnel | 0.15 |
| 5. Labor stability | 0.05 |
| 6. Technological leadership | 0.05 |
| 7. Community service | 0.10 |

These weights were then accepted by the team as basic data.

The company executive committee was considering three possible board policies which, in abbreviated form, were:

A. Projected 200 per cent expansion of the company's operations in two years, including new products and markets.
B. Maintenance of the present size of the company, with emphasis on improvements in models of existing products.
C. Maintenance of the present size of the company, with emphasis on the replacement of less profitable products by new products.

A company committee, composed of representatives of all of the major functions of the company, then evaluated each policy on a numerical scale with respect to each objective. More specifically, evaluations were assigned which were assumed to measure the probability that a specific objective would be attained under a given policy.

[3] For a description of the weighting procedure used, see Reference 7, Chapter 6.

The resulting evaluations were then appropriately combined (as with weighted probabilities) and the relative weight (*utility*) of each policy was determined, yielding:

| | |
|---|---|
| Utility of Policy A | 0.28 |
| Utility of Policy B | 0.38 |
| Utility of Policy C | 0.34 |

In other words, Policy B was judged to be of greatest expected value in terms of achieving the specific objectives of the company. By this means, the company was able to establish an "optimal" policy for its future planning. Note particularly that this policy, i.e., maintenance of the present size of the company with emphasis on improvements in models of existing products, is not the kind of policy usually associated with long-range planning. If the various policies had not been evaluated in terms of objectives, the company would probably have planned by means of Policy A, i.e., in terms of a projected 200 per cent expansion of the company's operations in two years including new products and markets. Such a planning policy would have been expected to yield results which would not necessarily have been compatible with the stated objectives of the particular company.

The appropriate standards and measures for long-range planning, once established, guide the next phase of the research along the proper path of company growth. Thus, in the preceding example, the selection of Policy A would have required that a planning program include consideration of new products and also new markets. Policy C would have required emphasis only on consideration of new products, whereas Policy B required only a concentration on improving the existing products.

In order to illustrate in specific terms the application of operations research to long-range planning involving some of the major paths of company growth, I shall summarize briefly several company case histories which reflect the use of the operations research approach.

## OPERATIONS RESEARCH IN PRODUCT SEARCH AND EVALUATION [4]

One of the most common paths of company growth is that involv-

[4] This section is a brief summary of an article on this subject written jointly by the author and Dr. Paul Stillson, Director of Operations Research, Shell Chemical Corporation, in the *Journal of Marketing*, July, 1957.

ing new products—whether required for the sake of keeping up with a rapidly changing technology, for expansion, or for diversification.

The well-known investment firm, J. H. Whitney and Company, reported that, of 2,100 new product propositions, only seventeen were considered by them to be of merit. Of these seventeen, only two proved to be conspicuously successful on the competitive market; five were moderately successful; six were considered to be of a borderline nature; three were still too young to appraise; and one was a distinct failure, even though its production was recommended. In this vital area of product expansion, product improvement, and product diversification, this is indeed a very dismal record. It would appear evident, therefore, that there is a great need for improved methods of product search and product evaluation.

The search process in obtaining new products for expansion or diversification is principally one of selection, in that many ideas and suggestions must be examined and those meriting further investigation must be evaluated. The final objective of the researcher is to obtain a group of alternate possibilities, each of which has been subjected to intensive research and deliberation, and has also passed various criteria of acceptance. A product evaluation procedure is then carried out for each of these remaining possibilities to determine the final choice.

Recently, the Oster Manufacturing Company, well known for its line of pipe and bolt threading machines, announced its entrance into the billion-dollar materials-handling field through a line of multi-purpose, hand-propelled, hand and battery operated portable lifts. This move by Oster culminated a three-year study into new products and their market potential which had been conducted in cooperation with the Operations Research Group at Case Institute of Technology.

The first stage of the Oster new product study consisted of establishing suitable criteria, standards, and measures. These items reflected the current status, facilities, capacities, and objectives of the particular company. Some of the initial criteria of acceptance were:

1. Can use be made of the existing distribution facilities?
2. Can use be made of the existing production facilities?
3. Can use be made of the present raw materials?
4. Can use be made of the present technical knowledge?

5. Can patents and copyrights be obtained for the product?
6. Has the new product been tested adequately—marketwise?
7. Has the new product been tested adequately—engineeringwise?

These criteria were ranked according to their relative importance by one of several procedures that have been developed and successfully applied.[5] Then, products obtained from such publications as *The Thomas Register of American Manufacturers* or from consideration of new materials and new manufacturing techniques were studied with respect to these criteria of acceptance.[6] This yielded a greatly reduced list of products which were initially acceptable and ready for further sifting.

Consideration was then given to the relationship of each proposed product with the existing company product line. Specifically, the following basic questions were answered:

1. Why is a new product being searched for at this time?
2. Will the inclusion of this new product affect the operational stability of the company?

A new product is usually considered for one of the following reasons:

1. Promotional: to extend the product line and increase the over-all sales volume for all products.
2. Aggressive: to extend the company's products into new areas and to diversify the product line.
3. Defensive: to provide an additional outlet for the company's facilities in the event of a market decline in the current product line.[7]

Only those products which conformed to that objective selected from the three were retained for further consideration in a second-stage sifting process.

[5] There are, of course, serious limitations on the use of such ranking devices as well as on the validity of the results obtained therefrom. These are considered in Chapter 6 of Reference 7. See also Reference 17.

[6] For a discussion of methods of evaluating such products with respect to criteria of acceptance, see Reference 7, Chapter 6, and Reference 17.

[7] This might also be phrased as seeking a product line which will compensate for the economic peaks and valleys of the demand for the current product line and which will provide a means of maintaining a certain degree of labor stability under all business conditions.

To answer the second question, it was necessary to consider the basic nature of the company's operations with respect to such items as:

1. Its ability to process certain raw materials
2. Its ability in tooling
3. Its ability in the finishing of products
4. Its ability in packaging
5. Its current marketing and distribution channels

Consideration of items of this kind entailed considerable analysis. However, the successful determination of the company's objectives and its philosophy of operation are essential ingredients of any scientific product search.

The selection criteria will vary with each company and with each product classification. However, the final result in each case is a much narrowed-down list of truly "acceptable" products, each of which must then be evaluated.

## Product Evaluation

The method of product evaluation can be stated in terms of three tasks:

1. Determine the minimum market requirements for each product.
2. Analyze these market requirements with respect to production planning, manufacturing facilities, man power, and supervision.
3. Determine whether these market and production requirements can be met.

*Task 1. Minimum Market Requirements.* In order to stipulate a minimum acceptance level for gross sales, it was necessary to make certain asumptions or estimates concerning manufacturing costs, sales mixture, administrative expenses, overhead, and the like. These costs, either historical or estimated, must reflect the adaptation of the present system to incorporate the new product. Factors such as dealer's discount, acceptable net rate of return, product mix, and others, may be unknown but can be expressed in terms of parameters. For example, there was some doubt as to the sales commission that should be allowed on a given new product as well as to the minimum acceptable net rate of return. The evaluation, then, was carried out for low, medium, and high values of each of these factors. The resulting evaluation was then a function of both parameters. Thus, a table of the following form (data fictitious) was prepared to exhibit the minimum market requirements as a function of the sales commission and the net rate of return:

|  |  | Sales Commission | | |
|---|---|---|---|---|
|  |  | 0.02 | 0.05 | 0.08 |
| Rate | 0.10 | 386,000 [a] | 455,000 | 555,000 |
| of | 0.15 | 516,000 | 650,000 | 873,000 |
| Return | 0.20 | 783,000 | 1,132,000 | 2,055,000 |

[a] All values within the table are based on gross sales per year.

*Task 2. Production Requirements.* The minimum market requirements thus established must then be translated in terms of specific production requirements. Here, one must consider problems of inventory, time, and man-power requirements, capacity allocations, planning and scheduling, and other elements. These problems can be solved by means of the many operations research techniques of production and inventory control, linear programing, queueing theory, and the like.

*Task 3. Market Analysis.* The third and last task in this evaluation procedure is to determine whether the market and production requirements indicated by Tasks 1 and 2 can be met. Here, one must consider the feasibility of capital investment, facility expansion, and material procurement, as well as the determination of the potential market for the new product through the use of sales forecasting, market research, and market testing.

## Observations on New Product Search and Evaluation

Once these tasks had been completed, management was provided with information and facts with which it could make an effective decision. In general, the method for searching for new products as outlined above subjects management to critical self-analysis concerning long-range objectives and goals and incorporates these policy decisions into future expansion plans. It defines an acceptance standard for present as well as future company operations, and it suggests other profitable areas for further research in the fields of product improvement, product expansion, and product diversification.

*Operations Research in the Long-Range Planned Expansion
of an Electric Utility System* [8]

Any electric utility company expands its system in order to be able to fulfill its customer demands for power with some prescribed measure of reliability. Since future customer demands can only be estimated and since generators and auxiliary equipment (boilers, turbines, and the like) are subject to forced outages (e.g., breakdowns), a utility system is required to maintain a reserve of installed generating capacity in the form of "extra" turbo-generator units. Therefore, the problem of system expansion is essentially equivalent to the problem of determining and maintaining a proper (or optimum) installed, reserve generating capacity. Failure to have a sufficient reserve (sufficient as measured by some criterion) leads to customer shortages with resulting customer dissatisfaction and loss of revenue, both direct and indirect. On the other hand, a surplus of generating capacity means additional inventory costs—costs associated with direct charges on idle or unnecessary capital equipment.

The "reserve" problem, then, is to ascertain the best balance between these two costs—the cost of a shortage and the cost of excess inventory. The determination of this optimum balance point then indicates when a new unit should be added to the system, thus giving the best reserve policy for the particular system and, hence, determining the optimum expansion program for the company.

In the electrical utility industry, the reserve question is usually phrased in terms of "What is the optimum reserve generating capacity?" wherein the existence of one single reserve percentage is implied. For example, a rule of thumb in the industry is that the reserve capacity should generally be no less than 15 per cent of the system capacity. However, as will be seen later in this paper, there is no *one* optimum percentage, since the optimum varies with the size of the generators in operation. Furthermore, since the reason one seeks to ascertain the optimum reserve is to know when additional capacity is required, it seemed much more reasonable to rephrase the research

[8] This section is, with only minor modifications, the paper described in Reference 3. It appears here with the kind permission of the editor of *Operations Research*. A more complete and technical version of this case study appears in the AIEE *Transactions*.

question in terms of "When should generating capacity be added to the system?" Then, having answered this question, one can readily determine the optimum reserve capacity for any given generating system.

An associated problem, and one for which the answer is, in a sense, already implied in the determination of the optimum reserve policy, is that of determining the optimum size of unit to be added to the system. Varying the size of the unit affects coal costs, maintenance costs, labor costs, holding costs, and other factors. Here, in considering large as opposed to small units, one seeks a "best" balance between installation cost savings, coal savings, and labor and maintenance savings, on the one hand, and increased costs of investment, on the other.

A method for answering the first question—that of determining the optimum time to add generating capacity to a system—will be discussed first. Then, the second problem, that of determining the most economical size of unit, will be considered, subject to restrictions stated later. The methods described here were developed in a study recently completed for an electric utility company.

## Determination of Optimum Reserve Generating Capacity

Analysis of the company system showed that the following factors affect the determination of the optimum time for acquiring generating capacity and, hence, must be taken into account:

1. *Available Capacity:*
   (a) The number and sizes of the generating units now in the system.
   (b) The size of new generating units to be added to the system.
   (c) The amount of additional power available from (1) interconnections and, to a much lesser extent, from (2) voltage drops, (3) drop-off of customers whose contracts permit reductions in power, and (4) large industries within the system area that have their own generating units.
2. *Requirements* (consumption of power or of power-generating capacity):
   (a) Customer demand (since this is not known, it must be forecast and errors due to forecasting must also be taken into account).
   (b) Scheduled, or preventative, maintenance.
   (c) Unscheduled, or emergency, outages due to breakdowns.

3. *Costs:*
   (a) Purchase price of the generating equipment.
   (b) Installation cost of the generating equipment.
   (c) Operating cost of the generating equipment: (1) coal, (2) labor, and (3) maintenance.
   (d) Fixed charges on capital equipment: (1) cost of money, (2) income tax, (3) real estate and personal property taxes, (4) depreciation, and (5) miscellaneous.
   (e) Costs due to shortages [9] (or maximum allowable risk of shortage)

Certain of these factors had fixed values and could be determined immediately: for example, the number and sizes of the existing units in the generating system. Additionally, the scheduled maintenance program is an established one and, thus, it is safe to assume, at least for the moment, that it will be continued in its present form during the period of time under study. (A variation of the scheduled maintenance program is also evaluated in a later section of this paper.) Finally, the costs associated with installation and operation of the generators are also known.[10]

Certain other factors could be assigned values, but these values were not unique. Such factors are:

1. *The probability of forced outage* (i.e., the probability that a generating unit would not be available owing to a breakdown). Studies conducted on a national scale by the Edison Electric Institute showed that the national average for forced outages, for weekdays only, for all types of generating equipment is approximately 2 per cent. Roughly, this indicates that one can expect generating equipment to be out of commission approximately 2 per cent of the time because of an emergency, or forced, outage, either because of turbo-generator or boiler trouble.

Analysis of the company system showed that forced outages were being experienced only 1 per cent of the time. Accordingly, both figures were used in the study. Using both the 1 and 2 per cent figures

---

[9] A shortage occurs whenever the sum of customer demand, forced outages, and scheduled outages (due to maintenance) exceeds the total system capabilities.

[10] Since the purchase price of any generating unit will vary with time, this factor was treated essentially as a variable, and results were obtained for various price levels.

also enables management to measure the value of its excellent preventive maintenance program, because forced outages are affected by the rigidity (i.e., frequency and nature) of the preventive maintenance program.

2. *The amount of additional power available* to an electric utility company is largely dependent upon contractual arrangements with interconnecting companies. Inasmuch as this amount can vary with respect to the future, several varying amounts of additional power were assumed, namely, 100, 200, and 400 megawatts (MW). Not only does this enable us to provide answers to the reserve question, but it also serves to measure the value of the interconnection and the amount of power for which one should contract from the interconnection.

3. Since a system would require an *infinitely large amount of generating capacity* in order to provide for no shortages whatsoever, management must decide upon a certain risk of shortage which is "acceptable" from a practical, operating point of view.

In the electric utility industry, a rule of thumb exists as to a *maximum acceptable risk of shortage*. This, of course, assumes much as to the homogeneity, from one system to another, of the type of customer, sizes of units in the system, costs of shortage, cost of holding excess inventory, and so forth. Within the industry, however, this shortage policy is not too well defined. Accordingly, several shortage policies were assumed and evaluated with respect to total expected cost. In particular, three policies were considered and evaluated. These assumed the maximum allowable risk of shortage to be (a) one day in two years, (b) one day in five years, and (c) one day in ten years.

4. Inasmuch as the research study also included the determination of the optimum size of new units to be added to the system, the alternatives of adding distinct *sizes of generating units* were studied. In particular, two systems were studied, involving the addition of units of 240-MW and 340-MW size.

5. Since the purchase price of new generators will vary with time, study was also made of the effect of various levels of incremental *costs of purchase*. Thus, for a comparison of the addition of 340-MW

units with the addition of 240-MW generators, cost differentials of 0, 1, 2, 4, and 8 millions of dollars were considered.[11]

Finally, there were the following factors whose values had to be established: (a) the probabilities of forced outages of varying amounts for the system as a whole, and (b) the determination of expected customer demand. From these two factors and the known scheduled maintenance requirements (as well as the system capacity and other factors) one must then determine (c) the probability of a shortage. Finally, since there will be errors due to forecasts of customer demand, one must determine (d) the amount of reserve capacity required to provide for various levels of protection against forecasting errors.

### Determination of Customer Demand

In the determination of expected customer demand, it is normally of interest to ascertain only expected daily peak demands, since the ability to satisfy customer requirements at peak loads implies the ability to satisfy off-peak demands as well. Furthermore, since weekend and holiday peak loads are only 50 to 75 per cent of the normal weekday peak load, it is assumed that, for all practical purposes, shortages will not occur on week ends and holidays. Hence, in the analyses to follow, only peak loads occurring during weekdays are considered.

To determine the distribution of peak loads, a method was developed that is based upon the company's forecast of annual kilowatt-hour (kwh) consumption. A study of this annual kwh-consumption, by months, revealed a consistent variation in monthly demands. Furthermore, study also revealed that the distribution of daily peak loads within any given month was also predictable.

Therefore, by means of statistical analyses, the distribution of daily peak loads within each month can be obtained and, hence, the nature of customer demand for each month. Following is an example of such a distribution of daily peak loads for a sample month.

### Determination of Probabilities of System Outages

Methods of calculating probabilities of outages for a given system

[11] These cost differentials include incremental installation costs.

range from the rigorous method of Calabrese to the approximation method of Lyman.[12] For a system such as that discussed here, where unit sizes vary over a very large range, a rigorous computation of system probabilities of outages would require the use of a large electronic computer. Accordingly, the following device was employed.

SAMPLE MONTH

| Peaks (MW) | Expected Number of Days |
|---|---|
| 1230 | 0.32 |
| 1240 | 0.57 |
| 1250 | 0.84 |
| 1260 | 1.28 |
| 1270 | 1.68 |
| 1280 | 2.00 |
| 1290 | 2.31 |
| 1300 | 2.35 |
| 1310 | 2.31 |
| 1320 | 2.00 |
| 1330 | 1.68 |
| 1340 | 1.28 |
| 1350 | 0.84 |
| 1360 | 0.57 |
| 1370 | 0.32 |

The actual system under study was represented by a system of generating units whose sizes (i.e., capacities) are multiples of 25 MW. This yields a model of the system whose joint probabilities are then easily calculated. Care was taken so that any errors due to this simplification would be in the direction of increasing reserve requirements.[13]

## Determination of When Units Are to Be Added to the System

Once having determined (1) expected customer demand, (2) expected frequency and amount of forced outages, and (3) scheduled

[12] See References 4, 5, 6, 13, and 15.

[13] Since the results obtained from the model of the system are assumed to represent the actual system, several models were tried and the results compared with observed (historical) values, from which the "multiple of 25 MW" system was selected.

maintenance requirements, these three factors can then be combined to yield the total expected demand on the system for each month.[14] Such a combination led to the type of total expected monthly demand tabulation shown in Table 1.

TABLE 1
TOTAL EXPECTED DEMANDS FOR "TYPICAL" MONTH

| Total Demand, Including Forced Outages (1) | Expected No. of Days for Month (2) | Expected No. of Days for Month, Indicated Demand or Greater (3) | Expected No. of Days for Year, Indicated Demand or Greater (12 x Col. 3) (4) |
|---|---|---|---|
| 1400 | 1.282 | 21.000 | 252.0 |
| 1425 | 1.361 | 19.718 | 236.616 |
| 1450 | 3.521 | 18.357 | 220.284 |
| 1475 | 4.400 | 14.836 | 178.032 |
| 1500 | 2.949 | 10.436 | 125.232 |
| 1525 | 2.511 | 7.487 | 89.844 |
| 1550 | 1.746 | 4.976 | 59.712 |
| 1575 | 0.854 | 3.230 | 38.760 |
| 1600 | 0.688 | 2.376 | 28.512 |
| 1625 | 0.508 | 1.688 | 20.256 |
| 1650 | 0.319 | 1.180 | 14.160 |
| 1675 | 0.228 | 0.861 | 10.332 |
| 1700 | 0.197 | 0.633 | 7.596 |
| 1725 | 0.147 | 0.436 | 5.232 |
| 1750 | 0.097 | 0.289 | 3.468 |
| 1775 | 0.073 | 0.192 | 2.304 |
| 1800 | 0.047 | 0.119 | 1.428 |
| 1825 | 0.024 | 0.072 | 0.864 |
| 1850 | 0.018 | 0.048 | 0.576 |
| 1875 | 0.012 | 0.030 | 0.360 |
| 1900 | 0.007 | 0.018 | 0.216 |
| 1925 | 0.005 | 0.011 | 0.132 |
| 1950 | 0.003 | 0.006 | 0.072 |
| 1975 | 0.001 | 0.003 | 0.036 |

Then, with the total expected monthly demand on the system determined, this demand is associated with total system capabilities and maximum allowable risks of shortage so that, finally, it is possible to

[14] Treating the expected forced outages as a demand on the system is a very useful device which enables one to consider the capacity of the system as fixed.

determine when new generating units should be added to the system. The procedure for doing so may best be explained by means of the following example.

## Example

Assume the following conditions to be true:

1. Maximum allowable risk of shortage: 1 day in 5 years. (I.e., the system is permitted to have a shortage no more frequently than 0.2 days per year.)
2. Internal system capacity: 1,725 MW.
3. Additional capacity (e.g., from interconnection): 100 MW. (It is assumed, therefore, that the total system capacity is 1,825 MW.)

Assume that we are considering the month depicted in Table 1. By referring to Table 1, we see that, for this month, a demand of 1,850 MW or more to occur at the rate of 0.576 days per year can be expected (Column 4). Since the total system capacity is only 1,825 MW, 0.576 represents the expected number of days per year that the system will be short. Since 0.576 exceeds the maximum allowable shortage of 0.2 days per year, more generating capacity must be added during this illustrative month.[15]

Thus for each month a table of total expected demand on the system is determined by combining (1) expected customer demand, (2) expected frequency and amount of forced outages, and (3) scheduled maintenance requirements. By comparing the expected number of days per year that the system will be short with the maximum allowable risk of shortage, it can then be determined when (i.e., in which month) additional generating capacity will be required.

Such an analysis was conducted for combinations of the following values of the factors:

1. Probability of a unit outage: 1 and 2 percent.
2. Additional power available from the interconnection, etc.: 0, 100, 200, and 400 MW.
3. Maximum allowable risk of shortage: 1 day in 2 years, 1 day in 5 years, and 1 day in 10 years.

[15] Were the expected number of days short less than 0.2, the system would be deemed sufficient, and the next month's demand would then be analyzed.

The results are summarized in Table 2, which shows not only when the next unit should be added to the system for various assumptions, but also the corresponding percentage of reserve available in the system at that time.

TABLE 2

INSTALLATION DATE FOR NEXT UNIT

| Prob- ability of Outage, % | Additional Power, MW | Risk of Shortage | | | | | |
|---|---|---|---|---|---|---|---|
| | | 1 day/ 10 Yrs. | % Res. | 1 day/ 5 Yrs. | % Res. | 1 day/ 2 Yrs. | % Res. |
| 1 | 0 | Dec. 57 | 22.0 | Apr. 58 | 18.6 | June 58 | 18.6 |
| | 100 | July 58 | 18.6 | Apr. 59 | 11.7 | July 59 | 11.7 |
| | 200 | May 60 | 6.2 | Dec. 60 | 4.6 | Mar. 61 | 1.8 |
| | 400 | Mar. 62 | − 5.0 | July 62 | − 5.0 | July 62 | − 5.0 |
| 2 | 0 | Dec. 56 | 31.3 | Apr. 57 | 27.4 | Dec. 57 | 22.0 |
| | 100 | Dec. 57 | 22.0 | June 58 | 18.6 | July 58 | 18.6 |
| | 200 | Dec. 58 | 13.9 | May 59 | 11.7 | May 60 | 6.2 |
| | 400 | Apr. 61 | 1.5 | Nov. 61 | 0 | Mar. 62 | − 5.0 |

The method just presented assumes, essentially, that there are no errors in the forecasting of customer demands. In practice, however, if adjustments are not made for errors in forecasting, shortages will occur with less frequency (in comparison to the forecast just developed) 50 per cent of the time (since the forecast will be high 50 per cent of the time), and shortages will occur with more frequency 50 per cent of the time (since the forecast will be low 50 per cent of the time). Accordingly, an additional amount of reserve capacity is required to provide a margin of safety against such errors, that is, in order to reduce the percentage of time with which more frequent shortages will occur or, equivalently, in order to increase the percentage of time during which fewer shortages will occur.

Calculations were made, based on a four-year forecast, showing the additional reserve capacity required for various percentage levels. Results are shown in Table 3.

Analyses were also made of the economics associated with various values for:

1. Probability of unit forced outage: 1 and 2 per cent.

TABLE 3

ADDITIONAL RESERVES REQUIRED BECAUSE OF FORECASTING ERRORS

| % of Time Fewer Than Max. Allowable No. of Shortages | % Additional Reserves Required |
|---|---|
| 60 | 2.1 |
| 70 | 4.3 |
| 75 | 5.6 |
| 80 | 7.0 |
| 85 | 8.7 |
| 90 | 10.7 |
| 95 | 13.7 |
| 97.5 | 16.3 |
| 99 | 19.4 |
| 99.5 | 21.5 |

2. Maximum allowable risk of shortage for 1 day in 2 years, 1 day in 5 years, and 1 day in 10 years.

3. Additional power available from the interconnection: 0 MW, 100 MW, 200 MW, and 400 MW.

4. Incremental cost of purchasing new 340-MW generating units as compared with 240-MW generating units: $0 million, $1 million, $2 million, $4 million, and $8 million. (I.e., a system which involved the addition of new 340-MW units was compared with one adding 240-MW units for various cost differentials.)

These analyses were based on the method discussed earlier and yielded the results to be discussed subsequently.

## Effect of a Rigid Preventive Maintenance Program

As mentioned earlier, the company system experienced forced outages only 1 per cent of the time, rather than the national average of 2 per cent, because of an excellent preventive maintenance policy. This has resulted in a reduction of forced outages that has reduced the capacity requirements and, hence, resulted in substantial gross cost savings. These savings must then be compared with the increased costs of maintenance required to obtain the 1 per cent forced outage rate in order to determine whether or not the rigid maintenance program is economically justified. The gross savings due to this more rigid maintenance program are given in Table 4. (The numbers in

Table 4 represent the annual savings obtained by comparing the costs for a 1 per cent unit, forced outage rate with those for a 2 per cent unit, forced outage rate.)

TABLE 4

ADDITIONAL COSTS, 2 PER CENT OUTAGE RATE VS. 1 PER CENT OUTAGE RATE

| Size of Units Subsequently Added | Maximum Allowable Risk of Shortage | | | | | | | | |
|---|---|---|---|---|---|---|---|---|---|
| | 1 day/2 Yrs. | | | 1 day/5 Yrs. | | | 1 day/10 Yrs. | | |
| 240 MW | 1.3 [a] | 1.1 | 0.4 | 1.8 | 1.3 | 0.5 | 1.9 | 1.7 | 1.0 |
| 340 MW | 1.2 | 1.0 | 0.6 | 2.2 | 1.7 | 1.2 | 2.4 | 1.9 | 1.2 |
| | 100 | 200 | 400 | 100 | 200 | 400 | 100 | 200 | 400 |
| | Additional Power available (MW) | | | | | | | | |

[a] Figures shown are in millions of dollars per year.

## Maximum Allowable Risk of Shortage

In this study, the "cost of shortage" and "maximum allowable risk of shortage" have been used rather interchangeably. Ideally, one would like to be able to determine the costs caused by shortage (including the impact on customer good will, loss of future sales, and the like) and thereby arrive at a definite answer to the reserve question. However, the costs caused by shortage are not known, nor are they easily determined. Hence, the alternate approach of analyzing several maximum allowable risks of shortage was used. Thus, although management is obliged to decide upon a suitable shortage policy, it is nevertheless supplied with a firm quantitative basis for establishing this policy.

Table 5 shows the cost reductions associated with shortage policies of 1 day in 2 years and 1 day in 5 years as compared with a policy of maximum acceptable risk of shortage of 1 day in 10 years.

## Additional Power Available from the Interconnection

Throughout this discussion, it has been apparent that a very important factor is the amount of power available from the interconnection. Thus, in applying Table 1, varying the level of the amount of power available from the interconnection would affect whether or not additional capacity must be added. In addition, as the other tables show, the costs and savings vary quite markedly with the

TABLE 5

REDUCTION IN COSTS FOR RISK OF SHORTAGE
GREATER THAN 1 DAY IN 10 YEARS

| Risk of Shortage | Size of New Units | Probability of Forced Outage | | | | | | | |
|---|---|---|---|---|---|---|---|---|---|
| | | 1% | | | | 2% | | | |
| 1 day/5 yrs. | 240 MW | 1.0 a | 0.8 | 0.3 | 0.2 | 1.0 | 0.9 | 0.7 | 0.6 |
| | 340 MW | 1.0 | 0.9 | 0.6 | 0.3 | 1.0 | 1.2 | 0.8 | 0.3 |
| 1 day/2 yrs. | 240 MW | 1.9 | 1.5 | 1.0 | 0.3 | 2.0 | 2.0 | 1.7 | 0.9 |
| | 340 MW | 2.4 | 1.7 | 1.1 | 0.4 | 2.3 | 3.0 | 2.0 | 0.9 |
| | | 0 | 100 | 200 | 400 | 0 | 100 | 200 | 400 |
| | | Additional power available (MW) | | | | | | | |

a Figures shown are in millions of dollars per year.

amount of such additional power. Accordingly, analyses were made
of the differences in costs associated with power available from the
interconnection in amounts of 0 MW, 100 MW, 200 MW, and 400
MW. The amount of 100 MW was used as a base, and all costs were
compared accordingly. The results are given in Table 6.

TABLE 6

EVALUATION OF INTERCONNECTION (BASE: 100 MW)

| Additional Power Available | Size of New Units | Probability of Forced Outage | | | | | |
|---|---|---|---|---|---|---|---|
| | | 1% | | | 2% | | |
| 0 MW | 240 MW | −2.0 | −1.9 | −1.6 | −2.0 | −1.9 | −2.0 |
| | 340 MW | −2.5 | −2.4 | −1.8 | −2.0 | −2.2 | −2.8 |
| 200 MW | 240 MW | 1.8 a | 1.3 | 1.5 | 2.0 | 1.9 | 1.7 |
| | 340 MW | 2.0 | 1.7 | 1.3 | 2.5 | 2.2 | 1.5 |
| 400 MW | 240 MW | 3.8 | 3.1 | 2.6 | 4.7 | 4.4 | 3.5 |
| | 340 MW | 4.2 | 3.6 | 2.8 | 5.5 | 4.6 | 3.4 |
| | | 1 day/ 10 yrs. | 1 day/ 5 yrs. | 1 day/ 2 yrs. | 1 day/ 10 yrs. | 1 day/ 5 yrs. | 1 day/ 2 yrs. |
| | | Maximum allowable risk of shortage | | | | | |

a Figures shown are in millions of dollars per year.

As mentioned earlier, a tabulation such as Table 6 thus furnishes
management with a sound basis for determining the amount of power
for which it should contract from the interconnection.

## Determination of Size of New Units to Be Added to the System

A highly essential question which must be answered in planning for the expansion of a utility system is that of determining the most economic size of unit to be added to the system.[16] Two basic plans of expansion were considered: (1) each new unit is of size 240 MW, or (2) each new unit is of size 340 MW. Since actual purchase costs were not known and would vary with time, computations were made for various incremental cost levels, thus permitting determination of those purchase cost levels for which one unit is more economical than the other. These comparisons, using the 240-MW unit as a base, are given in Table 7, and are obtained by taking into account (1) fixed charges on capital equipment and (2) differential costs in (a) coal, (b) labor, and (c) maintenance.

## Observations on Planned Expansion

The utility system case study illustrates a method for solving the problem of long-range planned expansion of a company. Specifically, the method enables a company to determine when additional generating capacity should be added to the system and, also, to ascertain the optimum size of these new generating units. These conclusions, however, presuppose that management has already made certain decisions as to:

1. The probability of unit forced outage to be used, that is, establishing the preventive maintenance policy.
2. The maximum allowable risk of shortage.
3. The amount of power to be made available through the interconnection.
4. The safety level deemed essential for protection against forecasting errors.

Once having answered these questions (with the assistance of the cost comparisons previously described), it can then be readily determined when new units should be added to the system, what the size of these units should be, and, hence, the best long-range expansion program for the company.

[16] See Reference 2.

## TABLE 7
### COMPARISON OF 240 MW AND 340 MW UNITS

| Probability of Outage % | Additional Purchase Cost of 340 MW vs. 240 MW | Maximum Acceptable Risk of Shortage | | | | | | | | | | | |
|---|---|---|---|---|---|---|---|---|---|---|---|---|---|
| | | 1 Day/10 Yrs. | | | | 1 Day/5 Yrs. | | | | 1 Day/2 Yrs. | | | |
| | | 0 | 100 | 200 | 400 | 0 | 100 | 200 | 400 | 0 | 100 | 200 | 400 |
| 1 | 0 | 3.7 a | 7.7 | 7.6 | 8.1 | 3.9 | 7.8 | 9.9 | 9.4 | 8.8 | 9.0 | 5.5 | 8.3 |
| | 1.0 | 2.3 | 6.3 | 6.5 | 7.3 | 2.5 | 6.6 | 8.9 | 8.6 | 7.5 | 7.8 | 4.6 | 7.5 |
| | 2.0 | 0.9 | 5.0 | 5.4 | 6.5 | 1.1 | 5.4 | 7.9 | 7.8 | 6.1 | 6.6 | 3.6 | 6.7 |
| | 4.0 | −1.9 | 2.4 | 3.3 | 4.8 | −1.6 | 2.9 | 5.9 | 6.3 | 3.5 | 4.2 | 1.7 | 5.2 |
| | 8.0 | −7.1 | −2.7 | −0.8 | 1.7 | −6.7 | −1.7 | 2.2 | 3.3 | −1.6 | −0.2 | −1.9 | 2.3 |
| 2 | 0 | 2.1 | 2.2 | 7.1 | 6.9 | 1.3 | 5.1 | 7.3 | 3.0 | 4.8 | 11.4 | 8.4 | 6.2 |
| | 1.0 | 0.7 | 0.8 | 5.8 | 6.0 | −0.1 | 3.7 | 6.0 | 2.2 | 3.4 | 10.4 | 7.3 | 5.4 |
| | 2.0 | −0.7 | −0.6 | 4.5 | 5.0 | −1.5 | 2.4 | 4.8 | 1.3 | 2.0 | 9.0 | 6.2 | 4.6 |
| | 4.0 | −3.5 | −3.4 | 2.0 | 3.2 | −4.3 | −0.3 | 2.0 | −0.4 | −0.8 | 6.4 | 4.1 | 2.9 |
| | 8.0 | −8.8 | −8.6 | −2.8 | −0.4 | −9.5 | −5.3 | −2.2 | −3.7 | −6.1 | 1.4 | 0 | −0.2 |
| | | 0 | 100 | 200 | 400 | 0 | 100 | 200 | 400 | 0 | 100 | 200 | 400 |
| | | Additional power available (MW) | | | | | | | | | | | |

a Figures are in millions of dollars for period 1958–67. The negative values indicate the conditions under which the 240-MW generator is preferable to the 340-MW generator.

## THE APPLICATION OF OPERATIONS RESEARCH TO OTHER LONG-RANGE PLANNING PROBLEMS

The following case history summaries reflect in further degree the broad applicability of the operations research approach to the problem area of long-range planning.

### Allocation of Sales Effort

In 1955, Russell L. Ackoff reported on a study conducted jointly by the Lamp Division of the General Electric Company and the Case Institute Operations Research Group.[17] This study was concerned with the allocation of sales effort and recognized that, before a salesman can operate most efficiently, three questions must be answered:

1. How frequently should a salesman call on a specific account?
2. How many accounts should be assigned to a salesman?
3. What kind of man makes the best salesman for what type of account?

The study concentrated on providing answers to the first question, namely, How frequently should a salesman call on any specific account? The study also provided data from which conclusions and suggestions were derived affecting the use of sales time. These are:

1. The breakdown of how a salesman spends his time
2. The allocation of sales calls to prospects
3. The breakdown of salesman time into sales and service activity

Specifically, the study showed that a considerable average reduction in the number of sales calls could be made without affecting the sales volume; that is, the existing number of salesmen in the Lamp Division could carry considerably more accounts without affecting their return per account.

At the time of the study, the Lamp Division was preparing for a reorganization which indicated the need for a greater number of salesmen than that currently employed. The study showed that, contrary to this belief, additional salesmen were not required. The operating cost implications of this result were considerable.

[17] See Reference 1.

## Planning for an Integrated Operation

The reorganization of the Lamp Division of the General Electric Company was reported by Walter Glover and Russell L. Ackoff early in 1956,[18] and is another illustration of the application of operations research to the problems of long-range planning. Glover and Ackoff discussed "Five-Year Planning for an Integrated Operation" and told how objectives were established, how policies were set, and how resources and organizational operations were coordinated for the entire Lamp Division.

The resulting five-year plan covered the following major areas:

1. Specification of objectives for the next five years
2. Specification of operating policies by which the objectives could best be attained
3. Specification of the resources required to carry out the policies
4. Specification of the resources required to carry out the policies within the framework of existing resources

The new organizational structure and the corresponding objectives were announced by the General Electric Company in January, 1955. Although it is obviously too early to completely evaluate this study at this time, it has been stated that the objectives set for the first of the five years were met and, in some cases, surpassed.

## Long-Range Planning by Means of Operations Research on the Consumer

There is a most important class of operations research studies on long-range planning in which the research is conducted on (and for) one's customers. An example of an extensive use of this type of approach to the problem of long-range planning is that reported by Roger Crane.[19] He describes how the Westinghouse Air Brake Company conducted research on consumers in order to help establish an effective company-wide research and development program.

Since most of the company's business was with the railroads, the initial objective of the research project was to carry out research on railroad operations in order to obtain a thorough and comprehensive

[18] See Reference 14.
[19] See Reference 8.

knowledge of railroad operations. As time progressed, the scope of this activity broadened to include the study of all present and potential customers of the company.

Among the problems considered by the Operations Research Group at Westinghouse Air Brake Company were the following: [20]

1. Analysis of the operations of a railroad classification yard
2. Determination of the optimum length (number of cars) of a train
3. Study of the distribution of freight cars in a large terminal area
4. Purchasing of new rail and its allocation on a railroad
5. The flow and utilization of information on a railroad

## LONG-RANGE PLANNING AND MANAGEMENT DEVELOPMPNT

In this final section, I should like to call attention to the fact that long-range planning must also include some program for the development of management personnel within the company. It does not suffice to consider expansion and growth only in terms of plant, land, and/or machinery, or solely in terms of balance sheets, working capital, and the like. Without trained, intelligent, and competent management, "the best laid schemes o' mice and men gang aft a-gley." Toward this end, many companies have recognized in operations research a valuable training ground for tomorrow's managers and have either selected men skilled in operations research for managerial positions or have assigned prospective managers to their operations research teams as part of a management development program. In either case, they are providing for a corps of inspired and trained managers—scientifically trained managers—who will be in a much better position to accept and use effectively the greater amount of information and answers about their present and future operations which is being provided for them through operations research.

The importance of having managers who are conversant with operations research and scientific methods is pointed out very well by Chairman of the Board of the Cummins Engine Company J. Irwin Miller, who writes:

If the head of a business indulges in research, as many do, just to solace his own fears of the future, and plays no personal part in this agonizing function, then he will only come to the end of his cycle all the sooner. If

[20] See References 9, 10, 11, and 12.

research is to be fruitful, it must be a daily concern of top management, and if it is to succeed, those who conduct the research must have a solid understanding of the true needs of their company, of its industry, and of its customers.[21]

## REFERENCES

1. Russell L. Ackoff, "Allocation of Sales Effort," *Proceedings of the Conference on "What Is Operations Research Accomplishing in Industry?"* Cleveland, Ohio, Case Institute of Technology, April 5–7, 1956.

2. "An Investigation of the Economic Size of Steam-Electric Generating Units," *Combustion,* February, 1955, pp. 57–64.

3. E. Leonard Arnoff and John C. Chambers, "On the Determination of Optimum Reserve Generating Capacity in an Electric Utility System," *Operations Research,* August, 1956.

4. G. Calabrese, "Determination of Reserve Capacity by the Probability Method—Effect on Interconnections," AIEE *Transactions,* 69 (1950), Part II, pp. 1018–20.

5. G. Calabrese, "Determination of Reserve Capacity by the Probability Method," AIEE *Transactions,* 68 (1949), Part II, pp. 1681–88.

6. G. Calabrese, *System Generation Reserve Requirements,* monograph submitted to the Subcommittee on the Application of Probability Methods to Power System Problems, July 9, 1953.

7. C. West Churchman, Russell L. Ackoff, and E. Leonard Arnoff, *Introduction to Operations Research,* New York, John Wiley and Sons, Inc., 1957.

8. Roger R. Crane, "Operations Research on Industrial Consumers, *Proceedings of the Conference on "What Is Operations Research Accomplishing in Industry?"* Cleveland, Ohio, Case Institute of Technology, April 5–7, 1955.

9. Roger R. Crane, Frank B. Brown, and Robert O. Blanchard, "An Analysis of a Railroad Classification Yard," *Operations Research,* August, 1955, pp. 262–71.

10. Roger R. Crane and Frank B. Brown, "Theory of Maintenance of Rolling Stock," *Mechanical Engineering,* December, 1954.

11. Roger R. Crane, "Some Examples of Operations Research Work," *Proceedings of the Railway Systems and Procedures Association Winter Meeting,* 1953.

[21] See Reference 16.

Note: The author wishes to express his indebtedness to Walter R. Van Voorhis for his valuable comments and constructive criticism contributing to the preparation of this paper.

12. Roger R. Crane, "A Discussion of Certain Maintenance of Way Problems," Seminar on Operations Research, Railway Systems and Procedures Association, February, 1954.

13. "Forced Outage Rates of High Pressure Steam Turbines and Boilers," *Combustion*, October, 1954, pp. 57–61.

14. Walter S. Glover and Russell L. Ackoff, "Five-Year Planning for an Integrated Operation," *Proceedings of the Conference on Case Studies in Operations Research*, Cleveland, Ohio, Case Institute of Technology, February 1–3, 1956.

15. W. J. Lyman, "Calculating Probability of Generating Capacity Outages," AIEE *Transactions*, 65 (1945), pp. 1471–77.

16. J. Irwin Miller, "Executive Planning for 1970," *Indiana Business Review*, May, 1956.

17. Paul Stillson, "A Method for Defect Evaluation," *Industrial Quality Control*, July, 1954.

# 21.

# Application of the Computer to Planning

## By Melvin E. Salveson [1]

Among the activities carried out in planning and preparing for "tomorrow's business," there are many problems for which OR [operations research] and the large-scale computer are most useful. Here are some of the less usual and more recently developed business applications. Note that in each case the situation at hand was analyzed in accordance with the method described earlier. The OR analysis and formulation precede, and provide the basis for, the computer solution.

*Economic analysis and forecasting.* Through the use of various econometric models, such as the Leontief input-output model, or certain of the structural or growth models of economics, an industry or a company can compute (and some do), according to a mathematical model, the probable timing and magnitude of change in its business due to changes in various sectors of the economy.

For example, suppose a company in the specialty metals business wished to estimate the magnitude of the effect on its business from the opening of the St. Lawrence Seaway. It sells to manufacturers of rolling stock, to equipment manufacturers, and to those who supply products to these manufacturers. The changes in its business would not be proportional simply to the expected reduction in freight-car usage. Rather, it would include changes due to the interaction of the railroad industry with many other industries.

A large problem of this type resulting in the "simultaneous" interaction of

[1] Reprinted by permission from Melvin E. Salveson, "High-Speed Operations Research," *Harvard Business Review*, July–August, 1957.

225

many variables requires a large-scale computer to solve the simultaneous equations in the mathematical model. Similar situations might be studied, say, for the effect of the road-building program, the effect of changes in the home-building industry, and so on.

*Budgeting.* The company budget represents an excellent instrument through which to study the aggregate effect of various marketing, manufacturing, and engineering policies, strategies, and plans. If properly designed, the method of budgeting can compute an "optimal" budget—that is, one which is best of the many alternatives and which takes into account the interactions of the various elements of the business.

The American Management Association recently announced an operational gaming model in which chief executives can practice competing in a simulated "game" of competition in an assumed industry. This model includes and computes the effect of each company's policies or choices in allocating its limited funds among research and development, advertising, plant expansion, production, and other needs. The game has proved to be highly realistic and results in genuine personal involvement and learning. It would be possible for any company to develop a game for its own industry and to use its budget model for strategy planning and top-management training.

*Location selection.* Often the factors affecting the profitability of a store, a plant, or a warehouse are numerous and complexly related. In order to find the best location it is necessary first to determine the relative importance of these factors and the extent of their interaction in a suitable model. A large-scale computer often is essential in solving the model for the relative importance of the factors and then in selecting the best location.

*Personnel selection and recruitment.* The problem of determining what personal factors affect work performance, and by how much, often may be formulated best into a problem in solving a system of simultaneous equations. Other personnel studies can be and are made with . ˙ rge-scale computer, such as analyzing accident records for accident pro. ˙ ˙ness, for equipment maintenance needs, and for other purposes.

*Plant layout.* There are many factors simultaneously involved in layout studies, including flow paths of the materials, size and location of the storage areas, amount and kind of equipment, length and balance of assembly lines, and degree of work specialization. Added to these there is always the problem of unexpected changes in product mix, product design, and market demand. The selection of a best plant layout and size under these conditions is complex and difficult, but it usually can be formulated as a mathematical model, in which case a fast, large-scale computer can be a real help in reaching a "best" solution.

*Inventory planning.* Often inventory and equipment policies can be established more effectively through the use of a large-scale computer.

Thus, in a recent study reported by K. C. Lucas of Thompson Products Incorporated,[2] the computer was used to simulate behavior of incoming orders and to test the result of different inventory policies on customer service and deliveries. This helped top management decide between the amount to invest in inventories and the level of service and deliveries. The computer was not used, in this case, for controlling current inventories but rather for planning inventory policies and assuring they would be consistent with and carry out top management policies. The computer made it possible to obtain simulated experience to test the policy before it was implemented by operating on a suitable "Monte Carlo" model of the total inventory operation.

Many other problems lend themselves to a similar type of analysis, including the well-known "queueing" or waiting-line problem. This latter is found in situations involving service to randomly arriving customers, such as at toll gates, airports, retail stores, and factories.

There are many other uses of computers for solving business planning problems beyond those just described, but the foregoing should serve to indicate what promising area there is for operations research and large-scale computers to serve all levels of management.

[2] K. C. Lucas, "Electronic Computer Simulation of Inventory Control," *Proceedings of Conference on Electronics in Action* (New York, American Management Association, 1957).

## 22.

# Forecasting Man-Power Needs — A Tested Formula

## By Wendel W. Burton [1]

Industry has devoted a great deal of time, effort, and money to the study of economic influences: past, present, and future. Sales forecasts, budgets, and plant and equipment expansion among many profit tools are determined by these studies. Unfortunately, this same time and effort have not been expended to study man-power forecasting. Most employment departments and cost departments throughout the country have overlooked or neglected this field. Perhaps the "feast or famine" nature of our work has kept us on the run too much in recent years, but I am not convinced that our own lack of planning has not contributed to this general confusion.

Although we in industry try to anticipate our needs in plant expansion with long-range programs, we normally wait until the last minute before instituting a request for the specialized man-power needed to operate these plants. Under the pressures of immediate need, a compromise is frequently made in the selection of a person or people to direct a part of our operations and as a result some of the gains we should expect are not realized. "Lead time" to get desired personnel is needed.

Minnesota Mining and Manufacturing Company is a growth company with a history of yearly additions. We, too, were subjected to the problems caused by war, postwar, Korea, and the pressures since

[1] Based on a presentation to the American Management Association, 1957. Reprinted by permission of the author.

then. We were not completely free from the influences of the "bulls" and "bears" of the employment market. With colleges and high schools releasing their graduates primarily in June, it was most important that we recruit large numbers early; otherwise we would have to pull our applicants from other companies. This situation pointed up very clearly the need for accurate facts and figures.

About four years ago on a visit to General Motors, I had the opportunity to discuss these problems with Merle Hale, Head of Salaried Personnel, and in turn a chance to preview their "lead time" program for replacements. This discussion gave me the idea that an accurate forecast could be made of future needs by a careful analysis of the past. I determined on my return to take the General Motors replacement program and statistically relate it to economic forecasts.

The first step in this program was to discuss my idea with our Director of Personnel and secure his approval for such a study. He recommended that the first study be made of part of our management payroll so that this information could be utilized by the Personnel Development Committee.

A five-year statistical history of this management payroll was made, dividing the group into five classifications: sales, laboratory, engineering, administrative, and production. A tabulation was made of the number in each group at the start of the year, and additions and deletions for the year and the total at the end of the year. (Although a detailed analysis was made of the additions and deletions, nothing significant developed.) Turnover percentages were determined and the possible retirements within the next five years listed. (See Fig. 1.)

Our company uses sales dollars as the basis for all forecasts and budgets. If a relationship could be established between man power and sales dollars, then it would be possible to forecast man power for as many years in the future as sales forecasts were available. With this in mind I tried relating the number of managers at the end of the year into parent company sales for the year. There was an excellent correlation on the first attempt. The average amount of sales per manager was quite consistent each year even in the various classifications. I then received a five-year sales forecast from our Economic Research Department. The total parent company sales forecast for each year was divided by the average sales per manager and the result was a total of managers for each year of the next five years. By

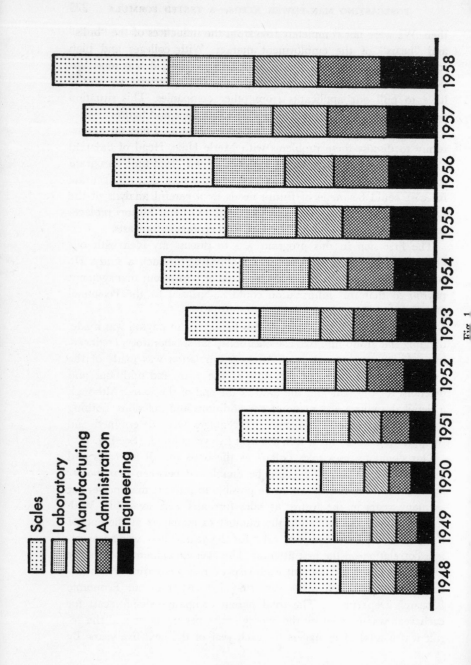

Fig. 1

Sales
Laboratory
Manufacturing
Administration
Engineering

1948 1949 1950 1951 1952 1953 1954 1955 1956 1957 1958

multiplying the total managers each year by the turnover ratios and adding the number of additional managers to be secured that year, we were able to determine the number necessary to develop. (See Table 1 and Fig. 2.)

TABLE 1

| Year | Salesmen End of Year | Average During Year | Sales Per Man Col. 2 (000) | Percent of Turnover | '55 Sales Forecast + Or − (000) | Loss Thru Turnover | + Or − Forecast |
|---|---|---|---|---|---|---|---|
| '50 | 72 | 70 | 211 | 7 | | | |
| '51 | 77 | 74½ | 220 | 5 | 1,387 | | |
| '52 | 87 | 82 | 219 | 11 | | | |
| | | | | | Avg. | | |
| '53 | 93 | | 234 | 8 | 212 | | |
| '54 | 92 | 90 | 210 | 6 | | 7 | None |
| | | 92½ | | Avg. | | | |
| | | | | 7 | | | |

In view of the fact that we hit a correlation on sales, it was not necessary to explore other areas such as units produced or sold, plant worth, and so forth.

Our charts were submitted to the Personnel Development Committee with a recommendation that a quarterly analysis be made to insure accuracy. The information resulting from this study gave them an accurate forecast on which to base their development plans. The question might well be asked, "How accurate has this forecast proven?" A check on December 31 each year starting with 1954 has shown the following margin of error:

December 31, 1954—less than ½ of 1 per cent
December 31, 1955—less than ½ of 1 per cent
December 31, 1956—8/10 of 1 per cent

Today, three and one-half years from the date of the original forecast, we are still following our historical pattern. Should manage-

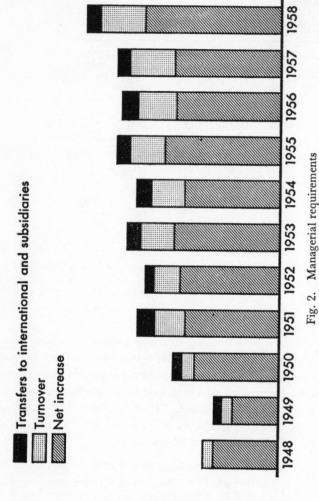

Fig. 2. Managerial requirements

Transfers to international and subsidiaries

Turnover

Net increase

1948 1949 1950 1951 1952 1953 1954 1955 1956 1957 1958

ment make any policy or procedural decisions that would affect this pattern, our calculations could be adjusted accordingly.

After the presentation to the Development Committee, I asked permission to study an operating division, and a member of the committee offered his division as a "guinea pig." An analysis of the management payroll in that division again gave us a fine correlation and our forecasts were made in the same manner as our first study.

In studying the division I was particularly anxious to try this method on salesmen, for management had experienced difficulty in meeting its sales forecasts. Our study quickly pointed out the reason. It took about six to nine months for a new salesman to start pulling his own weight and, as a result, unless men were added well in advance they could not contribute. To meet the sales goals for any year it was necessary to have $x$ men on the payroll at the start of the year for every million dollars of sales forecast. A suggested schedule for the addition of salesmen was prepared for the division. Periodic checks of the management forecast have shown about the same percentage of error as experienced in our first study.

These forecasting activities were a spare-time operation of the Employment Department and as a result nothing further was attempted until the fall of 1954. At that time, we were notified by our sales executive that a combination of sales forces might release a large number of men for assignment to other divisions. The suggestion was made that it might be desirable to withhold hiring additional men until these men were properly transferred. Permission was asked and given us to make a study, analysis, and forecast of all sales divisions.

Working with the statistical department, we tabulated a five-year history of each sales force. In establishing the amount of sales per man, both the number of men at the end of the year and the average number of men during the year were tried. We found our best results with the average number of men during the year. Using the year's sales for that division and dividing by the average number of men involved, the sales per man were determined. The sales forecast for the coming year was then divided by the number of men on the force at that time.

This new figure was compared to the present figure and past history in order to determine if additional man power would be needed.

The turnover percentages were calculated for each year and a reasonable percentage used to determine turnover for the coming year. The total number of men needed because of turnover and additions was then calculated and the result compared with the total of those who might be available for transfer. It was very apparent that we could continue hiring salesmen on a modified scale and easily absorb those available for transfer. (See Table 2.)

TABLE 2

| Year | Sales-men End of Year | Average During Year | Sales Per Man Col. 2 (000) | Per-cent Turn-over | '55 Sales Fore-cast + Or − (000) | Loss Thru Turn-over | + Or − Fore-cast |
|---|---|---|---|---|---|---|---|
| '50 | 54 | 52 | 96 | 18 | | | |
| '51 | 54 | 54 | 103 | 26 | | | |
| '52 | 72 | 63 | 118 | 28 | 2,585 | | |
| '53 | 81 | 76½ | 120 | 13 | | | |
| | | | | | Avg. | | |
| '54 | 78 | 79½ | 135 | 7 | 155 | 13 | 18 |
| | | | | 17 | | | |
| | | | | Avg. | | | |

This information was presented to our top sales officer and all sales managers. Permission was given the Employment Department to recruit or transfer as we determined best. It was pointed out to each sales manager that the trend in sales per man could give him an excellent picture of the size of his force. If the amount per man was getting too high, additional men should be added; if too low, perhaps some should be removed or at least additions stopped. The information is now analyzed every six months, and, if considered advisable, presented to the sales manager.

The statistical department and I next tried a study and forecast of our laboratories. With a ten-year history of personnel readily available from the budgets prepared by our Controller's Department, we decided to double our normal five-year analysis. We first tried to compare total laboratory personnel with sales each year, but found a poor correlation. When we eliminated the nontechnical employees from our calculations, however, we found a very good correlation. Every time we increased company sales a million dollars, we added $y$ number of technical employees. When we carried our calculations into the individual product laboratories and compared their technical man power with the sales of that product division, however, we found wide differences. The correlation that we experienced for the combined laboratories would not hold true for them individually.

In our analysis of this situation, we did not attempt to tell who was right or which laboratory had the better balance. It appeared on the surface that one laboratory had nontechnical personnel engaged in technical activities and another probably was forcing its technical personnel to do some nontechnical supporting work. A meeting was held with several of our laboratory heads in the controller's office. The results of the study were discussed and it was decided that some of the laboratories would try to experiment for a year or two and determine how much nontechnical help is required to effectively back up a technical man. It is quite possible that this study may affect our method of laboratory budgeting.

In the summer of 1955, our Vice-President of Engineering appointed a committee of engineers to analyze the man-power situation in the Engineering Division. They were concerned with a sudden shortage of man power and wanted to do something about it. At our first meeting, as consultant, I acquainted the committee with the results of previous studies and it was decided to approach this problem in a similar way. Members of the committee were assigned by the chairman the task of gathering certain statistics for the second meeting. We determined to analyze several factors such as engineering costs, plant worth, total expenditures, and operating expenses in relationship to man power. At the second meeting these comparisons were made, but again sales and technical personnel gave us our best correlation.

The committee presented this information to the Vice-President of Engineering with the suggestion that our hiring be brought back into balance with the sales curve. Approval was granted and our hiring program was stepped up.

My goal in man-power forecasting has always been the accurate preparation and use of forecasts by our operating divisions. The Controller's Division has had the same goals, so over a year ago they insisted on man-power forecasts as a part of each budget plan for the following year. When all man-power forecasts were received they were tabulated and then discussed with the Employment Department. With the ratios determined from our studies we jointly made some corrections on the technical requirements. The office requirements were not adjusted due to the fact that up to that time we had not made a five-year history of that division. The Employment Department then calculated the turnover figures for sales, technical, and salaried nontechnical. These figures were added to the increased man-power forecast and my department had an excellent picture of its recruiting responsibility. The factory and temporary estimates (not a problem) were included and the forecast for 1956 was complete.

# 23.

# *The Objectives of a Business*

## By Peter F. Drucker [1]

Most of today's lively discussion of management by objectives is concerned with the search for the one right objective. This search is not only likely to be as unproductive as the quest for the philosopher's stone; it is certain to do harm and to misdirect.

To emphasize only profit, for instance, misdirects managers to the point where they may endanger the survival of the business. To obtain profit today they tend to undermine the future. They may push the most easily salable product lines and slight those that are the market of tomorrow. They tend to short-change research, promotion, and the other postponable investments. Above all, they shy away from any capital expenditure that may increase the invested-capital base against which profits are measured; and the result is dangerous obsolescence of equipment. In other words, they are directed into the worst practices of management.

To manage a business is to balance a variety of needs and goals. This requires judgment. The search for the one objective is essentially a search for a magic formula that will make judgment unnecessary. But the attempt to replace judgment by formula is always irrational; all that can be done is to make judgment possible by narrowing its range and the available alternatives, giving it clear focus, a sound foundation in facts, and reliable measurements of the effects and validity of actions and decisions. And this, by the very nature of business enterprise, requires multiple objectives.

[1] From Peter F. Drucker, *The Practice of Management* (New York, Harper & Brothers, 1954), pp. 62–87.

What should these objectives be, then? There is only one answer: *Objectives are needed in every area where performance and results directly and vitally affect the survival and prosperity of the business.* These are the areas which are affected by every management decision and which therefore have to be considered in every management decision. They decide what it means concretely to manage the business. They spell out what results the business must aim at and what is needed to work effectively toward these targets.

Objectives in these key areas should enable us to do five things: to organize and explain the whole range of business phenomena in a small number of general statements; to test these statements in actual experience; to predict behavior; to appraise the soundness of decisions when they are still being made; and to enable practicing businessmen to analyze their own experience and, as a result, improve their performance. It is precisely because the traditional theorem of the maximization of profits cannot meet any of these tests—let alone all of them—that it has to be discarded.

At first sight it might seem that different businesses would have entirely different key areas—so different as to make impossible any general theory. It is indeed true that different key areas require different emphasis in different businesses—and different emphasis at different stages of the development of each business. But the areas are the same, whatever the business, whatever the economic conditions, whatever the business's size or stage of growth.

There are eight areas in which objectives of performance and results have to be set:

Market standing; innovation; productivity; physical and financial resources; profitability; manager performance and development; worker performance and attitude; public responsibility.

There should be little dispute over the first five objectives. But there will be real protest against the inclusion of the intangibles: manager performance and development; worker performance and attitude; and public responsibility.

Yet, even if managing were merely the application of economics, we would have to include these three areas and would have to demand that objectives be set for them. They belong in the most purely formal economic theory of the business enterprise. For neglect of manager performance and development, worker performance and public responsibility soon result in the most practical and tangible loss of market standing, technological leadership, productivity, and profit—and ultimately in the loss of business life. That they look so different from anything the economist—especially the modern economic analyst—is wont to deal with, that they do not readily submit to quantification and mathematical treatment, is the economist's bad luck; but it is no argument against their consideration.

The very reason for which economist and accountant consider these areas impractical—that they deal with principles and values rather than solely with dollars and cents—makes them central to the management of the enterprise, as tangible, as practical—and indeed as measurable—as dollars and cents.

For the enterprise is a community of human beings. Its performance is the performance of human beings. And a human community must be founded on common beliefs, must symbolize its cohesion in common principles. Otherwise it becomes paralyzed, unable to act, unable to demand and to obtain effort and performance from its members.

If such considerations are intangible, it is management's job to make them tangible by its deeds. To neglect them is to risk not only business incompetence but labor trouble or at least loss of worker productivity, and public restrictions on business provoked by irresponsible business conduct. It also means risking lackluster, mediocre, time-serving managers—managers who are being conditioned to "look out for themselves" instead of for the common good of the enterprise, managers who become mean, narrow, and blind for lack of challenge, leadership, and vision.

## How to Set Objectives

The real difficulty lies indeed not in determining what objectives we need, but in deciding how to set them.

There is only one fruitful way to make this decision: by determining what shall be measured in each area and what the yardstick of measurement should be. For the measurement used determines what one pays attention to. It makes things visible and tangible. The things included in the measurement become relevant; the things omitted are out of sight and out of mind. "Intelligence is what the Intelligence Test measures"—that well-worn quip is used by the psychologist to disclaim omniscience and infallibility for his gadget. Parents or teachers, however, including those well aware of the shakiness of its theory and its mode of calculation, sometimes tend to see that precise-looking measurement of the "I.Q." every time they look at little Susie—to point where they may no longer see little Susie at all.

Unfortunately, the measurements available to us in the key areas of business enterprise are, by and large, even shakier than the I.Q. We have adequate concepts only for measuring market standing. For something as obvious as profitability we have only a rubber yardstick, and we have no real tools at all to determine how much profitability is necessary. In respect to innovation and, even more, to productivity, we hardly know more than what ought to be done. And in the other areas—including physical and financial resources—we are reduced to statements of intentions rather than goals and measurements for their attainment.

For the subject is brand new. It is one of the most active frontiers of thought, research, and invention in American business today. Company after company is working on the definition of the key areas, on thinking through what should be measured, and on fashioning the tools of measurement.

Within a few years our knowledge of what to measure and our ability to do so should therefore be greatly increased. After all, twenty-five years ago we knew less about the basic problems in market standing than we know today about productivity or even about the efficiency and attitudes of workers. Today's relative clarity concerning market standing is the result not of anything inherent in the field, but of hard, concentrated, and imaginative work.

In the meantime, only a "progress report" can be given, outlining the work ahead rather than reporting accomplishment.

## MARKET STANDING

Market standing has to be measured against the market potential, and against the performance of suppliers of competing products or services—whether competition is direct or indirect.

"We don't care what share of the market we have, as long as our sales go up," is a fairly common comment. It sounds plausible enough; but it does not stand up under analysis. By itself, volume of sales tells little about performance, results, or the future of the business. A company's sales may go up—and the company may actually be headed for rapid collapse. A company's sales may go down—and the reason may not be that its marketing is poor but that it is in a dying field and had better change fast.

A maker of oil refinery equipment reported rising sales year after year. Actually new refineries and their equipment were being supplied by the company's competitors. But because the equipment it had supplied in the past was getting old and needed repairs, sales spurted; for replacement parts for equipment of this kind have usually to be bought from the original supplier. Sooner or later, however, the original customers were going to put in new and efficient equipment rather than patch up the old and obsolescent stuff. Then almost certainly they were going to go to the competitors designing and building the new equipment. The company was thus threatened with going out of business—which is what actually happened.

Not only are absolute sales figures meaningless alone, since they must be projected against actual and potential market trends, but market standing itself has intrinsic importance. A business that supplies less than a certain share of the market becomes a marginal supplier. Its pricing becomes dependent on the decisions of the larger suppliers. In any business setback—even in a slight one—it stands in danger of being squeezed out altogether. Competition becomes intense. Distributors in cutting back inventories tend to cut out slow-moving merchandise. Customers tend to concentrate their purchases on the most popular products. And in a depression the sales volume of the marginal supplier may become too low to give the needed service. The point below which a supplier becomes marginal varies from industry to industry. It is different in different price classes within the same industry. It has marked regional variations. But to be a marginal producer is always dangerous, a minimum of market standing always desirable.

Conversely, there is a maximum market standing above which it may be unwise to go—even if there were no antitrust laws. Leadership that gives market dominance tends to lull the leader to sleep; monopolists have usually foundered on their own complacency rather than on public opposition. For market dominance creates tremendous internal resistance against any innovation and thus makes adaptation to change dangerously difficult. Also it almost always means that the enterprise has too many of its eggs in one basket and is too vulnerable to economic fluctuations. There is, in other words, an upper as well as lower margin—though for most businesses the perils of the former may appear a good deal more remote.

To be able to set market-standing objectives, a business must first find out what its market is—who the customer is, where he is, what he buys, what he considers value, what his unsatisfied wants are. On the basis of this study the enterprise must analyze its products or services according to "lines," that is, according to the wants of the customers they satisfy.

All electric condensers may look the same, be the same technically, and come off the same production line. Marketwise, condensers for new radios may, however, be an entirely different line from condensers for radio repair and replacement, and both again quite different from the physically indistinguishable condensers that go into telephones. Condensers for radio repair may even be different lines if customers in the South judge their value by their resistance to termites, and customers in the Northwest by their resistance to high humidity.

For each line the market has to be determined—its actual size and its potential, its economic and its innovating trends. This must be done on the basis of a definition of the market that is customer-oriented and takes in both direct and indirect competition. Only then can marketing objectives actually be set.

In most businesses not one but seven distinct marketing goals are necessary:

1. The desired standing of existing products in their present market, expressed in dollars as well as in percentage of the market, measured against both direct and indirect competition.

2. The desired standing of existing products in new markets set both in dollars and percentage points, and measured against direct and indirect competition.

3. The existing products that should be abandoned—for technological reasons, because of market trend, to improve product mix, or as a result of management's decision concerning what its business should be.

4. The new products needed in existing markets—the number of products, their properties, the dollar volume, and the market share they should gain for themselves.

5. The new markets that new products should develop—in dollars and in percentage points.

6. The distributive organization needed to accomplish the marketing goals and the pricing policy appropriate to them.

7. A service objective measuring how well the customer should be supplied with what he considers value by the company, its products, its sales and service organization.

At the least the service objective should be in keeping with the targets set for competitive market standing. But usually it is not enough to do as well as the competition in respect to service; for service is the best and the easiest way to build customer loyalty and satisfaction. Service performance should never be appraised by management guesses or on the basis of occasional chats the "big boss" has with important customers. It should be measured by regular, systematic, and unbiased questioning of the customer.

In a large company this may have to take the form of an annual customer survey. The outstanding job here has probably been done by General Motors; and it explains the company's success in no small degree. In the small company the same results can be achieved by a different method.

In one of the most successful hospital-supply wholesalers, two of the top men of the company—president and chairman of the board—visit between them two hundred of the company's six hundred customers every year. They spend a whole day with each customer. They do not sell—refuse indeed to take an order. They discuss the customer's problems and his needs, and ask for criticism of the company's products and service. In this company the annual customer survey is considered the first job of top management. And the company's eighteenfold growth in the last twelve years is directly attributed to it.

## Innovation

There are two kinds of innovation in every business: innovation in product or service; and innovation in the various skills and activities needed to supply them. Innovation may arise out of the needs of market and customer; necessity may be the mother of innovation. Or it may come out of the work on the advancement of skill and knowledge carried out in the schools and the laboratories, by researchers, writers, thinkers, and practitioners.

The problem in setting innovation objectives is the difficulty of measuring the relative impact and importance of various innovations.

Technological leadership is clearly desirable, especially if the term "technology" is used in its rightful sense as applying to the art, craft, or science of any organized human activity. But how are we to determine what weighs more: one hundred minor but immediately applicable improvements in packaging the product, or one fundamental chemical discovery which, after ten more years of hard work, may change the character of the business altogether? A department store and a pharmaceutical company will answer this question differently; but so may two different pharmaceutical companies.

Innovating objectives can therefore never be as clear and as sharply focused as marketing objectives. To set them, management must first obtain a forecast of the innovations needed to reach marketing goals—according to product lines, existing markets, new markets, and, usually, also according to service requirements. Secondly, it must appraise developments arising or likely to arise out of technological advancement in all areas of the business and in all of its activities. These forecasts are best organized in two parts: one looking a short time ahead and projecting fairly concrete developments which, in effect, only carry out innovations already made; another looking a long time ahead and aiming at what might be.

Here are the innovation goals for a typical business:

1. New products or services that are needed to attain marketing objectives.

2. New products or services that will be needed because of technological changes that may make present products obsolete.

3. Product improvements needed both to attain market objectives and to anticipate expected technological changes.

4. New processes and improvements in old processes needed to satisfy market goals—for instance, manufacturing improvements to make possible the attainment of pricing objectives.

5. Innovations and improvements in all major areas of activity—in accounting or design, office management or labor relations—so as to keep up with the advances in knowledge and skill.

Management must not forget that innovation is a slow process. Many companies owe their position of leadership today to the activity of a generation that went to its reward twenty-five years or so ago. Many companies that are unknown to the public will be leaders in their industry tomorrow because of their innovations today. The successful company is always in danger of living smugly off the accumulated innovating fat of an earlier generation. An index of activity and success in this field is therefore indicated.

An appraisal of performance during the last ten years serves well for this purpose. Has innovation in all the major areas been commensurate with the market standing of the company? If it has not, the company is living off past achievements and is eating up its innovating capital. Has the company developed adequate sources of innovation for the future? Or has it come to depend on work done on the outside—in the universities, by other businesses, maybe abroad—which may not be adequate to the demands of the future?

Deliberate emphasis on innovation may be needed most where technological changes are least spectacular. Everybody in a pharmaceutical company or in a company making synthetic organic chemicals knows that the company's survival depends on its ability to replace three quarters of its products by entirely new ones every ten years. But how many people in an insurance company realize that the company's growth—perhaps even its survival—depends on the development of new forms of insurance, the modification of existing forms, and the constant search for new, better, and cheaper ways of selling policies and of settling claims? The less spectacular or prominent technological change is in a business, the greater is the danger that the whole organization will ossify; the more important therefore is the emphasis on innovation.

It may be argued that such goals are "big-company stuff" suitable for General Electric or for General Motors, but unnecessary in the small business. But although the small company may be less in need of a complete and detailed analysis of its needs and goals, this means only that it is easier to set innovation objectives in the smaller business —not that the need for objectives is less. In fact, the managements of several small companies I know assert that the comparative simplicity of planning for innovation is one of the main advantages of small size. As the president of one of them—a container manufacturer with sales of fewer than ten million dollars—puts it: "When you are small, you are sufficiently close to the market to know fairly fast what new products are needed. And your engineering staff is too small to become ingrown. They know they can't do everything themselves and therefore keep their eyes and ears wide open for any new development that they could possibly use."

## PRODUCTIVITY AND "CONTRIBUTED VALUE"

A productivity measurement is the only yardstick that can actually gauge the competence of management and allow comparison between managements of different units within the enterprise, and of different enterprises. For productivity includes all the efforts the enterprise contributes; it excludes everything it does not control.

Businesses have pretty much the same resources to work with. Except for the rare monopoly situation, the only thing that differentiates one business from another in any given field is the quality of its management on all levels. And the only way to measure this crucial factor is through a measurement of productivity that shows how well resources are utilized and how much they yield.

The Wall Street exercise of comparing the profit margin of Chrysler and General Motors is actually meaningless. General Motors manufactures most of the parts of the car; it buys only the frame, the wheels, and the brake. Chrysler until recently was an assembler; it made nothing but the engine, which is but a fraction of the value of the car. The two companies are entirely different in their process mix. Yet both sell a complete car. In the case of G.M. the bulk of the sales price is compensation for work done by G.M.; in the case of Chrysler the bulk of the sales price is paid out again to independent suppliers. The profit G.M. shows is for 70 per cent of the work and risk; the profit Chrysler shows is for 30 or 40 per cent of the work and risk. Obviously General Motors must show a much bigger profit margin— but how much bigger? Only an analysis of productivity which would show how the two companies utilize their respective resources, and how much profit they get out of them, would show which company did the better managing job.

But such a yardstick is needed also because the constant improvement of productivity is one of management's most important jobs. It is also one of the most difficult; for productivity is a balance between a great variety of factors, few of which are easily definable or clearly measurable.

We do not as yet have the yardstick we need to measure productivity. Only within the last few years have we found a basic concept that even enables us to define what we have to measure—the economist calls it "Contributed Value."

Contributed Value is the difference between the gross revenue re-

THE OBJECTIVES OF A BUSINESS

ceived by a company from the sale of its products or services, and the amount paid out by it for the purchase of raw materials and for services rendered by outside suppliers. Contributed Value, in other words, includes all the costs of all the effort of the business and the entire reward received for these efforts. It accounts for all the resources the business itself contributes to the final product and the appraisal of their efforts by the market.

Contributed Value is not a panacea. It can be used to analyze productivity only if the allocation of costs which together make up the figures is economically meaningful. This may require major reforms in the accountant's traditional concepts, figures, and methods. We have to give up such time-honored practices as the allocation of "overhead" on a percentage basis "across the board" which makes realistic cost analysis impossible. We have to think through what depreciation charges are supposed to do—charge for the use of capital, measure the shrinkage in value of the equipment, or provide for its eventual replacement; we cannot be satisfied with a "rule of thumb" percentage depreciation allowance. In short, we have to focus accounting data on management's needs in running a business, rather than on the requirements of tax collector and banker, or on the old wives' tales so many investors imbibe at their security analyst's knee and forever after mistake for financial wisdom.

Contributed Value will not measure productivity resulting from balance of functions or from organization structure, for these are qualitative factors rather than quantitative ones, and Contributed Value is strictly a quantitative tool. Yet, the qualitative factors are among the biggest factors in producivity.

Within these limitations, however, Contributed Value should make possible, for the first time, a rational analysis of productivity and the setting of goals for its improvement. In particular it should make possible the application to the systematic study of productivity of new tools such as the mathematical methods known as "Operations Research" and "Information Theory." For these tools all aim at working out alternative courses of action and their predictable consequences. And the productivity problem is always one of seeing the range of alternative combinations of the various resources, and of finding the combination that gives the maximum output at minimum cost or effort.

We should therefore now be able to tackle the basic productivity problems.

When and where is the substitution of capital equipment for labor likely to improve productivity, within what limits, and under what conditions? How do we distinguish creative overhead, which cuts down total effort required, from parasitical overhead, which only adds to costs? What is the best time utilization? What is the best product mix? What is the best process mix? In all these problems we should no longer have to guess; we can find the right answer systematically.

The Contributed Value concept should show us clearly what the objectives for productivity are:

1. To increase the ratio of Contributed Value to total revenue within the existing process. This is simply another way of saying that the first goal must be to find the best utilization of raw materials or of services bought.

2. To increase the proportion of Contributed Value retained as profit. For this means that the business has improved the productivity of its own resources.

## PHYSICAL AND FINANCIAL RESOURCES

What resources objectives are needed and how progress toward them is to be measured differs for each individual business. Also objectives in this area do not concern managers throughout the enterprise as do the objectives in all other areas: the planning for an adequate supply of physical and financial resources is primarily top management's job; the carrying out of these plans is mainly the job of functional specialists.

Yet, physical and financial resources are too important to be left out of consideration. Any business handling physical goods must be able to obtain physical resources, must be sure of its supply. Physical facilities—plants, machines, offices—are needed. And every business needs financial resources. In a life-insurance company this may be called "investment management," and it may be more important even than marketing or innovation. For a toy wholesaler the problem may simply be one of obtaining a seasonal line of credit. Neither, however, can operate unless assured of the financial resources it needs. To set objectives without planning for the money needed to make operations possible is like putting the roast in the oven without turning on the flame. At present objectives for physical resources, physical facilities, and supply of capital are only too often taken as "crash decisions" rather than as carefully prepared policies.

One large railroad company spends a lot of time and large amounts of money on traffic forecasts. But a decision to spend ten million dollars on new equipment was taken in a board meeting without a single figure to show what return the investment would bring or why it was necessary. What convinced the Board was the treasurer's assurance that he could easily raise the money at low interest rates.

A notable exception in respect to physical resources is the long-range forest-building policy of Crown Zellerbach, the West Coast pulp and paper manufacturer. Its aim is to make sure that the company can stay in business by providing the timber supply it will need in the future. Since it takes fifty years or more to grow a mature tree, replacement of cut trees involves investing today capital that will not pay off until the year 2000. And since the company expects the trend of pulp and paper consumption to continue to rise sharply, mere replacement is not enough. For every tree cut today, two are being planted to become available in fifty years.

Few companies face a supply problem of Crown-Zellerbach's proportions. Those that do usually realize its importance. All major oil companies work on the finding and exploration of new oil wells. The large steel companies, too, have begun to make the search for new iron-ore reserves a systematic, planned activity. But the typical business does not worry enough about tomorrow's supply of physical resources. Few even of the big retailers have, for instance, anything comparable to the planned and systematic development of "sources" that is so important an activity in Sears, Roebuck. And when the Ford Motor Company announced a few years ago that it would systematically build up suppliers for its new West Coast assembly plants, the purchasing agent of a big manufacturing company considered this a "radical innovation." Any manufacturer, wholesaler, retailer, public utility, or transportation business needs to think through the problem of its physical resources, and spell out basic decisions.

Should the company depend on one supplier for an important material, part, or product? There may be a price advantage because of bulk purchases; in times of shortage a big and constant buyer may get priority; and the close relationship may result in a better design or in closer quality control. Or should the company find several suppliers for the same resource? This may make it independent; it minimizes the danger of being forced to close down because of a strike at a single supplier; it may even lead to lower purchase prices as a result of competition between several suppliers. A cotton-textile manufacturer has to decide whether he should attempt to outguess the cotton market or try, in his buying policy, to average out fluctuations in cotton price, and so forth.

Whatever the decision, objectives should aim at providing the physical supplies needed to attain the goals set for market standing and innovation.

Equally important is good facilities planning. And it is even rarer. Few industrial companies know when to stop patching up an old plant and start building a new one, when to replace machines and tools, when to build a new office building. The costs of using obsolete facilities are usually hidden. Indeed, on the books the obsolete plant or machine may look very profitable; for it has been written down to zero so that it looks as if running it involved no cost at all. Most managers know, of course, that this is pure fallacy; but it is not easy to free ourselves completely from the spell of arithmetical sleight of hand.

Yet, clearly, both undersupply of facilities and their oversupply are extremely dangerous. Physical facilities cannot be improvised; they must be planned.

The tools for the job are available today. They have been developed above all by Joel Dean, the Columbia business economist.[2] They are simple enough to enable every business, large and small, to decide what physical facilities and equipment it needs to attain its basic goals, and to plan for them.

This, of course, requires a capital budget. And this raises the questions: How much capital will we need, and in what form; and where will it come from?

The life-insurance companies have had capital objectives for a long time. They know that they have to obtain a certain amount of money each year to pay off their claims. They know that this money has to come from the income earned on their invested reserves. Accordingly, they plan for a certain minimum rate of return on these investments. Indeed, "profit" in a

[2] See especially his *Capital Budgeting* (New York, Columbia University Press, 1951) and his brilliant article: "Measuring the Productivity of Capital," in the January–February, 1954, issue of the *Harvard Business Review*.

life-insurance company is essentially nothing but the excess of investment earnings over the planned minimum return.

Other examples of capital-supply planning are those of General Motors, DuPont, and the Chesapeake and Ohio Railroad. And the American Telephone and Telegraph Company, as already mentioned, considers this so important a job as to justify the full-time attention of a senior member of top management.

But, on the whole, managements do not worry over capital supply until the financial shoe pinches. Then it is often too late to do a good job. Such vitally important questions as: Should new capital be raised internally by self-financing, borrowed long-term or short-term, or through stock issue? not only need careful thought and study; they largely determine what kinds of capital expenditure should be undertaken. Decisions on these questions lead to conclusions regarding such vital matters as pricing, dividends, depreciation, and tax policy. Also, unless answered in advance, the company may well fritter away its available capital on the less important investments only to find itself unable to raise the capital for vital investments. In far too many companies—including some big and reputedly well-managed ones—failure to think through capital supply and to set capital objectives has stunted growth and nullified much of the management's brilliant work on marketing, innovation, and productivity.

## How Much Profitability?

Profit serves three purposes. It measures the net effectiveness and soundness of a business's efforts. It is indeed the ultimate test of business performance.

It is the "risk premium" that covers the costs of staying in business —replacement, obsolescence, market risk, and uncertainty.[3] Seen from this point of view, there is no such thing as "profit"; there are only "costs of being in business" and "costs of staying in business." And the task of a business is to provide adequately for these "costs of staying in business" by earning an adequate profit—which not enough businesses do.

Finally, profit insures the supply of future capital for innovation

[3] For a discussion of these terms see my *New Society* (New York, Harper & Bros., 1950), especially Chapter 4.

and expansion, either directly, by providing the means of self-financing out of retained earnings, or indirectly, through providing sufficient inducement for new outside capital in the form in which it is best suited to the enterprise's objectives.

None of these three functions of profit has anything to do with the economist's maximization of profit. All the three are indeed "minimum" concepts—the minimum of profit needed for the survival and prosperity of the enterprise. A profitability objective therefore measures not the maximum profit the business can produce, but the minimum it must produce.

The simplest way to find this minimum is by focusing on the last of the three functions of profit: a means to obtain new capital. The rate of profit required is easily ascertainable; it is the capital-market rate for the desired type of financing. In the case of self-financing, there must be enough profit both to yield the capital-market rate of return on money already in the business, and to produce the additional capital needed.

It is from this basis that most profitability objectives in use in American business today are derived. "We shoot for a return on capital of 25 per cent before taxes," is an accountant's shorthand way of saying: "A return of 25 per cent before taxes is the minimum we need to get the kind of capital we want, in the amounts we need and at the cost we are willing to pay."

This is a rational objective. Its adoption by more and more businesses is a tremendous step forward. It can be made even more serviceable by a few simple but important refinements. First, as Joel Dean has pointed out,[4] profitability must always include the time factor. Profitability as such is meaningless and misleading unless we know for how many years the profit can be expected. We should therefore always state anticipated total profits over the life of the investment discounted for present cash value, rather than as an annual rate of return. This is the method the capital market uses when calculating the rate of return of a bond or similar security; and, after all, this entire approach to profit is based on capital-market considerations. This method also surmounts the greatest weakness of conventional accounting: its superstitious belief that the calendar year has any

[4] Most effectively in the *Harvard Business Review* article mentioned above.

economic meaning or reality. We can never have rational business management until we have freed ourselves from what one company president (himself an ex-accountant) calls "the unnecessary tyranny of the accounting year."

Second, we should always consider the rate of return as an average resulting from good and bad years together. The business may indeed need a profit of 25 per cent before taxes. But if the 25 per cent are being earned in a good year they are unlikely to be earned over the lifetime of the investment. We may need a 40 per cent return in good years to average 25 per cent over a dozen years. And we have to know how much we actually need to get the desired average.

The tool for this is also available today. It is the "break-even point analysis," best described by Rautenstrauch and Villers in their book *The Economics of Industrial Management* (New York, Funk & Wagnalls Company, 1949). This enables us to predict with fair accuracy the range of returns under various business conditions—especially if the analysis is adjusted to express both changes in volume and in price.

For small and simple businesses this capital-market concept of the minimum profitability required is probably adequate. For the large business it is not sufficient, however, for the rate of return expected is only one factor. The other is the amount of risk involved. An investment may return 40 per cent before taxes but there may be a 50 per cent risk of failure. Is it a better investment than one returning 20 per cent with practically no risk?

Shooting for a 25 per cent return before taxes may be good enough for existing investments, investments that have already been made irrevocably. But for new decisions management needs to be able to say: "We aim at a ratio of 1.5 to 1, 1.33 to 1, or 1.25 to 1 between anticipated return after all costs (including those of capital) and estimated risk." Otherwise a rational capital-investment policy cannot be worked out.

And without a rational capital-investment policy, especially in the big business, no real budget is possible. It is a necessity for effective decentralization of management; for without it central management will always manage its components by arbitrarily granting or withholding capital and arbitrarily centralizing the management of cash. It is a prerequisite of the spirit of management; without it lower management will always feel that its best ideas get lost in the procedural maze of the Appropriations Committee "upstairs."

A rational capital-investment policy sets the range for management decisions. It indicates which of the alternative ways of reaching marketing, innovation, and productivity goals should be preferred. Above all, it forces management to realize what obligations it assumes when making decisions. That our business managers have for so long been able to manage without such a policy is as amazing a feat of navigation as Leif Ericson's feat in finding his way back to Vineland across the Atlantic without map, compass, or sextant.

A capital-investment policy must be based on a reasonably reliable assessment of the ratio between return and risks. These risks are not statistical risks like the odds at the roulette table or the life expectancies of the actuary, which can always be calculated. Only one of the four "costs of staying in business" is a statistical risk: replacement. It is no accident that it is the only one that is being handled as a cost, called variously depreciation, amortization, or replacement reserve. The other three—each of which is a more serious risk than replacement—are essentially not predictable by what happened in the past; that is, they are not predictable statistically. They are the risks of some new, different, unprecedented occurrence in the future.

Still we can today reduce even these risks to probability forecasts—though only with a fairly large margin of error. Several of the large companies are apparently doing work in the field; but the systematic job has yet to be done.

The real problem concerning profitability is not, however, what we should measure. It is what to use for a yardstick.

Profit as percentage of sales—lately very popular in American business—will not do, for it does not indicate how vulnerable a product or a business is to economic fluctuations. Only a "break-even point" analysis will do that.

"Returns on invested capital" makes sense, but it is the worst of all yardsticks—pure rubber of almost infinite elasticity. What is "invested capital"? Is a dollar invested in 1920 the same thing as a dollar invested in 1950? Is capital to be defined with the accountant as original cash value less subsequent depreciation? Or is it to be defined with the economist as wealth-producing capacity in the future, discounted at capital-market interest rates to current cash value?

Neither definition gets us far. The accountant's definition makes no allowance for changes in the purchasing power of the currency nor for technological changes. It does not permit any appraisal of business performance for the simple reason that it does not take the varying risks of different businesses into account, does not allow comparison between different businesses, between different components of the same company, between the old plants and the new plants, etc. Above all, it tends to encourage technological obsolescence. Once equipment is old enough to have been written down to zero, it tends to look much more profitable on the books than new equipment that actually produces at much lower cost. This holds true even during a deflationary period.

The economist's concept of invested capital avoids all this. It is theoretically perfect. But it cannot be used in practice. It is literally impossible to figure out how much future wealth-producing capacity any investment made in the past represents today. There are too many variables for even the best "electronic brain." There are far too many unknowns and unknowables. To find out even what would be knowable would cost more than could possibly be gained.

For these reasons a good many management people and accountants now incline toward a compromise. They would define "invested capital" as the amount it would cost today to build a new organization, a new plant, new equipment with the same productive capacity as the old organization, plant, and equipment. Theoretically this, too, has weaknesses—it would, for instance, greatly distort profitability in a depression period when new equipment prices and building costs are low. But the main difficulties are practical. For replacement assumptions, besides being not too reliable, are difficult to make; and even minor changes in the assumed basis will lead to wide divergences in the end results.

There is, in other words, no really adequate method as yet. Perhaps the most sensible thing is not to search for one but to accept the simplest way, to realize its shortcomings, and to build safeguards against its most serious dangers.

I have therefore come to advocate a method which has little in theory to commend it: to measure profitability by projecting net profit—after depreciation charges but before taxes—against original investment at original cost, that is, before depreciation. In inflationary periods the original investment figures are adjusted roughly for the rise in costs. In deflationary periods (this method has still to be tested in one) original investment figures would similarly be adjusted downward. In this way a uniform investment figure can be arrived at in roughly comparable dollars every three or five years, regardless of the date of the original investment or the purchasing power of the original money. This is admittedly crude; and I cannot defend it against the argument advanced by a friend that it is no better than painting over a badly rusted spot. But at least the method is simple; and it is so crude that it will not fool any manager into mistaking for precision what, like all "return on invested capital" figures, no matter how obtained, is at best a rough guess.

## The Remaining Key Areas

Little needs to be said here about the three remaining key areas: manager performance and development, worker performance and attitude, and public responsibility. . . .

However, it should be clear that performance and results in these areas cannot be fully measured quantitatively. All three deal with human beings. And as each human being is unique, we cannot simply add them together, or subtract them from one another. What we need are qualitative standards, judgment rather than data, appraisal rather than measurements.

It is fairly easy to determine what objectives are needed for *manager performance and development*. A business—to stay in business and remain profitable—needs goals in respect to the direction of its managers by objectives and self-control, the setting up of their jobs, the spirit of the management organization, the structure of management, and the development of tomorrow's managers. And once the goals are clear, it can always be determined whether they are being attained or not. Certainly the examination of the spirit of management, proposed in Chapter 13 below,[5] should bring out any significant shortfall.

No one but the management of each particular business can decide what the objectives in the area of *public responsibility* should be. . . . Objectives in this area, while extremely tangible, have to be set ac-

[5] See *The Practice of Management.*

cording to the social and political conditions which affect each individual enterprise and are affected by it, and on the basis of the beliefs of each management. It is this that makes the area so important; for in it managers go beyond the confines of their own little world and participate responsibly in society. But the overriding goal is common for every business: to strive to make whatever is productive for our society, whatever strengthens it and advances its prosperity, a source of strength, prosperity, and profit for the enterprise.

We are in a bad way, however, when we come to setting objectives for *worker performance and attitude*. It is not that the area is "intangible." It is only too tangible; but we know too little about it so far, operate largely by superstitions, omens, and slogans rather than by knowledge.

To think through the problems in this area and to arrive at meaningful measurements is one of the great challenges to management.

The objectives in this area should include objectives for union relations.

If this were a book on industrial society, the union would figure prominently (as it does indeed in my *New Society*). In a book on *The Practice of Management* the union is only one of many outside groups and forces management deals with—suppliers, for instance. But it is a powerful outside force. It can through wage demands wreck the business, and through a strike deprive management of control. The management of any unionized company therefore needs definite long-range objectives for its union relations. If it leaves the initiative in labor relations entirely to the union, it can be said not to manage at all.

Unfortunately that has been precisely the way too many of our managements have conducted their labor relations in the last fifteen or twenty years. They have left the initiative to the union. They have usually not even known what to expect in the way of union demands. They have, by and large, not known what the union is, how it behaves, and why it behaves as it does. When first told that certain union demands are about to be made, the typical management refuses to listen. It is sure that the demand will not be made—for the simple reason that it does not consider it justified. Then, when the demand is made, management tends to turn it down as "impossible" and as "certain to ruin the business," if not our free-enterprise system. Three days to three years later management caves in, accepts the demand, and in a joint statement with the union leader hails the agreement as a "milestone in democratic labor relations." This is not management; it is abdication.

What union-relations objectives should be concretely goes beyond the scope of this book. But they should first focus on returning the initiative to management. This requires that management must know how a union operates and why. It must know what demands the union will make and why; indeed it must be able to anticipate these demands so as to make their eventual acceptance beneficial to the enterprise or, at the least, harmless to it. Above all, it must learn to make demands itself; as long as the union alone makes demands, management will remain the passive, the frustrated, the ineffectual partner in the relationship.

Union relations, no matter how important, are however only a small and peripheral part of the management of work and worker. Yet, in the main areas we simply do not even know whether the things we can measure—turnover, absenteeism, safety, calls on the medical department, suggestion system participation, grievances, employee attitudes, etc.—have anything at all to do with employee performance. At best they are surface indications. Still they can be used—in some companies are being used—to build an Employee Relations Index. And though we can only guess what such an index measures, at least the systematic attempt to find out what goes on in the work force focuses management's attention on what it could and should do. While no more than the merest palliative it serves at least to remind managers of their responsibility for the organization of the worker and his work. Admittedly this is hardly even a stopgap, perhaps only an acknowledgment of ignorance. The goal must be to replace it by real objectives which are based on knowledge.

## THE TIME SPAN OF OBJECTIVES

For what time span should objectives be set? How far ahead should we set our targets?

The nature of the business clearly has a bearing here. In certain parts of the garment business next week's clearance sale is "long-range future." It may take four years to build a big steam turbine and two more to install it; in the turbine business six years may be "immediate present" therefore. And Crown Zellerbach is forced to plant today the trees it will harvest fifty years hence.

Different areas require different time spans. To build a marketing organization takes at least five years. Innovations in engineering and chemistry made today are unlikely to show up in marketing results and profits for five years or longer. On the other hand, a sales campaign, veteran sales managers believe, must show results within six weeks or less; "Sure, there are sleepers," one of these veterans once said, "but most of them never wake up."

This means that in setting objectives management has to balance the immediate future—the next few years—against the long range: five years or longer. This balance can best be found through a "managed-expenditures budget." For practically all the decisions that affect the balance are made as decisions on what the accountant calls "managed expenditures"—those expenditures that are determined by current management decision rather than by past and irrevocable decisions (like capital charges), or by the requirements of current business (like labor and raw material costs). Today's managed expenditures are tomorrow's profit; but they may also be today's loss.

Every second-year accountancy student knows that almost any "profit" figure can be turned into a "loss" by changing the basis of depreciation charges; and the new basis can usually be made to appear as rational as the old. But few managements—including their accountants—realize how many such expenditures there are that are based, knowingly or not, on an assessment of short-range versus long-range needs, and that vitally affect both. Here is a partial list:

Depreciation charges; maintenance budgets; capital replacement, modernization and expansion costs; research budgets; expenditures on product development and design; expenditures on the management group, its compensation and rewards, its size, and on developing tomorrow's managers; cost of building and maintaining a marketing organization; promotion and advertising budgets; cost of service to the customer; personnel management, especially training expenditures.

Almost any one of these expenditures can be cut back sharply, if not eliminated; and for some time, perhaps for a long time, there will be no adverse effect. Any one of these expenditures can be increased sharply and for good reasons, with no resulting benefits visible for a long time. By cutting these expenditures immediate results can always be made to look better. By raising them immediate results can always be made to look worse.

There are no formulas for making the decisions on managed expenditures. They must always be based on judgment and are almost always a compromise. But even a wrong decision is better than a haphazard approach "by bellows and meat ax": inflating appropriations in fair weather and cutting them off as soon as the first cloud appears. All managed expenditures require long application; short spurts of high activity do not increase their effectiveness. Sudden cuts may destroy in one day what it took years to build. It is better to have a modest but steady program of employee activities than to splurge on benefits, lush company papers, and plant baseball teams when times are good, only to cut down to the point of taking out the soap in the washrooms when orders drop 10 per cent.[6] It is better to give the customer minimum service than to get him used to good service only to lay off half the service force when profits go down. It is more productive to spend 50,000 dollars each year for ten years on research than to spend, say, two million one year and nothing the next nine. Where managed expenditures are concerned, one slice of bread every day is better than half a loaf today and none tomorrow.

Almost every one of these expenditures requires highly skilled people to be effective. Yet, first-rate people will not remain with a business if their activity is subject to sudden, unpredictable, and arbitrary ups and downs. Or if they stay, they will cease to exert themselves—for "what's the use of my working hard if management will kill it anyhow?" And if the meat ax cuts off trained people during an "economy wave," replacements are hard to find or take a long time to train when management, applying the bellows, suddenly decides to revive the activity.

Decisions concerning managed expenditures themselves are of such importance for the business as a whole—over and above their impact on individual activities—that they must not be made without careful consideration of every item in turn and of all of them jointly. It is essential that management know and consciously decide what it is

---

[6] Lest this be considered hyperbole, it actually happened, in this country, and in 1951.

doing in each area and why. It is essential that management know and consciously decide which area to give priority, which to cut first and how far, which to expand first and how far. It is essential finally that management know and consciously decide what risks to take with the long-run future for the sake of short-term results, and what short-term sacrifices to make for long-run results.

A managed-expenditures budget for a five-year period should show the expenditure considered necessary in each area to attain business objectives within the near future—up to five years or so. It should show the additional expenditure considered necessary in each area to maintain the position of the business beyond the five-year period for which concrete objectives are being set. This brings out the areas where expenditures are to be raised first if business gets better, and those where they are to be cut first if business turns down; it enables management to plan what to maintain even in bad times, what to adjust to the times, and what to avoid even in a boom. It shows the total impact of these expenditures on short-range results. And finally it shows what to expect from them in the long range.

## BALANCING THE OBJECTIVES

In addition to balancing the immediate and the long-range future, management also has to balance objectives. What is more important: an expansion in markets and sales volume, or a higher rate of return? How much time, effort, and energy should be expended on improving manufacturing productivity? Would the same amount of effort or money bring greater returns if invested in new-product design?

There are few things that distinguish competent from incompetent management quite as sharply as the performance in balancing objectives. Yet, there is no formula for doing the job. Each business requires its own balance—and it may require a different balance at different times. The only thing that can be said is that balancing objectives is not a mechanical job, is not achieved by "budgeting." The budget is the document in which balanced decisions find final expression; but the decisions themselves require judgment; and the judgment will be sound only if it is based on a sound analysis of the business. The ability of a management to stay within its budget is often considered a test of management skill. But the effort to arrive at the budget that best harmonizes the divergent needs of the business is a much more important test of management's ability. The late Nicholas Dreystadt, head of Cadillac and one of the wisest managers I have ever met, said to me once: "Any fool can learn to stay within his budget. But I have seen only a handful of managers in my life who can draw up a budget that is worth staying within."

Objectives in the key areas are the "instrument panel" necessary to pilot the business enterprise. Without them management flies by the "seat of its pants"—without landmarks to steer by, without maps, and without having flown the route before.

However, an instrument panel is no better than the pilot's ability to read and interpret it. In the case of management this means ability to anticipate the future. Objectives that are based on completely wrong anticipations may actually be worse than no objectives at all. The pilot who flies by the "seat of his pants" at least knows that he may not be where he thinks he is.

# 24.

# *For Operation Success*

## By CLINTON F. ROBINSON [1]

It is axiomatic that many factors beyond the control of any company have a significant bearing on its success. It is also true, if not axiomatic, that the proper planning of a business will result, within fairly narrow limits, in a positive control of its degree of success irrespective of the outside factors.

Defining objectives and planning their fruitful conclusion is a high-sounding phrase indeed, but when translated into more practical terms it is the comfortable practice of beating to the punch the accident of failure.

The contemporary industrial age is inexorably becoming more restrictive as compared to the era in which most American firms were born and thrived. While there is much to be learned from the past, it is the future to which we must now turn.

The nation's economy has emerged from a significant transition whereby it is no longer possible to secure success with relative ease. Pressures within the industrial complex itself, as manifested by factors such as increased costs of operation and sterner competition, are continually mounting. Local and national political influences are no longer remote and cannot be dismissed in the course of an evening's debate among friends. Foreign affairs are at best uncertain, and the multitude of problems inherent in them have a decided effect upon the well-being of any business.

[1] From Clinton F. Robinson, "For Operation Success," *Dun's Review and Modern Industry,* January, 1954, p. 1. Reprinted by permission.

Those widely divergent considerations are among those that comprise a set of "guiding stars" under which the average business thrives or not, as the case may be. These influences must be added together for composite analysis to get to the basic task of any sizable commercial organization—that is, survival followed by progress and increased profitability.

All of this is easily said, but it is obvious that the melt to be worked upon is a potpourri of such complexity as to astound even the better astrologists.

It is a certainty that the problem has been viewed from just about every conceivable angle. Many tangible approaches to the question have undoubtedly been taken or are in various stages of application. Unfortunately, note must also be made of the considerable body of firms that do not consider attempts at planning, particularly long range, of any import.

To determine the most meaningful method of attacking the task of comprehensive planning is undoubtedly controversial. There is, however, an initial conclusion that may be drawn that should engender very little debate. That is, the subject is not only susceptible of division into two parts, but must be so treated.

The first part or phase is the broad and relatively unchanging determination of the primary purposes and general objectives of any business organization. The second phase embraces the follow-on and ever-changing rationalization and detailed planning necessary to successfully realize the stated objectives within a stipulated period of time.

Viewed one way, the two phases actually constitute the time-honored chicken-and-egg sequence. In this case the egg is regarded as the objectives, from which must spring the chicken which is defined as successful planning. Taken alone, neither are of particular value or significance. Accomplished in inverse order the value of each is surely to become diffused.

The task of getting a definable purpose and set of objectives can be stated in absurdly fundamental terms. The vast majority of industrial enterprise has been created to make money. However, this rudimentary definition is of no real value in assisting in the very real chore of actually making the money. If, as a matter of fact, it is used as the sole guide it may well produce disastrous results.

With respect to the first part of the subject, there are eight significant points around which any outline of purpose and statement of objectives should be built:

1. Profits desired.
2. Internal endeavor required to realize the profits.
3. Markets to be exploited.
4. Obligation to customers.
5. Obligation to stockholders.
6. Obligation to employees.
7. Obligation to community.
8. Ethical standards for the conduct of all phases of the company operation.

Development in concise and meaningful terms of the eight points just mentioned provides the common knowledge and understanding that are so mandatory to success in planning. It is the tangible basis for management teamwork directed toward a common goal.

## Follow Through

The task of developing the objectives belongs to anyone in an organization that can properly be identified as part of management. As a practical matter, a broad outline of the purpose and objectives must be prepared at the top of an organization. The outline then can be handed down and back through the lowest possible level so that all of the best thinking and competence available within a company are utilized in its further development or expansion. Long and studied consideration should be afforded the results by the president, his principal officers, and finally the board of directors.

From this endeavor there should emerge a document, the context of which would separately enumerate both the primary purpose and general objectives of the company.

In the primary-purpose category the significant areas covered are outlined below:

1. Geographical limitations of the business.
2. Acceptable economic and political conditions under which activities of the company would operate.
3. A general statement of basic product lines.
4. A general statement of limitations with respect to product lines not

now manufactured but which may or should be undertaken at some future time.

In summary, general objectives would be treated in the final document as follows:

1. A general statement with respect to the operations of the company, to include an unquestionable level of integrity, product quality, technical skill, and dependability.

2. The minimum acceptable profits to be expected.

3. The markets to be undertaken.

4. General rules governing the establishment of product lines, to cover the complete line consideration and standards for manufacturing.

5. A general statement with respect to sources of supply.

6. A general statement with respect to company organization, principles, distribution, practice, and related considerations.

7. A general statement with respect to the conduct of a research program.

8. General statement with respect to finance, to include consideration of working capital, utilization of funds in excess of the operating needs, the company debt conditions, and dividends.

9. General statement with respect to personnel, to include levels of employment, morale, enthusiasm, wages and salaries, training, career advancement, safety, working conditions, and welfare.

10. General statement with respect to public relations, to include perpetuation of the company's reputation, its standing in the community, and sale of its products.

Having developed the primary purpose and general objectives of the company, a firm set of ground rules is therefore provided for the necessary detailed planning. As previously indicated, the methods and approaches to the follow-on planning may vary, and sometimes widely. Nonetheless, there is a system of programing which, when completely developed, is certain to make the well-defined purposes and objectives into a reality.

## Detailed Work

This system of planning is on a five-year program basis. The program is "sliding" inasmuch as it is reviewed annually and at each revision another year is added. It is most detailed and exact for the first year of the period. Balance sheets, sources and application of fund statements, capital expenditures, research projects and expenses, and so on are the type of detail utilized for the first year's program. The following four years are based upon trends which are actually the best estimates with respect to sales dollars available to the company, the cost of producing these sales, the profit ratios involved, and projects involved in making the sales possible.

During the construction of the initial five-year program, and at the time of each annual revision, two guideposts are employed. First, the statement of "Primary Purpose and General Objectives" in order to keep all controlled activities of the company on the track previously determined to be the most desirable. Secondarily, a "Concept of the Future" is utilized. This Concept is prepared annually prior to programing activities. On the one hand, the Concept attempts, so far as it is humanly possible to do so, to collect and analyze the outside uncontrollable factors influencing the business—the "guiding stars" previously alluded to. On the other, the Concept presents all of the controllable projects and trends that are going on outside of the company. Illustrations of the latter category would be the probable effects of company research on its product line at stipulated dates in the future, and the estimated impact of, say, today's training on next year's sales.

In addition to the specific guidance made available for programers in the Objectives and Concept, there is an unalterable ground rule to be followed. All programs must be realistic and susceptible of reasonable attainment. Use of this axiom as against the philosophy of "hay before the donkey" avoids the hazards of effort diffusion and morale impact that haunt the unsuccessful overoptimist. It should be noted, somewhat wryly, that the reasonable approach must be carefully watched lest it, too, become a cropper in the other direction.

## CONSOLIDATION

On the basis of this Concept, and within the limitations established in the General Objectives, every operating segment of the company builds a five-year program. After study, approval, and consolidation there becomes one major program to guide the five-year operation of the company. During the course of consolidation each individual program must be balanced and adjusted with all the others to insure feasibility, not only from a financial standpoint, but also in light of limitations that may exist with respect to research capabilities, personnel, facilities, or any other pertinent reason.

As a result of this work there are developed for every element of the company tangible and identifiable tracks along which it must run. These "tracks" are in reality a set of programs covering the major activities noted below:

1. Sales.
2. Cost of sales.
3. Cost of products sold.
4. Administration.
5. Capital expenditures.
6. Advertising and promotion.
7. Research.
8. Product development.
9. Career development and personnel recruitment.
10. Training.
11. Profit.

It would not be proper to conclude without mentioning a most important offshoot of the programing activity. In the application of the programs to all major operations there is provided through periodic reports a yardstick for measuring accomplishments toward the desired objectives both long and short term. Through this means, trouble areas may be flagged and firm action taken toward problem identification and solution. Constant surveillance of actual performance against a reasonable but progressive program is the most positive way available to assure ultimate success.

A concluding reference should be made as to the size that a business should attain before its activities are programed. It can be said that no enterprise is so small that it should not have available a well-thought-out and defined purpose. Similarly, specific plans, formal or otherwise, should be available somewhat above the level of a desk drawer to provide success to the purpose. Short of the fact-finding "operation bonanza," planning techniques are the life blood of any industrial enterprise.

# 25.

# *The Primary Purpose and the General Objectives of the Carborundum Company*[1]

### FOREWORD

This Statement of the Primary Purpose and General Objectives of The Carborundum Company has been approved by the Board of Directors as the governing doctrine for the operation of the Company.

It is furnished to you for your information, study, and guidance. Only through complete common knowledge and understanding of what we are trying to do can we, as the management team of Carborundum, be successful. All our decisions and actions as executives of the Company should be directed toward the achievement of these General Objectives.

In the future it is intended that specific annual and longer-term programs covering the various activities of the Company, based on these General Objectives, be prepared and placed in effect to bring the Company to their full realization.

CLINTON F. ROBINSON<br>President

*May 1, 1952*

### PRIMARY PURPOSE

To conduct throughout the world, under all economic and political conditions consistent with the corporate nature of the Company, a

---

[1] Reprinted by permission of The Carborundum Company.

profitable, continuous, independent business in the manufacture and sale of

1. silicon carbide, aluminum oxide, and similar and related basic materials,
2. a complete line of abrasive products, a complete line of super refractories, metal additives, electrical heating elements and resistors, and other products containing or produced from those basic materials,
3. similar, related, and auxiliary products, and
4. other products consistent with the general nature of the Company, which can be undertaken successfully by the existing organization or an appropriate expansion thereof, with resulting growth in profits, financial stability, essential productive facilities, quality and quantity of products, reputation, and equitable benefits to the Company's stockholders, customers, and employees.

## GENERAL OBJECTIVES

1. Operations
    a. To generate adequate profits at least equivalent to those of similar enterprises.
    b. To obtain for the Company the maximum possible participation in the available markets for its products. To foster and improve sound and mutually profitable relations with the Company's distributors. To conduct appropriate advertising campaigns to reach all profitable markets.
    c. To create new and enlarged markets through the introduction of new and improved products and new uses and tools and methods for existing products.
    d. To expand the sale of the profitable products of the Company. As a corollary to eliminate unprofitable items, except where otherwise justified for competitive and advertising purposes.
    e. To increase the return from sales by greater efficiencies in manufacture, distribution, and administration and through sound sales policies and practices.
    f. To produce an unsurpassed quality of products in profitable quantity, at lowest costs consistent with that quality, to meet the needs of the Company's customers. As a corollary "substandard" products generally have no place in the Company's line.
    g. To maintain, at all times and under all conditions, adequate reliable multiple sources of supply at lowest costs, consistent with necessary quality, for the Company's requirements for raw materials, semifinished and finished products, and services.
    h. To produce a satisfactory and continuous volume of products for

sale with minimum productive cycles; to maintain inventories consistent with good customer service, sound practices, and manufacturing procedures; to develop firm long-term commitments to cover the requirements of major customers; so that a continuity of efficient plant operations and minimum labor turnover can be achieved.

   i. To adapt promptly and smoothly the Company's activities as an essential industry to emergency conditions in the event of mobilization or war.

2. Research

   a. To conduct a vigorous planned program of scientific and technical research to improve and lower costs of the technical processes of manufacture, to develop an unexcelled quality of products, to take the lead in meeting the needs of the Company's customers for improved and new products, to develop new uses for existing products, and to develop new high-profit products for introduction to existing and potential customers. As a corollary to collaborate with and properly utilize other appropriate research organizations.

   b. To conduct a vigorous planned program of commercial and economic research, to assist in maintaining and increasing the Company's participation in the available markets for its products, to discover profitable new products and markets for exploitation by the Company, to determine the trends and growth factors in the industries served by the Company, and to formulate and evaluate reliable estimates of present and future economic conditions.

3. Finance

   a. To maintain necessary working capital to support sales volume and adequate funds with which to operate the Company, with appropriate reserves to meet swings in economic conditions.

   b. To utilize funds excess to the needs of the Company to reduce and finally eliminate the Company's long-term debt. Consistent with economy and other objectives, to retire debt prior to maturity.

   c. To pay regularly the common stockholders of the Company fair and reasonable dividends on a stable basis and to increase their equity in the Company, thus strengthening the confidence of the stockholders and the public in the common stock of the Company as an investment of high caliber and broadening the common stock ownership.

   d. To invest the earnings of the Company over and above requirements for working capital, debt retirement, and dividends in improved productive facilities and new profitable undertakings.

4. Personnel

   a. To provide superior personnel in all key positions and to attract and hold qualified and efficient managerial, professional, technical, skilled, clerical, and other employees.

b. To train and develop the Company's personnel for improved performance and greater responsibilities within the Company.

c. To maintain high morale, enthusiasm, and loyalty to the interests of the Company. To promote good understanding and cooperation among the Company's personnel. To create a sense of belonging so that all employees are working toward a common goal.

d. To adequately compensate the Company's employees through sound wage and salary administration, and appropriate incentives, pensions, and other benefits.

e. To maintain high standards of safety and working conditions and facilities consistent with the nature of the Company's operations. To maintain at all times a definite interest in the health and welfare of the Company's employees. To make Carborundum "a better place to work."

5. Public Relations

a. To foster the Company's reputation for fair dealing, prompt service, dependability, integrity, courtesy, quality of products, outstanding ability, and technical skill. To make the Company's trade mark "Carborundum" stand for these characteristics.

b. To foster the Company's position as a good citizen of the countries in which it operates and a good neighbor in the communities where it is located.

c. To cooperate lawfully with similar enterprises and industry generally for mutual betterment.

d. To conduct all operations of the Company in the highest ethical manner and with proper revelation of its operations to its stockholders and governmental agencies appropriate to a publicly owned corporation.

6. Management

To realize these objectives through the periodic preparation of specific short- and long-term programs, carried out through a simple and effective organization, employing proven management techniques and procedures and based on the principle of decentralized operations with centralized control of performance.

# IV

## SPECIAL PROBLEMS

Be not the first by whom the new are tried,
Nor yet the last to lay the old aside.

—Alexander Pope

# 26.

# *Introduction*

• Systems engineering is the effort to assess the technological needs of the future and to plan how best to meet them. In some businesses it may be profitable to have an entire company department devoted to systems engineering.

• "Commercial" management's voice in selecting future research projects is growing stronger, particularly in industries where the technological race is tensest and the assessment of market needs is most important.

• At least one company has found it possible to develop a normal growth pattern for new products that can be used in planning sales.

• In marketing strategy, the steps to be taken and their timing may depend importantly on relationships between end users of the product, suppliers, and other groups in the distribution picture.

• In managing overseas operations, long- and short-range planning should be treated differently. It may be wise to concentrate the first in the United States while leaving much of the second for the field offices abroad.

• So-called scientific methods and formulas for planning the ideal size of a plant or business are generally impractical.

These are a few items from the hopper of ideas in this section. These ideas have an obvious bearing on the conduct of long-range planning. They also have a subtle—but no less important—bearing on the development of skillful thinking about planning problems. This is a point worth considering.

As we have seen earlier, long-range planning often involves managers in jobs that they have not done before. The articles in this section are dramatic evidence of this fact. For instance, in the lead article we see executives at Bell Labs attempting to see the technological future twenty or more years in advance (so far they have been successful). In Mr. Corey's interesting case on the Aluminum Company of America, we see a materials producer leaving its traditional role and going into production of an end product. Again, in Mr. Holst's article we see an American company working out a procedure for setting long-term objectives for its offices in foreign countries. In all of these cases the planner is looking forward in time. He is appraising today's strengths and weaknesses in terms of tomorrow's opportunities. He is mentally putting his company in the fourth dimension, so to speak.

Needless to say, problems of this sort are about as challenging as any management can face. They call for the utmost skill in analysis and imagination. They require a very high order of good judgment. They bring out the "superman" in us—if we have any! But no matter how demanding long-range planning is, we must solve its problems in the same old way we solve any other problem—out of our experience. For in a sense, we are no better than our pasts. We can apply only the facts we have understood, only the lessons we have learned, only the values that have made an impression on us.

The real question is: How perceptively shall we apply them? Will we be aware of the subtle impact of various experiences in our lives on our standards and ways of thinking? (I once had an English instructor who argued that a shoeshine boy could do a better job of it if he had an appreciation of classical music—the idea being, of course, that music appreciation entered into his values about what constituted perfection, good taste, etc.) Will we be able to talk intelligently about our assumptions in discussing planning problems with other executives?

Let me be more specific. The question is raised in Mr. Hunt's article on Bell Labs whether people will ever want television with their telephones. Now, the typical reaction to this question today would be, "Of course not! Why would anyone have any use for TV with a telephone?" Such a response might be broken down this way: (1) People don't want TV with their telephones today. (2) Therefore they won't want TV with their telephones tomorrow. The first is a fact. The second is a conclusion from the fact. Few will argue with the first, but the systems engineers at Bell Labs would argue with the second. They think that the time is coming when people *will* want TV with their telephones—and are beginning to plan for it, according to Mr. Hunt. We don't know yet whether the systems engineers are right or not. But we must at least give them credit for going over their reasoning—undoubtedly *they* had a negative reaction to the question at first, *too*—and separating observed facts from conclusions about those facts.

Take another example. Mr. Corey notes in his article that managers sometimes assume that if a product or application is basically good, it will find its way into the market. In the typical case where someone takes this for granted, he probably has in mind several examples of good products that *did* succeed with a minimum of promotion. From this observation he generalizes that any good product can succeed likewise. The danger is clear. Part of the time he may be quite right, but part of the time he will be wrong, because new products are launched on the market under such widely varying circumstances.

Most good marketing managers know this; they are not dumb. Yet they sometimes fall into the trap of making the generalization anyway. They make the same simple everyday mistake that we all do: they "assume their assumptions." If they did not—if they took the time to scrutinize those assumptions—it is hard to see how there could be so *many* tragic cases on record of good products that failed to "sell themselves."

All of this has a very pertinent bearing on long-range planning. A good management training program has a very great deal to offer it, and planning in turn can be of very great use in training. In case discussions and in on-the-job coaching, the continual inquiry can be, "Why do you think that? Can you give an example? Is that situation like the one we are facing?" And so forth. Such a background for planning should be invaluable. At the same time, planning should serve well as an advanced testing ground for training. No other management job offers so many opportunities for rigorous testing of one's reasoning and for meaningful exploration of one's managerial experience.

Moreover, since in long-range planning we are looking forward to an uncertain future, we must make even more use than usual of values and standards. We must continually resort to phrases like "good job" and "safer course" and "sound financing." What do we mean by a *good* job? What bench marks from past experience do we have in mind when we think of a *safe* course? How did we get our ideas about what makes for *sound* financing? Unless we can discuss such questions frankly with associates, our long-range planning will rest on a shaky foundation. We will not be able to "crank in" depth of experience, to refer back to Bruce Payne's concept in an earlier chapter.

## CONTRIBUTORS TO THIS SECTION

*Morton Hunt,* a free-lance writer, is the author of about 140 articles in *Fortune, Life, Reader's Digest, Harper's, Saturday Evening Post,* and other magazines. He was President of the Society of Magazine Writers in 1956.

*Robert K. Stolz* is a Senior Consultant with the management consulting firm of McKinsey & Company, Inc. He became interested in research planning because of the growing concern of his firm's clients with the size of their research budgets and the question of how well the money was being spent.

*Harry L. Hansen* is Professor of Business Administration at the Harvard Business School. He is the author of *Marketing: Text, Cases, and Readings,* published in 1956 by Richard D. Irwin, Inc., and the coauthor, with Malcolm P. McNair, of *Problems in Marketing,* published by McGraw-Hill Book Company, Inc. He was instrumental in the development of the Harvard Business School's new course in Creative Marketing Strategy.

*E. Raymond Corey* is Associate Professor of Business Administration at the Harvard Business School. Active as a teacher of marketing, he is the author of *The Development of Markets for New Materials* and *Direct Placement of Corporate Securities,* both published by the Harvard Business School Division of Research, and of articles in the *Harvard Business Review.*

*Willem Holst* is Manager, Economic Coordination, Standard-Vacuum Oil Company. His article is based on his remarks at the 26th Annual National Business Conference of the Harvard Business School in 1956. His company's experience in the remote control of overseas operations dates back to 1933.

The late *Edward H. Hempel* was Assistant Professor of Industrial Engineering at Columbia University. He was also Research Secretary of the Management Division, American Society of Mechanical Engineers.

*Richard Austin Smith* is Associate Editor of *Fortune*. The author of numerous articles and one book, he has served in the past with *Time, Life,* and *Think* magazines and with the United States Department of Labor. He is a member of the National Press Club.

# 27.

# Bell Labs' 230 Long-Range Planners

## By Morton M. Hunt [1]

The contemplation of the future has long been a favorite pastime of poets and dreamers. For industrialists, however, it is a serious and workmanlike business. One of the most remarkable organized efforts to foresee the future is being made, day in and day out, by the long-range planners and the "systems planners" of the Bell Telephone System—a thousand or more specially oriented scientists and executives scattered strategically throughout its huge laboratories and affiliated companies.

These down-to-earth seers grapple with the future from nine to five daily, trying to outguess the vagaries of unwritten history. For obvious reasons, successful prophecy is far more important in the communications business than in the diaper, auto, paint, or paper businesses. The telephone first made possible easy contact between separated people— and the sweeping impact of that commonplace facility is almost impossible to gauge. Hardly anyone realizes, for instance, that the telephone on his desk is but one set of controls in a single electric machine that lies spread across the three million square miles of the U.S.; his phone is physically linked with over 50 million other telephones by 185 million miles of wire and 200 million complex electric relays. An individual conversation by telephone is an act one takes for granted; but last year Americans made 56 billion phone calls, and quite ob-

[1] Reprinted by special permission from the May, 1954, issue of *Fortune;* © 1954, Time Inc.

viously a major part of the affairs of the nation could not have been conducted without the transmission of this ocean of talk.

The U.S., with only 6 per cent of the world's people, owns 59 per cent of the world's phones. Britain has only one-third as many phones per million, West Germany one-sixth as many, and Russia one-sixtieth as many. To what extent this is responsible for the U.S. being the world's richest and most productive nation, one can only speculate; yet since man is distinguished from the beasts principally by the facility with which he communicates, it must be that the telephone network has been vastly influential in making American civilization what it now is.

For such reasons, officials of the Bell System feel the weight of destiny on their shoulders, and pay well for the services of expert planners. The Bell System consists of the American Telephone & Telegraph Co., the headquarters organization; Western Electric, which makes and installs the equipment; Bell Telephone Laboratories, the research-and-development outfit; and twenty-one "operating companies," which actually provide the telephone service. In each of these parts of the Bell System there are specialists in planning, from the businessmen of A. T. & T. to the scientific directors of Bell Labs, to the managers of the local companies, who try to keep up with the growth of their cities but not outrun them.

In addition to all this, Bell Labs has in recent years set up an entire department whose sole function is to assess the probable needs of the future, and to make judicious speculations as to how those needs can best be met. Systems Engineering, as the department is called, consists of over 230 thoughtful, inquisitive engineers, physicists, and mathematicians who are occupied full time with the express duty of acting as scientific seers and architects-of-the-future.

The boss of these engineer-dreamers is a short, amiable, balding man named George Gilman. His planners are an assortment of scientists of all ages, shapes, and backgrounds, from old experienced telephone engineers to shiny-faced lads with fresh Ph. D.'s. All of them are clean of hand and shirt; they sit in offices, reading, arguing, doodling endless diagrams, and collecting masses of data, but seldom doing physical work. "We avoid inventing things," Gilman says. "It prejudices our neutral position."

"Anyhow," he adds with an Olympian wave of his hand, "we don't have to actually *build* a new mechanism to know that it is possible. When we need a new thing, we think out what it should do, talk over its hypothetical characteristics with the development engineers, and they build it for us."

Gilman's systems planners are scattered about the upper floors of the Bell Labs building on West Street, overlooking the New York waterfront. A future-predicter at work is nothing exciting to watch. He sits at a desk, reading technical reports and memoranda; he scratches his chin thoughtfully, tilts back in his chair, lights and re-lights a pipe monotonously, scribbles a few equations, and doodles a few diagrams. Sometimes he shuffles in and out of the great laboratory at Murray Hill, New Jersey, looking for new theories and inventions to help him, asking innumerable questions, and nodding in unconvinced affability. He cannot talk without a pencil or a piece of chalk; he spoils hundreds of sheets of notepaper, tablecloths, menus, and napkins with scribbled diagrams. He may perform a study known as "systems evaluation" to see how well some part of the Bell System is currently functioning, and he may go on to use the mathematical tools of operations analysis, to disclose which factors can best be altered in the interests of greater efficiency; but systems planning—the architectural designing of the future—goes far beyond both of these.

## Automatization, Vintage 1910

Long-range planning is an old and honored policy in the Bell System, going back long before there was any special department entitled Systems Engineering. Originally the key planners were simply high-level engineers scattered about the Bell System in various jobs. Just about the shrewdest, yet simplest, piece of forecasting in telephone history was made some forty years ago. The subject in question was the use of operators versus some new and seemingly visionary devices for automatic (dialed) telephoning.

A few of the more farsighted telephone engineers began to wonder about the far future. (This was about 1910.) They looked at the curves of telephone growth; they dared to wonder if someday every family might have a phone; they pored over charts and worked on equations of probability. After a while, a few of these genteel radicals put down their pencils and agreed on one thing. "Unless we put in dialing by the customers themselves," they told the vice-presidents, "the telephone system will someday collapse of its own growth. Within a generation you won't be able to hire enough girls to run the phone system even if you could get every eligible girl of the right age and education in the whole country." Within ten years automatic exchange equipment and dial phones were perfected and being installed throughout the country.

Since that time the number of phones in the U.S. has grown sixfold; if no automatic switching equipment had been developed, the phone company today would need 1,500,000 full-time operators—and it currently has a hard time finding and keeping a mere 250,000 of them.

Equally remarkable foresight was displayed in a few small laboratory rooms at Bell Labs twenty-eight years ago, when inventor Herbert Ives and several associates began to tinker around with whirling disks, spirals made of little lenses, and other improbable-looking mechanisms in a system called "television." In 1927 they invited a delegation of newsmen into the offices of Bell Labs and let them goggle at a flickery picture of Commerce Secretary Hoover, speaking from a brightly lit telephone booth down in Washington, his face and voice being sent to New York over telephone wires. Within the next three years they had also transmitted two-way telephone television, color television, and had even foreseen the future to the extent of transmitting a movie over a TV circuit from Philadelphia to New York.

None of this was for the purpose of getting the telephone company into the TV-producing business. (For that matter, nobody in Bell knew whether there would ever be a TV business, or how it could compete with movies and radio.) But the planning specialists of the Bell System had figured out that this thing logically had to become big in the future; when it did, the images and sound would have to be carried around the country via the telephone network, and it behooved them to find out how it would work, and what kinds of long-distance wires, amplifiers, filters, and the like would have to be built into future telephone installations to make that possible.

## THE TV SYSTEM NOBODY KNOWS

It is likely that many people believe (if they think about it at all) that the TV networks themselves developed, installed, and operate the coaxial cables and radio-relay towers that carry TV across the country. The actual facts are quite different. Broadcasters have rented the long-distance facilities of the Bell System since the early days of radio, and TV has followed the same pattern. In almost all cases, when the picture and sound leave the control room of a TV studio, they travel downstairs in telephone-company wires, under city streets to a "TV operating center" run by telephone engineers, and are transmitted cross-country by Bell System radio relay or coaxial cable—both of which the Bell System owns, and which its own engineers designed over fifteen years ago, in response to the earnest pleading of the planners to make radio relay and coaxial cable capable of carrying not only great new loads of phone conversations, but television as well. At the far end, other telephone engineers receive and reroute the impulses via underground lines into the local TV station's own control room, where the studio engineers finally take charge of shunting it into the local transmitter.

Neither radio relay nor coaxial cable, excellent as they are for carrying TV signals cross-country, is economically feasible for this local distribution of the signals within a city from the TV operating center to control room, or vice versa. The fine-gauge paper-covered wires that carry ordinary telephone conversations around a city could be pressed into service only by using expensive special repeaters (amplifiers), and even then two miles would be the practical limit because of introduced distortions. So back in the early 1940's the design engineers developed for this special purpose a husky shielded wire called a "video pair." Video pairs, far cheaper than coaxial, were still expensive; moreover, they would take up valuable space in telephone conduits that might be better used for ordinary telephone wires. Yet at a time when no huckster, producer, or business analyst was willing to bet his reputation on the future of TV, the systems planners of Bell Labs advised the directors of the telephone companies to start putting video pairs into the ground as part of every new telephone-cable installation when those cables ran past stadiums, theaters, or radio-studio buildings. Long before TV was a paying proposition the telephone companies had stuffed into the ground millions of dollars' worth of video pairs—useless for anything but TV—in the firm belief that the special wires would be needed mighty soon.

All this sounds simpler than it really is. The systems engineers of

A. T. & T.'s Operation and Engineering Department and systems engineers of Bell Labs had to do more than merely conclude TV was a coming thing. They had to estimate what demands it would make on a national communications system, and put together a theoretical system—based on equipment that would become available in time— that could handle these demands, be compatible with the rest of the Bell System's business (which is, after all, basically one of handling telephone conversations), *and,* beyond that, be economically justifiable.

The biggest trouble with TV, from the engineer's point of view, is that it takes up too much space. Each channel occupies as much room on a radio-relay or coaxial-cable circuit as would serve 600 to 1,000 simultaneous long-distance telephone conversations. And *that* is a serious matter; for frequency space is a valuable and hard-won commodity.

"Television," the planners warned the management of A. T. & T. in the mid-thirties, "now looks as though it would use up anywhere from two to four million cycles of bandwidth—the equivalent of 600 conversations. That much bandwidth can't be crammed onto ordinary wires." Management wanted to know what to do about it. The planners said that several researchers in the laboratories had an idea that although wide bands of frequencies would leak off a regular wire, they would stay on the inside surface of a tube with a wire down the middle of it. Other researchers, they added, had some notion that high-frequency radio waves, carrying a wide band of frequencies, could be focused like light and beamed from tower to tower. Either method would solve the problem of future telephone traffic—and of TV at the same time. After listening to these alternatives the A. T. & T. management boldly spent an additional $10 million to perfect coaxial cable (the hollow tube) and nearly as much on radio relay, though neither of these systems would be needed for nearly ten years.

A special feature of systems planning known to most canny businessmen is the strategy of hedging one's bets. Lesser men than systems planners might, fifteen years ago, have occupied themselves with the question of *which* system—radio relay or coaxial cable—was the better one, and which should therefore receive the full force of future development. In the truly long-range view, however, both seemed excellent, lacking only the perfection of special unknown devices to make either one a whole workable system. So both were pursued; both were perfected; and today both operate together—compatibly—serving the same functions within the transcontinental telephone network. In soft, level soils, where a plow can speed along easily, cable goes in cheaper; in mountainous regions, radio-relay towers perched on ridge crests are a better solution. As for the future, the best minds at Bell Labs will venture no guess as to which system will eventually win out. Right now, 11,000 route miles of radio relay are strung across the country, and 9,500 miles of coaxial cable are buried beneath its soil.

## Before Color, a Scrubbing Job

Color TV raised a whole new complex of problems. The big trick in color is to crowd much more information into no more frequency space than that allotted to black-and-white TV. Ideally, black-and-white TV is allotted a bandwidth of about four megacycles; but in actual practice, especially when coaxial cable is used, it gets somewhat less. That does not matter much, since the upper third of the bandwidth carries information which doesn't affect the picture perceptibly. Even when the upper 1.3 megacycles are chopped off, the televiewer can barely perceive any difference in picture quality.

Color TV, however, has to be sent on four full megacycles, and even so, the only place where TV engineers can squeeze in additional signals to signify hue and intensity is in the upper part of the band, just where loss and distortion are most pronounced.

For this reason, a group of systems engineers have been working out plans for new terminal equipment, repeaters, equalizers, and methods of maintenance to make the present coaxial-cable and radio-relay circuits capable of passing the color TV signal without distortion or loss. "We're doing what you might call 'scrubbing up the circuits,' " says one of the group. To date, the Bell System has "scrubbed up" circuits for color TV between New York and California; other circuits will be improved as the broadcasters need them—but plans are so far advanced that upgrading any particular circuit would take only a month or two.

## Frequency Space: A Limited Resource

Such matters are the legitimate province of systems planners; but actually the finest grist for their intellectual mill consists of far larger issues, problems that exist over periods of decades. One of the largest is the matter of a vanishing natural resource—frequency space. Every message sent over radio occupies a certain range of frequencies, and the more traffic there is, the more difficult it is to fit everything in.

By modern techniques, it is possible to send and receive radio signals covering a range from about 100,000 cycles per second (the 3,000-meter wave length) clear up to 30 billion cycles per second (the one-centimeter wave length). That seems like room enough for all, especially in view of the fact that Morse code needs only about 100 cycles, and a phone conversation needs only about 4,000 cycles. Radio, however, needs up to 15,000, and TV about four million per station. As a result, the FCC has already divided up and parceled out the entire useful range of radio frequencies. There is practically no empty space left, except at extremely high frequencies that the engineers don't yet know how to use.

If the radio waves are so crowded, perhaps the better answer for the phone company is to expand along the lines of improved coaxial cables and wires. But this is no easy answer either; the wider the band of frequencies put on wire or cable, the more amplifiers the engineers have to insert into the circuit, or the bigger they have to make the cable. That soon becomes cripplingly expensive.

In another generation, from past indications, the volume of telephone talk may easily double or triple, the number of mobile radiotelephones increase tenfold, the volume of transatlantic telephone business grow a dozenfold, and TV expand into fields only dimly foreseen. Such facts might give any systems planner pause. But having so paused and reflected, several of Gilman's men and others from A. T. & T. recently worked out plans in which it appears possible that the enormous potential load (even including theater network television) could nevertheless be shunted around the country by Bell System facilities, by modifying present cable, radio-relay, and switching systems. "We expect to be able to meet whatever load may arise," one of Gilman's assistants says, "and without lousing up the whole radio spectrum, either."

## Waves Beamed Through Pipes

One of the inventions that figure heavily in their long-range thinking about the frequency-space problem is called a "waveguide."

Above 30 billion cycles per second, there is a great area of radio frequencies that aren't used. Unfortunately these frequencies begin to act a little like light—they are stopped not just by solid objects, but by clouds, smog, or even rain. Bell inventors started over twenty years ago designing hollow pipes in which the radio impulses could travel in their own atmosphere. Confined within their waveguide—which will be only a couple of inches in diameter—these waves will neither be affected by outside radio waves, nor affect any outside receivers. In contrast to older systems, which carry several dozen to several hundred phone conversations at one time, a single waveguide pipe could easily carry many thousands. One hitch, unfortunately, is that the copper pipe must be microscopically precise, both in manufacture and in installation; also, each will require a fortune in terminal facilities to stack up and later unscramble the thousands of simultaneous messages. (Waveguides a few hundred feet long are actually in use nowadays on radio-relay towers, and cost about $12.50 per foot. No Bell System engineer will even hazard a guess as to the cost of a transcontinental waveguide.)

Other frequency-saving mechanisms are now in the experimental stage. These handle human voices and TV pictures the way the Army handled milk and eggs in the last war—powdering them, shipping them, and reconstituting them later on. How this could be done was explained in "The Information Theory," *Fortune,* December, 1953.

Another major concern of the systems planners is the customer—a cantankerous, ornery, and noncontrollable piece of the system. A small group of Gilman's men is continuously trying to analyze the ways in which customer habits affect the telephone network.

## PHONES IN A JAM

One of the things they worry about is the possibility that too many customers will choose the same moment to pick up their phones to place calls. Ordinarily the telephone system is geared to handle about one phone in twenty, at any given instant. If one phone in every ten were to be picked up at once, a serious jam could ensue. If one exchange were to be so jammed, the automatic equipment in other exchanges would hold its calls, waiting to get through, and so the jam might fan out from one exchange to another throughout parts of a city, or even a whole city.

This is no theoretical nightmare. During World War II a Washington, D.C., radio station announced free nylons to the first few callers; the resultant eruption of calls swamped one central exchange, backspread to others, and seriously snarled phone connections in the nation's capital and some adjoining points for more than two hours.

The job of the planners, of course, is to specify systems large enough, and with safeguards enough, to prevent this kind of thing in everyday use; on the other hand, for good economic reasons, they dare not overdesign the capacity of the system by any huge factor. In general, their planning is sufficiently adroit so that attacks of paralysis in the phone system have been extremely rare and short-lived.

But the big question is: what would happen if a major disaster or surprise bombing attack were to cause millions of people to make a frantic dash for the phone? The resulting snarl might temporarily immobilize all defense and rescue efforts. After considerable study, the planners suggested and the operating companies have adopted a safeguard to be used only in the gravest emergencies. In each major telephone exchange of the nation, an attendant by merely flipping several switches can temporarily cut off outgoing calls from some or all of the nonessential phones, allowing the civil defense setup, the military, the Red Cross, and other critical agencies to go about their business unhampered by fears of an overload. This emergency system has been tested in a few local situations, such as storm and flood, and has worked beautifully.

Officials of the operating telephone companies do the same kind of planning on their own, often without the assistance of Gilman's group. They have been planning the routes of new cables and radio towers so as to avoid paralysis if any one city were wiped out. For instance, all national TV programs, all overseas telephone calls, and until recently all long-distance calls in and out of New York passed through one switching center in a building on lower Sixth Avenue. One good blast over that part of the city would have cut North and South apart, and isolated us from Europe. Today a series of alternate exchanges in Newark and other points are handling about one-third of New York's long-distance business. Similar plans are being carried out in a dozen major cities.

## AN ASH CAN FULL OF PLANS

Among the sundry uncertainties with which Gilman's department has to contend, perhaps the greatest of all is the unpredictability of new discoveries and inventions. A few years ago, for example, several physicists at Murray Hill got interested in the odd properties of the metallic element germanium. When they got through investigating it, they had invented the transistor—a pea-sized object that will do most of the things vacuum tubes do, last perhaps twenty times as long, use almost no power, and take up almost no space. As a result, several hundred pounds of plans, which had been worked out with excruciating care, and which dealt with such matters as the amplifiers, modulators, varistors, and such that boost your voice in loudness $10^{1,500}$ times (i.e., 1 followed by 1,500 zeros) as it crosses the country, may soon be ready for the ash can.

The transistor did little, however, to alter the larger outlines of the biggest and finest scheme ever concocted by the prophets of the telephone company. That scheme is called FACD ("foreign-area customer dialing"), which means long-distance dialing by the customer. In the full-fledged FACD system, a subscriber will pick up the phone, dial three digits plus the local number of any other subscriber in the country, and that's all. No fuss, no operators, no waiting; all America in his own backyard.

That idea, so simple and appealing, is actually the longest-range piece of planning ever undertaken by the Bell System. It dates back to 1933, when Dr. Frank B. Jewett, then president of Bell Laboratories, invited his associates to consider the problem of long-distance automatic dialing.

The heart of the problem was the nature of central-office switching equipment. The early automatic machinery for handling dial calls consisted of banks of fast-moving rotary switches and relays called "step-by-step" equipment. This equipment is logical, but unimaginative; it has to be told everything, including not only the destination but the best route. If it were to be used for long-distance dialing, a subscriber might have to dial a number like this: 057 076 097 157 2345. Even so, the machine could not automatically take any bypaths or alternates.

The planners concluded that a completely different type of central-office equipment was needed. They told the development engineers in broad terms what they wanted to do. "Make a system," they said, in effect, "that can accept the dialed numbers from the customer; hold them in an electrical memory while it figures out the ultimate destination; look over all the routes from its own position to the destination; pick out and test the shortest or best one; if that one is busy, pick out the next shortest one or the next until it finds a free circuit; operate all the necessary switches; make sure it has the right number; and then disengage itself and get busy with someone else." As though that weren't enough, they also wanted it to be able to call a human operator when the customer dialed an impossible number, wait for him if he forgot the last couple of digits and had to look them up, pull the plug on him if he took too long about it, and in general do everything in a judicious, intelligent manner.

The machinery that was finally perfected to fit this prescription is called the "crossbar system." The first toll crossbar installation went into operation in Philadelphia ten years after the engineers started trying to make it. A more recent version of crossbar required a patent application as big and heavy as a copy of *Gone With the Wind*.

## NOTHING HAPPENS OVERNIGHT

Although FACD has been in the works for nearly a generation, it is emerging slowly because such a vast amount of expensive equipment in the U.S. was made and installed to do the local switching job before the planners had begun concocting their great plan. The cost of the change-over will run into many hundreds of millions of dollars. As a result, FACD is going to have to be born a finger at a time.

To some extent, it's born already. Formerly, anywhere from two to eight operators had to talk to each other to put through a long-distance call. Today, because of the installation of many crossbar exchanges and toll offices, 44 per cent of all long-distance calls are being dialed directly by the first operator the customer talks to. The next step will simply let the customers in those same areas (where the operators now dial long-distance calls) do the dialing themselves. This ultimate achievement is no longer just a paper dream: it went into effect in the suburban community of Englewood, New Jersey, in November, 1951.

Since that time, the 10,000 telephone customers of Englewood have been able to dial directly any one of some 13 million telephone numbers in the U.S., covering large areas of the East, Midwest, and West. They dial the ten digits and wait about fifteen seconds [2] while the incredible nationwide machine makes its thousands of split-second decisions, tests its routes, double checks its own handiwork, and then rings the other phone, anywhere up to 3,000 miles away. Another 10,000 customers just outside Detroit and 10,000 more outside Pittsburgh got FACD during 1953, and more communities will get it each year from now on. The job should be completed within fifteen or twenty years.

## WHO MAKES OUT THE BILLS?

The FACD plan solved many problems, but raised new ones. Who, for instance, would record and charge the customer for the long-distance call, if no operator were involved? The planners foresaw this need and predicted long ago that an automatic billing mechanism would have to be developed. Ten years of work in Bell Labs have since resulted in AMA (automatic message accounting). On a wide tape, AMA machinery records your phone number, the number you dialed, and the beginning and ending time of your conversation. Later other machines rerun the tape, pick out your call from all the other calls recorded on it, figure out how much to charge you, and write out a charge slip.

And how, the planners wondered, could a wholly automatic long-distance system be guarded from mechanical failure, with no operators checking on each call? (Actually, there will be even more employees than there are today, because business will be so much greater.) The solution lay in giving the crossbar machine and the big automatic toll centers the ability to recognize when something goes wrong in their intricate mechanisms. When any part of their many circuits goes wrong, certain automatic checking devices fail to get the right response to coded testing signals they continually send out. The faulty part causes the automatic testing brain to punch a mark on the appropriate part of a long ticket, which graphically portrays in terms of preprinted code symbols thousands of possible trouble conditions.

[2] In 1920 the average long-distance call was put through in fourteen minutes; in 1953 it went through in ninety seconds.

## ROBOT REPAIRMEN?

The obvious next step—and one that would surprise no one in the planning department—would be the development of servomechanisms that will analyze the printed trouble report and make simple repairs automatically, plugging in spare relays and tubes, pending the semiannual visit of the repairman.

All this sounds like plenty to work on for years to come. But in their more expansive moments around the conference table, the planners talk about even bigger things. Their FACD plans already make room for Canada and Mexico in the ten-digit dialing setup. But that's not all. "You may think worldwide dialing sounds silly," says one switching expert, "but we've thought about it a good bit, and aside from the backward state of telephone systems in some countries, it's well within the framework of our present plans."

Another remote subject of planning efforts involves a system that might, for the lack of any other name, be called "televisiphone"—the sending of TV images along with the voice signal. Bell engineers first hooked up a two-way telephone-and-television combination in 1930. The picture was miserable, and the cost would have been staggering to any customer. But it was a fascinating idea.

Today, twenty-four years later and with TV a nearly perfected art, the Bell planners are still thinking hard about televisiphone. It would put a terrific new demand for frequency bandwidth on the telephone wires and undoubtedly cost a good deal. One idea that planners have recently been considering involves sending not a moving image but a series of stills at five-second intervals; this would use up only a narrow band of frequencies and be much cheaper.

Dr. Ralph Bown, vice-president of Bell Labs, feels that the use of vision on the phone is as little appreciated today as the use of speech was when Bell invented the thing three-quarters of a century ago. "People used to ask who'd want to talk into a tin box," he says. "Today they can hardly get along without it, but they ask who needs TV with his telephone. But in today's world, sight and sound go together. Some form of vision with the phone is inevitable."

Other new devices that already exist, or should exist in the future, and for which the planners have great hopes, include an automatic telephone-answering machine to take your calls for you when you're out; a machine that understands the numbers zero to nine, and can ring a phone number upon spoken command; an electronic calculator that will design and draw plans for new pieces of technical equipment when told what that equipment has to do; and another calculator that will be able to translate from one language to another.

"However all that may be," Gilman said recently, staring at the ceiling with his hands clasped behind his head, "we can't afford to deal in idle dreams. We're simply trying to use every reasonable idea and prospective invention that may fit into the broad picture, so as to help solve the problems that will be arising in the future.

"The main thing is not to get too smug."

# 28.

# Steps in Research Planning

## By Robert K. Stolz [1]

Research planning has two distinct phases: programing and project selection. *Programing* develops specific research objectives and guidelines that make possible sound decisions on project selection. It defines the fields that should be studied and the emphasis that should be placed on the different kinds of research within each field. Within these guidelines *project selection* picks out the technical problems which bear most closely on the success of the company.

This distinction between programing and project selection is important. Too often a company plunges into the selection process without first setting up the outlines of the research program needed. This is like building a house room by room, without first developing a blueprint of the structure.

### CLEAR COMPANY GOALS

Rational research objectives rest on clearly defined business objectives. Just any statement of company objectives will not do; we are dealing here with a very special situation. To be meaningful to research, business objectives must reflect management's thinking on:

Social and economic factors affecting long-range profitability in the industry.
The competitive situation in the industry.
Activities critical to company success.
Company strengths and weaknesses.

[1] From "Planning—Key to Research Success," *Harvard Business Review,* May–June, 1957, pp. 82–88. Reprinted by permission.

The company's ambitions and resources with respect to expansion into other fields.

There are at least two broad criteria that can be applied to test the adequacy of a company's stated objectives as guides to research planning.

*Action Needed.* First, objectives must go far beyond the simple statement of broad financial goals, such as "to increase sales volume by 50 per cent in five years" or "to increase earnings per share by 10 per cent annually." These may have some general inspirational value, but they fail to spell out for research what needs to be done. To be really useful, company objectives should name the specific steps that need to be taken to meet financial goals. To illustrate:

An eastern manufacturing company stated its objective simply as "to increase net profits 10 per cent annually." But, over a five-year period, profits had increased only 1 per cent or 2 per cent per year.

This company's research and engineering department had been working mainly on improving product line A, which contributed the lion's share of sales and profits; but when management made a complete study of the company's outlook, it found that demand was gradually shifting from product line A to product line B, a subsidiary line in which company performance had been weak.

The study also brought out that product line A was so superior that it was not threatened by routine product improvement of competing products, but that it could be wiped out by major technical advances, unquestionably in the wind, that would permit use of much cheaper materials.

The company set new objectives, including:

To broaden product line B to meet market requirements.

To capitalize on the company's quality reputation in product line A by building quality into product line B.

To protect position in product line A by keeping in the forefront of major technical advances.

To maximize profitability in product line A through streamlining product coverage as competitive conditions permit.

With the help of such objectives as these, research revamped its entire program, cutting improvement work on product line A to one-third of its former size, but at the same time making provisions to keep abreast of developments of new materials that might affect the line. The main emphasis of the research program shifted to the development and improvement of products in the B line. Although the total size of the new program was only about 80 per cent of the previous one in terms of cost, it was far more effective in terms of profits and sales potential.

*Expansion Policy.* The second criterion for company objectives is that objectives must clearly define management's intentions on expansion into new fields. Without such a statement research personnel may feel that they have carte blanche to explore where they see fit. Further, management's stated intentions must be based on realistic evaluation of the company's financial and personnel resources, or the door will be thrown open to unproductive research, and research personnel will become frustrated. Thus:

One president encouraged his research people to spend up to 25 per cent of their budget on exploratory work, no matter where it might lead. "We want to capitalize on anything you fellows can come up with," he would say. "We are broadminded. We'll try our hand at anything."

Over a period of time the research group came up with a number of interesting leads, each of which would have brought the company into businesses quite unrelated to its own. Each development was taken up with the president who, after what seemed like an interminable delay, decided that the company was not in a position to pursue it further. The result: the research group saw that effective exploratory work was not going to be used, it lost confidence in management, and finally abandoned its exploratory efforts.

Before a company encourages its research group to spend substantial work on investigations that are likely to lead into new fields, it should answer such questions as:

Are there sound reasons for moving into new fields? Are markets for present products stabilizing, declining, or becoming less profitable?

Which fields of business are most closely related to our own? What is their rate of growth? How do their long-range profit outlooks compare to our own and to each other?

Who are the present and probable future competitors in the most attractive related fields? What are their strengths and weaknesses? Are there needs in these fields that are not now being met by available products?

What are the capital requirements for getting established in a new field? What are the requirements for success in the most attractive related fields? Do we have a sufficient number of the kind of people required to manage a successful business in these fields?

Would it be more practical to enter these fields through acquisition or by developing our own products?

The company that thinks through the answers to such questions is not likely to lead its research group astray with high-sounding objectives that cannot really be pursued.

## TRANSLATION OF TARGETS

The second major requirement of sound planning is that research managers have the business sense to translate business objectives into laboratory objectives. This calls for good judgment and the willingness of research managers to satisfy over-all company needs and not be swayed by the demands of individual groups. The following example illustrates how one research director translated his company's business objectives into research objectives:

First, the research director accepted the budget indicated by the percent-of-sales guide long used by the company. (He did not like it, but was "stuck" with it.) In determining how this budget should be allocated to meet competing research needs, he had to decide how to break the total sum down between research on present fields of business and research for products to lead the company into new fields. He began by analyzing the company's total situation and its objectives.

For a number of years, company management had wanted to expand into at least two related fields. This expansion, however, would have taken well over half the total research budget; and company objectives showed clearly that the company's future depended primarily on its performance in its present fields, in which the technological pace was so rapid that to maintain or improve company position required considerable research effort. The director therefore allocated research effort between present and new fields on a 65–35 basis.

Such a budget clearly allowed too little to support research in both outside fields of interest to the company. Therefore, he insisted that management select one outside field as the initial area of exploration, postponing work in the other for some years to come.

His second major programing step was to divide the funds for work on present fields among the company's three product lines. Company objectives established the relative long-range profitability of each line. Thus, using profit potential and rate of technical advance as his criteria, he split the 65 per cent portion of the budget into three units of 30 per cent, 20 per cent, and 15 per cent each.

He then decided how much should be spent on product improvement and new product work for each product line. For example, in the product line receiving 30 per cent of budget, a number of factors argued strongly for new product work: growing lack of consumer brand loyalty, many new products introduced by competitors, and consumer indifference to the usual product improvement. Thus, the research effort in this field was broken down between new product and product improvement work on a 24–6 basis. After similar analyses he was able to make the same kind of breakdown for the other two product lines.

Exhibit IX shows the total program.

One observation needs to be made here. The change in the research program that results from an approach such as the foregoing is likely to be substantial. Consequently, the research director should take the position that the program has to stand the test of time, particularly in areas where it contrasts sharply with the old program. In actual practice the program will, of course, probably require some

EXHIBIT IX.   Director's Final Breakdown of Research Budget

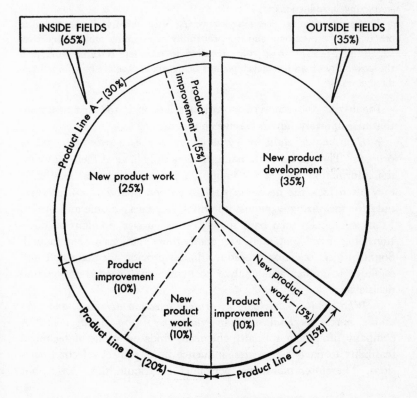

modification to adjust to the specific opportunities that present themselves in the project selection process.

## PROJECT SELECTION

Definite *procedures* need to be set up to ensure that adequate consideration is given to all factors that should enter into a project selection decision. In making the ground rules, four questions are of special importance.

1. *What criteria should be used for selecting projects and setting project priorities?* Criteria will vary from company to company, as will the emphasis placed on an individual criterion. But, in general, two different classes of criteria should be set up:

*To measure economic potential*—weighing such factors as sales and profit potentials, return on investment, intensity of competition, and costs of marketing introductions.

*To assess technical feasibility*—covering such factors as the technical obstacles to be overcome and the probability of attaining project objectives successfully, research costs, time required to complete research work, and the possibility of project developments being made obsolete by competitors' discoveries.

Identifying the criteria for project selection is the first assurance that all important factors receive consideration.

2. *How should data be gathered on the economic potential of projects?* Though research managers generally have at their fingertips the information needed for judging a project's technical feasibility, they often lack the necessary staff to gather, analyze, and interpret data for measuring economic potential, i.e., sales volume and profits. Many companies then have to rely on executives' opinions on questions of economic potential. Frequently these opinions are not factual. Sound project selection procedure should provide adequate staff and facilities to gather and analyze economic data needed for factual decisions.

3. *Who should participate in project selection decisions, and who should make the final selection—research or top management?* A company producing specialty chemicals finds questions of technical feasibility to have the greatest influence in its project selection decisions. Therefore, marketing personnel contribute their ideas, but

research managers have final responsibility for project selection. The same would hold true of numerous other firms.

In general, however, it can be said that "commercial" management's voice in project selection decisions is growing stronger, particularly in industries in which the technological race is tensest and the assessment of market needs is most important. For example, in the case of a company in the packaged food field, top management and marketing personnel actively participate with research management in project selection decisions, with top management making the final selection.

4. *How should projects be reviewed?* The review and re-evaluation of projects in process is an integral part of the selection procedure. It is reselection; it reaffirms or rejects the original decision to work on the project, after a study of up-to-date information on market potential and an assessment of the technical obstacles that have arisen since the project got under way.

## MAKING CONNECTIONS

It is evident that sound research planning requires effective liaison between research managers and other members of the management team. Lack of effective liaison between research and marketing personnel has already been mentioned as a common obstacle to planning. One marketing executive, for instance, complained:

The last time research held a project selection meeting, they called me in at the last minute. Then they shoved this list of projects under my nose and asked if I approved. I saw it was the same old stuff they've been working on for years and never get finished. But then I saw my boss sitting there, and I said to myself, "Has he approved this? Do I make a monkey out of myself if I say no?" I didn't know which way to jump. Research pulls the same stunt every year. When are they going to start working on the things we really need?

To ensure that effective liaison exists between research and the functions it serves, a number of companies have established research planning committees. For example, a famous food company recently set up a research planning committee consisting of the president, the executive vice-president, and the vice-presidents for research, marketing, and production. It also set up several subcommittees consisting of research, marketing, and production personnel to evaluate specific proposed projects.

Other companies have set up similar programs to integrate research and development effort with the needs of the business as a whole. For example:

A successful ethical drug company achieves effective coordination through a development-liaison committee. Attended by the president, executive vice-president, and key marketing, production, and research and development executives, it meets weekly for a full half day. Although not a decision-making body, it brings together all the basic data, points of view, and judgments necessary to guide the executives responsible for selecting and re-evaluating research projects. It also enables marketing and production executives to anticipate the problems they will face in the manufacture, promotion, and sale of new products.

Of course, the mere establishment of committees is no assurance that the resulting research effort will be soundly programed. But it is a step in the right direction; committees serve to tear down the "iron curtains" that have surrounded the research effort in many companies, and establish a basis for effective liaison.

## CONCLUSION

To summarize, sound planning of research is not easily achieved. Top management frequently fails to define clearly the business objectives that are needed to guide research. Or it sets broad financial targets that company personnel consider to be largely inspirational and rarely attainable.

With no specific objectives, research planning is frequently pulled and hauled among different groups, each pressuring for attention to its own short-term needs. Research planning becomes a matter of negotiation, rather than an orderly process of evaluating needs and capabilities.

The liaison between research and the other major divisions of the company essential to sound planning is also hard to achieve. The traditional management attitude persists: research should be put in a corner and left to its own devices with the hope that "the boys will come up with something worth while."

The company that strives for sound planning of research will not, therefore, find the going easy. But the rewards will be worth the effort. An intelligent definition of top management's objectives and their means of achievement can have a salutary effect on the business as a whole as well as on research. Especially when business objectives are translated into realistic research targets, the payoff can be even greater than it would be if management went out and hired more expert scientists and engineers to staff the laboratory—assuming, of course, they could be found!

A final word about the organization of research management: many companies today need to make special provisions to assure that research planning gets the time and attention it needs. Often this means that the research director should have an assistant in charge of research planning. There may also be a need for a special assistant to the president to direct company planning as a whole and coordinate it with the planning of research.

Lastly, today's research director should be a much broader-gauge executive than we have visualized heretofore. We have long recognized that his difficult job requires both managerial and technical skills. Now we see that he must first be a businessman. Along with the president, he must be able to see the needs of the business as a whole. And he must be a person of the stature necessary to be admitted to the inner councils of top management. These are the essential requirements of his rigorous task.

# 29.

# *Timing of New Product Introduction*

## By Harry L. Hansen [1]

A difficult problem in timing . . . is whether or not a company should be the first one to offer a new type of product on the market. What are the advantages and disadvantages of being the first or being the follower?

Undoubtedly a great deal depends upon the nature of the product, its uniqueness, and the question of whether or not the company has any long-run advantage, as for example through the control of patents. In thinking about a problem like this, take for example the question of frozen orange juice. Supposing Minute Maid Corporation, a newly formed company and one of the first (as Florida Foods, Inc.) on the market with frozen juices, was attempting today to break into the field. In all likelihood the company would have a difficult time competing against today's well-established sellers, such as General Foods, Inc., and Libby, McNeill, and Libby. In contrast the California Fruit Growers Exchange, which came late into the frozen orange juice field, encountered only normal difficulty in getting retail stores to handle its frozen orange juice, because its brand, Sunkist, was well known on fresh oranges.

Take another illustration. Suppose the executives of a large paper company, such as West Virginia Pulp & Paper Company, well established in selling printing and industrial papers, might think that it would be desirable for the company to enter the consumer facial

[1] From Harry L. Hansen, *Marketing: Text, Cases, and Readings* (Homewood, Illinois, Richard D. Irwin, Inc., 1956), pp. 115–19. Reprinted by permission.

tissue field. Here we have a field dominated by several strong brands of which one of the strongest is Kleenex, made by the International Cellucotton Products Company. In some markets Kleenex is very substantially ahead of all other brands in consumer acceptance, probably outselling all others combined. In such a situation, West Virginia, despite its large size, would have an extremely difficult time in offsetting consumer preference for Kleenex.

Take as another example the marketing of electric blankets. General Electric was the first seller in this field, entering it in an attempt to try to expand the sale of its electric wiring. What difference does it make to a company like the Chatham Manufacturing Company, a blanket manufacturer, if Chatham enters the field later? Can General Electric establish so strong a brand preference that it would be difficult for Chatham to break into the market? Probably not, since presumably market acceptance of this product would be so slow that a seller entering the market late could expect consumers to shop and compare electric blankets.

Take, for example, a record which, it is claimed, will induce sleep through hypnotic suggestion. Does it make any difference here whether or not the seller is the first one to make available such a record, or is this fact immaterial?

Large sellers may be able to afford to delay in introducing new products. An illustration of this is Dictaphone's entrance into the field of electronic dictating machines. For several years this company, with an older type of dictating machine, lagged behind the smaller companies in their development of such machines; but when it finally developed a machine, it had overcome certain of the disadvantages or difficulties that were evident in earlier competitive makes. With its well-known name it had little difficulty in regaining its market position. Another illustration might be taken from the field of the electric razor. The first electric razors to be popularized were sold by Schick; but when a large company, Remington Rand, followed, it rapidly assumed a position of leadership. These illustrations suggest that the small seller does not have an easy time merely because it is first in the field. Typically it escapes only temporarily the job of combating large competitors, and it has the difficult job of developing demand by itself. Some small companies will attempt therefore "to ride on the coattails" of larger sellers. For instance, many small frozen food packers have capitalized on the acceptance for frozen foods created by the pioneer frozen food seller, Birds Eye Division of General Foods, Inc.

Since new products are often a gamble, a company can lessen its risk by avoiding radically new products or by following the moves of competitors and letting these sellers make the mistakes of market appraisal. A frequently quoted example of the risk in the introduction of new products that require buyers to think in radically different ways was Chrysler's move in the 1930's in introducing a streamlined line of cars. The design turned out to be too radical for consumers to accept. On the other hand, it is sometimes a greater risk not to be the first company in the field with a new product. For example the financial rewards were high for those who pioneered chlorophyll toothpaste and antihistamine cold remedies, even though the continuing markets for these products turned out to be far smaller than originally they were heralded to be.

Thus it is difficult to generalize whether the risk is greater to be first or later in the field. To find the answer one must estimate total market size (a difficult job for a new product), and predict the speed at which buyers will accept the product (no less difficult a job).

One general observation can be made even though there will be exceptions to it, namely, that generally buyers, both consumer and industrial, are generally slower to accept new products or services than the seller expects, even though in the seller's eyes these new ideas are obviously desirable. This buyer hesitation or skepticism is often minimized by the seller in his enthusiastic belief in his product or service. Naturally, there are all degrees of buyer skepticism. Buyer reaction to an electric rattrap is likely to be more cautious than toward more conventional rodent killers. Paper bathing suits for women are viewed with some misgivings, whereas a new synthetic fiber woven into men's suits may cause only momentary doubts.

The seller therefore often has the difficult appraisal to make: How far ahead of buyer product experience can he afford to get? A minor product improvement, like a wrap-around windshield, may be accepted by buyers quickly; a major change or an entirely new product, like a garbage-disposal unit, may require years of selling effort before it is widely accepted.

## New Product Growth Curves

How long should it take to establish a product on the market? The answer depends upon the strength of the underlying demand for the product, the financial resources of the seller, and the skill which he brings to bear upon the problem. Despite the probable overriding control of the individual case situation, there always is an interest in the possibility of approximating a normal new product growth curve. There is not much known about such curves. This general lack of information is probably traceable to a series of considerations. Basically, sellers usually regard individual product sales figures as confidential. If the product has been evaluated as unsuccessful, the seller does not normally want to reveal data that may properly or improperly be taken to be a reflection on his business judgment and performance. Apart from these considerations, many sellers look upon the study of past experience as of only limited value for future experience in a world where there have been so many dynamic changes in the last quarter century. World depressions, wars, booms, strikes, and major technological bursts tend to discourage reliance on statistical curves. Despite these difficulties the basic idea in theory is an intriguing one.

Butler, moreover, writing in 1946 on this subject, indicated that in his company, a cotton textile manufacturing company, normal growth patterns could be defined. The technique was relatively simple. In order to compare products selling in different volumes and with different potentials, sales were converted to "per cent of objective" calculated by years. The objective might be set at three, five, or ten years depending upon the situation. When the data were plotted on a grid with the per cent of objective on the vertical scale and years on the horizontal scale, a normal growth pattern was observed. Actual per cent of objective for new products was then compared with the normal curve. If a product appeared to be growing more slowly or rapidly than normal, study was then made to determine the reasons. Experience indicated that there were different normal growth patterns depending upon the merchandising effort used. Exhibit X illustrates the technique employed by Butler. In order to smooth the actual growth curve, he has used a three-year moving average.[2]

[2] Ralph Butler, "Growth Pattern for New Specialty Products: A Case Study," *Journal of Marketing*, July, 1946, p. 27.

EXHIBIT X

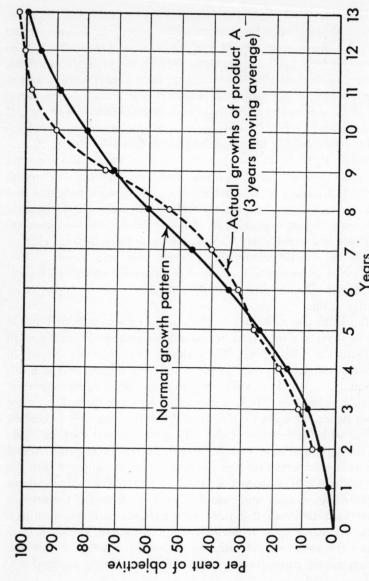

Source: Ralph Butler, "Growth Patterns for New Specialty Products: A Case Study," *Journal of Marketing*, July 1946, p. 29.

# 30.

# *The Strategy of Market Introduction for Industrial Products*

## By E. Raymond Corey [1]

In planning the introductory marketing program, it may be difficult to anticipate the reactions which various market groups may have toward the appearance of the new product in the market and hence to determine where to concentrate sales effort. In addition, the appearance of the new product in the market may generate unanticipated forces of resistance which obstruct the creation of initial demand and delay the integration of the new product into established channels of manufacture and distribution. Such complexities were present in the history of Alcoa's development of a market for aluminum sleeve bearings.

In 1936 the Aluminum Company of America had initiated laboratory work on the development of an alloy suitable for use in aluminum sleeve bearings. This work was undertaken after Alcoa personnel had learned that both the British and the Germans were successfully using such bearings in aircraft engines. Within a year Alcoa laboratory technicians had developed Alcoa alloy 750 as the material most suited for use in bearings. This alloy contained $6\frac{1}{2}$ per cent tin, 1 per cent copper, 1 per cent nickel, and $91\frac{1}{2}$ per cent commercially pure aluminum by weight.

[1] From E. Raymond Corey, *The Development of Markets for New Materials* (Boston, Harvard Business School Division of Research, 1956), pp. 82–98. Reprinted by permission.

Experimental bearings made of alloy 750 were made available in 1937 to a large diesel engine builder to be installed for testing on a few diesel engines. Alcoa's management believed that the testing should be restricted because of the functional importance of engine bearings and because of the damage that faulty bearings could do to large engines. Sufficient test data, it was believed, would take two to six years to accumulate.

The shortages of tin during World War II precluded the possibility of further development work, although the diesel engine builder's test installations were still operating. By 1944, however, when limited amounts of tin again became available, the performance characteristics of aluminum bearings had been thoroughly studied, and test data had proved the suitability of aluminum in this application. In 1945, therefore, the diesel engine builder ordered solid aluminum bearings from a bearing manufacturer for all its diesel engines.

The logical market for aluminum bearings, the Alcoa management had concluded, was the large diesel field, all diesel engines over truck-size diesels. There were approximately ten large manufacturers of diesels for large tractors, locomotives, and power plants. The reason for ruling out smaller type diesel and gasoline engines was that their design called for a thin-walled bearing, and aluminum had to be used in a bearing that had a ratio of wall thickness to diameter that was greater than could be accommodated in smaller engines. It was possible, however, that either through further alloying development or through changes in engine design, a solid aluminum bearing might at some future date be developed for small diesels as well as automotive engines.

In large diesels, however, pronounced advantages were claimed for aluminum. Solid aluminum bearings resisted corrosion by chemicals much better than conventional bearing materials. Corrosion was a matter of increasing concern with the greater usage of engine lubricating oil additives. Second, aluminum dissipated heat rapidly so that when any possible high spots on the inside bearing surface and on the shaft rubbed against each other, the frictional heat was dispersed before the two metals could expand and the bearing freeze on the shaft. Third, solid aluminum bearings, it was claimed, would outwear other bearings many times over, and there had been no instances in any tests of "fatigue failure." [2] The chances of fatigue failure occurring had increased as engines were designed for greater power output. A fourth, and particularly important, advantage claimed for aluminum was that in case of failure for such reasons as inadequate oil supply or insufficient clearance between the bearing and the crankshaft, the bearing would not damage the shaft. In large diesel engines, an engine shaft might cost as much as $4,500 to replace.

Aluminum bearings, furthermore, would cost less to make than the types of bearings they were designed to replace. An aluminum bearing was made from a cylindrical casting, machined on an automatic lathe, and finished to close tolerances in a boring machine.

Two processes, each requiring more skill and more tooling than the above process, were used in making conventional bearings. In the one process, flat sheet steel (to serve as the backing or outside surface of the bearing) was bonded to a thinner sheet of inside bearing surface material, such as babbitt metal. Pieces of the bonded metal were sheared off, and these flat blanks were formed into bearing halves in a punch press. The inside dimensions of each half were machined to close tolerances, and then the entire piece was plated with an alloy of copper, lead, and tin.

A second process for making bearings used seamless steel tubing. molten copper and lead alloy, machining this inside surface, and then Such a bearing was made by coating the inside of the tubing with a coating all bearing surfaces. The application of the inside bearing surface material required a great deal of skill. Consequently, this type of bearing was the most expensive to make.

Although no adequate estimate of the cost of making an aluminum bearing was available in 1944, one aluminum bearing manufacturer subsequently reported that his cost for making such bearings was 25 per cent to 50 per cent less than what he would have to pay to purchase a babbitt metal steel-backed bearing and between 35 per cent and 60 per cent less than the price of a copper-lead bearing.

## Initial Market Development

Satisfied, then, on the basis of both its own laboratory tests and the

---

[2] Fatigue failure was a fracturing of the inside bearing surface which spreads, causing pieces of the inside bearing surface to break off.

early diesel engine builder's experience that alloy 750 aluminum bearings was a sound application, the Alcoa management made plans in 1945 to market bearing castings. The decision to market castings rather than alloyed metal in ingot form was based primarily on the desirability of doing as much as possible to maintain bearing quality. Alloy 750 required special foundry techniques, and it was likely that even if Alcoa was not to make castings, most cases of bearing failure would reflect ultimately on the company. In addition, foundries that might make such castings would almost invariably have no technical service facilities to help customers with application problems, so that this function would be likely to fall on Alcoa's staff. Another reason for the decision to make castings was the hope that as volume of business increased, prices could be reduced. This possibility was all the stronger if all casting was done by one organization rather than scattered among a number of foundries. Finally, by making bearing castings rather than supplying ingot to foundries for this purpose, Alcoa would realize a higher dollar volume of sales and accordingly would increase its opportunities for profit.

In 1945 Alcoa undertook a national advertising campaign on aluminum bearings. The advertisements were designed to generate customer inquiries. These requests for further information were answered with letters listing the largest bearing manufacturers in alphabetical order and suggesting to the sender that an order for a trial set of bearings be placed with one of these companies or with his present supplier. Alcoa Development Division personnel also called on large diesel engine builders and, after creating some interest, suggested that these companies contact their normal bearing suppliers. When Alcoa could learn who the bearing supplier was, a salesman was detailed to call on this supplier and advise him of his customer's interest in aluminum. Bearing manufacturers indicated a great interest in the new development and asked about the introductory work that was being done with bearing purchasers. Shortly thereafter it was learned that salesmen for some bearing manufacturers were following up Alcoa calls and were frequently recommending their own bearings rather than aluminum bearings.

In the meantime, many smaller bearing manufacturers indicated a great deal of interest in aluminum bearings. Alcoa representatives tried to work with these concerns, but it soon became evident that their customers did not include the manufacturers of large diesel engines.

Alcoa then shifted the direction of its promotional work. On calls to bearing users, Alcoa offered to make a test set of bearings in its laboratory machine shop for trial purposes. When the bearings had been tested, Alcoa designers made up sets of blueprints which the engine builder could use to order bearings from his normal supplier. Instances in which this approach was successful included those cases where the user made his own bearings and did not buy from a bearing manufacturer. Three diesel engine manufacturers had made their own babbitt metal bearings and were well equipped to take on aluminum. A fourth diesel engine builder had machine capacity which he could use for this purpose, and when he became convinced of the desirability of using aluminum he decided to make his own bearings. These four companies then used aluminum bearings exclusively.

This last company of the four had previously been the customer of Tyler Bearing Corporation,[3] a large supplier of bearings for diesels. When the decision to convert to aluminum was made, therefore, orders placed by this company with Tyler had been canceled. In the meantime (early 1946) Sawyer Diesel,[4] another Tyler customer, had given Alcoa an order for a test set of alloy 750 bearings. Tyler's president therefore requested the Alcoa management to let him take over the order for this test set. Alcoa readily consented to this arrangement.

In the next year, Tyler submitted many sketches of different types of bearings to Alcoa and requested bearing prices on each. In the meantime, Sawyer Diesel did not receive the set of aluminum bearings it had ordered. In early 1947 a letter was received from Tyler saying that the company had had great difficulty in taking test measurements on some aluminum bearings it had tried to make, and its readings were completely inconsistent with each other.

An Alcoa representative working with the Tyler plant manager, however, straightened out the machining difficulties. Sometime thereafter, Tyler informed Alcoa that the company still found aluminum

[3] Fictitious name.
[4] Fictitious name.

impossible to machine accurately. This concluded any activity on the part of Tyler with aluminum bearings as far as Alcoa was concerned.

With these delays, interest at Sawyer Diesel, Inc., in aluminum bearings had waned considerably. Alcoa representatives in their contacts with the Sawyer Purchasing Department were not able at that time to revive interest in solid aluminum bearings.

Several years later, however, it developed that some users of Sawyer diesels were having bearing trouble. The problems had arisen in part from the fact that Sawyer was designing new engines with increased power output, and that standard bearings could not always stand up under the greater loads.

In the late summer of 1952 the Alcoa Development Division received word from one Sawyer customer that the company was purchasing a new diesel engine and would like to have a set of aluminum bearings installed. The bearings were machined in the Alcoa laboratory shop and then installed at a cost of approximately $1,000. Shortly thereafter another bearing company reported a bearing failure on a Sawyer diesel. The faulty bearing had badly scored a $4,500 crankshaft, and this engine user, too, wanted to get a set of aluminum bearings from Alcoa. Subsequently, operating people from two other companies using diesel engines made similar inquiries at Alcoa after learning of these instances in which aluminum bearings had been successfully installed.

Another attempt to get aluminum bearings adopted at Sawyer seemed timely, therefore, and a meeting was then arranged with Sawyer executives. In this meeting the company's general manager stated that Sawyer was not using aluminum bearings because the engineers had not recommended it. The chief production engineer then said that there was a belief that aluminum bearings would damage a crankshaft in the event of seizure.

The Alcoa representatives indicated that this was a misconception, and that laboratory tests would prove the opposite to be true. It was then arranged to run such tests, and it was agreed that if the results were satisfactory, Sawyer would order trial sets of aluminum bearings for further testing. Accordingly, bearings were placed on a crankshaft set up for test purposes in the Sawyer shop, and the oil supply was cut off. The bearings seized but in failing did not damage the shaft.

In a short time, Alcoa received an order from Sawyer's purchasing department for ten sets of aluminum bearings to be tested in actual use. This order was subsequently canceled because of some differences of opinion among Sawyer executives with regard to the test program. At a later meeting between Alcoa and Sawyer representatives, however, the order was reinstated.

In the meantime, Alcoa had learned of numerous other companies which were interested in solid aluminum bearings. The Alcoa Development Division management believed, therefore, that such an important testing program ought to be broadened in scope to include more concerns than those Sawyer had planned to select. This matter was taken up with the Sawyer management, and it was agreed then that an Alcoa representative should visit various additional companies using diesel engines. It was also agreed that Sawyer would give Alcoa a list of the power companies at which it planned to install trial bearings, and in all cases both Alcoa and Sawyer engineers would be on hand to watch the installation of trial sets.

The first company which an Alcoa representative visited was interested in the possibility of testing a set of aluminum bearings but did not want to take action until the district sales manager for Sawyer could be consulted. The Alcoa representative then called on the Sawyer district manager, who expressed a desire to cooperate as fully as possible in this program. At his suggestion a Sawyer salesman was assigned to make calls with the Alcoa representative on Sawyer customers. This salesman, however, sometimes told customers on these calls that Sawyer was recommending one of its regular bearings; that solid aluminum bearings were being tested, and if they proved to be satisfactory Sawyer would so inform its customers. In another of Sawyer's sales areas, the Alcoa representative was asked not to visit Sawyer customers since one set of aluminum bearings had already been allotted to this area for trial purposes, a fact of which Alcoa had not been apprised.

As time went on, interest in aluminum bearings seemed to be increasing as certain diesel engine users, having encountered difficulties in some instances with conventional bearings, successfully replaced them with aluminum bearings. Nevertheless, certain diesel engine builders exhibited a great reluctance to add aluminum bearings to their present lines.

In spite of these difficulties, Alcoa's sales of aluminum bearing castings had been rising steadily since 1947. Annual sales as of 1954, however, were only a small fraction of the annual sales potential this application was estimated to hold for aluminum. The great bulk of sales was being made to diesel engine builders who made their own bearings. One large bearing manufacturer was accounting for some of the volume because he had had firm specifications calling for aluminum bearings from one of his customers. Under these circumstances, the Alcoa management was considering four alternative courses of action: (1) continue the present work with engine builders and other bearing users; (2) try to persuade as many engine builders and other bearing users as possible to undertake the manufacture of their own bearings; (3) build a machine shop that could handle production orders for finished bearings; (4) acquire an interest in an established bearing manufacturing firm.

The history of Alcoa's efforts to build the market for aluminum bearings illustrates the difficulty of appraising at the outset all the factors and conditions which may affect the success of a marketing program. While Alcoa originally planned to function as a supplier of bearing castings, lack of success with this approach required the company to try other approaches, sometimes singly and sometimes in combination, over a period of time from 1945 to 1954. As in this case, inability to predict market reception of the product may leave a company no other alternative than to try a variety of approaches until one is successful.

The philosophy has been expressed that when a new application is basically a good one, the product will eventually find its place in the market. That aluminum bearings represented a "good application" is supported by the facts that several diesel engine manufacturers have been using aluminum bearings for large diesels, that aluminum bearings have been successfully installed in numerous instances where conventional bearings failed, and that sales of bearing castings have continued to grow after the war until the present time. Nevertheless, with benefit of hindsight, it may be pertinent to speculate as to why Alcoa's introductory marketing program did not succeed, quickly and easily, in creating as great a measure of demand for aluminum bearings as Alcoa's management had hoped might be developed.

In this instance, four market groups may be identified as having a potential interest in aluminum bearings. These groups are large bearing manufacturers, small bearing manufacturing concerns, diesel engine builders, and diesel engine users. In commenting further on Alcoa's experience in this case it may be useful to consider each of these groups in turn—its reactions to the idea of aluminum bearings and possible reasons for these reactions.[5]

## RESISTANCE OF THE BEARING MANUFACTURERS

Alcoa's introductory marketing program for solid aluminum bearings had encountered resistance from bearing manufacturers shortly after its inception. Through its advertising program, Alcoa had generated inquiries from engine builders, which were referred to large bearing manufacturers for action. Certain bearing manufacturers had then responded to Alcoa's efforts by attempting to divert the expressed interest in aluminum bearings to an interest in the types of bearings which they regularly made and sold.

While this response may have seemed to be aimed at undermining the Alcoa program, it may more usefully be interpreted as an effort on the part of bearing manufacturers to pursue a program in accord with their own interests. Large bearing manufacturers would probably have no strong incentives to promote the use of aluminum. Any sales volume that could be built up in the new line might simply replace sales of the other types of bearings they regularly sold. In addition, since the manufacturing process for aluminum bearings differed from processes by which conventional types were made, any shift in emphasis away from conventional types to aluminum bearings might require important changes in the production program.

In addition, the introduction of an aluminum bearing more simple to make than other bearing types possibly presented somewhat of a challenge to an important element in the bearing manufacturer's competitive strength, his technical know-how, and his production skills. The fact that it required less machinery and less processing skill to make aluminum bearings from castings than to make conventional bearings created the possibility that bearing customers might adopt

[5] The analysis which follows is an effort to interpret, from the point of view of the materials producer, the significance of the reported facts. This interpretation is the author's own analysis, based on the information provided by one company. It was not practical, within the scope of this study, to obtain facts and opinions from all groups and companies concerned in this case history.

aluminum bearings and then choose to make their own instead of purchasing them from bearing suppliers. One engine builder's decision to make his own aluminum bearings from Alcoa castings might easily have sufficed to turn disinterest in the new product on the part of bearing suppliers into active resistance to it.

It is likely, too, that the bearing manufacturer would not be completely in favor of a market approach by Alcoa which involved the latter in the bearing manufacturer's relations with his customers. It would probably be a matter of some concern to him that, if an improved product was available, he should be the one to introduce it to his customer. The bearing manufacturer's technical reputation is likely to be based in part on his ability to keep abreast of new product developments and, when these developments have been evaluated, to make them available to his customer. It is logical therefore that when the initial introduction of the new product does not come through the framework of this supplier-customer relationship, the first reaction on the part of the supplier might be to discredit it.

Another reason for resistance on the part of large bearing manufacturers might possibly have been some uncertainty with regard to the future role of the aluminum producing companies in the bearing market. The development of demand for aluminum bearings might possibly attract the aluminum companies to compete for a share of the market for bearings, particularly if a satisfactory aluminum bearing should be developed for use in automotive engines.

The growth of active resistance to a new product on the part of established manufacturers, once started, may tend to be self-perpetuating and may be difficult to overcome. Once the established manufacturer has taken the position with his customers that he does not recommend a new product, it may be psychologically difficult for him to reverse his stand.

## Market Position of the Small Bearing Manufacturer

Failing at the outset to enlist the active support of large bearing manufacturers, Alcoa had the possible alternative of approaching market development through the smaller concerns. Smaller bearing manufacturers might have utilized the new product to increase their market shares and hence would have reason to work aggressively on establishing aluminum bearings in the market. This approach has been successful in other cases. Why might it not have been effective in this instance?

Alcoa's experience indicated that small bearing manufacturers did not typically sell to large diesel engine builders. There were also indications that relationships between the large bearing manufacturers and their customers were exceptionally strong, and hence that it might be difficult for outside suppliers to sell to these customers. In many instances diesel engine builders probably relied greatly on the technical assistance of bearing manufacturers both to design their bearings and to recommend specific types for their use. Furthermore, the supplier-customer relationship in many instances was probably one of long duration and may have been one around which strong personal ties had developed.

Unless there were compelling reasons for making changes, the engine builder could be expected to rely, then, on his regular bearing suppliers for bearings and for technical service and technical advice. As long as a diesel engine, and the bearings in it, performed satisfactorily for the user, there would be no impetus for change even though aluminum bearings had superior performance characteristics. Under these circumstances smaller bearing manufacturing concerns may have found the development job a somewhat difficult undertaking.

## REACTIONS OF DIESEL ENGINE BUILDERS

When Alcoa first began to offer to supply trial sets of finished bearings to diesel engine builders, the company enjoyed some initial successes with four engine building concerns which were interested in making their own bearings rather than purchasing them from established bearing manufacturers. The comparative simplicity of finish-machining aluminum bearings was a consideration strongly favoring their adoption. In these cases, evidently, the only finished bearings which Alcoa sold were trial sets, and thereafter it supplied bearing castings to this group of engine builders.

Efforts to interest some other diesel engine makers in converting to the use of aluminum bearings were notably unsuccessful. It seemed difficult for Alcoa salesmen to interest these concerns in taking bearings for trial use. When engine builders could be persuaded to conduct either field tests or shop tests, these trials were sometimes carried out under something short of favorable conditions. Why was it that, with the exception of those firms interested in making their own bearings, diesel engine builders as a group did not exhibit greater interest in adopting aluminum bearings?

To understand the engine builder's position, it might be useful first to define the product as it relates to *his* selling program. Understandably, the type of bearing in a diesel engine might not be an important sales point for the engine builder to stress in sales to customers, since it would normally be assumed by his customer that the engine builder would use bearings which, with proper care, would last the life of the engine. Cost of the bearing would probably have a relatively insignificant effect on the cost of the engine itself and consequently would not be translated into a lower price to the engine user.

Type of bearing used in an engine may become important only when users experience particular difficulties with this engine part. Under such circumstances, the bearing would then achieve an importance that goes beyond the part itself. Bearing failure might do damage to an engine that would be considerably more costly than the bearing. Additionally, excessive difficulties encountered with this one part can reflect unfavorably in the user's mind on the over-all quality and design of the engine.

Hence, it might be said that bearings may be important in somewhat of a *negative* sense to the engine builder. The *positive* appeal of the product for *some* engine builders was the fact that it was relatively simple to machine finished bearings from castings. Hence, engine builders for whom this consideration was important would have a strong reason, in addition to the advantages of the product itself, for adopting aluminum bearings.

For other diesel engine manufacturers, there might be a natural reluctance to make a change. In the absence of particular problems with conventional bearing types, engine builders have no compelling incentive to adopt aluminum bearings. If, on the other hand, customer difficulties with bearings bring up the question of whether a new type of bearing might be used, engine builders might tend to rely for technical advice on bearing suppliers—both because of the highly technical nature of the part and because of the close relationships that may have developed between engine builder and bearing supplier. It might be unlikely under the circumstances that bearing manufacturers would recommend the use of aluminum bearings.

In addition, engine builders might be inclined, of their own accord, to develop some resistance to aluminum bearings when this product appears in the market as a remedy for the difficulties customers have experienced with engines they have made. The failure of one engine builder to develop strong enthusiasm for a field testing program which involved his customers and to work harmoniously with the Alcoa representative in this undertaking may easily have been due to a sensitiveness about such difficulties.

## INCENTIVES OF ENGINE USERS

Engine users seemed to exhibit real interest in adopting aluminum bearings. With the development of diesel engines with high power output and with the increased use of engine lubricating oil additives, engine users began to encounter difficulties with the use of conventional bearings. Their interest in aluminum bearings therefore sprang from a recognized need to find a type of bearing that would require less frequent replacement and would not cause engine maintenance problems.

It is significant that engine users came initially to Alcoa and that orders received from this group were evidently unsolicited. Had these purchasers not recognized a strong need to find a better product than the bearings then in use, it might have been difficult to focus sales effort at this level in an attempt to create demand for aluminum bearings. Engine users might tend to follow the technical advice of engine builders on matters such as bearings. Hence, it is of particular interest that some engine users were willing to try aluminum bearings although it was necessary to obtain these sets from a source other than their regular sources of supply.

If engine users could be identified as that group of customers having both the greatest incentive to adopt the new product and the least resistance to it, initial efforts to introduce aluminum bearings might logically have been expected to be most successful in this segment of the market. If it is likely then that the engine user's existing supply sources would tend to be an influence opposing adoption of the new product, the approach to end users might have been more effective than it was if it had been a direct approach—one not taken through, or in the name of, the end user's regular supply service.

When an Alcoa representative visited the customers of one diesel engine building concern to solicit their participation in a bearing test program, his efforts in creating demand for the new product were possibly less effective than they might have been in the absence of this tie-in with the engine builder. Had the field salesman simply been selling finished bearings and representing Alcoa alone, he might have been in a position to emphasize to a greater extent than he may have done both the cost and the functional advantages of aluminum bearings. As it was, he may have hesitated to draw critical comparisons between aluminum bearings and the conventional bearings which the engine builder was then using.

Hesitancy to approach end users directly may arise from an unwillingness to jeopardize relations with the end user's regular suppliers if it is anticipated that at some future time this group will be the one through which the product will regularly sell. Thus Alcoa representatives may have been hesitant at the outset to approach engine builders out of consideration for the maintenance of good relations with bearing manufacturers. Later on, hesitancy to approach engine users directly and aggressively might have been based in part on a desire on Alcoa's part to maintain good relations with diesel engine builders.

Such hesitancy, however, may possibly prolong the achieving of initial acceptance of the product in the market if it means minimizing the aggressiveness of the selling program. Approaching the market as they did, first through bearing manufacturers and then through engine builders, Alcoa representatives were not enabled to sell "against" conventional bearings and to take full sales advantage of the difficulties which were being encountered with conventional bearings in certain makes of diesel engines. Prolonging the initial stages might have had the effect then of permitting the development of increased resistance at all levels of the market to the new product.

When the new product can be introduced quickly and effectively at an end-user level, it may be psychologically easier for other groups in the market to concede its advantages and to incorporate the new product advantageously in their own operations. Once groups in the market have time to generate resistance to the product and have an opportunity to sell against it, ultimate adoption tends to become a concession and may therefore be long in coming. Reports discrediting the new product have an opportunity to circulate. Such reports become the basis for explanations as to why manufacturers and end users are *not* selling or using the new product, as the case may be.

Successful sales efforts with end users, however, may be expected to create pressure on their chain of supply (in this case the engine builder and the bearing manufacturer) to have the new product available. Whereas these suppliers may have hesitated originally to sponsor an unproven product, they would now be motivated by the desire to preserve market share by keeping abreast of technical developments.

When it seemed apparent that demand had been created at the end-user level and that adoption by the chain of supply was in process, it might be appropriate at that point to shift the focus of sales effort away from end users. Serving the end-use market directly may not in the long run be either satisfactory or economical for the materials producer. If not, then distribution through the established chain of supply may provide broad coverage of the market and may put the new product in channels where a sales and a servicing program can be carried out effectively.

## SUMMARY

In the initial stages of market development the materials producer's efforts to create demand for the new product may be focused either on potential manufacturers of the new product or on potential end users. Some conscious choice needs to be made, therefore, with regard to which of these groups can most effectively be approached on a direct basis.

The choice ought probably to be based, first, on a definitive analysis of the product, the process by which it is manufactured, and its end-use applications. Second, the choice should be based on a judgment as to whether potential manufacturers or potential end users of the new product will have the greatest incentives to adopt it initially and which groups in the market can be expected to register the greatest resistance to its adoption. Finally, some appraisal should certainly be made of the character and the strength of the relationships between potential end users and their suppliers. When incentives to adopt the new product at the end-use level conflict with the influences of a strong end user-supplier relationship, the incentives may not be strong enough to assert themselves in the face of these contrary pressures.

On the basis of such an appraisal a decision may then be made as to whether the creation of demand for the new product can best be achieved by focusing sales effort at an end-use market level in an attempt to *draw* the new product into, and through, the chain of supply. Alternatively, the materials supplier may choose to *push* the product through this chain by seeking to interest manufacturers in assuming major responsibility for developing demand at the end-user level.

When there is potential resistance in the market to the new product, the introductory marketing program may lose effectiveness if it is complicated by efforts to reach more than one group of customers at the same time. In attempting to preserve his relations with both potential end users and their suppliers, the materials producer may find that he has modified the aggressiveness of his marketing program. The result may be to reduce the competitive impact of the new product on products which it seeks to displace.

If the materials producer chooses to focus initial sales effort at the end-user level, the success of this program may be signaled in time both by increasing sales to end users and by the growing interest of other concerns in making and selling the new product. At this point a second stage in the marketing program might evolve out of the first phase. In the second stage the materials producer may change his focus of sales effort from end users and may concentrate his sales program on the end user's regular sources of supply.

At what point in time the transition should be made between the first and second phases is a matter of judgment. On the one hand, the materials producer may not long wish to jeopardize relationships with his eventual customers by competing with them in the end-product market. On the other hand, he will want to be assured that growth of the market will not be deterred by the discontinuance of his own direct sales efforts to generate demand at the end-user level. The over-all selling effort may conceivably lose some of its aggressive flavor when the product becomes integrated in the established chain of supply. Continued market growth may then depend upon whether the level of end-user demand is self-sustaining and on whether some suppliers will want to sell the new product aggressively in order to increase market share against their competitors.

# 31.

# *Long-Range Objectives*

## By Willem Holst [1]

One of several aspects of control—remote or otherwise—is the establishment of targets, or objectives, by the top management of a company. In overseas operations such targets may be arrived at in a number of ways—for example, on the basis of American experience, or by a comparative analysis of a number of overseas units, or by an individual analysis of conditions applying to a single operation in a particular country. Frequently a combination of these approaches is used. But whatever route is taken, whether past performance or some other criteria are employed, these two conditions must be met if the goals are to be set successfully and if subsequent control is to be maintained:

There must be a continuous flow of information between the field and the central office.

The information must be consolidated and analyzed in reference to given standards of performance.

I will limit my discussion in the following pages to the longer-range aspects of remote control, concentrating on the planning and coordination of supply and demand for five to ten years ahead, and the associated financial problems. Long-range planning is just as dependent on a continuous flow of information between the fields and the central office as is short-range planning. But the type of information and the relationships between the overseas units and head-

---

[1] By permission from *Management Guide to Overseas Operations,* Edited by Dan H. Fenn, Jr. Copyright, 1957, McGraw-Hill Book Company, Inc.

quarters are likely to be somewhat different in short-range planning, where an appraisal of past performance is usually involved. Before describing Standard-Vacuum's control system in this context, however, I would like to digress briefly to describe the company's operations.

## SCOPE OF ACTIVITY

From the 1890's to 1933, the Standard Oil Company (New Jersey) and the Socony Mobil Oil Company had been operating as separate firms in the Eastern Hemisphere. Jersey Standard had only producing and refining facilities there, while Socony Mobil was limited to a marketing organization. The two companies felt that they could achieve better service and greater operating efficiencies by combining operations. So in 1933 they formed the Standard-Vacuum Oil Company, which was to operate in the Asian and African countries east and southwest of the Persian Gulf. This portion of the world includes more than fifty separate political entities and has a population of almost 900 million, exclusive of the mainland of China.

Today, Standard-Vacuum operates as a fully integrated, separate oil company. It has its own officers and directors, and formulates and administers its own policies. It has just completed a new headquarters office in White Plains, New York, which houses the 700 employees who comprise the company's headquarters staff.

Overseas, Standard-Vacuum has 40,000 employees. About 95 per cent of them are nationals of the countries in which they work. The company has established twenty-one wholly owned subsidiaries and fourteen branches abroad; in addition, it has one affiliate in which it owns a majority interest, and seven in which its interest is less than 50 per cent. These operating units cover all phases of the oil industry —exploration, production, pipeline transportation, refining, marine transportation, and marketing. At present, the company's principal exploration activity is in Indonesia, India, Pakistan, Western New Guinea, Papua, British Somaliland, and the Philippines. Standard-Vacuum currently operates refineries in Indonesia, India, South Africa, Australia, and Japan. Marketing activity throughout the so-called "Stanvac Area" is conducted through twenty-two branches and subsidiaries. In addition to its own production, Stanvac is a purchaser of both crude oil and products in the Middle East, where its parent companies have a share in petroleum operations in Iran, Iraq, Saudi Arabia, and Qatar. For transporting the petroleum, the company owns and operates twenty-three vessels totaling about 340,000 dead-weight tons. In addition, it usually has another thirty to forty ships under period charter.

Stanvac's branch and subsidiary offices are located at points as far apart as Capetown, South Africa, and Yokohama, Japan, and Karachi, Pakistan, and Wellington, New Zealand. Some 10,000 miles separate these locations. Singapore, close to the center of the Stanvac area, is 180° both east and west of New York, where the company has its headquarters; hence the adjective "remote" is particularly applicable to Standard-Vacuum's operations.

The company's rapid postwar growth, combined with the vastness of distance and variety of activities it embraces, has made the problem of remote control an exceedingly complex one for us. Our volume of business increased from about 70,000 barrels per day in 1938 to 200,000 barrels per day in 1955. Consequently, the topic of this chapter represents an operating problem which demands our continuing attention.

## PLANNING AGENCIES

Standard-Vacuum's long-range planning is done through the cooperation of several agencies in the central office, which consolidate field information and translate it into company-wide plans for the future:

The functional departments—exploration, producing, manufacturing, marketing, and marine transportation—act as technical liaison agents between their field counterparts and other central office control agencies.

The economic coordination department provides the supply-and-demand framework for the company's long-range logistical planning, evaluates possible alternatives of supply through the preparation of economic studies, and establishes the basis for a long-term capital investment program.

The treasurer's department translates the investment program into its financial implications. Included in its reports are a consolidated forecast of cash available from profit and depreciation, a breakdown by currencies, and a statement of sources for additional funds, if such are needed to arrive at a balance with the company's over-all capital requirements.

The coordination committee is responsible for reviewing all forward plans, associated budgets, and appropriation requests before recommending action by the board of directors.

## THE CONTROL MECHANISMS

We can now look at Standard-Vacuum's machinery for long-range planning and control in somewhat greater detail. There are four main mechanisms:

1. The establishment of definite objectives with regard to areas of operation, degree of integration, product quality improvement, and similar matters.

2. A forecast of petroleum consumption five to ten years ahead on an area-wide basis, with an estimate of the company's sales opportunities based on that probable consumption.

3. The determination of an optimum supply and demand balance by individual years.

4. The preparation of a cash and currency forecast, taking into account capital investment requirements, crude and product pricing, freight rates, and the profitability of each phase of the company's operations.

The long-range objectives are established at two levels—the policy level, where the political stability and economic climate of particular regions determine their acceptability as areas of large-scale future investment; and the operational or budgetary level, where the long-range logistical and financial framework determines how much each phase should be expanded or contracted, or what degree of integration should be sought, taking into account parent company supplies of crude and product in the Persian Gulf.

The determination of the economic climate is accomplished in various ways. Many governments publish pamphlets describing incentives for foreign investment, and these are most helpful. Also, agencies of our own government prepare excellent material on foreign industrial opportunities through local embassies and consulates. Stanvac's own field offices periodically submit pertinent data to guide the central office in matters affecting both the economic and political climate. In addition, when a large new investment is contemplated, direct contact is established between directors of the company and high government officials to explore the economic conditions further and to discuss terms.

## FORECASTING DEMAND

The second planning mechanism is one which I am sure is familiar to all readers: the forecasting of future business volume. Standard-Vacuum has continuously modified its forecasting techniques over the past ten years. In the process we have markedly changed the character of our relationships with the field, especially in this matter of appraising future outlook.

Prior to 1947 forecasting of demand was almost exclusively the responsibility of overseas marketing units and was confined to Stanvac sales as opposed to industry-wide prospects. The New York office did little reviewing or revising beyond the consolidation of individual field forecasts, which were largely based on local knowledge of sales contracts for the near future, combined with an attempt at simple projection of past sales trends for individual petroleum products. While this method yielded reasonably good over-all results for the two or three years immediately ahead—with errors averaging only 2 per cent to 5 per cent for aggregate demand—estimates for five to ten years into the future were always far too low. For example, a projection made in 1946 for the year 1955 proved to be 40 per cent below the actual tenth, or terminal year, of the forecast period.

In order to improve such forecasts—particularly those for individual products—and to permit a more careful New York review, the field units were given new instructions. These programs suggested the preparation of forecasts by an "end-use" technique—that is, an estimate of the number of passenger cars, buses, trucks, and tractors that would be in operation and the average amount of petroleum each would consume. Such forecasts, prepared on an industry-wide basis for two to four years ahead, made possible a more careful New York appraisal of field estimates and provided a good basis for a reasoned exchange of views when New York felt the estimates required revision. However, longer-range estimates for over four years continued to be made largely on the basis of the simple projection technique, a device with limitations which readily became apparent.

More recently, therefore, the New York staff has adopted a technique which is coming into ever more widespread use: the determination of long-range trends in petroleum demand by an analysis of the entire energy balance of an area. This means forecasting the *total* demand for all forms of energy from primary sources such as coal, hydro-power, natural gas, petroleum, and, eventually, nuclear sources. Then an estimate is made of the part that petroleum is likely to play in meeting that total demand. This requires an appraisal of the probable rate of industrialization and economic development generally, of future balance of payments problems, and of the availability and rate of exploitation of competing energy sources. With New York's encouragement, a few of our major field units are beginning to adopt this technique; smaller units, however, simply do not have an adequate staff to carry through such a relatively sophisticated approach.

Japan provides an illustration of the operation of this energy-balance method of forecasting demand:

About five years ago, when we first tried this approach, we looked at the Japanese government's estimates of future coal production. Their figure was something like 55 million tons a year. As time went by, Japan's actual coal production dropped from a level of 48 million tons down to 43 million. At that point, of course, we became quite worried about our balances. We made a local survey and discovered that the coal situation seemed to be getting even worse, indicating that the government's higher coal production forecast was likely to be nowhere near correct. Consequently, we turned our plans around completely, basing them on the more realistic figure of 43 million tons of coal. The difference in consumption of fuel oil was enormous and we had to make drastic changes in our expansion plans for the next five years.

## BALANCING SUPPLY AND DEMAND

The determination of supply and demand is a complex problem, involving an infinite number of permutations and combinations. We have more than a dozen crude oils available, at least eight refinery sources of supply including the Persian Gulf, and over twenty marketing entities to satisfy with products covering a wide range of quality specifications.

Our third control mechanism, designed to balance supply and demand, is based generally on estimates of product output by overseas operational units, but any plan extending beyond three years can be modified if necessary by selection and construction of appropriate refinery equipment. The final determination of what may be regarded as an optimum over-all balance for the company as a whole is therefore essentially an economic problem, involving a comparison of major alternatives. By its very nature, this is a centralized New York office function. In large measure, the staff work is carried out by the economic coordination department, which works in close collaboration with the New York functional departments. Of course some trial and error is involved in arriving at optimum solutions, but a new supply-and-demand balance must be prepared once every six months because of the ever-changing aspects of the petroleum industry as a whole.

The fourth and final mechanism of long-range planning is the translation of the supply-and-demand balance into financial terms, and the reappraisal of various major alternatives in the light of over-all financial feasibility. Costs, requirements for investment in fixed capital and working capital, and cash generation through profits, depreciation, self-insurance, and other reserves must be projected by major functions.

Standard-Vacuum's overseas units are responsible for the initial preparation of such cash forecasts for periods up to four years into the future. However, these estimates are subject to general guidance from the New York office, which determines the assumptions that should be used with regard to prices, freight rates, and so on. Some New York adjustments usually prove to be necessary. Generally we have found that these modifications suggested by the central office and based on its comparative analysis of past field forecasts are helpful in improving future field accuracy.

The New York staff tends to assume primary responsibility for the preparation of longer-range financial forecasts—that is, forecasts extending beyond four years. Individual field units are not in a good position to determine the size and location of needed new refineries, or to judge the relative priorities to be assigned to various regions in terms of their comparative political stability or investment climate. As in the case of demand forecasting, however, it is hoped that the larger field units can make an increasing contribution to such longer-range financial projections.

In closing, I would like to make a few general observations, based on Stanvac's experience, about the relationships between field and central office with respect to long-range forward planning:

Standard-Vacuum's system of remote control is not static, but is subject to constant development, experimentation, and change.

What appears to be a highly centralized long-range planning control function belies the fact that in many other respects, and even in short-range planning, Standard-Vacuum encourages an ever-increasing degree of decentralization in order to free top management for major policy issues.

Because of the complexity of the company's operations, certain appraisals and decisions can be made only in New York; nevertheless, here too an attempt is made to keep information flowing in both directions between the field and the central office. A continuous interchange is essential for improving the accuracy of longer-range forecasting and for logistical coordination.

In planning a sound program for the future, Stanvac feels that the central office agencies should always have the courage to look as far into the future as is necessary to discern the major trends. Because it may well take up to five years to negotiate, plan, and build a new refinery from scratch—and even longer to develop a new producing field—Stanvac believes that forecasting and planning should extend up to ten years ahead.

# 32.

# *Planning the Size of an Enterprise*

## By Edward H. Hempel [1]

The decision, how big an enterprise should be conceived and made, when to enlarge and how much, or when to mark time, is definitely the most fundamental and vexing task of top management. The problem will confront not all, but most managements in the near future. For many decades one could try to start small, hoping for progress and good luck, to build more when the time would be favorable, and thus could "hope" to grow. In the years to come more cautious and more aggressive procedure will be needed. The owner or manager of a company who desires it to grow will have to plan its size for quite some years ahead; he will have to work toward this goal, and try to achieve it by continued planning. Success is as possible as it always was. But it is more difficult to achieve. If an enterprise is not planned for at least some time ahead, it will not be organized for this goal in due time; it may grow, but others who plan for future size will organize better and grow faster.

### Long-Range Size Planning

The conceiving of a long-range and far-future size for a company does not mean that from the very beginning a definite size should be chosen, to be achieved twenty or thirty years later. Even today most plants and enterprises are designed only in a size suited to near-future conditions, but in all well-planned enterprises top management also has a long-trend concept of size that is being kept in mind and aimed

[1] From Edward H. Hempel, *Top-Management Planning* (New York, Harper & Brothers, 1945), pp. 25–45.

334

at as an ultimate long-range goal. In this manner the various near-future sizes actually installed are in reality only temporary sizes, chosen so as actualities make possible the achievement of the long-range size objective. To many, especially to those who have never tried to plan the size of an enterprise for more than the immediate future, this long-range size planning may appear as an absurdity and impossibility. But it is neither absurd nor impossible.

## The Reasons for Long-Range Size Planning

Nearly all industrial enterprises are being founded to exist for many years, at least for twenty or more years, which may represent the rest of the life span of the founder, the length of the usual life of buildings and equipment, or the length of time for which a president and intelligent manager should try to think ahead before he decides to invest his or someone else's money in a plant in a certain industry, in a definite locality, and within a given environment. By doing this he shows that he is willing to become with his enterprise part and parcel of the community and part of its economic future. Naturally, the good manager tries to think ahead as far as possible and, vague as the possibilities of conceiving the ultimate size of an enterprise may be, he should, and actually usually does, try to form this concept, not only for his own sake but for the sake of those whom he expects to have associated with him.

If he conceives only a small enterprise, he will select few or no executive collaborators; he will elect to operate with foremen; he will buy land and build the plant without concern for much expansion, choose equipment and machines for near-future needs; he will not conceive an extensive distribution system, nor look for dealers in far-off places; he will, in brief, organize and work for small-scale operation, and ultimately he will have to be content with achieving it. It takes time to train and make men and organizations ready for expanded activities, and that is why top managements usually determine, at least vaguely, how far they gradually intend to go. Thus, there is a definite need for trying to conceive an ultimate size, and it can be done!

## The Possibilities of Long-Range Size Planning

As yet there is no definite theory on how to determine the potential ultimate size of enterprises, but there are at least some fairly certain and time-tested principles, gathered from observation, which help in trying to do it. With special studies and interest centered on this problem, we probably shall someday have truly reliable methods which can be used. For the time being one can only indicate how this sort of management thinking generally runs.

(a) *Local Operation Size.* The most simple size planning is that for an enterprise conceived for limited local operation only: a city including suburbs; a county or a few counties; or part of a big city. In this category is the greatest number of companies. They are usually called "small" enterprises, stores, service workshops, branch offices, branch plants, local warehouses, and such like. The term "small," however, is not always properly chosen, since local operation size may range from a few to hundreds or thousands of employees.

The main point in planning for local operation size is that from the start the management intends to make the enterprise serve only its given economic environment, without any further thought to give it a wider operating radius or expansion beyond this most effective and economical sphere of activities. Within its limited location, however, the enterprise is planned to grow as big as possible and as much as economic actualities permit. This purposeful limitation of activities is neither wrong planning nor need it involve sacrifice of maximum size.

There are quite a few industries and plants which almost must be planned that way in order to be organized best: bread bakeries, confectionery plants, central kitchens for chain restaurants, laundries, newspapers, public utilities like gasworks or waterworks; automobile central repair shops, tire recapping plants; gasoline stations and distribution points; central warehouses; milk distribution centers, meat warehouses, small ice cream plants.

At closer analysis one soon finds that local operation size is indicated when:

1. Frequent (daily, twice daily) contact with a relatively great number of outlets or customers is required;

2. Close attention has to be paid to demand details, and changes thereof have to be taken care of quickly and reliably;

3. The product is perishable within a short time, or the service has to be rendered quickly;

4. Prices have to be kept low because of regulations, competition, or in order to tap the maximum market;

5. Freight charges have to be kept at a minimum for the same reasons.

(b) *Small Territory Operation Size (one state or a few).* Legal reasons and the fulfillment of different state regulations in intrastate and interstate activities, sometimes tax reasons, and similar considerations may make it advisable to conceive ultimate operation size as limited to a "small" territory composed of one or a few states.

The scope of activities is conceived somewhat wider than for local operation and they are definitely and in all details adjusted to the territory. This sort of ultimate size can be found applied in brewing and soft drink manufacturing; automobile assembly plants; large ice cream plants; biscuit and cracker bakeries; smoked meat, sausage, and fish establishments; by makers of refrigerated products; in dyeworks and quite a few other chemical industries; in coffee roasting establishments; paint and allied product plants; and in fertilizer mixing establishments, just to give examples.

In all these instances it will be found that the small territory size is being planned for because:

1. The character of the products (taste, composition, etc.) has to be adjusted to prevailing needs or preferences;

2. Delivery or contact must be available to customers at least twice per week or more, but not daily;

3. The price need not be exactly a minimum price, but must be kept on the low side;

4. Transportation is mostly by truck and within the usual 150-mile truck routes within which this transportation is most economical;

5. Production for the chosen state territory is achieved cheaper in one plant than in a number of smaller local plants;

6. The demand originated in the state territory just about justifies the plant;

7. The perishability of the product is partly but not fully overcome.

(c) *Large Territory Operation Size.* Whenever a considerable number of states is necessary to create a sufficient market or demand for the products of one plant, the formation of large territories to be served by a strategically located plant is indicated.

In planning for this size of operation, considerable ultimate plant size must be provided for from the start, considerable expansion must be anticipated, and the entire organization must be gradually built up accordingly.

In this category of production are most mechanical, electrical, chemical products, necessarily made in standard or typical grade qualities, which have to be made in large quantities within one plant in order to be low in price: iron and steel products; electric equipment and apparatus; standard chemicals; gasoline. Naturally, in such plants also nonstandard grade products may be made in order to increase the volume of business.

Generally, the following points will be found to be significant:

1. Perishability has fully been solved or does not exist in the product;

2. Delivery or contact with consumers or buyers of the product is at infrequent intervals, and not necessarily of the "plant to consumer" variety, but mostly to middlemen or large buyers;

3. The product is difficult to make in small plants and requires complex production facilities, skill, and expert knowledge, which are developed best and obtained most economically in a rather large plant;

4. The price of the product, because of competition from similar products, cannot be too high, but need not be unnecessarily low. Most of these products are in the "cost plus fair profit" class and are sold at prices in line with the quality and technical perfection built into them;

5. Transportation costs play a minor role in relation to the price proper and are carried willingly by the buyer.

(d) *National Operation Size.* One can and should aim from the start at ultimate national size, even if the enterprise is still small and only beginning, provided the product is suited for it. National operation does not just happen, it is painstakingly developed, planned, and worked for. The fact that relatively few companies achieve national size is not due to lack of consumers nor is it dependent on economic circumstances. Their products either do not lend themselves to such ambitious planning or the managements do not care to plan for it.

National operation size can be achieved in one centralized plant (whisky distilleries, wineries, Ford River Rouge, aircraft, etc.), or through multiplant operation (National Biscuit Co., Du Pont, tire plants, Standard Oil, U.S. Steel, Singer Sewing Machine).

The key to achieving national success and size will be found in the fulfillment of at least three or all of the following prerequisites:

1. Uniqueness of product, in engineering features, design, construction, composition, or quality in general, which must be distinct from and at least partially but definitely superior when compared with similar products;

2. Uniqueness of price, invariably on the low side, for the product and quality offered. Rarely are the prices of national success products high, if compared with prices asked for the same product made by smaller producers;

3. Uniqueness of organization, technical and commercial, in general concept and execution, mostly including excellent service to product and to user;

4. Uniqueness of management and leadership, expressing itself particularly in effective long-range and near-future planning of most management actions;

5. Uniqueness in the development of the demand and of sales, always aimed at mass consumption.

(e) *International Operation Size.* In past decades relatively few industrial top managements were interested in possibly and actually extending their activities into international size. Most of them were willing enough to export any of their products, if it was not too difficult to do and payment was certain, but few actually aimed at the establishment of American plants abroad.

There was no need for it. The American market was big enough, lucrative, relatively simple to work in, and above all, safe in every way. Foreign activities caused much more trouble and always some political, economic, and financial risks, which top managements were hesitant to take; even if the returns on investments were considerably higher than in the United States, there were always some new restrictions or regulations which made profit collection difficult if not impossible, and thus most companies did not desire to grow into international activities, even if potentially they could have.

The few that did were exceptionally successful: Ford, General Motors, Firestone, Grace, Anaconda, Guggenheim, General Electric, Westinghouse, Caterpillar, Singer Sewing Machine, Du Pont, Eastman Kodak, International Business Machine, typewriter companies; they all succeeded in extending their sales and production activities into international dimensions. It may seem puzzling that side by side with these giants relatively small companies succeeded in building up considerable and profitable international activities: drugs, medicinals, hair tonics, hair dye manufacturers; perfumeries, silk stockings, and small machinery; bathing suits, office supplies, kitchen gadgets, and similar odd articles brought fortunes to those who dared to plan for ultimate international size.

How did companies achieve international success?

1. Always their products were unique in international competition, at least somewhat superior, better, more useful than offered by other nations or by native producers; most of them were patented.

2. The prices charged were not necessarily low, nor even adjusted to the relative purchasing power, but they were reasonable.

3. The main point, however, always was that the urge or need to buy these products was latent and strong, so strong that the foreign buyer felt he simply had to have the product, to satisfy his urgent need, his vanity, egotism, prestige, or whatever advantage it gave him.

Since in [World War II] great sections of the world have been opened up and people throughout the world have become accustomed to many products to which they otherwise would have given little attention for years to come, it is definitely certain that after this war exceptional opportunities will be available to managements who will find it worth while to think not only in local or somewhat larger sizes of enterprise, but who will have the courage to extend their thinking and planning beyond the borderlines. Unlike after the last war, the considerably heavier tax load which in the United States will limit profit possibilities for many years to come will provide a new and most potent stimulus to expand into foreign activities.

It is hoped that these comments have proved that it is possible to determine and plan for the ultimate size of an enterprise, at least in sketchy outlines. No one will try to do this sort of thinking in definite figures for plant size and potential volume of sales. But he will try to vision the ultimate potential, organize and manage toward it, and use every opportunity to bring the struggling company step for step toward its ultimate goal. . . .

## In What Terms Should the Size of an Enterprise Be Planned?

The size problem appears not only in different forms, it also can be thought of in different terms: capacities of various kinds, investment, assets, man power, or number of employees. All of them have their advocates and place in management thinking; budgeting has attempted over and over to use these concepts in and for "planning," and therefore the investigation of their suitability for top-management planning ought to be especially worth while.

## The Various Kinds of Output Capacities

Business and technical men are given to express the size of an industrial enterprise in terms of capacity, mostly meaning some potential production output. However, in whichever form capacity may be used or referred to: "normal capacity, maximum capacity, excess capacity, dead capacity, or any other capacity," when it comes to considering, determining, and expressing the capacity of any plant as the measured and representative size of a company, one soon finds that usually neither the capacity nor the size is properly expressed. Capacities can be expressed in terms of products or production, in terms of common measures, or in man-hours. What do they indicate and what do they mean?

## Capacity in Terms of Products

Only if one single kind or similar kinds of products are being made in the shop or plant can one readily determine how many units can be produced per hour, eight-hour shift, per week of forty or any number of hours. Which one of these is "normal" capacity has to be specified, and thus one can get from the number of units mentioned an idea of how big a plant the company has or would like to have; by assuming or ascertaining that all will be sold, one may guess at the size of all activities involved. One can do the same even if different sizes of the same product should have to be made, but for planning purposes it will be wise to ask: Is capacity in terms of products to be made a primary factor? or is it dependent on others? If it is dependent, the other factor or factors must be considered as the objects of planning.

## Capacity in Terms of Common Measures

In order to budget, it has become customary to express capacities also of plants which turn out or are supposed to turn out a considerable variety of products, as most plants have to do. These capacities are stated in terms of common measures, so that a total size or total capacity may be ascertained. Whatever the production variety may cover, the output or size is expressed in pounds, yards, square feet, or other common measures, and then it is stated that a company has or should have that capacity or size. It will be readily understood that this is a somewhat unreliable way of doing it. Figures of this kind are expedients, they represent mixtures of different kinds of products, and the same capacity figure of 100,000 square feet of veneer wood per day may be true for some days but hardly for all, if various kinds of veneer are produced. Again, this is not a good way to discuss or plan the size of a company.

## Capacity in Terms of Man-Hours or Production Units

There is in use still another method of expressing the physical capacity of production, even if it should involve absolutely different products: for instance, artificial flowers, the making of which requires different times; braid and ribbon production, which is variety enough in itself, but may have to be expressed combined with the production of ordinary cotton cloth and cotton print; the assembly of coupés, two-door sedans, four-door sedans, ½-ton, 1-ton, and larger trucks; the output of iceboxes of entirely different kinds.

In order to express and measure the size of such enterprises in one common measure, the method uses the man-hours required to make one unit of the main product; the basic unit, often called *product unit or production unit,* is made the basis or measure for expressing all other units in a common manner. Using the number of man-hours required to make one unit of all the various products, and relating these man-hours to the basic unit man-hours, one obtains conversion factors which are used to express entirely different production in one common measure or capacity. (See Table 1.)

By using this method one can express the daily production of nearly any kind of product mixture and still refer to a "capacity"; also one can use this information for quite a few production control purposes. But even this capacity based on man-hours is hardly a suitable basis for planning.

The man-hours required to make various products are subject to changes, which often are considerable. Especially when new products have been made for a few weeks, capacity improves through better experience or because of methods developed in the meantime. Doubling or trebling of production by better methods has been

## TABLE 1

### THE DETERMINATION OF THE DAILY CAPACITY OF AN ICEBOX PLANT

| Products | Man-Hours per Unit | Conversion Factors | Production Units | Boxes Made per Day | Production Units per Day Basic Units |
|---|---|---|---|---|---|
| Basic Unit = Icebox Model 40 | 120 | — | 1 | 125 | 125 |
| Production May 15 | | | | | |
| Model 45 | 140 | $\frac{140}{120}$ | 1.167 | 20 | 23.34 |
| Model 51 | 182 | $\frac{182}{120}$ | 1.516 | 30 | 45.48 |
| Model 40 (basic) | 120 | $\frac{120}{120}$ | 1.000 | 50 | 50.00 |
| Model 30 | 80 | $\frac{80}{120}$ | 0.667 | 10 | 6.67 |
| Total May 15 | | | | 110 | 125.49 |

achieved. On the other hand, it happens in some shops that production is slowed down because of any of many reasons. Besides, physical capacity can be increased considerably by overtime, second and third shifts, new layout, wage incentives, or changes in foremen.

All these capacities and how they are determined have been discussed, because in many instances they are used to describe the size of plants and enterprises, and because projects often call for the planning of a definite capacity. This practice is satisfactory for physical plant projects but should not be confused with the planning of the size of the activities of a company, which is the planning top management has to do first and above all in order to determine the size of its operations. The physical plant size is only one part of the entire scheme and plant sizes should be engineered to suit the plans of management rather than vice versa. Plant size, no matter how expressed in terms of capacity, is, therefore, not a primary factor; it is or should be governed by other size concepts which have to be evolved in order to plan.

## Size in Terms of Investment

Often one hears enterprises described and plans discussed in terms of investment. "There are invested in the company $x$ dollars now. We plan to spend $y$ dollars on expansion to increase capacity, business, and profits." This sounds as if investment could create size and that one could plan in terms of investment. It may readily be that company B, with an investment of $1 million and good planning, outgrew company A built with an investment of $5 million.

Capital investment by itself, no matter how big or small, cannot create size, nor does it describe the size in which management actually operates. Especially if the investment is stated in "capital values," which are nominal values of stocks or bonds sold, this size concept is definitely unsuited for planning.

## Size in Terms of Assets, Net Worth, etc.

Enterprises are actually operated with their assets—cash, open accounts, inventories, machines, buildings—and their total value sometimes greatly exceeds the capital invested, because some assets are obtained either on credit or through the use of undistributed profits, which then explains the "surplus" of the company.

The total value of assets of a company is more significant and reliable an expression of size than is capacity or capital investment, because it shows at least how much actual money was used to achieve what the company did in terms of production, sales, and profits. Capacity refers only to plant size; capital investment only to part of the financial size; assets reveal the total of funds which are used, but even then, in talking and thinking of assets, it is necessary to know which assets are meant: book assets, showing every item at cost or market, whichever is lower; or net assets, which means book assets minus reserves set up to show their actual present-day value after depreciation and other value deductions. Net assets, meaning the amount of all book values minus all reserves, are for management purposes important figures to have at hand, since they show the amounts exposed by the management to economic risk, and thus can be used for checking on plans and planning.

In spite of their importance, however, net asset figures are in the same category as capacity or capital investment when it comes to planning the size of an enterprise. While covering more elements of management activities than capacity or capital investment, net assets still are not factors fundamental and important enough to be singled out as those factors which painstakingly should be planned and which would help in making a company grow and prosper.

In top-management planning it would be folly to plan inventories, open accounts, plant assets, etc., in terms of dollars and to expect that this would help to achieve best company size at all times. The control of these items will contribute toward that end, but size planning ought to be concentrated and based on even more important things.

## Size in Terms of Man Power

In economic statistics and in the listings of the magnitude of states, counties, or cities, the number of people, and especially of those gainfully employed, is often taken as a measure for "size." Those who actually work with these figures are not quite agreed on how useful such figures really are. While they help to formulate a size concept, they reveal actually only one, and a rather indefinite, aspect of activities.

In reference to industrial organization and magnitudes of plants, man-power figures have almost lost the significance they had forty and more years ago. At that time it was almost true that a plant with 200 men turned out ten times as much as one with twenty men. Nowadays, with mechanization and automatization of equipment advanced to almost uncanny perfection, but not equally applied in plants and industries, it is entirely feasible that in one plant 500 men turn out as much as 800 do in another. The different characteristics of men in different parts of the country, and above all the inequalities of managements and organizations, make man power produce differently, and thus man power is not a factor helpful in planning size.

This is especially interesting since in the years to come a maximum of man power is to be employed by planning.

## THE "PRACTICAL" METHODS OF SIZE DETERMINATION

While so far only size "concepts" were discussed, in view of the fundamental importance of determining size it should be useful to review and analyze also some of the more common "methods" which have been recommended and used for the determination of company or plant sizes in past years.

### The Size of Minor Additions and Expansions

In an already going concern desirable or necessary minor additions in shop or organization capacity are usually decided upon without much scientific procedure. There is a need for them, the size of the necessary addition is estimated, and then it is determined how much machinery, man power, floor space, or plant should be added. Rarely are additions overdone. Where oversizing occurs, it usually happens because someone was too ambitious, but this is soon discovered and attempts are made to correct the situation.

Often, however, one can find that new sections are purposely oversized, but this then means that the management has definite reasons for it and plans to bring the related sections up to corresponding capacity and size. For instance, if a company has so far bought its forgings from a supplier, and the volume has grown so that the installation of a forge shop becomes worth while, such a shop will nearly always be built bigger than for immediate needs. How much bigger and for how much more work, no one really knows or tries to figure out scientifically, but a similar increase as in the past is assumed and a forge is built which can take care of present needs as well as of some additional ones.

Rarely are such additions sized to long outlooks. They are caused by recognized advisability and are mostly sized to suit immediate and probably near-future needs, which can be foreseen fairly accurately. The classic example of the most carefully undertaken expansion was furnished by Du Pont in the gradual increase of nylon manufacture. To start with, they produced and sold only one-fifth of one day's demand for stockings, in spite of knowing full well that nylon could ultimately expect to replace at least 50 or more per cent of all silk stocking sales. When the capacity was enlarged, it was done only as observation of results justified the expansions, and they are still far from having reached their limit or from being overdone.

## Financial Limitations of Size

There is no doubt that financial considerations often govern the size decision of practical managers, especially in smaller companies and projects. The physical size of the small company must by necessity be conceived in line with available funds. Whether the small industrial producer desires to make shirts, to found a bakery, smoke fish, or manufacture a chemical specialty, he usually has only a certain sum of money available for the undertaking, banks are reluctant to lend much, and only equipment manufacturers are ready to sell part of the equipment on installment.

In either case the designing of a plant and of an organization to a given sum of money is not difficult, and only in the selection, kind, and quality of the equipment will differences of judgment and wisdom be shown. Some industrial newcomers insist on buying the latest and best, and so they have to be content with little; others shop for secondhand equipment and a far-off corner to get started. *The right solution lies in striking a happy medium and in selecting the equipment, location, and organization that will allow for sound growth on the basis of what has been selected for the start.*

At all times it is good to remember that plant size, meaning the expenditure for building, machines, tools, etc., is only part of the entire financial requirement. There must be cash, raw material inventories, stocks of finished products to be kept on hand; there will be open accounts not paid immediately, emergencies and difficulties of various sorts, and always salaries and wages to be paid, regardless of the early fortunes of the enterprise. The practical man will take all these facts into account in organizing the size of an enterprise which must be kept in line with available funds.

While newcomers often overlook these points, it is significant that the most experienced companies observe them carefully. The big chain baking companies—Continental Baking Company—and the big chain store companies—Atlantic and Pacific—always establish a plant, warehouse, or supermarket in such size that there will be success in operating it. They choose location, physical size, equipment, total assets, personnel, radius of operation, and everything else so that each plant or store can well take care of its own needs and of its territory, and that it contributes to achieving national size, progress, and profitability for the company, and provides permanence of employment for its employees. This proves really good top-management planning.

## Estimated Big-Size Operations

Where financial limitations do not exist and funds can be obtained to create any size of plant or organization, it has become the tendency in highly competitive industries to conceive and build big-size plants and organizations from the very beginning. Papermaking and rayon plants; automobile and tire factories; aircraft companies; breweries; even modern paint, soap, and cosmetics production; nitrogen and alkali manufacture; steel, aluminum, and manganese companies— all are conceived big or are not undertaken at all.

This practice is based on the recognized fact that a small company would have little chance for success, and would be doomed to almost certain lethargy in its particular field, in which usually two or three big companies have already set such high operating standards that anyone not matching them adequately would waste his money. The managers of such new big-size enterprises usually make sure that the big size is justified by bringing out superior products, by diversifying the product range, by better methods of sales, by affiliation with consumer companies, or by other measures which help to achieve the success otherwise unattainable.

The size they choose is usually based on statistical data, on studies, and economic analyses, but the size they actually establish is always only estimated. It is not based on immediate or near-future considerations, but tries to suit at least a five- or ten-year program of intentions and hopes. The stakes for which these sizes are designed are no mere trifles. They sometimes aim from the start at outdoing the first or second or third largest company in the industry, to match a competitor in products, activities, and size. It is known that this cannot be done in the first year, nor in two or three years. The management plans accordingly, and has, in addition to large size, which provides cost superiority if sufficient volume is obtained, sufficient capital reserves to meet any temporary reverses.

Just as the size and outcome of major battles cannot be planned or predicted in all details with certainty, but all efforts and preparations are made to win, so these creations of large and largest companies are not based on any one theory or fixed formula, but on daring and careful approximation of how much of an enterprise might be necessary to achieve the desired goal, to get leadership in a city, within a small or large territory, on a national or international scale.

It may be surprising that top managements in their size planning of such magnitude do not use scientific methods or formulae, but one comes to understand this as soon as one analyzes and tests these methods for their practical usefulness.

## The Scientific Methods of Size Determination

Since it is always desirable to replace judgment methods by better ones, the scientific or semiscientific procedures which have been proposed will be presented and described. This is the more worth doing as they show quite a variety and interesting differences of approach. It should be kept in mind that all these methods have been recommended for use and in many cases have been used at the time of planning, when as yet hardly any definite information on the prospective enterprise in form of reliable data is available, and when the management faces its most difficult task, which is to determine the size of the enterprise it should develop and organize.

### Maximum Profit Size

The most direct, simplest, and apparently indisputable method for proposing or selecting the best size for an enterprise is the one which recommends that it be made as big as the class of enterprises earning the highest profits in that particular industry.

The technique is simple, requires hardly any work, and consists in securing financial statistics—which can be obtained from quite a few financial services and other sources. From these statistics classes of enterprises are formed, either on the basis of sales, capital, or net investment; the profits and profit percentages actually obtained are calculated for each class; the size group which shows the highest percentage of profit is considered as the best size. (See Fig. 1.)

In graphic presentations of this method the $x$ axis usually shows sales or capital investment by size classes; the $y$ axis shows the percentage of profit reported in relation to either sales or capital investment, as illustrated above.

The conclusion drawn and recommended is that the new enterprise should be sized so as to obtain top profits. For skilled promoters it is relatively simple to obtain the funds for a plant of this size, but it is an entirely different matter to obtain the sales to support it. It took the companies in the best profit class decades probably to get there, and it required a great deal of effort to organize their enterprises for best profitability and most profitable sales, but it looks like trying the impossible to get enough sales away from them for a new company of their own size. Thus the method can hardly be recommended for actual work and general application.

## Lowest Product Cost Size

Even more frequently referred to than the previous method is the theory which declares that a company or plant should be sized so that the cost per unit produced is the lowest. The argument is convincing. It usually is presented in form of the well-known "cost curves," which are readily drawn up but are difficult to establish in responsible figures. The curves look usually more or less like those in Fig. 2.

How good is this method? Costs are always difficult figures. They are difficult to determine, even in a well-organized company with many years of experience in calculating costs. There are many cost elements involved, some predictable, others changing so suddenly and so widely that it is next to impossible even in going concerns to tell what costs per unit of a specific product will be for a few years ahead.

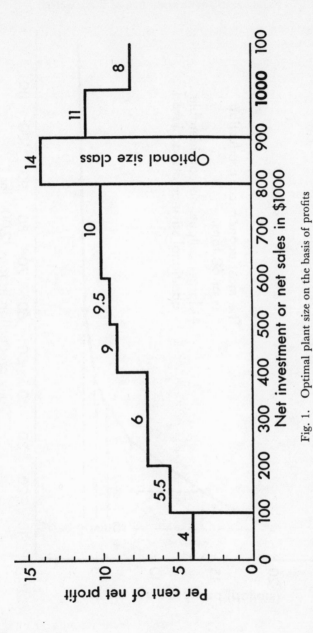

Fig. 1. Optimal plant size on the basis of profits

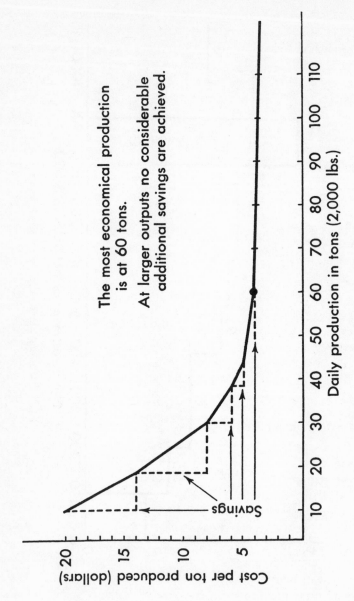

The most economical production is at 60 tons.

At larger outputs no considerable additional savings are achieved.

Savings

Cost per ton produced (dollars)

Daily production in tons (2,000 lbs.)

Fig. 2. Optimal plant size on the basis of cost per unit

But costs can be established, at least approximately and with a good deal of assumptions, if only one kind of product is being made in a not much changing process: flour milling, cement manufacture, etc. It is also well known that *in theory one can get cost figures for any volume of sales,* by segregating the costs into fixed and variable elements and by assuming various unit sales.

*In spite of all care applied in calculating such costs, however, the actual cost figures, obtained two years later, are always different and sometimes considerably different;* also, in cases where different products have to be made, different costs at assumed different volumes can be figured, but it would hardly be wise to place great faith in them. They definitely will be different at actual volumes and actual costs.

The weakest point in this size theory is in the "assumption" of sales. One can assume any volume and find, say, that at 2,000,000 unit sales the costs would be lowest. But what good does that do if only 1,000,000 units can actually be sold, and one has a plant and organization with 50 per cent idle capacity?

Thus it is not the lowest cost, but the obtainable volume of sales that should decide plant size, and this consideration makes sales prediction much more important than the lowest-cost method of size planning. A theoretical lowest cost, no matter how mathematically correct, is still only theory, and not a workable proof for management decision.

## Lowest Technical Investment Size

Quite a few top managements are inclined to be guided in their decisions on the size to be given their project by the amount of investment required for plant and equipment. They are "fixed cost"-minded, and theory has for them another curve to convince, and to prove, such size.

The method does not attempt to ascertain operating costs, nor does it determine product costs at various volumes, but it singles out the cost of buildings, machinery, mostly includes the cost of essential equipment, and determines how much various sizes of these items would cost to produce various volumes of products.

In making the studies it is often found that the costs of plant and equipment per unit produced do not decrease steadily with increasing volume as shown in the cost-per-product unit study, but that in order to produce an increasing number of units, the first costs of the necessary technical investment begin to rise per unit produced after a certain number is achieved. Thus, the theory claims, a point of "optimal fixed investment" is clearly indicated where the total cost of fixed investment is the lowest per unit which can be produced with it. Such a curve, showing cost of technical investment per unit produced, is shown in Fig. 3.

Assuming that the fixed costs and costs per unit produced are correct, as they well may be, because it is not too difficult to get costs of equipment and plant buildings of increasing sizes, what does the curve prove? And is it correct to build a plant and enterprise to the size indicated by the lowest fixed investment per unit produced?

Actually, a management which does build a shop, plant, and organization to that size will be building it only in consideration of investment economy. True, the company will invest in a financially highly desirable size, but its output may or may not represent or be in line with its sales possibilities. To state it more bluntly: a management trying to save investment dollars will freeze its company's activities to a physical capacity rather than keep the investment in line with its economic and sales possibilities.

Besides, it should be kept in mind that production facilities are not always best expressed in terms of dollars. No two engineering firms will design the same $500,000 plant, and while the firm whose equipment may cost the least per unit to be produced may fulfill its promise, another firm, by providing different structures, different equipment, different layout, and perhaps by use of some secondhand equipment, might build a plant just as efficient but considerably larger, more flexible, or otherwise more serviceable.

## Most Efficient Operating Size

Another technical concept of ideal plant size is the one which conceives every section utilized at work capacity (which is at about 90 per cent of its maximum eight-hour-day output), with every type of equipment chosen so that the work of the various sections harmonizes into an ideal flow, ideal space economy, and therefore

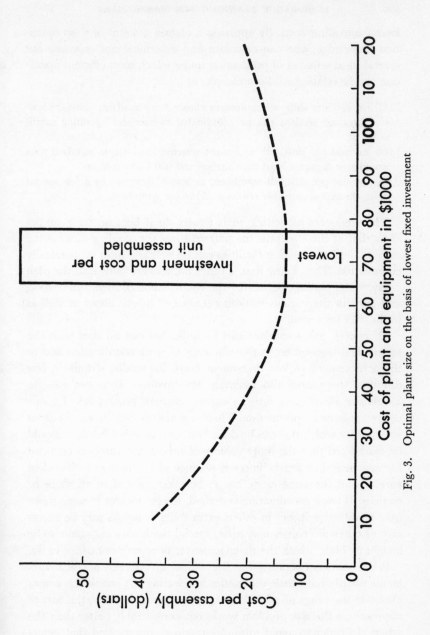

Fig. 3. Optimal plant size on the basis of lowest fixed investment

lowest operating costs. By applying a certain amount of shop operation knowledge, one can calculate and determine not only one but several ideal volumes of production under which most efficient operation can be established. For example, at

2,000 castings per shift, all equipment chosen from available standard low-cost sizes, all sections can be coordinated to excellent operating conditions; at

5,000 castings per shift, all equipment selected from larger standard sizes would give the same ideal coordination and still lower cost; at

6,500 castings per shift, all equipment as before, increased by a few special units, the best conceivable results could be brought about.

The engineers suggesting such figures do it because their studies show that at these outputs the pattern shop, the molding and casting sections, and the melting facilities can be well and most economically coordinated. They know that if other outputs are built into the plan —say, 3,500 castings per shift—the coordination of men, time, work, and costs in the various sections cannot be brought about as well as in the sizes suggested.

Of course, any size plant can be built, but not all sizes with the same advantageousness in the efficiency of work coordination and in the achievement of low investment costs. Especially, if quite a few different shops and also assembly are involved, it is not easy to harmonize all of them into an equally efficient process flow for any desired volume of production. There are always definite daily output volumes for which this can be done best. On the other hand, it should be considered that the daily volume of production rarely is constant for any period of years. There is a range of production to be taken care of and the same range has to be taken care of in all shops or sections. If work coordination is desired, the equipment in some shops may readily give it, but in others extra shifts or layoffs may be necessary or other difficulties may arise, special machinery may have to be bought or built, which the management may or may not desire to do.

When various operating size suggestions are worked out, managements usually have little difficulties in selecting the one which comes closest to the range of sales they expect to obtain. Usually, this sort of approach to the size problem works out considerably better than the others. In order to avoid misunderstanding: the method that determines the most efficient operating sizes is not the same as any of the previous ones. It is a combination of all of them and in addition to the costs of plant and equipment considers the possibilities of operating all of it in harmony, which means that it considers shop management in addition to costs.

# 33.

# *Business Espionage*

## By Richard Austin Smith [1]

One sunny day last autumn, the Washington vice-president of a $300-million manufacturing corporation was informed that a Mr. Jackson wished to see him on an urgent and confidential matter. Mr. Jackson, a burly ex-cop, perspiring under a load of synthetic bonhomie, came to the point at once: he was on a mission of industrial espionage. Ten days earlier a West Coast competitor of the vice-president's company had hired Mr. Jackson to make tape recordings of everything that went on in the latter's Washington office. He had already established himself in the adjacent Gordon Hotel with another private investigator, and just the night before had entered the vice-president's private office in the Cafritz Building with a tailormade set of keys. There, after a leisurely reconnaissance, the two of them decided the best location for their microphone was behind the venetian-blind valance—but then a more provident idea came to mind. Why not fake the recordings through the cooperation of the vice-president and his staff, and thus avoid the risk of getting jailed for illegal entry? Mr. Jackson went on to explain in confidential tones that he was a family man with three children, and though a tiger on adultery cases, he just didn't like the look of this, his first assignment in the frightening world of big-business espionage. Hence his proposal of a fix, with all its advantages for both the spies and the spied-on.

Though the vice-president didn't realize it at the time, he was getting a firsthand glimpse of the subterfuges, the mendacity, the

[1] Reprinted by special permission from the May, 1956, issue of Fortune; ©, 1956, Time Inc.

wheels-within-wheels of a practice that today reaches into almost every industry. His experience was to differ from hundreds of instances of business espionage only in two respects: the relative inexperience of the spy and the disarming disclosure of his mission. Battalions of more seasoned operators are regularly at work stealing business secrets undetected by management. In scale, their operations range from spying out a competitor's multimillion-dollar bid on a government contract to paying a Safeway mimeograph man $5 a week for an advance copy of the Thursday Specials. The automobile, chemical, and oil industries particulary attract these operators, but they can be found in any spot where information is worth cold cash: drug and cosmetic firms (see "Revlon's Jackpot," *Fortune*, April, 1956), real-estate offices, art galleries, styling studios, banks, investment houses, publications, communications companies, steel mills, and so on. Few persons, of course, will admit they practice espionage (and not many more admit to being victims). It is enveloped in hypocrisy, and the companies that use espionage as a regular competitive weapon resonantly deplore its existence or deny that it does exist. Almost nothing has been written about the practice generally, though there was voluminous press coverage of its wire-tapping phase during the trial of "Steve" Broady, a private detective, in New York last year. Yet, in the opinion of some of those engaged in this unsavory business, there is more industrial espionage going on in the U.S. today than in any other period in our history.

In the Jackson case, however, the vice-president was not bothering his head about the country-wide spread of industrial espionage; he was solely concerned with his individual involvement. To him, industrial espionage, like personal tragedy, had always been something that happened to the other fellow, in another industry, in a pleasantly removed locale. That it had materialized under his nose and, worse, that he was the object of it, made him both indignant and uneasy. He was also unsettled by practical considerations. His office was bulging with competitive information of great value to his company, besides confidential material from the AEC and the Department of Defense, all of which he and his executives were accustomed to discuss freely in what they had considered the privacy of their suite. The presence of a microphone, even by permission, would impale him on the horns of a dilemma. If company personnel were to become hyperconscious of the recorder, business would come to a standstill; yet if there were any relaxation of vigilance, confidential material would surely go down on the tape. Feeling a little as if he had been suddenly transplanted behind the Iron Curtain, the vice-president decided to stall Mr. Jackson—at least until he could determine what the man's game really was.

The subsequent investigation did little to restore his peace of mind. A request for advice addressed to a friend, an investigator in a federal agency, brought an admonition to notify the FBI rather than the Washington police, against the possibility that the latter might be in on the deal themselves, as they had been in previous cases. (During the ugly vendetta against Howard Hughes' T.W.A. by Owen Brewster, then a Senator from Maine, Metropolitan Police Lieutenant Joseph W. Shimon tapped the Mayflower Hotel telephones of the Hughes attorneys, and suffered no stiffer punishment than a departmental transfer.) At the FBI, the vice-president was told to go along with the Jackson proposition so as to collect incriminating evidence. For his part, Mr. Jackson was not impatient; he was getting $25 a day and expenses, and he and his colleague spent a convivial week end with a brace of local belles. Reports substantiating the Jackson story soon began to come in from the FBI. But by Thursday the vice-president had had a bellyful of "all this cloak-and-dagger stuff" and informed Mr. Jackson the deal was off. The office underwent a meticulous search for microphones, the locks were all changed; and a wire from the Gordon Hotel, discovered dangling in happy anticipation just above the vice-president's window, was torn down. But to this day the vice-president isn't sure that no information was stolen. Shortly after he had broken off with Mr. Jackson, the Washington grapevine carried the word that a stack of the vice-president's confidential letters and memos (photostated) had turned up in the hands of the West Coast competitor.

## The Appetite for Information

The current upsurge of industrial espionage, which is employing many thousands of Mr. Jacksons, is mainly attributable to a toughening of competition, with a resultant increase in the pressure on ethics. But two less obvious developments are also responsible, and these, like the heightened competition, are essentially postwar in origin.

The first is the terrific premium American industry now puts on all kinds of information. Ask the average executive what preoccupies him most, and he'll be obliged to say: information. From the moment he enters the office, his central concern is collecting it, evaluating it, acting upon it. The volume and scope of government data have increased enormously since the war. Trade journals and newsletters, themselves proliferating in the postwar boom, regularly bring to his desk specialized information on taxes, financial trends, political possibilities, trade situations. From within his own establishment he gets valuable sales data, expansion studies, cost analyses, and the reports of that recently recognized genre, the marketing specialists. Information about his competitors arrives with less formality but in substantial volume. Suppliers furnish it, often as a sales fillip, or it may come from an incautious word dropped by the competitor himself. For example, an American Motors executive, in between putts, let fall that next year's Nash would be of a certain over-all height; this single dimension would enable a competitive designer, knowing the trend Nash was working on and the cowl-cab-rear-deck ratios involved, to evolve an astonishingly accurate side view of the forthcoming car.

Naturally, much of business' new appetite for information is satisfied by routine and quite ethical procedures ranging all the way from staff studies to industrial intelligence. Industrial intelligence itself encompasses activities that extend from innocuous practices, like pumping a competitor, to reprehensible ones employing fake polls and phony letterheads. Comparative shopping is an example of intelligence in its acceptable form and sometimes reaches a high order of development, as in the case where Macy's, bound to observe manufacturers' minimum prices until it could prove others broke them, cracked the price-tag code of Masters Inc., the giant New York discount house. But the line between business intelligence and business espionage is sometimes vague, and depends on what has come to be accepted practice. In the oil industry, regularly employed scouts, really spies, are expected to try to beat the successful well driller out of part of his rewards. They steal telltale core samples while posing as equipment salesmen, college boys, itinerant preachers; or they just watch a drill rig through field glasses until oil is struck, then hightail it to the nearest phone and take up options on the surrounding land.

That's the way the game is played by all companies concerned, and the economic incentives being what they are, it would be sheer sanctimony to expect anything else. In Detroit, on the other hand, some motorcar people photograph whatever they see on the road that looks like a disguised prototype, yet they would condemn as espionage any peeking through a styling-studio window with a long-range telescope. Thus business intelligence may be considered as the getting of competitive information by all *legal* means. Industrial espionage, however, has no justification either in ethics or in law; it is a culpable contravention of the basic right to privacy in one's person and property.

What brings some businessmen to cross the line into industrial espionage is the inability of business intelligence to satisfy their voracious appetite for information. No amount of routine intelligence work would have been able to adduce, say, the contents of the $250,000 cost study made of Packard at the time James Nance took over its presidency. But industrial espionage might have delivered it within a fortnight. Industrial espionage makes it possible for unscrupulous managements to get million-dollar information at bargain-basement prices. Instead of developing their own marketing data, industrial processes, and contract-bid figures, they find it profitable, and relatively safe, to steal their competitors'. Thus the practitioners of industrial espionage not only get information at nominal cost, but acquire along with it the invaluable knowledge that that information is the basis of their competitors' strategy.

While businessmen were working up the informational appetites that for some culminated in industrial espionage, there was an equally spectacular development in the *means* of getting somebody else's secrets. These techniques, already well advanced by World War II, were improved and elaborated as the cold war brought into being our first big peacetime espionage system. Over the past fifteen years thousands of FBI, OSS, CIA, Signal Corps, and military-intelligence men have been trained as spies, and in the use of complicated electronic equipment. They picked up much industrial information in their wire tapping, surveillances, and so on, and got their first clear understanding of the lucrative possibilities of business espionage. Then, as higher salaries of industry attracted them, many left to set up shop as independent operators or to take corporate jobs as undercover investigators—"security men" is the preferred euphemism.[2] Detroit, for instance, has become a Mecca both for corporate security men and independent operatives. Though the ex-agents on piecework assignment are prone to grouse that car manufacturers reserve "the big jobs" for their regular employees, the free-lancers have nevertheless done quite well. A group of ex-FBI men now forms Michigan's biggest "professional" investigative agency (all accountants or lawyers), and one ex-agent in Detroit recently refused to discuss his espionage activities for the illuminating reason that to do so "would jeopardize $50,000 worth of business a year." This influx of highly trained operatives, on top of the normal development of undercover men from within the nation's 5,000-odd detective agencies, has enormously increased the effectiveness of industrial espionage.

## EASY DOES IT

The typical approach of an undercover man to his work, like that of any other pro, is to exert no more effort than absolutely necessary. Very often a great deal can be learned about a business simply by bribing a janitor or charwoman to save the contents of office wastebaskets. Stenographers habitually throw away spoiled letters, contracts, etc., intact, while the average executive is so unmindful of what he puts into his "round file" that one investigator recently remarked, "Give me a company's waste paper for a couple of weeks and I'll tell you all about its operations." Other more or less standard procedures include the use of a horn-shaped listening device, sensitive enough to pick up conversations through the open windows of offices or parked automobiles across the street; telephoto movies of business conversations, subsequently "translated" at lip-reading schools; or telescopic close-ups of test tracks and styling studios from low-flying planes and helicopters. (G.M.'s new $175-million Technical Center is being equipped with electronic devices that will automatically draw the curtains over its studio windows at the near approach of any aircraft; outside, a similar system in the amphitheater will summon attendants to cover up new models being displayed to management.) Then of course there is "hooking," a sort of confidence game

[2] The Society of Former Special Agents of the FBI, Inc., claims a membership of 3,500, last year signed up 500. It is estimated that Ford alone employs over thirty ex-agents.

with information rather than money as the goal. Two classic examples:

An undercover man, assigned to ascertain the (unpatented) chemical process of a competitor, determined the habits of a likely source, an assistant plant manager, "Mr. Clark," and managed to meet him. In their first conversation the agent, posing as a chemical executive, mentioned that good chemical men were hard to get, and that his own company was having the devil of a time finding a manager for a plant being built in the Middle West—did Clark know of anybody who might be interested in a $15,000 job? Indeed he did: himself. Well, the operative reluctantly explained, the new plant was to be in a quite different branch of the industry (an important point in allaying the quarry's suspicions); had he had any experience in that kind of production? Clark had not, but the agent pretended to be so impressed with his general capabilities that, at a second "chance" meeting, he suggested Clark work up a detailed description of his own plant's processes, and his part in them, "so that I can convince our technical people you know your stuff on this job." Clark, no doubt prepared to put his knowledge at a new employer's disposal anyway, assented. With the proudly detailed process description in his pocket, the agent disappeared; as for Clark, even if he were to deduce the identity of the real company behind the swindle, he would be the last man to complain of what had happened.

Seismograph Service Corp. of Tulsa learned from one of its customers that a talented young Virginia electronics engineer had developed a system that established the exact offshore position of seismographic mapping ships, an essential to the collection of exact geological data. The bearer of this important intelligence was Seismograph's chief customer, Phillips Petroleum, for which Seismograph had itself been trying unsuccessfully to produce an effective positioning apparatus. The engineer's name, said the Phillips man, was Charles Hastings, and he went on to describe in detail the disclosures Hastings had made about his Raydist system. Phillips' suggestion: Seismograph should consult Hastings about their problems. What happened then has been luminously described by New Orleans Judge J. Skelly Wright in an opinion handed down last year:

"Instead of going to Hastings as upright businessmen, Seismograph determined to steal his work. [Dr. James E.] Hawkins, an officer and director of Seismograph . . . immediately applied for patents on the system and variations thereof in the hope that the inexperienced and impecunious Hastings had not already done so. But Seismograph did not stop there. It sent its executive vice-president to Virginia to learn more of Hastings' secrets and to offer him a brave plan by which they would form a joint venture to exploit the system. The brave plan was even reduced to writing and presented to Hastings for his consideration. Seismograph invited Hastings to its home office, further to pick his brains and milk him of the information on Raydist he had been so long acquiring. During the time Seismograph was deluding Hastings with the offer of a joint venture, its own technicians, led by Hawkins, were perfecting their own version of the Raydist system based on the information Hastings had given them. By August 1, 1947, Seismograph felt it had no longer any use for Hastings, having obtained all the information it needed. Still it held the lure of joint venture before his eyes, so that he would not give his information to Seismograph's competitor, Offshore Navigation, and so that it, Seismograph, would have time to perfect its patent position. . . . Seismograph's president, Westby, even conjured up a fake demonstration, and had Hastings prepare equipment for the demonstration for Phillips representatives who were never even advised that a demonstration was to take place. Indeed, Seismograph even stooped to espionage on Hastings' patent counsel. Thus it was that Seismograph was able to perfect its Raydist system, which it called Lorac." With Lorac patented, Seismograph then had the audacity to sue Hastings for patent infringement with Raydist. This suit Judge Wright dismissed on grounds that any patent "obtained through fraud and dishonest dealings is unenforceable in a court of equity."

## INSIDE INDUSTRY

All of the foregoing measures are possible without ever crossing the victim's threshold. When an invasion of the premises does become desirable the business esponiage game gets dirtier and more complicated, but here again the industrial spy can count on a great deal of technical help. Tiny portable transmitters, hardly bigger than a package of cigarettes, can be taped under an executive's desk, and for the two weeks' life of the batteries will broadcast all conversations to a receiver located a block or so away. (The late Serge Rubinstein, who often boasted his most profitable ventures were the result of electronic eavesdropping, even brought espionage into the boudoir by attaching one of these little devices to the springs of a lady friend's bed.) A somewhat similar instrument can be fitted into a wall or' floor plug, from which it transmits through the building's electrical system to a receiver. Wire taps, of course, are the meat and potatoes of the industrial spy, but even these have undergone startling improvements. They will now pick up a voice even when the phone receiver is on the hook; moreover, a recently developed switch starts the recorder only when a voice comes over the line—eliminating costly monitoring and reducing frequency of reel changes.

In situations where such mechanical means are unsuitable or ineffective, the agent simply gets himself into the plant or office by a ruse, preferably at night, for night workers usually are several cuts below the day shift in alertness or intelligence. One operator gained free run of a well-guarded factory by showing the badge lent him by an obliging fire battalion chief. Another posed as a state official, with a set of bona fide departmental car tags "borrowed" for the occasion. A building inspector, charged with enforcing weight restrictions on factory floors, has also been of service, the agent either assuming his identity or accompanying him as an "assistant." Few agents, however, pass themselves off as policemen. The police are not only universally ill-tempered about anyone's "impersonating an officer," but some policemen, properly approached, have shown a remarkable disposition to be helpful.

## O.K. There, Joe?

"My job," recalls a New York investigator, "was to get my client a sample of a special kind of [unpatented] sewing-machine spindle a competitor had developed in a middle-western factory. I got in touch with an agreeable city detective and we went out to the plant in a patrol car. There he and the driver showed their badges to the night watchman and told him they had seen a suspicious flashlight up on the roof: they'd like to have a look around. The plan was for me to tag along as if I were one of them and then when they took the watchman up to the roof, I was to stop off on the second floor where the machines are set up. I found the spindles easily and slipped one into my pocket. Pretty soon I heard one of the detectives call to me:

'Everything O.K. there, Joe?' If I needed more time, I was to say: 'I'd like to look around a little longer,' then they'd take the watchman off to some other floor, but I had the spindle, so out we went."

The true test of an accomplished industrial spy, however, is getting into plants and offices not for one-night stands, but rather for months at a time. This, the so-called undercover operation, is as rich in its rewards as in its complications. Most of it is done through secondary agents, for private detectives themselves are too easily spotted through routine investigation. If possible, contact is made with some susceptible person already employed by the company concerned. In the main, such individuals never intended to become spies when they were first hired, but turned to espionage through boredom, dissatisfaction, need of funds, or friendship for a colleague now employed by the competition. For all of that, they are the most effective of espionage agents, very hard to detect, and likely to continue their operations for years unless they carelessly let themselves become identified with information that later turns up in the hands of a competitor.

## BONUSES FOR TIDBITS

If there is no established source inside the company, one is "planted" there. John Leon, a Washington, D.C., private detective, specializing in undercover operations in the small experimental electronics companies of the surrounding area, usually begins such an assignment by putting a want ad in the paper for a suitable job classification. Technicians, engineers, electricians, and maintenance personnel are preferred to desk men because of their ability to move freely about without attracting suspicion.

A satisfactory applicant is selected by personal interview from those responding to the ad; then the pitch begins: a certain type of "general" information is needed from the "Electroray Co."; if the applicant can land a job with them (a relatively easy task in this high-turnover industry) the detective will supplement his income by as much as $60 a week, with bonuses for especially valuable tidbits. With the prospective spy going on the detective's payroll immediately, awaiting employment, indoctrination begins: "I tell him how to write reports, what to look for, how to photograph documents, or get them out at night and bring them back in the morning. If the man is a technician, I interest him in being a detective someday and I pretend something quite different from what I'm actually trying to do. You gradually work him into what you are doing and tell him as little as possible. He doesn't know who your client is, or why you want the information, or which information is really important. That way, if he gets caught or outlives his usefulness you have no trouble. On cases where there's only a limited amount of money available, I advertise for a man to do part-time work on Sunday or in the evenings. Sometimes in the answers I find a man actually employed in the bank or business I want to get into. This is the guy I'll hire, give him some innocuous make-work until I can win his confidence enough to get the particular information my client is after."

## COLLECTING "EVIDENCE"

By and large, undercover operations are assigned by lawyers (in whom the principals have unbounded confidence) and executed by individual investigators or the smaller detective agencies. The biggest agencies avowedly engage in it only to collect evidence for patent-infringement cases. The stated reasons for their abstention are moral, but no doubt practical considerations carry some weight. Potential customers for plant-protection service (a lucrative part of a big agency's business) are understandably leery about buying it from any agency that also engages in business espionage. (In a ludicrous foul-up some years back, one of an agency's guards unwittingly arrested one of its undercover men at work in the same plant.) Even so, the techniques in patent-infringement cases, as illustrated in these examples from the Pinkerton files, do not differ from those employed in "standard" undercover operations:

To get samples of a fine white clay in various stages of processing for a client who thought his patents were being infringed, a Negro investigator was sent to a remote section of Florida where the suspected competitor had his mines. He moved into one of the shanties on the outskirts of town, among a group of Negro mine employees. To one of these he posed as a voodoo doctor whose special power lay in the "conjuhs" he could perform with the fine white clay. The employee, assured of secrecy, compensation, and immunity from boo daddies, hags, and other "ha'nts," furnished the essential samples, which were soon on their way to the client.

To collect process data from a Texas food company, suspected by their client of infringing its patents, three youthful Pinkerton investigators posed as local college boys hopeful of writing up the company for their college paper. The prospect of free publicity so beguiled the company's management that a foreman was assigned to the three investigators with instructions to take them on a plant tour and answer any questions they might ask. Openly taking notes, and helped over the tough spots by the eager foreman, the Pinkerton men jotted down the entire process, even to temperatures and pressures. The resulting infringement suit was a snap.

At the opposite pole, ethically, from undercover work is what might be called "white espionage." This is the widespread practice of hiring the man who has the desired information. He is expected to deliver, and usually does. Many employers, like Westinghouse Electric, recognize that what a man knows is his stock in trade, and so they put no restriction on any disclosures he may make to his new bosses. Some, like chemical companies, require employees to sign formal secrecy agreements. Where white espionage enters the picture in actionable form is through an ex-employee's breach of these agreements or his use of trade secrets in a business of his own. Linde Air Products, now part of Union Carbide, successfully sued a former employee who had worked on Linde's process for making synthetic star sapphires and then left to use the same process in his own company. Last year a Maryland judge ruled that Colgate-Palmolive Co. had wrongfully appropriated the trade secrets of Carter Products Inc., after it hired a young Carter chemist who had promised not to disclose a secret process for making pressurized shaving soap (Rise).

## The Irregulars

But the ethical aspects of industrial espionage, while they may bother the amateur, trouble the pro hardly at all. The latter draws much comfort from the single fact that the Department of Justice, the agency charged with responsibility for prosecuting illegal wire tapping, refrains from so doing because it too indulges in the practice. His reservations are thus almost entirely material. "I wouldn't think of doing a thing like spying on a client's competitor," explained an ex-FBI agent recently, "unless, of course, the client gave us some more business." What does bother the pro is espionage by "irregulars," the self-anointed spies recklessly hawking their wares on the open market.

Some Detroit teen-agers recently sidled up to a G.M. public-relations man, proffering snapshots they had taken of "a Ford prototype." He sent them packing without so much as a peek. Far more serious was the 1954 camera work of a Roseville, Michigan, policeman who, as a G.M. protection guard, had slipped into the company's old styling studio and photographed the '56 models of Buick, Chevrolet, Olds, and the supersecret turbine car, the Firebird. But when he and two confederates tried to peddle their pictures to a competitor (at the bargain rate of $1,000) the competitor prudently declined and notified General Motors. G.M. had had the spy under surveillance while he worked for them—their suspicions aroused by his over-eagerness to be transferred to the styling studio—and they went into action at once. The films were soon recovered by the ruse of having them purchased by an independent designer, and the culprits arrested (though not prosecuted, for that would have required public presentation of the evidence—the pictures). Unlike his "professional" colleagues, all the irregular can expect for his perfidy is exposure.

## PERILS OF SPY HUNTING

As one might anticipate, the means by which management may combat espionage are sometimes as pernicious as the practice itself. Wholesale investigations of personnel, such as a spy hunt Chas. Pfizer & Co. put on in 1954, are self-defeating. Even if one were to establish the source of the information leaks, and Pfizer failed to do so even after spending over $60,000 to pry into the personal life of several hundred employees, the damage to morale is likely to bring on a recrudescence of espionage by the remaining staff. For loyalty to the company keeps many potential spies in check; when this is destroyed, personal attitudes change: what would have been considered the betrayal of a friend becomes intelligence against an enemy. The setting up of TV cameras on assembly lines, putting "open" microphones in executive offices, or the planting of "mice"—telephone-company slang for management informers—are equally indefensible and costly to morale. Certainly a boss cannot be expected to turn a deaf ear to internal informants but he should apply the same ground rules to his office that he uses at home, viz., that tattling by a member of the "family" is not encouraged as a matter of policy and puts the informer in the wrong, except where Johnny has been seen lighting matches in the woodbin.

## The Best Defense

The first step in establishing a sensible security system is mental. Executives must begin thinking of information for what it is, money. Valuable data should no more be permitted to lie around on a desk top, tempting the susceptible, than a sheaf of hundred-dollar bills. (U.S. Steel, for example, requires its Executive Committee members to turn confidential material back to the Secretary at the end of each meeting.) Once this point of view is accepted, simple physical measures can make it tough for the spy: where confidential information must be given over the phone, "scramblers" at both ends of the line will neutralize wire tapping; paper shredders can be installed in individual offices, or a central trash system with a shredder set up for "sensitive" departments. But the best security of all comes from having good people. This means more than keeping them happy on the job, it means the careful screening of each applicant. All too frequently company personnel departments fail to check back on an applicant's work history or talk to his former employers. In one case, where an electronics engineer was being paid by one firm to spy on a dozen others, such a check would have uncovered so many falsehoods that no prudent company would have hired him.

Once American business has taken all reasonable measures to protect itself from industrial espionage, it should not be unduly alarmed that some leakage continues. Human nature being what it is, absolute business secrecy is impossible, even undesirable. The most any company has a right to expect is adequate lead time. Corporate energies, then, should not be absorbed in protecting archaic secrets but in producing new ones. Dynamism is a superb offensive measure against espionage. For espionage, a state of dependence on what others know is debilitating to its practitioners and the faster the quarry moves the quicker the initiative of a spying competitor will be destroyed. Said the old sea captain, voicing the advantages of a clean pair of heels in Kipling's *The "Mary Gloster"*:

> And they asked me how I did it,
> And I gave 'em the Scripture text,

"You keep your light so shining
A little in front o' the next!"
They copied all they could follow,
But they couldn't copy my mind,
And I left 'em sweating and stealing
A year and a half behind.

# V

## LIMITATIONS

Far better it is to dare mighty things, to win glorious triumphs, even though checked by failure, than to take rank with those poor spirits who neither enjoy much nor suffer much, because they live in the gray twilight that knows neither victory or defeat.

—Theodore Roosevelt

# 34.

# *Introduction*

• Perfect economic forecasting will always be beyond the ability of mortal men. The ancient folk saying that "business is a gamble" hasn't lost its profundity. But an executive is crazy if he doesn't try to get the best odds in that gamble. Present techniques of forecasting can greatly reduce uncertainty about the future—and they show promise of getting much better.

• The most common way to detour around unreliable forecasts is to separate those parts of the operation that will not be affected by the uncertain factor and plan only for them in considerable detail.

• Planning is expensive and time-consuming, the more so as it is projected further into the future. There comes a point when a decision must be taken, when a course of action must be selected, and when plans must be translated into action. Whether ready or not, the management may be forced to move.

• Every management believes that it is relentlessly pursuing the goal of sound growth, but the weaknesses of human nature somehow tend to get in the way.

So say the contributors to this section on the limitations of long-range planning—and they point up many other problems as well, along with suggestions for coping with them. It is a very good idea to keep these limitations in mind. By thinking positively *and* realistically about planning, we can keep it from becoming another fad.

Earlier in this book we saw that outlining a company's future strategy means looking at the business in a very analytical, factual, and critical way. We saw that the planner must appraise the firm's strengths and weaknesses as well as trends in the industry and in the economy. Obviously, if this is done there will be many mistakes made.

Some goals will be too high, others too low; errors in timing will occur; and so forth. Difficulties of this nature will not always be due to human nature, for there is not only the handicap of uncertain forecasts to worry the planners but the practical impossibility of making a timetable for ideas, or of knowing for sure which up-and-coming executives will be able to take over a job that needs to be done, and how soon they will be ready to handle it.

But while all this is true, it is important to understand that the limitations of planning are not inelastic. They may not always be so severe as they are at first in a company's history. Experience in planning, especially if it is shared by many executives in the company, is bound to reduce the number of mistakes that are made in the future. The work of today's planners will be a valuable legacy for the planners of tomorrow. It will increase their skill, maturity, and confidence.

But *doing* is the key, not knowledge. I believe it was the novelist James Cain who remarked that you can't teach a writer to write by describing the process to him any more than you can teach a woman how to have a baby by letting her watch somebody else have one; the only way he can really learn is by going through with it himself. The same may be true of long-range planning. The literature will be helpful. It will provide ideas. It will show how somebody else looks at the problem, which is always helpful. But its values will not materialize until the reader personally gets into planning and actually helps translate a program into action. When that happens he will really be able to make some headway against the limitations of planning.

## Contributors to This Section

*The Editors of Business Week* put out a magazine which needs no introduction to businessmen or business students. The article reprinted in these pages is but one of a long series of interesting *Business Week* stories on forecasting, economic projections, and long-term trends.

*William H. Newman* is Samuel Bronfman Professor of Democratic Business Enterprise at Columbia University; and *Harold Koontz* and *Cyril O'Donnell* are with the School of Business Administration, University of California at Los Angeles. (For further details about these men, see earlier sections of the book.)

*Keith Powlison* is Vice-President and Secretary of Armstrong Cork Company. Active in many business organizations, he has served as a Director of the American Management Association, a Trustee of the Controllership Foundation, and a Trustee of the Joint Council on Economic Education.

# 35.

# Business Forecasting

BY THE EDITORS OF *Business Week* [1]

At the first United Nations Conference in San Francisco in 1945, the late Edward R. Stettinius, Jr., once chairman of U.S. Steel, and at the time Secretary of State, was posing for a picture. The photographer was Joe Rosenthal, who not long before had shot the classic picture of the flag-raising on Mt. Suribachi.

"How do you want me, Joe?" asked Stettinius.

"Look as if you're peering into the future," said Rosenthal.

"How do I do that?" asked Stettinius, and looked stricken.

"Okay," said Rosenthal, "so just peer."

Like Stettinius, many a businessman and government official has experienced a hopeless, hapless feeling when confronted with the necessity of gazing into mists of the future—but has, nevertheless, composed his features into the proper expression of executive omniscience and gone on making decisions, whether he could see anything ahead or not.

For every policymaker knows that, like it or not, he lives in the future. His every decision must be based on some forecast. And action based on a wrong forecast can be fatal.

That's why the common and most fundamental question every businessman asks is, "What's the business outlook?" He seeks the answer from his business cronies, his banker, his broker; from newspapers, bank letters, tipsheets, magazines; from the U.S. government; and from a corps of economists.

[1] Reprinted from the September 24, 1955, issue of *Business Week* by special permission.

*Desperate Chance*—Since these seers frequently seem to speak in as many tongues as did the hod carriers at Babel, a harried businessman is often tempted to give up and flip a coin to get a forecast on which he can base decisions.

Coin-tossing as a forecasting technique might once have made sense. But now it makes less sense all the time, as economic forecasting moves from charlatanry to science.

Perfect economic forecasting will undoubtedly always be beyond the ability of mortal men, since economic events are part of the chance-ridden skein of history. But techniques of forecasting, capable of greatly reducing uncertainty about the future, exist now and show promise of getting considerably better.

U.S. business these days is increasingly basing its major decisions on careful and detailed economic forecasts. Says Cecil Burrell, who directs the eighty-man economic staff of Standard Oil Co. of New Jersey, "I don't see how you can run any business without them."

This is the approach that's changing the job of the entrepreneur. Classically, he was a risk-taker. But now modern management, backed by professional economists, is coming to see that risk reduction is a key part of its job. Because of this change, you can define management's function today as one of blending forecasts and programs. Every sound economic forecast implies a sound program.

*Two Fields*—To make the blend, then, the businessman must have the forecast. And, to find the forecast he can get into the realms of either art or science.

For most of recorded time, the world got along without much science. So it's certainly no insult to any human activity to call it an art and not a science.

The nature of an art, however, is such that the quality of its product depends mainly on the talent of the artist. What he does cannot really be explained or taught. There have doubtless been some magnificent business forecasters in history, but they were artists, and their talent—or their luck—cannot be communicated to others.

Today, economic forecasting is part science, part art. This report, however, will attempt to explain only the scientific aspects of economic forecasting.

## CHOOSING THE PITCH

There are three basic strategies for economic forecasting. You can call them: (1) loaded-deck, (2) oaks-from-acorns, and (3) test-tube.

*The loaded-deck* strategy may look spurious, but it's extremely important in business forecasting. To work with it you must know what has happened or is happening before anyone else knows, or else you must be able to catch the future just as it arrives at the present. If you know how a deck of cards is stacked, then you know how they'll be dealt—here, the present is identical with the future. The strategy won't work without inside information and fast accurate reporting. But when these are available the results can be impressive. For instance, advance news of the outcome of the Battle of Waterloo, brought through their own carrier pigeons, gave the Rothschilds their chance to make a fortune on the London Stock Exchange in 1815.

*Oaks-from-acorns* forecasting is based on the concept that the future is not identical with the present, but is an outgrowth of it. So, if you know how the present is germinating or growing, you can figure out what the future probably will be. Closely related to this idea is the notion that change through time is rhythmic or cyclic—and that, like the life and death cycles of plants and animals, business activity also has its expansions and contractions. With this strategy, you forecast by detecting the symptoms of a change of phase.

*Test-tube,* or systematic, forecasting stems from the concept that, though changes in the natural world seem confusing and chaotic, scientific analysis can reveal certain underlying regularities. The way to find these regularities (or laws, principles, or theories) is to black out much of reality and hold only to the abstractions. Though the theories that result will be "unreal," they'll still possess tremendous power to affect the real world, provided that they are sound theories. You find out if a theory is sound by testing how it measures up when it meets with the real world: An atomic explosion confirms Einstein's $E = mc^2$; an increase in employment following a reduction in the rate of interest confirms Keynes.

*For Mystics, Too*—All scientific economic forecasting depends on one or another, or a combination of these three strategies. Even those who make forecasting an art and cloak it in mysticism probably depend on them, too.

That's been the case with forecasting for thousands of years. The high priests of ancient Egypt preached nonsensical gobbledygook to the masses when prophesying future levels of the Nile, but secretly performed careful calculations of the river's movements. Today, many a businessman conceals or is not entirely conscious of the observations and reasoning behind his "hunches" and "instincts."

## I. Who Can Use It?

Ultimately, every businessman must make his own judgments. Whether he wants to employ a professional economist, or economic staff, or outside consultants to prepare forecasts on which he can base his judgments, depends mainly on the nature of his business and of the problems he faces. He can probably use expert counsel:

If, like U.S. Steel or R. H. Macy & Co., his business swings a lot with the business cycle.

If, like Westinghouse Electric Corp. or Armstrong Cork Co., he sells to a great many customers, not to just a few big ones.

If, like General Motors, Ford, or Chrysler, he makes a product with a long production lead time.

If, like Standard Oil of New Jersey, or Socony Mobil, he's got to look several years into the future to plan capital expansion programs.

If, like all those mentioned, he can afford to hire good economic talent that can tell him more about the general business outlook, and the future of his own particular business, than he can get from other sources. (Those "other sources" can include: a couple of good newspapers and magazines, business colleagues, a trade association, or government publications.)

*Man for the Job*—Companies vary enormously in what they pay economists and what they budget for economic staffs. The National Industrial Conference Board made a survey of forty-two companies in 1950 to find out about these salaries and budgets, and the survey's results still seem valid. It showed that annual budgets for economic staffs ranged from $10,000 to $375,000, with the average at $38,000. Salaries paid to economists ranged from $5,000 to $36,000, with the median at $12,000. The top figure would, of course, be exceeded by some professional economists, like Theodore Yntema, Ford's treasurer, who have graduated from the technician class to the highest echelon.

Many companies look for their economists to rise as Yntema has done. They try to hire a man who is not simply a good technician but who looks as if he might eventually make a first-rank company officer.

But, whatever other material you might look for if you hire an economist, you want to make sure you get one who knows his trade—and knows how to forecast. This isn't necessarily easy.

Economists have a way to go before they get their forecasting techniques straightened out. Right now, there are almost as many ways of business forecasting as there are forecasters. Four causes lie behind this fact: (1) Business forecasting grew up largely on "the wrong side of the tracks"—i.e., in Wall Street and in industry—where it escaped academic codification; (2) you need different techniques to solve different forecasting problems; (3) many forecasters apparently seek to build their personal prestige by marginal differences in their product; and (4) competence and training vary widely among the forecasters.

It would take volumes to explain all the forecasting techniques used these days. It's possible though, to find the chief techniques that economists use when they're working with any of the three basic strategies of forecasting.

## GETTING DOWN TO BUSINESS

Many economists—among them some who have physically left the academic cloisters—still regard economic forecasting as a low and disreputable pursuit for learned men. "We don't know enough about the past to know anything much about the future," they say. So, they suggest, business must wait another hundred years or so before it can expect the savants to say anything meaningful about the future. Meanwhile, they maintain, it is proper that they should qualify all statements about the future to the point of meaninglessness.

But the number of economists who hold to this pure patient view of their calling is shrinking. More and more of them feel that if economics is to have any pretense of being a useful study its claim must rest on its ability to predict developments, and to provide solid foundations for policymakers to build on.

*Pushed Into It*—One of the chief reasons for the fact that more of them are overcoming their inhibitions about forecasting, and are concentrating on improving its techniques, is that they're being immersed deeper and deeper in government and business, where eyes are always on the future.

## Grabbing the Future

For the "loaded-deck" strategy, there are four techniques:

*Inside Information.* The technique is simple: Be an insider, know an insider, or pay money to somebody who says he will get inside information for you.

*Fast Information and Analysis.* Typical problem: Should we step up production next week, and, if so, in what product lines? What kind of orders will we be getting from our dealers? Technique: Find out what the dealers are selling this week by getting immediate reports on all sales; tabulate the answers by high-speed calculators and relate the data to inventory records.

*Knowledge of Limits* that can't change much through the forecast period. Typical problem: What will be the volume of durable goods production during a period of great defense expansion and booming demand? Technique: Find out how much steel the government intends to make available for civilian production.

*Spotting the Initial Phase* of a lengthy process. Technique: Investigate your field, working with such knowledge as: (1) construction contracts awarded are the first phase of future building starts; (2) orders received by manufacturers are the first phase of the coming volume of production; (3) plans for capital spending programs precede new investment.

In all such loaded-deck forecasting, it sometimes happens that the deck is unloaded against the forecaster. Life never runs out of surprises. But if the information is sound, a forecast based on present facts and linked closely to developments in the near future will generally be realized.

So these techniques have, and always will have, importance for anticipating particular situations and problems. But their usefulness in forecasting a broad and complex economic picture is limited. You can't necessarily get the scoop on the next development of the American economy by being a personal friend of the Secretary of the Treasury. On the other hand—don't cut him.

## II. Watching It Grow

You get four chief techniques in the "oaks-from-acorns" strategy, too.

*Trend Extrapolation.* Extrapolation is a six-bit word borrowed from the mathematicians. In this case it means predicting the future movements of an economic factor by projecting into the future the trends you know it has taken in the past. On a chart, an extrapolation looks like this (Fig. 1).

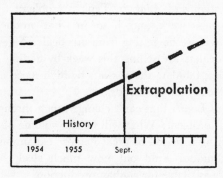

Fig. 1.

**Gap in the System**—What makes an extrapolation useful to a forecaster is the statistical fact that a trend that's advancing will keep advancing—at least until something else happens. Unfortunately, the technique won't tell you when the "something else" will come. For instance, a wage series that's pushing upward will tend to push prices upward, and that will tend to push wages up again—only not ad infinitum. Eventually, some other series, like a falling sales volume, may halt or reverse the upward wage-price spiral.

But if, in your business, you don't need to care much about cyclical swings around a trend—if, for instance, you're figuring out the number of telephones or kilowatt hours the American people will want to use in the next ten years—trend extrapolation is a useful technique.

Of course, you can put trend extrapolation to work in a more sophisticated way than simply by laying a ruler over the past direction of a business indicator and projecting it on into the future. If you sell books or whisky you may find your sales correlate nicely with the trend of disposable personal income, or if you sell oil or copper your sales may link up well with the Federal Reserve Index of Production.

*"Leading" series.* Andrew Carnegie constructed his own leading series for economic forecasting—by counting the smoking factory chimneys he saw. His was the archetype of the technique.

In the 1920's a hot search was on for a sort of economic philosopher's stone—a single business indicator that would always lead general business development. Some thought it lay in stock market activity; others saw it in interest rates, pig iron production, carloadings, or Dun & Bradstreet's index of business failures. Debate still rages over which of these are "old wives' indicators" and which possess real leading characteristics.

**Search Goes On**—The outstanding hunter for indicators with forecasting value is the National Bureau of Economic Research. It has been scrutinizing masses of business cycle data for more than three decades. Before World War II, Wesley C. Mitchell, the bureau's guiding genius, and Arthur F. Burns, now chairman of President Eisenhower's Council of Economic Advisers, examined hundreds of series, picked a set of twenty-one leading, coincident, and lagging indicators, whose movements had regularly traced the course of the business cycle.

After the war, the bureau's Geoffrey H. Moore set to work updating Mitchell's and Burns's work. Moore examined 801 monthly and quarterly indicators, selected twenty-one, some of which were the same as those chosen by Mitchell and Burns. Of the twenty-one, Moore's eight leading series are: residential building contracts, commercial and industrial building contracts, new orders for durable goods, prices of industrial common stocks, wholesale prices of basic commodities, average work week in manufacturing, new incorporations, and business failures.

These indicators do regularly lead the business cycle's turns—though there's argument over just why this happens. But the chief trouble with them is that they are all extremely sensitive. They oscillate a great deal from month to month. So it's hard to know, when making a forecast, whether an up or downturn in one or another of the leading series means the real McCoy, or whether it's only a temporary wiggle.

*Diffusion Indexes.* To find the meaning of those upturns and downturns, the bureau has invented a thing called the diffusion index. The bureau developed the index after it discovered that business cycle movements "have invariably been preceded by a remarkably regular cycle in the proportion of industrial activities undergoing expansion or contraction."

Forecasters make the index by counting the number of indicators in a given group that are rising at a given time. They convert this into a percentage of the number of indicators in the group. The bureau labels this percentage as a diffusion index because it believes it shows how widely diffused economic movements are. The bureau's diffusion indexes generally reach their peaks and troughs six months to twelve months ahead of the peaks and troughs of general business activity.

**Doubtful Quantity**—not all economists think the diffusion index is much of a step forward. Arthur L. Broida, a Federal Reserve Board economist, maintains that it isolates cyclical turning points from all other changes in the economy's direction some time after the event. He holds that the index shows nothing different from what statisticians have long achieved by noting rates of growth and decline of a series of indicators. Their notes have already shown that a slower rate of increase in an index generally precedes its downturn.

*Wright's Indicator.* This device for determining real turns in the business cycle is named for its inventor, Ashley Wright, a Standard Oil Co. of New Jersey economist.

Wright's gimmick is to make shrewd use of the normal distribution curve, which looks like this (Fig. 2).

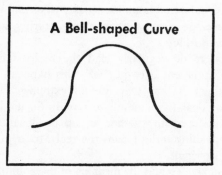

Fig. 2.

Because of its appearance, this is also called the "bell-shaped curve." The statistical concept behind it is simply this: Divergences from a "norm" or average will tend to cluster in a bell-shaped curve, because the small divergences are more frequent than the large ones, the very large divergences are rare, and divergences of the same size are equally likely to occur on the plus or minus side of the norm.

Wright put the theory to work when he found that upturns and downturns of a large number of business indicators tend to cluster in a bell-shaped curve, and that the peaks and troughs of the curve show up the turning points of the general business cycle.

**Recession by Numbers**—For instance, suppose that forty business indicators begin to turn downward, as follows:

|  Month  | Number of Series That Turned Down |
|---------|:---------------------------------:|
| January | 2 |
| February | 4 |
| March | 6 |

There it is March, and twelve of the series have already turned down. You must be headed for a turn in the general business cycle soon. It will come at the point where the mass of downturning business indicators cluster. Sure enough—

|  |  |
|------|:-:|
| April | 9 |
| May | 8 |

You've undoubtedly passed the turning point, because twenty-nine of the forty business indicators are now dropping. From now on they'll thin out—

|  |  |
|------|:-:|
| June | 5 |
| July | 4 |
| August | 2 |

And there you are—in a recession, at the point where all your business indicators have turned down. You can start watching now for upturning indicators.

**Handling the Figures**—Wright bases his forecasts on his estimate of where the center of the bell-shaped curve, outlined by the rise and fall of the indicators he has chosen, will be.

Several of the forty business indicators that Wright uses—slab zinc shipments, wholesale prices of hogs, gum rosin, and inedible tallow—are of trivial importance in relation to broad economic developments. But Wright frankly selects them, not for their general economic significance, but for their consistent behavior during turns in the business cycle.

**Difficult, But . . .**—The turn-spotting techniques are admittedly imperfect devices. They are often difficult to interpret. When they show a downturn it's often hard to know whether it's to be a mild or severe one. And, when you allow time for gathering the necessary data, they usually give only a few months' lead on cyclical turns.

These are serious limitations. Nevertheless, a man whose business lives or dies by his skill at anticipating major turns in the business cycle will ignore at his peril the signals he might get from these leading series devices.

## III. Ranging the Field

Test-tube or systematic forecasting is the classic strategy of economic analysis. The technique here is to discover enduring relationships among economic factors and apply them to situations in the past, present, or future.

Analyzing the general business picture and making quantitative estimates of what conditions may be like a year or more ahead requires all the theoretical training, knowledge of institutional and statistical facts, technical skill, and political insight that an economist can command.

*Aid for the Searchers*—In dealing with comprehensive forecasting problems, economists today have two tremendous advantages over those who worked twenty years ago.

The first is economics' own "unified field theory." It's the product of the Keynesian revolution (BW—January 8, 1955, p. 104). Before John M. Keynes wrote his *General Theory of Employment, Interest, and Money,* economic theory tended to be fragmented into separate theories of wages, money, foreign trade, and so on. None of these separate principles had much relationship to each other. Economists may argue how much of the Keynesian revolution is attributable to Keynes himself. But there can be little doubt that general comprehension of how all the parts of an economy mesh together has advanced greatly since the mid-1930's.

The second advantage is the system of national income accounts developed since the early 1930's by the Commerce Department and the National Bureau of Economic Research. These give the economist a detailed and comprehensive picture of the national economy.

From unified economic theory and national income accounting stem the two most important techniques for systematic economic forecasting.

The "Lost Horse" Technique is the first. That, anyway, is how it was christened by Sidney Alexander, Columbia Broadcasting System economist. He took the name from the old gag about how to find a lost horse. You do it by going to where the horse was last seen and asking yourself where you would go from there if you were a horse.

When you take that theory off the farm and put it to work in general business forecasting, each component of the gross national product (consumption, expenditures, gross private domestic investment, net foreign investment, government purchases of goods and services) plays the part of the lost horse. The analyst first finds out where each of these was when last reported by the Commerce Department's National Income Division.

But how he answers the question of where each section of GNP is going depends on his skill, patience, insight, and information.

An economist who wants to fake impressively can simply guess figures for each part of the coming year's GNP. (Projecting gross private domestic investment at $49.6 billion is obviously more impressive than projecting it at $50 billion.) If there were state licensing boards for economists, a forecaster caught doing this would be convicted of malpractice and sentenced to run a checkout register in a supermarket for the rest of his days.

*Honesty's Realm*—But the honest economist will go deeply behind each component of GNP when he prepares his forecast. He will study government plans and policies, analyze budget estimates, weigh the likelihood of the passage of important legislation, and attempt to estimate the price tags the various bills will bear.

He will look behind private investment at the factors affecting the capital goods industries, study ratios of inventories to sales and of production to capacity. He will look at the factors that affect building construction, such as credit terms, availability of mortgage money, vacancy rates, rents, and price movements. He will measure his analysis against the findings of capital spending surveys.

He will try to gauge the effect of government fiscal policies on private investment and consumption, estimate the relationship between the growth of investment and consumption. Then he will see how money credit conditions may affect people's spending or saving, their liquid assets, their supplies of durable goods. And he will measure this against the finding of consumer intention surveys.

He must put all these parts together to make a whole—but he must also carry in his mind an image of how the whole will affect the parts. He will also have to sense how noneconomic factors—like international relations and national elections—will affect the picture.

*Endless Job*—Since the task of preparing a forecast of the national economy can be almost endless, the economist must figure out the point at which he has all the information he can handle. But, at best, the time he has for these analyses is always pretty short, since he must base his forecasts on the most current information. If he takes too long, his facts grow cold. The best course for the forecaster is to stay at his task continuously, constantly modifying his forecast on the basis of new information.

The only way to judge whether an economist has done a thorough sensitive forecast—or blooped his way through one—is to examine carefully the details of his analysis. Of course, a lost-horse analysis depends a lot on the economist's subjective judgments about the data he receives and on his somewhat "artistic" perception of relations. So all of his analysis may not show on paper.

## IV. The Elegant Way

A more rigorous way of tackling the problem of what will happen to the millions of factors and relations that make up the national economy is to build an econometric model of the economy. The method here is related to the lost-horse technique, but it's a lot more elegant, for the practice of econometrics is one of blending economics, mathematics, and statistics.

*Step by Step*—An economist starts to build a model by first selecting an economic theory, or set of theories, that he believes will take into account all the significant factors likely to affect the general business or particular industry situation that he is forecasting.

He translates the theory into a set of mathematical equations (see Fig. 3) that make up his econometric model. The equations relate the factors he wants to discover (the dependent variables) to the factors he already knows, or can estimate easily (the independent variables). These independent variables can be of two types: first, those that are historic facts, such as last year's profits or inventory spending; and second, future elements, such as government spending, that can be estimated from advance information.

The econometrician bases his forecast on the past relations between the dependent and independent variables. He assumes that relations that were stable in the past will remain stable in the future. Of course, the relation between large economic aggregates, like consumption and income, won't be perfectly stable. So the question the forecaster must first answer is: "Will they be stable enough, within some estimated range of probability, to be used for forecasting?" If it turns out that they aren't stable enough for the job they're supposed to perform, the forecaster can assume that the theory behind his equations is not valid. Even then he has achieved something—and, in this way, econometrics can be a useful technique for junking false economic theories.

*Not All Approve*—Econometric models come in for plenty of criticism from forecasters who stick to other techniques.

One of the chief complaints against them is that they make complex mathematical operations on data that are too rough to permit such manipulation. Stephen M. DuBrul, a General Motors economist, says that to apply intricate econometric techniques to the rough data that are available is "gold-plating crowbars."

Other charges leveled against econometric models are that they:

Are based on static, not dynamic, theories.

Deal in large, meaningless, catchall concepts, such as consumption, instead of dealing with markets for specific types of consumer goods and services.

Imply an economy based on "economic man" and don't allow for the often unpredictable reactions of people, which can make for big changes in an economy.

But econometricians keep building their models and trying to improve them. They try to fit more factors into their figuring to overcome the complaints that their models are mechanically unsound and insensitive to social movements.

*National Picture*—There are plenty of econometric model-builders at work to handle this task of improvement.

At Michigan University's Research Seminar in Quantitative Economics, three econometricians, Lawrence Klein, Daniel Suits, and Arthur S. Goldberger, have built a twenty-five-equation model of the U.S. economy. They've been operating it for three years and its forecasts for 1953 and 1954 came close to actuality.

They don't look on their model as a once-and-for-all job, but are continuously testing and strengthening it. When a forecast turns out to be off the mark, the Michigan group probes into the machinery of the model to find out just where the fault lies, changes the model to try to correct the mistake next time. And to make the model more realistic, the group is also making intensive studies of particular sectors of the economy, including the construction industry, foreign trade, agriculture, and the money market.

Econometricians at other U.S. universities are working on models of their own. The nation's econometric capital has just shifted from Chicago to Yale University, with the migration there of the Cowles Commission for Economic Research. Along with the commission, the headquarters staff of the Econometrics Society shifted to Yale, too.

*Models All Over*—Abroad there's plenty of research going on with the models. The Dutch, Norwegian, and Canadian governments are developing models of their own economies to help them with their economic policy-making.

The Dutch model has been operating since 1952. Opinion among economists in Holland is that the model has forecast the general direction of Dutch economic developments fairly accurately and that it has contributed to the molding of a more rational government economic policy. The model was put together by a noted Dutch economist, Jan Tinbergen. It was he who built the first econometric model of the U.S. economy for the League of Nations in 1939.

Chief man working with the Norwegian model is Ragnar Frisch, to whom Harvard University has just awarded the first Schumpeter Prize for "genius and leadership in the use of rigorous scientific methods in the social sciences." Three research centers have a hand in the Norwegian model—Oslo University's Institute of Economics, the Central Bureau of Statistics, and the Finance Ministry's Budgets division. As of now, some ninety variables have been built into the model—and it's still being tested.

Lawrence Klein designed the econometric model that the Canadian government is developing. It, too, is still in the experimental stage. The Canadian government plans eventually to use it for forecasting but this probably will not happen for several years.

*Simpler for Business*—Industry's own economists are beginning to get into the model-building field. For industry's purposes the models have been simplified. Management has found them useful for doing one of the principal jobs for which business is turning to economists: helping guide planning for capital spending and expansion programs (BW—March 5, 1955, p. 66) by producing long-range projections of specific industries' places in the national economy.

Some industry economists like Standard Oil Co. of New Jersey's Cecil Burrell, Allied Chemical & Dye Corp.'s Avram Kisselgoff, CBS's Sidney Alexander, and Ford's William Flaherty believe econometric models will in time prove of great value to business as well as government. They say the models provide the best technique yet developed for organizing massive and complex statistical data, for cumulating knowledge and profiting from past errors and successes, and for systematizing the whole forecasting process.

## IT'S ALL YOUR BET

Each of the forecasting techniques set forth in this report (and the many variant methods) has its weaknesses and disadvantages for dealing with particular problems of economic prediction. So it would be foolish for a businessman or an economist to bet his future on one method to the exclusion of others.

Each is useful for confirming or refuting the picture that's revealed by other methods.

*Quick Selection*—If there's neither the time nor the resources for a businessman to use all the techniques simultaneously, he can choose among them easily—by working on the principle that the method that gives him his answer most simply is the best one.

If his business is to supply whoosies for General Motors, and for General Motors alone, the obvious way to get a forecast is for him to ask General Motors how many whoosies it thinks it will need.

If he's making a product, like color television, that's new and has a market that doesn't correlate well with any broad economic movements, it probably makes more sense for him to forecast his business from what his salesmen or his market research outfit can tell him, rather than to expect his economist to give him a firm answer.

On the other hand, if a businessman has an inventory, production, or long-run demand problem, and if the movements of a dozen or more factors can affect his future, the job of forecasting may call for some high-class economic analysis—either by the company's own economic staff or by an outside consultant.

*Man with the Chips*—But ultimately, every businessman must be his own forecaster. He's the one who makes the decisions. And his decisions must be based on his own final forecasts. His decisions will show the extent to which he has accepted or rejected—or ignored or misunderstood—the forecasts prepared for him by others.

The ancient folk saying that "business is a gamble" still hasn't lost its profundity. But a man is a sucker if he doesn't try to get the best odds in that gamble.

His odds must improve if he acts on the basis of full information, knowledge of the movements of economic indicators, and careful analyses of how changes in the big economic picture may affect his business.

# 36.

# *The Limits of Planning*

## By William H. Newman [1]

Administrators who wish to enjoy the benefits of planning can at least partially overcome the limits imposed by unreliable forecasting in two ways. First, they may make studied attempts to *improve* their *forecasts*. Thousands of companies subscribe to one or more forecasting services or employ some economic consultant to advise them. Many companies have made great strides in the compilation of data upon which to base predictions; for example, the automobile companies receive from week to week the sales, automobiles on hand, used car prices, and other market information from all of their dealers throughout the country. Several of the larger companies have a separate division whose sole mission is to prepare business forecasts. Of course, if the uncertainty relates to internal conditions, forecasting can often be improved by exercising closer control—as will be discussed in later paragraphs.

A second way to deal with unreliable predictions is to *detour* around the areas of greatest uncertainty. For instance, if securing an objective within a definite time is of sufficient importance, as it often is in military operations, alternative programs may be developed and started in operation; then, when it becomes apparent what the operating conditions actually will be, the most effective alternative is followed to its conclusion. Obviously it would be more economical to follow only the one alternative finally used, and in most business

[1] Reprinted with permission of publishers from *Administrative Action* by William H. Newman. Copyright, 1951, by Prentice-Hall, Inc. Published by Prentice-Hall, Inc., 70 Fifth Avenue, New York 11, New York.

enterprises the pressure for economy dictates that a single course be followed even though it is admittedly more risky.[2]

In a few situations unreliable forecasting may be counteracted by hedging; that is, by arranging operations so that losses in one area will be offset by gains in another, or vice versa. In a narrow sense, hedging is applicable only to protection against price changes for a limited number of commodities; the general principle, however, is sometimes applicable in other situations, such as offering two or more styles of products with the expectation that if one does not appeal to customers the other will, or locating plants both in the United States and abroad so as to be able to serve the foreign market regardless of the changes in foreign exchange rates.

The most common way to detour around unreliable forecasts is to separate those parts of the operation that will not be affected by the uncertain factor—volume, style, weather, or whatever it may be— and then make a tentative plan for the remaining segment in considerable detail. When the uncertain factor is finally settled, it is, relatively, a simple job to pull the various parts of the program together. It is quite possible, for example, to do the design work and develop engineering specifications for a product before it is practical to decide when, and perhaps in what plant, it will be produced. Many an advertising campaign has been mapped out, copy prepared, media selected, and all completed except for the timing which depended upon factors difficult to appraise when the planning was initiated.

These means of overcoming unreliable forecasts are at best only partial remedies. Improved forecasting technique may push forward the time span of confidence, but the practical limits are soon reached for most enterprises. The detours around unpredictable elements are only applicable in certain circumstances, and even then apply only to part of the operations of the enterprise. Consequently, the inability to forecast accurately remains one of the factors that limit the period and the detail in which planning is practical.

---

[2] The danger of following a single though risky course may sometimes be partly offset by insurance. As a rule, however, insurance is practical only for catastrophes that are quite unlikely to occur, and hence are not covered in the regular planning.

# 37.

# *The Limits of Planning*

## By Harold Koontz and Cyril O'Donnell [1]

A discussion of the managerial function of planning would not be complete without special recognition of the limits of planning in practice. These limitations are not so great as to reduce seriously the effectiveness of making complete and adequate plans, and they should not be interpreted as reasons for not bending every effort to plan. Nevertheless, awareness of them can remove many of the frustrations and inefficiencies of planning.

### The Problem of Accurate Premises

One of the limiting factors in planning is the difficulty of formulating accurate planning premises. Since these premises are the background against which a set of plans is made, they necessarily deal with the future. Since the future cannot be known with accuracy, premising must be subject to a margin of error. As was pointed out earlier, accurate and reliable forecasting is necessary for good planning because it is the basis of most planning premises. As forecasting techniques advance and as an enterprise gives more time and attention to working out a careful prophecy of the future, premises are naturally improved.

It is possible for the planner to reduce the risks involved in uncertainties of the future. One way of doing so is to have alternative sets of premises, and alternative plans based on them, so that major changes in future events can be readily reflected in action. Another is to be ready with detours in planning to allow for unforeseeable events. Both of these require flexibility in future plans. This may take the form of utilizing plant facilities for an operation not originally intended, shifting an advertising program to reflect a revised sales policy, or changing radically a product line, to mention only a few examples of swift changes necessitated in plans by later events.

Flexibility is, however, only possible within limits. In the first place, an enterprise cannot always put off a decision long enough to make sure of its rightness in the light of future events. Decisions must be made sometimes well in advance of the environment for which they are required. For example, a company planning to build a new plant to serve a future market may be forced to make decisions that will bind it to a given course of action for years in the future. In the second place, built-in flexibility of plans may be so costly that the probable benefits of hedging are not worth the expense involved. For instance, a company may spend so much to make a new plant useful for producing products other than those intended as to make the costs not worth the advantages. Or a company may keep so financially liquid in preparing for the possibility of a business recession that the advantages of having large cash reserves may be less than the advantages of deferred opportunities for profitable expansion.[2]

## RAPIDITY OF CHANGE

Another important limiting factor in effective business planning arises from business dynamics. In a highly complex and rapidly

[2] An interesting example of this kind of hedging may be seen in the cases of Montgomery Ward and Sears, Roebuck in the period after World War II. Montgomery Ward, under the leadership of Sewell Avery, built up cash reserves of approximately $250 million through 1952 but saw its share of the mail-order business fall from 40 per cent in 1942 to 28 per cent in 1951. Sears, on the other hand, under the leadership of Robert E. Wood, adopted an expansionist program and increased its share of the mail-order business from approximately 50 per cent to 66 per cent in the same period. Similar differences in position existed in the retail-store field for the two companies. Sears has also increased its profits relative to Ward's, its net income as a percentage of net worth having been significantly higher than Ward's. While the stock of Sears rose in price during the period, the stock of Ward's fell. Had a depression occurred in the immediate postwar period, Montgomery Ward would have been in an excellent position to capitalize on its liquidity, and Sears might have been in a vulnerable position. For details on the operation of these two policies, see "Betting on a Depression," *Business Week,* September 27, 1952, pp. 60–66.

changing industry, planning becomes extraordinarily difficult. The rapid succession of new problems attending change are often magnified by complexities so that planning assumes almost impossibly difficult proportions. The development of plans in the aircraft manufacturing industry during World War II, when the industry grew from one of a few small businesses to one of very large companies, was extremely difficult. When this growth was coupled with the fact that the product was exceptionally complex and rapidly changing, the planning problem during the first few years of expansion was almost beyond comprehension.

Essentially the same kind of difficulty has existed in many other industries. The rapid change and expansion of the airline industry after World War II and the growth of the electronics industry after 1948 are noteworthy recent examples of highly dynamic business situations in which the job of effectively developing plans has been exceedingly difficult. One might contrast the job of planning in these dynamic businesses with the task in such stable businesses as a local water utility in New England or a flour mill in Minneapolis. While all businesses are subject to problems of change, the degree of instability and complexity caused by business dynamics varies considerably from industry to industry and as among firms within an industry.

Even in a highly dynamic industry, however, it is surprising how many problems are of a recurring nature. In every new problem, there may be the same cost elements, and a well-developed pricing formula may be useful for widely different problems. Likewise, the problems of manufacture and utilization of plant and machinery may have common elements despite the differences in product. If the common elements in new problems can be sought out and separated, the complexity of planning in a highly dynamic situation can be simplified.

## INTERNAL INFLEXIBILITIES

There are many tendencies toward inflexibility in business operations that serve to thwart and limit effective planning. These may be divided between inflexibilities internal to the firm and those external to the firm. Among the major internal inflexibilities are those related to human psychology, policies and procedures, and capital investment.

## Psychological Inflexibilities

One of the important internal inflexibilities is psychological. Managers and employees develop patterns of thought and behavior sometimes hard to change. A company may be so imbued with a tradition for operating flamboyantly or expensively that a program of retrenchment is difficult. For example, the attitudes of production at any cost developed during World War II in many war plants became a psychological point of view difficult to overcome in the more competitive cost-conscious era following the war. Also, the frame of mind, engendered by the excess-profits taxes in effect during and after the war, that a dollar of expense was only really eighteen cents became a serious threat to efficient operation of many businesses in 1954.

In other cases, particularly in old, established businesses, there is a tendency for people to develop resistance to change. Managers and employees may eschew new methods, new products, and organization changes. Or a long period under close government regulations may bring about an attitude of running the business to avoid breaking the law, rather than to emphasize the quest for low cost and high profits. Persons familiar with the railroad business, for example, cannot help being impressed by the efforts taken to assure that freight bills are completely accurate. The original quotation and pricing made by the receiving agent is normally audited by the delivering agent, further audited by the regional accountants, again audited, at least on a sample basis, by the central office, and sometimes further audited by representatives of the Interstate Commerce Commission. One of the writers has seen small bills audited and checked to the extent where the cost of making sure the charges were accurate must have exceeded the amount of the bill.

That these psychological inflexibilities place blocks in the way of business planning is easy to understand. Many managers have been frustrated in their attempt to institute a new plan simply by the unwillingness or inability of people to accept the condition of change. Moreover, this is a difficult planning limitation to overcome. To do so requires patient selling of ideas, aggressive leadership, careful dissemination of information, and intentional development of a tradition of change among the members of the organization.

## Procedural and Policy Inflexibilities

Closely allied to psychological inflexibilities are those rigidities inherent in established policies and procedures. Once established, policies and procedures tend to become ingrained in the enterprise, and their change becomes difficult. A way of doing things, a chain of reports or invoices, and the place of people in following out procedures often become so established that it is exceedingly hard to modify them. During World War II, for example, one of the large aircraft companies developed from a small operation to one of fourteen divisions and some 200,000 people. Its procedures, paper work, and checks were developed for this large, far-flung operation. When the war ended and the company shrank to two divisions and 25,000 people, the procedures of the previous large operation lingered on. So drastic was the change in scale and nature of the operations that what was needed was a complete revamping of procedures for guiding research and development, manufacture, and servicing of customers. Yet to do this would have required major overhaul of the company's operations, and this was not practicable. The result was a long and partially ineffectual program of gradual change of procedures, which certainly did much to thwart some of the new planning of the company's revised operations.

The resistance of policies and procedures to change was interestingly illustrated in the Hoover Commission study of the organization of the federal government, begun in 1947.[3] The Commission found that essentially the same procedures were used for small government purchases as for large and that on over half of the three million purchase orders issued annually by civilian agencies the cost of paper work exceeded the cost of the items purchased. It found that the disposition of surplus property was governed by over 369 separate statutes, with new statutes being added to old until the weight of policy and procedure was stifling initiative and hamstringing efforts to improve handling the problem. The Commission also found most supply agencies overburdened with a surplus of complicated statistical and other records, many of which were obsolete, though few

[3] The summary of the Commission's findings has been published as *The Hoover Commission Report* (New York, McGraw-Hill Book Company, Inc., 1949).

agencies had the kind of data needed for effective management of the function.

One of the most convincing evidences of bureaucracy, whether in business or government, is the existence of complicated procedures designed to make sure that mistakes cannot be made. The existence of these procedures, many of which tend to become obsolete, especially in established enterprises, places a serious block to the institution of new plans and the development of new ideas. Progressive planning requires an environment of change with some reasonable degree of freedom and a willingness to assume the risks of mistakes. These are qualities difficult to find in an enterprise bound by the strait jacket of policy and procedural inflexibilities.

## Capital Inflexibilities

In the discussion of planning, reference was made to the inflexibility inherent in invested capital. A new plant constructed or a new machine purchased and installed represents an investment of company resources, which are, to varying extent, "sunk" in the enterprise. Sometimes, if a company wishes to change its plans affecting such investment, it can sell the plant or the machine at a favorable price and thereby liquidate its investment. But in most cases, once capital is invested in a fixed asset, the ability to switch courses of future action becomes limited, and the fact of the investment itself becomes a planning premise for the future.

Capital inflexibilities also exist where investment is sunk in items other than what is normally regarded as a fixed asset. If a company makes an investment in training of a particular kind or spends its resources in building up a certain kind of customer reaction to its product through advertising, packaging, or other devices, the funds so invested tend to become sunk. As such, unless the company has ways to liquidate its investment on a reasonable basis or change the course of action intended, or unless it can afford to write off the investment, the very fact that these costs are irretrievable may place important blocks in the way of change. While it is a good axiom to disregard sunk costs in planning, since nothing can be done about them, it is nonetheless true that their existence does influence planning. If a management can retrieve any of these costs by bending its plans to recognize them, it gains an advantage in so doing, unless the course so selected is not as advantageous as one that forgets these costs. But whether it is good planning and good economics to disregard sunk costs in a given circumstance, their presence tends almost invariably to act as a factor influencing planning.

## EXTERNAL INFLEXIBILITIES

Other limits to planning arise from inflexibilities external to the firm. These are essentially the characteristics of the external environment over which the manager has little or no control. Among these are the social institutions, with their folkways, mores, codes, and laws within which the enterprise, as a social unit, must operate. While social institutions do change, they sometimes change slowly. But whether they change slowly or rapidly, the extent to which they resist the will of the business manager gives rise to inflexibilities that stand in the way of his planning.

To discuss completely the nature of these external inflexibilities would be to describe the entire social environment, including, in addition to social factors, the accompanying technological, geographic, and economic elements of the environment. A brief description of three major external factors will, however, be made.

### Political Climate

Every business, to a greater or lesser degree, is faced with inflexibilities of the political climate that happens to exist at a given time. If the local, state, or national government has an active policy of business regulation, or if the national government adopts a high-tariff policy or otherwise restricts free trade, these are elements that must be taken into account in planning. Likewise, tax policies cause inflexibilities, as do antitrust and fair trade policies. Moreover, the basic attitude of government as reflected in investigations of business practices has significant effects. Furthermore, in this day, when government has become business' largest customer, the procurement policies and programs of government agencies cause rigidities in business planning.

### Labor Organization

The existence of strong unions, particularly those organized on a national basis, tends to restrict the freedom of the business manager in planning. The numerous wage- and working-condition provisions of union contracts and the influence of union policies on employee productivity and attitudes must be taken into account. In addition to being important environmental influences, they often give rise to definite inflexibilities. In the railroad industry, for example, management and unions entered into an agreement in 1936, providing for specific restrictions on a railroad's right to combine or to abandon service. These restrictions, in the form of dismissal compensation and preservation of job rights and influenced by the thinking of the Great Depression, place an important limitation on the ability of railroad managers to combine with other railroads or to abandon service; and the restrictions have been given the standing of law by the policy of the Interstate Commerce Commission of requiring such labor safeguards as a condition for approval of combinations or abandonments.

## Technological Change

The rate and nature of technological change also are effective external limitations upon a firm's planning. There are perhaps few things as unyielding as the state of technological development. Not that technology does not change. It, of course, changes rapidly, and one new development begets another. But at any given time, the status of technical progress is a relatively inflexible thing. Even though a particular technical problem may be solved in making a planned course of action possible, the manager may find that another technical problem remains unsolved and that the full use of the solved one depends upon the unsolved. In developing an electronic fire-control system, for example, the way of guiding a projectile toward a target may be well understood, and it may be possible to engineer the necessary circuits, but the lack of proper development of a single tube or the susceptibility of another to vibration may delay the accomplishment of the entire plan.

## TIME AND EXPENSE

Planning, like any other extensive use of time or materials, is costly. The effort that could be spent on forecasting, evaluation of alternatives, development of derivative plans, or other aspects of planning is almost limitless, the only effective brake being the cost to the firm and the time available to the manager before action must be taken.

From the standpoint of expense, the underlying principle that should be applicable to planning is simple: no firm should spend more on planning than the value of the benefits that might be expected. But the application of this principle is more complex, for a manager cannot easily know whether the amount of planning he undertakes will be worth the cost incurred.

But there are certain guides to planning expense that are useful. In the first place, a large firm can almost certainly engage in more thorough planning than a small one, for the reason that the ratio of planning expense to operating expenses or to the capital resources of the firm will be small. Many of the planning problems which face the small firm are almost as complex and varied as those which face the larger firm. Indeed, it is probably in the area of planning thoroughness, and the resources to accomplish it, that the large firm has an important advantage over its smaller counterpart.

In the second place, the more detailed planning becomes, the more expensive it will surely be. There is ever the existing danger, in large as well as small firms, that analysis of plans and formulation of the details of derivative plans may be so great as to be more costly than the benefits. One of the difficulties of modern engineering and production planning is that a small project may receive the same attention as a large project. One of the authors recalls a case where a project undertaken by a large aircraft manufacturer for a minor modification of an airplane required some 3,000 man-hours of engineering and production planning time to accomplish a job requiring 50 direct-labor-hours, when, had the job been done on a relatively unplanned basis, the planning time could have been reduced to some 30 man-hours, with only a doubling of the direct-man-hours involved.

In the third place, it is a characteristic of planning that, the longer in the future plans are projected, the more costly they are likely to be. Unless forecasts for a long time in the future are to be little more than informed guesses or if long-term plans are to be worked out more than in outline form, the cost of investigation and of fitting plans together, especially to arrive at a tolerable margin of error, is likely to be extremely high. Here again, the strategic factors are the importance of the plan to the future of the business and the resources that the firm, in the light of this importance, can afford to spend to perfect its long-range plans. To a large business and for major plans, this stretching of the planning period for years in advance may well justify heavy expenses. But, for the small firm, the costs involved may justify the manager's doing a careful job of planning for the near term, while relying on hunches and judgment for the longer term.

In addition to the sheer expense of planning, which necessarily at some point places a limit on planning, the time available is also an important limiting factor. There comes a time when a decision must be taken, when a course of action must be selected, and when plans must be translated into action. Whether ready or not, the management may be forced to move. However, time will not be so limiting for the manager who plans adequately and well in advance. Good planning reduces the occasions when the manager may be forced into snap decisions under the pressure of crises or the necessity for fighting business fires.

# 38.

# *Obstacles to Business Growth*

## By Keith Powlison [1]

A company cannot stand still. If it stops growing, it starts going downhill; there is no in-between. Of course, it is the normal expectation of every company under vigorous management to keep on growing, provided it does not run up against external circumstances beyond its control. That is part and parcel of the dynamic nature of business.

But there are many obstacles to growth within the company, which are not always recognized for what they are and purposefully dealt with. See them and take action on them, and the company should continue growing. Overlook them and do nothing about them, and the company may fall so short of its due growth that it is in fact on the downgrade.

What are these obstacles to growth, and what can be done about them? Let me try to set forth some of the more typical, more important ones, as I have observed them, and suggest an approach to their removal that others may find useful.

But first of all, because no management can tackle this problem until it has a clear idea of what its present rate of growth is (or is not) and what kind of growth it wants for the future, let us look at the underlying question of measures and goals.

### MEASURES AND GOALS

Nearly every management points to its company with pride as an

[1] Reprinted by permission from *Harvard Business Review*, March–April, 1953, pp. 48–56.

example of *growth*. At the same time the lament of investment coun-
selors and institutional investors is that real growth companies are so
rare. This paradox indicates that there is widespread difference of
opinion as to what growth in business really is. A closer look, however, reveals some fundamental points on which we can agree.

## Mere Expansion

Does business growth mean mere expansion—"progressive increase
or enlargement" as the dictionary definition has it?

For twenty years the·tide of business in this country has been rising.
Record all-time highs have been set by every important measure of
business activity. With very few exceptions the companies which
have been in business throughout this twenty-year span have increased
in sales, number of plants, employees, and variety of commodities
handled. As a matter of fact, most of those which did not share in the
upward swing of business are not here today; they fell by the wayside.

Broadly speaking, the dollar volume of business in this country is
today six times what it was twenty years ago. This means that if a
company's sales are now six times what they were in 1932, the company has just held even; it is an average concern. Again, since it will
be marketing its wares at prices which are at least twice as high (if
it has done a typical job on pricing), in *physical* volume the average
company will be handling now between three and four times as much
business as it did twenty years ago.

A company which is no more than average is hardly a growth company. It needs something more than mere expansion—a whole lot
more—to qualify as a real growth company. It seems only logical that
growth should be in terms of the goal or objective of business.

The purpose or goal of a company is to make a profit by employing
assets as effectively as possible to meet the needs and desires of customers. This definition, in turn, involves three factors: (a) assets or
capital, (b) sales, and (c) profits—profits being the difference between sales income and all costs, including taxes. These three factors
constitute the *eternal triangle* of business, and real growth depends
on all three together. The measuring stick or tool used for this purpose is the "return on capital employed" or the "return on investment," as some call it.

## Return on Capital

The final measure of the performance of an established company is the answer to the question: How effectively is the company employing all the capital or assets available to it? Capital or assets, as we use the term in my company and as I apply it here, means the total of all assets, principally cash, receivables, inventories, and property, plant, and equipment, regardless of where they come from or who supplies them. The total asset figure appears at the bottom of the left-hand side—the asset side—of the conventional balance sheet. The fact that it thus embraces all the basic factors of business is what makes this tool the common denominator by which companies can be measured and compared as to performance and growth.

In order to have a satisfactory return on capital employed, a company must use its assets hard. The harder assets are used, the more the sales obtained for each dollar of capital will be. This is the turnover factor.

The assets must also be used efficiently. The more efficiently assets are used, the lower costs will be and the higher the margin of profit on sales will be. This is the profit on sales factor.

Return on capital employed is *turnover times profit on sales*. Some companies, notably merchandising companies, make their return on capital employed with high turnover and low profit on sales; other companies, notably those in the extractive and heavy manufacturing industries, make theirs with low turnover and high profit on sales; and some are in between on both. No matter how they do it—and the characteristics of the business have a lot to do with it—they must have the right combination of these two factors for the kind of business they are in if the return on capital employed is to be adequate.

Now what has been the average performance as to return on capital employed? The Securities and Exchange Commission and the Federal Trade Commission, working together, have published figures representative of all *manufacturing* firms in the United States. These figures apply to the postwar period only. They show that from 1947 to 1952 the average manufacturing company (there are no comparable figures for the average merchandising firm) increased its total assets by approximately 50 per cent, boosted its sales by 45 per cent, but in 1952 earned 5 per cent less in profits after all taxes than in

1947. The annual rate of turnover fell from 1.61 to less than 1.5; the profit on sales (after taxes) fell from 7 per cent to less than 5 per cent; and return on capital—the final measure—dropped from 11.3 per cent to less than 7 per cent. (The figures for 1952 have been in part estimated.)

This shows that most companies experienced mere expansion, not business growth. The real kind of growth apparently is as rare as the investment people say it is. Where there is real growth, the return on capital is also increased or held at a high level while expansion takes place. Where there is outstanding growth, all three indicators—turnover, profit on sales, and return on capital employed—are raised or maintained at a satisfactory level. Some companies have done this, but they are few indeed.

The raising of earnings to a satisfactory level and the maintenance of earnings at that point while expanding is of critical importance. A real growth company keeps its development work in balance with its established business so that earning power does not deteriorate while capital expenditures are being made. This is important to investors and management alike. In these critical times, when we seem to be tottering uncertainly on the thin line between war and peace, no company can afford to run the risk of establishing a low base for excess profits taxes, whether or not such taxes are in force at the time.

But more important than the tax consideration, in my view, is the psychological factor. Very seldom, if ever, is management on sound ground in permitting an organization to use expansion as an excuse for poor operating results. Expansion is too alluring already—for reasons which will be under discussion subsequently—without adding any further inducement or incentive such as an exemption from operating accountability.

## Basic Ingredients

For the most part, so far, I have been talking simply about the figures, the accounting and financial data, which reflect growth; I have not said, in so many words, exactly what growth is. I wish I could. But I cannot, any more than the physicist can say exactly what electricity is. He tells us that electricity is an imponderable and invisible agency, capable under different circumstances of producing light, heat, chemical decomposition, and other physical phenomena.

And when he has said that, he is through with definition. But more important than definition is the fact that the physicist knows how to recognize electricity, measure it, produce it, control it; and he knows a little about how to use it—just a small fraction of what will be known a few years hence.

The secrets of growth in business are just about as imponderable. We do not know precisely everything that goes into it, but we can recognize it, we can measure it, we can produce it. The approach through return on capital employed—embracing the eternal triangle of business, capital employed, sales and profits—is fundamental. But there are other ingredients, other considerations, in the growth recipe. I should like to mention just a few of them:

1. Attention might well be paid to the rate at which new ideas, new products, or new processes are flowing into the business, and the rate at which the old, obsolescent, or unprofitable are flowing out. Putting the new in without giving it an opportunity to grow by pruning away the old results in an enlarged, swollen, stagnant business, just as in a shrubbery garden the old, dead, and dying holds back and stifles, and the uncontrolled sucker growth saps the strength needed for sound growth.

Periodically, some companies tell us what percentage of their products were not in the company's line at some earlier time. These figures are usually net—that is, the total of additions minus the deletions. It would be helpful if additions and deletions were shown separately, thus giving a feel of the rate of flow *in* as well as flow *out*.

We all recognize, of course, that growth in business, as in all other areas of human experience, is seldom continuous and constant. Usually it is by spurts with leveling off or consolidation periods between. The chart of a typical growth company, when plotted over a long period, usually resembles the profile of a stairway.

2. It is important, again, to know to what extent the products of the business are related to the means of serving man's needs and desires—the means by which living is made safer, healthier, and more satisfying. Labor-saving machinery and appliances, electronics, pharmaceuticals, chemicals, oils, TV, air transportation, just to cite a few, come to mind in this connection.

We might even ask: What about chlorophyll? Is it a heaven-sent potion which will forever relieve all mankind from the intolerable odors of human and animal existence? If so, it is destined to be a goose that lays golden eggs. Otherwise, it may prove to be no more than a quick gimmick.

3. We must also find out to what extent a company will participate in rising standards of living, in a war as well as a peace economy; to what

extent it will be affected by long-term tendencies, such as the trend toward an ever-growing old segment in our population or the trend toward socialization of economic effort.

All of these factors plus many others well known to readers are significant. The important thing is to be aware of them.

It is good general principle that one of the best ways to find what you are looking for is to watch those who have the biggest incentive to find it. No one stands to gain more from finding growth companies than investors. For this reason, real growth is anticipated and reflected in stock values. Of course a lot of other things enter the picture too. Just the same, with skillful analysis a high degree of discrimination between growth and nongrowth companies is possible. Here is just one clue: If you have to stand in line or know somebody to get a few shares of a new offering, that is a pretty good indication that there is some real growth in the picture.

We have seen that growth is performance toward profitability—the effective use of assets to make money—as measured by the return on capital employed; that it is not measured by mere size; and that it is constantly renewing itself by adding new vital growth products and pruning away the old and obsolescent. Now that we have an understanding of what growth is, let us see what prevents it.

But remember that in analyzing what prevents growth we are concerned only with what management *can* control. There is no use discussing what we cannot control as individual businessmen—such as war-created shortages and governmental restrictions, adverse legislation, long-term trends toward socialization, and so on—until we have done the best we can where we are free to act.

## THE UNPROFITABLE ITEM

Every business is continually taking risks. Profit is the incentive and reward for risk taking. Whether or not a company earns that most coveted of all reputations—that of being a real growth company—depends to a large extent upon what it does with its risks or ventures which do not pan out.

Suppose a company has a product line composed of two items. They are manufactured in one plant and distributed by the same sales force. One of the items is a good earner; the other fluctuates in a narrow range above and below the break-even point. This situation has existed for some time, but is now recognized as needing major attention. What does the company do about the weak item?

There are three alternatives: (a) to drop it—go out of that particular business; (b) to put it on a satisfactory basis; (c) to bail it out by adding something else. Let us take each of these in turn.

## Drop It from the Line

Of these three alternatives, the first is the most difficult and least frequently selected course of action. The reasoning may go something like this:

1. Progress is always the order of the day. One does not make progress by giving up—by going backward. Going out of a business is an admission of defeat.

2. Other companies make money on this commodity; we are at least as smart as they are; we can do it too. In other words, what anybody else can do, we can do, and we usually add "better."

3. It is nearly always possible to cite some other product that was worse longer and then finally blossomed out into a fine profitable business, and this one will do the same if we just give it time. After all, the product has not had a fair trial; conditions have been so abnormal.

4. We cannot afford to drop the item until we find something to take its place. It absorbs burden that cannot be carried by the remaining commodity. If we discontinue this item, we will have an unsatisfactory return on the whole investment.

5. An important part of the profit made on the profitable items would not be earned if we did not have the unprofitable item to attract customers.

6. The unsatisfactory item is highly competitive. The capacity to produce is bigger than the market. If we drop out, our volume will put our competitors on easy street. We cannot afford to let that happen. This is the gin rummy game in business: we can't do anything with it, but somebody else can, so we'd better hang on to it.

## Put It on a Sound Basis

If the product is continued for whatever reason, then we should put it on a sound basis. Solomon indicated the approach when he said, "Whatever thy hand findeth to do, do it with thy might." In copybook maxim style it can be stated, "If it's worth doing at all, it's worth doing well."

But it is very hard to correct a bad situation with which we have lived for a long time. If we knew how to fix it, we would have done so a long time ago. The situation is just this: since we do not know what is wrong, we cannot take for granted that anything is right. Everything has to be questioned, until the situation is corrected. This is an uncomfortable approach. Everyone who has had anything to do with the product is threatened with the possibility of having been wrong.

It is worse than that. It can even raise questions about panaceas. In business, as in medicine, panaceas are very soothing—even if they do not cure. To challenge a widely accepted and long-applied cure-all can be disturbing, even disorganizing. Incentive wages are a case in point. To some they are the answer to every ailing situation. If results do not improve or if they continue to deteriorate after the installation of incentive wages, is the soundness of incentive wages questioned? *Hardly*—or perhaps *seldom* is the word.

The more usual response is that the incentives are all right; we just need more of them. The medicine is o.k., we just did not take enough of it. The questioning of the other ingredients in the situation is potentially no less unsettling. This is true because many of them usually are of broad application—affecting other commodities beyond the one immediately under consideration. For these reasons, the correcting of the problem, as it is, frequently gives way to the third alternative—that of bailing out the item by adding to it or making it bigger.

## Bail It Out

This is usually by far the most inviting of the three alternative approaches. It eliminates the pain of going out of a business—the pain of seeing sales decline, cutting back on personnel, realigning organization. In effect, it places the stamp of approval on what has been done in the past. The operation, we say, was soundly managed, but it was intrinsically untenable. Nobody is at fault because only experience could prove that.

The situation is untenable because, for example, we do not have a whole family of products. The line is too short; it needs to be rounded out by the addition of new items. Or the situation is untenable because it is a *big kind* of business. It cannot be handled profitably on a small basis. It requires bigness to do adequate advertising, research, and engineering. So, it is decided to grow out of the problem by adding products, commodities, or lines—by growing larger.

This is a very palatable solution. From the time it is decided upon, a sigh of relief goes through the organization. Everybody is off the hook. Frustration gives way to the feeling that "now we're getting somewhere."

## LURE OF BIGNESS

This is characteristic of expansion—of getting bigger—no matter what the reason. Its allure is so nearly irresistible that it constantly threatens to displace profitability as the payoff goal in business—for a number of reasons:

1. The feeling that what is bigger is better is so widespread that it has come to be almost axiomatic.

2. Growth occurs quickly, is easy to see, and is impressive. It is apparent that something is going on in the erection of a building from the time ground is broken. In contrast, the steps which lead to profitability are subtle; you cannot see them; they are difficult and are relatively slow in coming to fruition.

3. It is exhilarating. It is a spending binge—like shopping (ask any woman).

4. Personnel problems disappear like snow in the tropics. People are hired, not fired; advanced, not demoted. Every administrator knows from painful experience how great these differences are.

5. Everybody is busy. The place literally hums with activity. The purchasing department becomes a mecca for eager salesmen. Engineers, architects, designers, draftsmen are doing the creative work that makes them happy. The treasurer busies himself making the rounds with the commercial and investment bankers for the needed funds. The top executives are swamped with invitations to tell luncheon clubs of the policies and principles that have led to the growth of the business. In other words, the "joint is jumpin'."

6. Everybody in a company has a warm feeling toward his associates who are expanding. It is the friendly kind of a feeling you have toward any one who helps you buy a deep freeze or an air-conditioning unit at wholesale. He saves you money. In like manner, it is pleasing to hope that, with the additional business, you will have a smaller share of the president's, the controller's, and the treasurer's salary to carry. Who likes to pay a driver, a checker-upper, and a penny-pincher anyway?

The person who relieves you of these unpleasant burdens is a friend indeed. You will support whatever he wants as long as it involves expansion—and pretty soon you find that he smiles with favor upon your proposals to grow out of your commodity, factory, and personnel problems. This is working together for everyone's advantage. In a way it is a sort of automatic, unpremeditated "log-rolling" for growth—for anything that involves decreasing the overhead burden.

What is wrong with this picture?

It is spending the company's money to distribute costs over a wider area by expanding and growing—rather than decreasing costs. It is looking backward to protect what the company already has that is weak—rather than looking forward to develop new business which holds promise for future success on its own. It is, in other words, defensive. It is playing to weakness.

## Burden Absorption

The arguments about rounding out the line or adding new operations can seldom be proved right or wrong. It is all too easy for the proponents to point to somebody else who presumably is making good money on one or more of the same products or activities in question. (Actually, the other fellow may be having the same trouble.) But the clinching argument for expansion is the old, perennial *burden absorption*. By adding more volume, the argument runs, fixed charges will be made lighter for every other operation.

Of course, whenever burden absorption is claimed, it is automatically assumed that there is already excess capacity in personnel and in physical facilities to handle added business without incurring further fixed costs, and that these excesses are practically in balance —indeed that they are just what will be needed for the new operation. Or it is assumed that the new business will be handled more efficiently than the old.

That both of these assumptions are frequently invalid is indicated by the fact that fixed costs per dollar of sales often fail to show the downward trend that was anticipated and claimed to justify the expansion move. In other words, after a reasonable consolidation period, it is not unusual to find that the ratio of fixed costs to sales tends to seek the level which has been normal for that business (provided its basic character is not completely changed), or at least fails to decline significantly.

So often the burden argument appears to be the perfect reason for expanding (or for not dropping a weak item), and so often it is accepted and then fails to materialize, that I think it should be called "the one-way street which leads to nowhere" except to the dead end of bigger volume and lower profits.

It is no accident that in some of our best-managed growth companies the burden-absorption argument is not accepted as valid either for going into or out of a business. Rather the assumption is that the business will be run efficiently at all times and that capacity will be balanced effectively against sales volume. This approach is far less dangerous than that of burden absorption.

Defensive growth—rear-guard expansion—does two serious things to a company's chances for real growth:

1. It fixes profits at a low level—costs at a high level—by freezing inefficiency permanently into the company.

2. It leads to cumbersome and unwieldy complexity. When, in the name of burden absorption, so many different kinds of products and technologies are brought together in one business family that they cannot be handled effectively within the practical limits of organizational decentralization, then diversification has gone too far. When this happens, mediocrity in earning power is almost certain to result.

## DOWNSTREAM MANAGEMENT

Another category of obstacles or hazards can be gathered under the title of "downstream management."

One example is the practice of using new job opportunities to find places for problem personnel rather than to find the right man for the job. By so doing, it is hoped to kill two birds with one stone. Unfortunately, this approach more often than not only postpones facing the personnel problem and, in addition, creates an added problem in the new job function. Availability is only one—and not the most important—criterion for selecting men for important assignments. This is taking the course of least resistance—coasting with the current—in other words, "downstream management."

Another example can be observed in the splitting up of productive operations, putting them at separate locations, even at higher costs, with the specific purpose of avoiding exposure to strike stoppages and other labor dislocations. This is "downstream management" in the sense that it tries to go around—to lighten the impact of—an inadequate labor relations program, rather than to do the job that ought to be done on labor relations in the first place. Many companies have demonstrated that sound labor relations—though not easy or cheap to achieve—really pay off. Of course the indispensable basis for sound employee relations is an efficiently run company. This is a big order. Yet without it, no matter how fancy the frills, employee relations cannot be satisfactory.

## Common Characteristics

These examples of what prevents growth, and many others that might be mentioned, have a few characteristics in common about which we can generalize:

1. They masquerade or wear the disguise of real growth; they make the company look bigger.
2. They seem to obviate the necessity of doing a pruning or a fundamental corrective job.
3. They make specific weakness or inefficiency less obvious by dispersing it throughout the organization—like a boil which does not come to a head but is gradually absorbed by the whole system. Instead of having isolated bad spots which can be identified, treated, and cured, the whole business area becomes mildly sick and operates at the level of mediocrity—not profitable enough to be strong, not weak enough to die.
4. They result eventually in a company which has so many different kinds of problems that it can specialize on nothing—it is a "Jack of all trades and master of none." This means that it does an average or compromise job while being forced to compete with a number of companies, some of which are expert at what they do.

### Danger Signals

We have just been looking at some of the things which prevent growth. When anything is as difficult to recognize, measure, and achieve as business growth, it is helpful to have danger signals or red lights along the way to tell us when we may be getting off the straight and narrow path to growth.

No signal, of course, is conclusive. Every one of them has to be verified and evaluated in terms of all the conditions—just as the medical diagnostician has to check and recheck symptoms and findings in order to be sure that he understands what is ailing his patient.

Let me mention, in the form of test questions, just a few of the signals that you may find it helpful to look for, since they may mean that there are serious obstacles to growth in your business:

1. *Do you depend upon a wide diversification of old products rather than upon efficiency and dynamic product and process development to sustain your earning power throughout the cyclical swings of business?* If so, there is serious question about your having a real growth company, and you are in danger of decadence.

2. *Has a substantial part of your expansion been achieved by adding more and more of the same thing rather than by adding new products or processes?* If so, you may be exposed to heavy obsolescence or even dry rot in a few years.

3. *Do you hang on to, instead of obsoleting, spare equipment or parts for which you have no known use, in the hope that they may be useful some day?* If so, you are using more capital than you need, and your return on capital employed is needlessly low. It is possible also that this is a symptom indicating that it pays better to be right than it does to be profitable in your company.

4. *Are rewards in your company based primarily upon how hard a man works, the size of his responsibility, his rank or status in the organization, or the fact that he is "in line" for bigger things, instead of being based invariably upon contribution to profitability?* If so, you are being lured off the growth beam.

5. *Do you make some capital expenditures, because you have the money, that you would not consider worth while if you had to borrow or sell stock to finance?* If so, you are possibly placing convenience—the availability of money to spend—above profitability as a criterion for new product or process ventures.

6. *Do your investments for cost reduction show big savings while earnings of the company are declining?* If so, possibly operating inefficiencies are increasing costs more than investment for cost reduction is decreasing them —and the stockholders are being asked to subsidize or pick up the tab for management's ineffectiveness.

7. *Does your company evaluate technical skills in handling materials and equipment higher than it does the ability to handle people?* (The tip-off on this is revealed in the kind of appointments made to the assignments involving large segments of employees.) If so, your company may be creating costly employee relations problems.

8. *Are capital expenditures to improve present businesses out of proportion to investments in new developments?* If so, you are losing your offensive, forward-looking pace.

9. *When the soundest calculations you can make do not support what you want to do, do you go ahead anyway, reasoning that there are "intangible" values and benefits that will justify your action?* If you do, you are kidding yourself. Intangibles are unfavorable at least as often as they are advantageous.

10. *Is "unfavorable" assortment becoming a more and more frequent reason for unsatisfactory margins—particularly since the end of the sellers' market in the early part of 1952?* If so, you are just getting volume whether it is profitable or not; you are picking up the crumbs, taking the orders that are easy to get, while the aggressive merchandisers are getting the high profit sales. In short, you are doing a "downstream" selling job.

11. *Do you do things for a part of your business that you would not do if that part were all the business you had?* If so, you may be allowing bigness to obscure the real economics of the situation.

12. *Do your top-management people spend most of their time working on the unsatisfactory parts of the business rather than the profitable parts?* If so, your company is playing to weakness and may be starving the golden goose.

13. *Do you excuse low profits today on the ground that the high costs now being incurred will pay off handsomely in future profits?* If so, you may be indulging in a form of rationalization that is very popular in periods of high taxes.

14. *Do many of your best young men leave to make more money elsewhere?* If so, maybe the cost of giving career men security regardless of performance is being paid for at the cost of superior men who have to go to other companies to find adequate reward for making a real contribution to profit.

15. *Is your diversification so broad that, like the old woman who lived in a shoe, you have so many situations you don't know what to do, especially about long-range development work?* If so, your effort is being diluted, and obsolescence may become systemic—for lack of new ideas and opportunities.

16. *Is the most rapid increase in such things as sales volume, number of employees, number of plants, and capital employed in the relatively low-profit areas of your business?* If so, you are probably bailing out what is weak—being defensive—rather than developing and exploiting new opportunities on their merits.

17. *Are more of your executives, principally those in so-called middle management, engaged in money-making ventures on the side?* In other words, are your executives selling their administrative services to the company and employing their creative money-making talents in their own, outside enterprises? If so, and I imply no criticism of anyone, it is an indication of the extent to which some big businesses are losing the essence of free

enterprise and assuming the characteristics of huge administrative units. Nothing could be more detrimental to business growth.

Significantly—not just incidentally—where are the lush expense accounts, where are the snazzy offices? In the personally owned businesses operated on the side, or in your publicly owned company? And do you ever hear it jokingly said from time to time—or is it jokingly?—"Don't mind me, I just work here."

## CONSTRUCTIVE ACTION

Up to this point we have found that growth is the process of employing more and more capital with increasing effectiveness—as measured by return on capital employed—in a company which is constantly being renewed by the addition of the new and the elimination of the obsolete. We have also found that every business is beset by very alluring and attractive alternatives which constantly threaten to prevent sound growth. Now, what constructive action can be taken?

Not for a long time has it been so important as it is now for businessmen to understand how to get growth. After four or five years during which the upward course of business was so strong that it was almost impossible for management to make an obvious mistake, economic forecasters tell us that we are now, for the first time in the postwar years, coming into a period in which operating results will accurately reflect the effectiveness of management and nothing else. The tide of business itself will no longer be the dominant factor eclipsing and covering up the weaknesses which have crept into management during the long years of swing-out from the depression of the 1930's.

We all know *what* to do to achieve growth. Set it as the goal, organize for it, and pursue it relentlessly. It is as simple as that—in principle. True as this is, it is not the answer we are looking for. Every management believes in its heart that it is doing this now—has been doing it for years—and yet so straight is the path and so narrow the gate that few, very few indeed, have entered into the Promised Land. The secret that has escaped us in our pellmell race for bigness is not *what* to do, but *how* to do it.

How can we get our employees to work for sound growth and to work for nothing else? Boil it down, and that is the question. Let us approach it by considering a few simple truths:

1. A company will get what it pays for, provided the payoff is consistent. If the choice jobs always go to the expanders in the business, the company will get bigness in sales, in plants, in products, in organization—but not profitability. If the big rewards are always for technical proficiency, it will get that—but not profitability. And so on with political sagacity and other alternative goals.

2. If the company vacillates between goals—i.e., cannot select one and adhere consistently to it—then the company will get nothing but confusion, frustration, low morale, and mediocre profits.

3. Management has to decide what it wants to pay for. It cannot let the matter be solved by default, cannot back away from the problem.

4. A vacuum is abhorred in business just as violently as it is in nature. If there is the slightest lapse in the rigid, continuous, and unrelenting adherence to the goal of growth, one or more of the false goals we have considered will rush in to fill the void.

Now, in the light of these considerations, how do we get a whole organization to work as effectively as it can for just one goal—namely, growth?

## Rewarding Performance

The only answer that seems sound to me is to find in business the most nearly perfect example of what we want and then to discover what makes it tick. In my view, the successful, small, owner-operated enterprise has got what we are looking for. The secret of its success is the direct, positive, immediate, and proportionate reward for effort in the profits of the business, to the extent that the effort is sound— and in the certain loss through the deterioration or collapse of the business if the effort is not sound.

Most big companies do not have these rewards and consequences. Salary administration does not provide it. It is too slow and cumbersome; it is bound by the need for uniformity, for standardization, and so on. Promotions cannot do it. There just are not enough jobs into which to promote everyone who makes the kind of contribution to profitability that is the essence of growth. If incentives are to be effective, the payoff must not depend upon deaths, retirements, resignations, or anything else which cannot be controlled; the reward and consequences must be as direct as in the owner-operated business.

In the typical business which does not have a well-worked-out and administered program of incentives, the consequences of unsatisfactory performance are much more direct and powerful than are the rewards for positive contributions to the goal. You can fire, demote, or cut the pay of a man in ten minutes; but you cannot give him a bonus, raise his pay, or promote him just like that. It practically takes a board meeting to reward him. The result of this is that there is much more incentive to *avoid mistakes* than there is to *venture,* to take the kind of risks that are essential to growth in business.

If we really want growth in big business, we are going to have to pay for positive action in larger measure than we penalize for mistakes. If we do not, we shall have big, safe, unprofitable administrative units called businesses.

The late Lammot du Pont told me several years ago that, in his opinion, the growth of his company throughout the many business generations of its long and successful history was attributable to the system of rewarding good performance, as well as holding individuals accountable for unsatisfactory performance, more than to any other one factor. But, he went on to say, in order to do it, much more hard work is required than to do just the usual or ordinary tasks with which an executive busies himself. Nothing is so important, he emphasized, and nothing is so difficult.

## Penetrating Scrutiny

From the time a company installs an incentive program, every act of management has to be consistent with the company objective in terms of which extra compensation will be paid. Everything has to stand up under the penetrating scrutiny of a smart organization to which every move means money. This is a wholesome thing for management just as audit by public accountants is good for controllers and should be welcomed in the same way.

It is not only wholesome for management, but essential to the free-enterprise system. This system is under attack from the outside; many of those who would destroy it have no understanding of how it works. We, the managers, must clearly understand it, and we must make it just as strong as we can. We can do this by gearing the rewards and penalties of performance directly to the one objective—the growth objective which we are all striving to achieve.

# VI

## STRATEGY

We cannot fix our security in a changing world by attempting to fix things; and the more we attempt to fix, the deeper our anxiety, because the more rigid we are, the more inept we are in dealing with life. Subconsciously, if not consciously, we know that it isn't working. . . . Confidence is what we want, not to fix tomorrow but to be sure that we can handle tomorrow.
—Duncan E. Littlefair, D. D. (from an extemporaneous sermon)

# 39.

# *Introduction*

• A confident aggressive spirit, backed up by intelligent planning and hard-hitting management, can be contagious.

• The five-year plan is a living document which never becomes static. At no time is it bound together between two covers as an "approved program" for the company. Most of the time it is in the form of rough layout sheets which are under constant revision.

• Effective planning often requires management to choose a course of action in the light of what a competitor is likely to do.

• Does the company market products in enough areas where important discoveries are likely? If not, it should broaden its technological and economic base by entering a number of "growth industries."

• All of our great industrial enterprises grow on the strength of a leading "image of the future." Optimistic ideas, dynamic aspirations, and cohesive ambitions are perhaps even stronger factors than we have thought in bringing about conditions making up a company's future.

These are a few of the ideas that the authors in this section consider important in making long-range strategy. If we look at this topic in perspective, we may see an important force working in favor of these ideas. For possibly the most significant thing about planning is the most obvious thing, when we recall the earlier discussions of organization, steps, and techniques. A carefully reasoned, comprehensive master plan provides an organized body of knowledge about where a company is going, how, and when. The moment managers admit the existence of such a plan, and especially if they have helped develop it, they also admit the priority of its goals and steps over personal power and advantage. In essence, this is a concept which Lyndall F. Urwick has put in broader terms in discussing scientific management,[1] but it is especially pertinent here.

What are the implications of this concept for making planning work? It means that the power of an executive does not depend alone on his ability to sell himself, to manipulate others to his point of view, to see a temporary advantage. There is more to his influence than personal charm and a sharp eye for short-term profit. He and all other managers are committed to a plan of action. It provides a broad framework for their policies and decisions. It lays down goals, standards, and criteria.

Consequently, no longer must men at the middle and lower management levels feel that direction from the top is subject to the momentary tides and currents of "politics." Politics there will be as always, but the plan operates as a sort of common law which, in the broad stream of decisions, exerts a powerful and *predictable* influence. A well-communicated, well-understood program for the next five years should counteract cynicism about how top-management decisions are made. It will give supervisors down the line the feeling that "We know where we're going"—not just that "We're going somewhere." Such an attitude may well have an incalculable effect on the success of planning in practical everyday operation. Reading through the chapters that follow, one may sense this assumption being made again and again.

Of course, none of this detracts from the need for strong leadership and good administration, as the authors here point out so well. Top management must be aggressive. It must continually review and revise. It must communicate. It must have a dynamic picture of the future. In other words, it must do all of those things which have always been needed in order to breathe fire and life into an organization that is going places. The plans themselves are only pieces of paper—"rough layout sheets," as Mr. Percy calls them—which are worth no more without people to implement them than statutes are without judges and lawyers.

Indeed, one underlying theme of these chapters seems to be the

[1] See *The Pattern of Management* (Minneapolis, University of Minnesota Press, 1956), pp. 14–18.

importance of maintaining the *initiative* in making planning work. Executives have to keep stepping out of the line of day-to-day operations to check, review, restate, spur the work on. This is no simple job. It is probably true that good long-range planning will make current operations and control easier, just as good operations and control will make planning easier, but there is also little doubt but that in the end planning will take extra time. We can ask: How will executives find this time on top of their already busy schedules? Or we can ask: Should current operations and control consume as much of a top executive's time as they do? I think the latter inquiry is more fruitful. It is interesting and significant that one very often finds, when he becomes acquainted with progressive companies, that the president and other key line executives regularly break away from operating routines "just to talk and think." They do not let themselves get "paced" by their administrative jobs like a worker on an assembly line.

## CONTRIBUTORS TO THIS SECTION

*Ernest R. Breech* is Chairman of the Board of Ford Motor Company. In his distinguished business career he formerly served as President of Bendix Aviation Corp., Chairman of the Board of North American Aviation, Inc., Vice President of General Motors Corp., and in various other positions.

*Charles H. Percy* is President of Bell & Howell Company. He has also served as a Director of Burroughs Corp. and of Harris Trust & Savings Bank, and as a Trustee of Boys Clubs, Chicago, The University of Chicago, and Illinois Institute of Technology.

*William E. Roberts* is Executive Vice-President of Bell & Howell. He is also Executive Vice-President and a Director of Bell & Howell, Canada, Ltd., and a Vice-President and Director of the National Lecture Bureau.

*Harold Koontz* is Professor of Business Policy and Transportation at the Graduate School of Business Administration, University of California at Los Angeles.

*H. Igor Ansoff* is a development planning specialist with Lockheed Aircraft Corporation. Formerly a mathematician with the Rand Corporation, he was head of the operations group of the company's missile division and a project officer on several major projects.

430     LONG-RANGE PLANNING FOR MANAGEMENT

*Weldon B. Gibson* is Associate Director of Stanford Research Institute. He has been active in the development of two leading conferences on long-range planning which the Institute has sponsored —the Industrial Economics Conferences of 1956 and of 1957.

# 40.

# *The Large Company: Basic Strategy*

## By Ernest R. Breech [1]

We at Ford Motor Company have been preparing for almost a decade to hold our own in what we foresaw would be a rich but hotly competitive market. We believe that we have a new kind of market today, that we are dealing with a more prosperous and more selective consumer, and that we must plan our business accordingly. We are acutely aware also of many external social and political forces which condition the environment of business and will affect our planning. We are confronted on all sides by difficult, almost imponderable questions. What will be the effect upon our business in five or ten years of the fast developing new technologies, of automation, electronics, atomic energy? Of defense planning? What about the great and swelling demand of American working people for greater employment stability? And so on.

I can't hope even to begin exploring all these questions in a few brief moments. I can try to give you my impression of what it takes to make a go of your company and mine in today's and tomorrow's competitive market. I will draw for that purpose upon our own experience with the reorganization of Ford Motor Company. Our whole story, basically, is one of preparation for a tough buyers' market. Moreover, I believe our company to be an almost classic example of the introduction of modern management methods and the results thereof.

Our strategy for the future was laid out ten years ago. It has stood up well under the test of time and we are still broadly adhering to it.

[1] Reprinted by permission from *Harvard Business School Bulletin*, Summer, 1955, pp. 26–29.

## A Bad Situation

When a new management team under Henry Ford II undertook the reorganization of Ford Motor Company, it found itself short on everything but determination. It faced the postwar market with run-down plants, obsolete products, almost nonexistent financial control, an inadequate engineering staff, and just sufficient cash to meet its daily operating requirements.

As we looked forward to the future, we saw that we would be unable to last when the competitive market returned, unless we remade ourselves completely into a strong, modern, going concern.

What guided us then, still guides us today. What we went after was precisely what it will take for your firm or mine to be competitive in the rich but hard-fought market of today and tomorrow. And what it takes, above all, is competent management, flexible and big enough to respond swiftly to changing market conditions; research and engineering adequate to meet the enormous strain of modern product competition; plants and machinery efficient enough to compete with the best of the industry; and a financial control system which provides sound forecasting, keeps operations efficient, and is geared to produce peak profits.

Let me point to just a few highlights of our experience and try to extract from them some general applications.

## Decentralization

One of our first steps back in 1946 was to set up a modern organization featuring a program of decentralization—breaking up our business into many smaller profit centers, each run like an independent business and held accountable for its profit performance. Along with this process naturally went the delegation of responsibilities to managers and the authority necessary to carry out those responsibilities.

In order to make that system work—and this was vital—we set up an incentive system based on supplemental compensation, and made it clear that rewards would be commensurate with performance.

We also set up an orthodox line and staff organization with an Administration Committee and various operating subcommittees to deal, for example, with product planning, merchandising, industrial relations, purchasing, scheduling, manufacturing, foreign operations, industrial and public relations. Each group develops basic programs and recommends them to the executive committee.

I wish I might tell you that once the organization is set along these lines, it remains put. It doesn't. So far as we're concerned, no book on organization has ever been written that can be applied dogmatically to any given company. A theoretically sound and logical organizational setup can and often does founder on the hidden shoals of human nature.

While the modern executive may seek guidance from the textbook, he remembers always that he is dealing with individuals and not with theoretical abstractions. Organizations are nothing more or less than groups of people with a common purpose. They must be rearranged from time to time so that the abilities of the management personnel at hand may be used to the greatest effect.

Management organization, like medicine, probably will always be as much an art as a science.

The corporation is like a living organism. All of you gentlemen have watched with much fascination, I'm sure, the changes and evolutions that have taken place in your own business organizations over a period of years. There seem to be recurrent cycles in which management power and influence flow in toward the center and then out to the extremities. Strange, hard-to-diagnose illnesses occur in various parts of the organism; unsightly bulges appear anywhere that fat is permitted to accumulate. (I suppose that's why they call that common affliction a "corporation.")

If the organism is permitted to sit still too long, it begins to develop hardening of the arteries, shortness of breath, and atrophy of the imagination. The executive must be constantly and critically sensitive to the health of the corporate organization, and experimental, intuitive, and imaginative in dealing with it.

## OUR AIM: OBSOLESCENCE

After we had set up our basic organization, we turned our attention to our engineering and product planning establishment. Unless you have the right product at the right time to meet consumer demands, you will not have much of a business.

In my opinion, the main goal of product engineering in any consumer goods company is obsolescence. Our job at Ford Motor Company is to obsolete every car on the road—not by superficial changes but by dramatic and fundamental engineering and styling improvements.

To do that job in a company with diversified products requires a very substantial research and engineering setup. We must be able to work out simultaneously the design of many different current and future models, push out ahead of competition in basic scientific research, and have an organization large and flexible enough to meet crash emergency demands for special engineering projects.

To give you an example, in 1946 we had a total of only 2,300 engineering employees, including draftsmen, clerks, and sweepers, and the activity was budgeted at $14 million annually. Compare that with today [1955], when our engineering personnel total 9,500, and the annual engineering budget is close to $95 million.

Over the same period, we have made available to our research and engineering men some $88 million for new facilities. In addition to building new research, styling, and testing facilities, we have invested heavily in a superbly staffed scientific laboratory which is working years ahead on the development of new and better means of automotive transportation.

The development of product planning—like organizational planning—depends much upon individual personalities and the type of products to be designed. Our own procedures have come about through a gradual evolution. Maybe I should call it "trial and error."

In our industry, we work at least three years ahead on new models. Normally, we should have final management approval of basic new-model styling and design characteristics more than two years before the actual production year. Right now we are placing our bets on what we think the public will want to buy in 1957 and 1958.

Does that policy pay off? Look at today's automobile sales. Had the automobile industry been content to ride along with its 1949 or 1952 models, I venture to say that this would be much closer to a four-million-car year than to the six-and-one-half-million-plus retail sales we presently anticipate. The big reason for today's booming car sales is that the 1955 models are far ahead of their predecessors in mechanical excellence, performance, and styling.

Rapid obsolescence is of course an expensive proposition. Tools, dies, fixtures—whole production lines or systems—might have to be scrapped in order to take advantage of some desirable improvement. It calls for a top-flight engineering and research organization, adequate and up-to-date facilities, plus careful planning and coordination with other components of the company.

## Modern Equipment

Next, we come to the vital problem of proper facilities planning. In order to maintain and improve our competitive position, we must of course have adequate and modern plant and equipment.

In our business, long-range facilities planning, to put it simply, means analyzing the market for our products over a certain period of years, determining what percentage of the market we think we can get, determining the type of products that will be characteristic of those years, and translating those findings into plant requirements. We ask what facilities will we need, in other words, to produce standard volume.

Broadly speaking, we define standard volume as the average annual output of cars, trucks, and other products which we expect to maintain over a long period—five years or more.

Since standard volume is the basis not only of all our facilities planning but also for all prices and budgets, it becomes a critical determination. If we overestimate our standard volume and wind up with excess plant capacity, we of course pay the penalty of lessened profits. If we estimate on the low side, we incur the added costs and inefficiencies of overtime work to meet peak markets.

There is some theoretical dispute as to whether it is wiser to estimate conservatively or to build the capacity to handle peak loads. We at Ford prefer the former course. The profit on added volume in excess of standard volume more than offsets the overtime premiums during peak operations. Moreover, in any industry with a high seasonal factor, such as the automobile business, the use of overtime to secure peak volume is a valuable means of promoting more stable employment and better incomes for our working people.

While long-range planning is a matter of recurring study, short-range facilities planning—one or two years ahead—must receive constant attention. Each component of each new model automobile requires facilities planning from metal stampings to automatic transmissions and engines.

Control of this effort is a vast job. All plans submitted for new products or models must be accompanied by rather detailed analyses of the facilities required. Obviously product planning and facilities planning must go hand in hand.

To do the complex job of both short- and long-range planning, the rearrangement of existing facilities, the engineering and integrating of new facilities, requires a vast and competent technical organization. Currently Ford Motor Company employs more than 5,300 manufacturing engineers, as we call them, including our plant, facilities, design, and methods engineers.

Our cost control system operates as a spur to every plant manager and foreman to analyze his operations continuously to determine whether more modern methods and machinery will do the job more efficiently.

Our current appropriations for modernizing and improving our machinery and methods run into many millions of dollars annually. We frequently find it to our advantage to replace two- or three-year old machinery with newer and more costly machines. We keep a close watch over such modernization; every appropriation for the purpose must show clearly the anticipated cost savings and the return on investment resulting. Later, actual performance is checked against these estimates.

## FINANCIAL CONTROL

The success of the entire business depends ultimately on sound financial planning and reporting. A financial control system must have a clear objective—a yardstick against which to measure performance. In our case, as I have mentioned, all financial forecasts are made on the basis of standard volume rate of operations. Each year every manager of a profit center must submit a profit plan for that year based upon standard volume.

These profit forecasts are reviewed individually with each manager and his principal assistants by the top officers of the company. All expense budgets of organizations that are not profit centers, such as those covering administrative and commercial expenses, engineering, and so on, are submitted annually and reviewed thoroughly in the same manner. In the monthly financial reviews all managers are present when the results of their operations for that month and the year-to-date are presented to the entire Administration Committee, all compared with the previously submitted financial forecasts, or profit plans.

In addition to the actual monthly and year-to-date profit statements, each month all operations furnish a forecast covering the next four months of the year, based upon the expected performance at anticipated volume.

## Pricing Philosophy

Although most companies of any size are strong, some of them outstandingly, on cost control, many of the same companies may be startlingly casual about pricing, or revenue control. It has been our experience that large dividends of added sales and profits can accrue from a careful and systematic attention to revenue control. Pricing procedures for all our products are based on anticipated costs and revenues at standard volume, without regard to temporary fluctuations in the market. However, revenue control involves much more than setting sales prices—it involves the whole area of pricing philosophy, the determination of desirable product mix, and the selection of buy or make products on the basis of obtaining maximum profitability.

Under the profit center system, revenue control of intracompany sales between various divisions of the same firm gives invaluable guidance in make-or-buy decisions, provides a check on supplier prices, and is a useful test of performance. Moreover, requiring our own producing divisions to sell competitively to the end-product divisions (car, truck, and tractor divisions) has contributed enormously to the improved profit position of Ford Motor Company.

What I have said here suggests that the whole financial control system must be so designed as to highlight profitability. In our business we do that through a combination of the profit center system and incentive in the form of a supplemental compensation plan in which more than 3,800 members of management participate according to their own performance.

In the course of reorganizing Ford Motor Company, by 1948 we had set up a modern cost control system and a supplemental compensation plan. Having done so, we were startled to find that nothing in particular happened. We had built, or so we thought, a log fire under the company. But we had not, up to that point, applied the torch of internal competition.

In the fall of 1948 we called together several hundred of our top-management men. We analyzed and compared the profit performance of each key operation, and showed how performance was reflected in the supplemental compensation fund. It was quite a show, and each man went out of that meeting determined to put his own house in order. Each man in turn set up similar meetings of his own supervisors and the process continued on down the line. These meetings were held, and still are, at regular intervals. The results were almost unbelievable.

Our direct labor costs were reduced from an off-standard of 65 per cent in July of 1948 to only 6 per cent off-standard in 1951, and manufacturing overhead improved 48 percentage points during the same period. We never could have achieved that performance without a real incentive system and internal competition that reached deep into our management structure.

## THE CRYSTAL BALL

Obviously, business planning for the future involves the all-important functions of merchandising and distribution. Are we riding the crest of a boom that may taper off a few months or years from now, or is this the new norm of American economic activity? How big is our market and how big is it likely to grow?

I think our expansion program indicates how we at Ford look at the situation. We see a constantly expanding market for cars and trucks and other automotive equipment over the long pull and, frankly, we intend to take an increasing share of that market for our own products.

We believe it is our business, and that of other large companies, to *make* trends, not to follow them. A confident aggressive spirit, backed up by intelligent planning and hard-hitting management, can be contagious. I'm sure most of you noted the recent upturn in steel production to meet the sustained sales performance of the automotive industry. It has served as a powerful stimulus to over-all economic activity.

## GAW—THE REAL STORY

There is one item I have not touched upon, but which I suspect you gentlemen may be curious about. It could be called "Planning the future strategy of your business in terms of labor relations."

We have long been completely sympathetic toward the desire of our employees to lessen the risks of unemployment resulting from seasonal factors in the auto industry. We have sought consistently to stabilize our production and employment, to minimize lay-offs due to model changes by better planning, to use overtime pay, wherever possible, to meet production peaks rather than hire temporary workers. We have made much progress in this direction.

We began some time ago [prior to 1955] to work on the details of a proposed plan of private supplementation of unemployment compensation that would give substantial added security to our workers in ways consistent with sound private enterprise principles.

We believe that such a plan should not shackle management's freedom to manage. It should be a definite determinable cost item with a definitely limited liability. It should not offer unemployment benefits so great as to remove the incentive to work.

The present plan meets every one of those requirements.

We believe it is a good plan—good for the workers, good for the company, good for the whole country. When you have had a chance to study the plan in detail, I'm sure you will agree that it solves a knotty problem which concerns not only American industry but the general public as well.

## TOMORROW'S MARKET

In summary then, gentlemen, let me say this: The market of the future promises to be unlike anything we have known before. We see no ceilings to that market except the ones imposed by our own shortness of vision.

That market, needless to say, will be hotly competitive.

In planning the strategy of the larger business—particularly in the consumer goods industries—clearly we will not be competitive in the year 1965 with the products or tools or methods of 1955.

Staying competitive will mean a bold, venturesome outlook on investment in new products, new plants and equipment. It will mean

seeking constantly to make obsolete existing products and being ready
to adapt our businesses to the needs of the atomic age.

Business management must be stronger than formerly in such areas
as scientific research, product and manufacturing engineering, financial forecasting, and control. It must have real flexibility and strength-
in-depth so that it can respond hard and fast to changing competitive
situations. It must be imaginative. It follows then that management
must provide enough incentive to attract and hold really capable men
at all levels—and in the last analysis, all else depends on this.

With a well-staffed management team in which an aggressive risk-
taking spirit is backed up by cool-headed, analytical planning, there
will be no problem too tough to be solved.

# 41.

# Planning the Basic Strategy of a Medium-Size Business

## By Charles H. Percy and William E. Roberts [1]

The foundation of "profit planning" is the company's sixty-month program. In setting our goals we take a retrospective look at where we have been, an objective look at where we are, and a hopeful look at where we want to go. We then chart a course which we believe will get us there. We keep an eye on economic forecasts, but I must admit that we do not let them influence our thinking too much. If the economic outlook is good, we are encouraged to go ahead with our plans. If it is foreboding, we try to determine how to buck the trend.

An important step is to analyze carefully our relative position in each field in which we compete. After a careful comparison of our past and present financial ratios—earnings to sales, return on investment, and inventory turnover—we establish goals to improve our position during each of the succeeding five years.

With the goals set, the detailed preparation of a sixty-month program begins. We analyze our existing product line and review our new product development and research program. A sales forecast is made by months for the next fifteen-month period and on an annual basis for the following four years. Increases in hourly labor rates and salaries are projected, as is the lowering of unit costs through the

[1] By permission from *Planning the Future Strategy of Your Business,* edited by Edward C. Bursk and Dan H. Fenn, Jr. Copyright, 1956, McGraw-Hill Book Company, Inc.

anticipated effectiveness of cost-reduction programs. For expansion and capital equipment, future needs are analyzed, schedules are made, and financing is planned.

The sixty-month program is a living document which never becomes static. At no time has it ever been bound together between two covers as an "approved program" for the company. Most of the time it is in the form of rough layout sheets which are under constant revision.

The objective of the program is not only the program but also the thinking and planning that go into it. We are never satisfied with it, and I hope we never will be. Working constantly on a sixty-month program makes the preparation of our current year's profit and loss forecast a great deal easier, more accurate, and more satisfactory than it might otherwise be.

The merchandising division establishes a detailed sales forecast by months for all products and models, and submits it to manufacturing, financial, and administrative management for critical analysis. This same procedure is repeated frequently throughout the year. Desired inventory levels are established and manufacturing schedules drawn up. Cost of sales and divisional expense levels are established by the budget board in consultation with division managers. Programs and expenses are continually revised to maintain the current year's profit objective. The forecast profit and loss statement and the anticipated balance sheet position projected one year ahead are submitted to the board of directors at its December meeting. . . .

## ACTUAL VERSUS FORECAST PROGRAM

Flexibility is a must in a sixty-month program. Looking ahead five years from a constantly moving current date makes planning for the immediate twelve-month period easier. Both our long-range and short-range programs are constantly modified to meet new competitive products, the unforeseeable results of some of our own engineering and research efforts, the consolidation of newly acquired businesses, and other factors incalculable in advance.

Actually, our five-year planning is not directly measurable in terms of "batting averages." But in keeping us aimed in the right direction it has helped to achieve a good batting average in our short-term, twelve-month planning.

Over the past four years we have varied only slightly from our planned sales, expense, and profit budgets. Variation in expenses against budget, for example, ranged from 4.4 per cent in 1952 to 1 per cent in 1954. The variation from the preyear profit budget to actual was only 3 per cent in 1954.

When deviations occur, as they frequently do during the year, we apply no magic formula for corrective action. Deviations are rapidly detected through weekly meetings of our sales analysis board. Then pertinent division heads and executives are gathered to determine what action is necessary. The answer may be overtime, the addition of double or triple shifts, duplicate tooling, new capital equipment, or around-the-clock engineering effort; it may be a price change or the appointment of a special task force to nurse the situation back to normal.

We try to make our near-term budgets for profits, sales, and manufactured products realistic and attainable. They are rarely missed although it sometimes requires ingenious and unusual effort to keep the program in balance.

Should some problem arise that cannot be remedied in time, we review earnings goals in the light of changed circumstances, and we immediately initiate steps to bring expense budgets into line.

Time will not permit a detailed review of our capital equipment planning. However, in brief, each division head develops and submits by November 1 a detailed list of his anticipated capital expenditures for the following year. The requested budgets are broken down in several ways. They are divided according to whether they are replacement, supplementary, or cost-reduction equipment. Each of these categories is, in turn, divided into two groups—"mandatory" and "desirable." The data are assembled by the controller, reviewed, and balanced by the budget board, and then submitted to the president and the board of directors for approval.

Once approved, it becomes the total company dollar capital equipment budget for the ensuing year. However, each individual expenditure against the budget must be fully justified by the division head and approved by the controller before actual purchase. Cost-reduction equipment must presently meet a rigid rule of paying for itself within eighteen months. The measuring stick is almost always: What is the rate of return on investment?

### COORDINATION OF MANAGEMENT EFFORT

At Bell & Howell we believe firmly that our business should be the expression of the ideas and objectives of our entire management group and, as far as humanly possible, of our employee group. We have experimented with many ways to encourage the free expression of opinion throughout the company, and have developed a pattern for coordinating our management effort and keeping us all running on the same track. The best way, we have found, is to have the top-management group help lay the track by participating in the development of the sixty-month and current year forecasts.

But occasionally it helps to get far enough away from the program to take an objective look at it. To do this our officers and division managers literally move to the Fin 'n Feather Club in nearby Elgin, Illinois, once each quarter. Here we spend several days working together without the interruption of telephones or the pressure of supervisory responsibilities. The setting is beautiful, the atmosphere informal. Sports clothes are the order of the day, and, despite the customary skeet shoot, we have never lost an executive! In addition to crystallizing our thinking about our future program, this meeting helps to ease tensions that may have built up between purchasing and manufacturing, manufacturing and engineering, or engineering and sales.

For some time afterward the atmosphere is completely relaxed back in the organization—and then, suddenly, we know we have to go back to Fin 'n Feather again.

Round-robin reports by division managers at our monthly staff luncheon keep each of us informed on all major developments within the company. Recent accomplishments can be reviewed and near-term forecasts analyzed.

We lean heavily on various management boards to coordinate the functional phases of our program. They are not committees. We feel about committees a little like the description by the chancellor of one of our large universities:

The first time he saw a camel, he got out of his jeep, stood right next to this ugly looking thing with its drooling jowls, baggy skin, and great humps, and he thought, "Good Lord, that looks like it was put together by a committee."

Although the responsibility of these boards is entirely advisory, they are effective in achieving a more closely knit operation and in tapping the specialized knowledge of top-management people.

The heart of our management program is the research board. All ideas for new products are first submitted to this board, which helps to guide new product ideas to fruition. The members of the board include the president, executive vice-president, and treasurer, the engineering, manufacturing, and merchandising vice-presidents, the head of our product planning activity, and the assistant vice-president in charge of production engineering and tooling. Thus, all major operating divisions are able to contribute their viewpoints and participate in discussions and decisions on new product development.

Market research and merchandising department ideas on product features, appearance, and price are usually obtained before the first line is made on a sheet of drafting paper.

Sales, engineering, manufacturing, and financing problems get a thorough going-over before—not after—new product development work is begun.

## RESPONSIBILITIES OF SPECIAL BOARDS

Our sales analysis board, which includes top merchandising, manufacturing, purchasing, and market research people and the executive vice-president, meets once a month. At these meetings individual product projections for the next fifteen-month period are studied month by month and compared with planned manufacturing and projected inventory schedules. The sales, manufacturing, and inventory programs are reviewed, and confirmed or modified in the light of changed conditions; weak areas are detected and corrective action planned. All statistical data are presented graphically.

Supplementing the sales analysis board, a smaller group meets each Monday and briefly reviews sales and manufacturing progress toward budget goals. Negative trends are thus detected in time to bend them back to meet or exceed budget.

The manufaturing board is composed of manufacturing, planning, tooling, production engineering, quality control, and methods engineering personnel. Acting as a two-way information channel and a sounding board for unusual problems or new manufacturing ideas or techniques, it coordinates the functions of the manufacturing division.

The budget board, which includes the president, executive vice-president, treasurer, controller, and vice-president of manufacturing, controls the purse strings of the company. It develops all budgets, in cooperation with the division heads, and recommends them for approval. Annual divisional expense budgets, manufacturing schedules, capital equipment budgets, inventory objectives, and the cash forecast are its responsibilities. It must operate within the current earnings target, with the sixty-month goals constantly in sight.

Our boards have become a device for overcoming the specialization that tends to divorce the outlook of operating experts in engineering from that of experts on sales or manufacturing. But they don't take major planning chores out of the operating people's hands; they don't take away from the division head the responsibility which is his for meeting company objectives; they don't become substitutes for the regular line and staff organization. The boards are merely superimposed on the operating organization as a device to make possible wider interdivisional participation by top executives.

## Execution of Program

We would agree, I am sure, that the basic purpose of a free society is to develop the individual to the greatest possible extent. Should we not also conclude, then, that a company's chance for success is greatest when it encourages such growth and development on the part of each individual within the organization? We believe so, and therefore our objective is to try to create the proper working climate and sufficient incentive for every person to work as conscientiously and intelligently as if he were working for himself. This is the goal we keep constantly before us.

Once our target has been established, our job is to shoot for it—and to shoot with an expectancy of success. We are entirely dependent upon the people of our organization, to whom we delegate all necessary authority and responsibility. Decisions are made at the lowest possible level. We try, as much as possible, to manage through the rule of exception; that is, once a plan has been established and the authority delegated for its execution, no further authority is required from any higher source unless an exception must be made because of changing circumstances. This removes 90 per cent of the routine work from the manager's desk.

But top management would be remiss if it assumed that its job was now done. For in addition to the never-ending job of future planning, the president and the executive vice-president must go to work for the operating divisions of the company to help implement plans and programs already made. This job has many facets, but I will mention only two: the communications program and the continuing task of evaluating divisional and individual performance.

We have proved again and again Thomas J. Watson's words: "None of us is ever enthusiastic about anything until we understand it. Knowledge creates enthusiasm, and it is enthusiasm which inspires us to work and move foreward."

When the organization, from top to bottom, understands the overall aims, objectives, problems, hopes, and aspirations of the company, then it can do a better job of carrying out the company program. . . .

## QUESTIONS AND ANSWERS [2]

*From the floor:* I am interested—and somewhat puzzled—by one aspect of Bell & Howell's "participation" management.

My organization has about 500 people in it, and is pretty small in comparison with some of the large companies. We have a lot of talented young men, however, who are charged with ideas and raring to go, and we are anxious to hear their suggestions. And I couldn't help thinking, as Mr. Percy reported on the way his company operated, how bogged down we get when we try to get all these people into the act, how even our little organizational problems seem to get choked in committee sessions. Yet I understood from his presentation that Bell & Howell had around 300 people getting together every month. How is it possible, as a practical matter, for a company to drag everyone into the act? And how can it control a management committee?

*Mr. Percy:* I became very enthusiastic about management participation—we had never had anything like it in the company before—but I must confess that at one point I made the unpardonable mis-

[2] The preceding sections are based on the authors' addresses at the Twenty-Fifth Annual National Business Conference at the Harvard Business School. In a subsequent meeting, Mr. Percy answered questions pertaining to his formal presentation; this section is drawn, more or less verbatim, from the discussion that took place at this meeting. George P. Baker, James J. Hill Professor of Transportation, Harvard Business School, acted as moderator.

take of letting it go too far, and it was hard to pull it back on the track again. You just cannot let this type of thing get out of hand.

After we started having everyone at the meetings, these conferences had to be held after working hours. This made arrangements much more difficult, of course. When we found that meetings were unnecessarily long and that reasons for calling them were often invalid, we instituted a training program on conference leadership. We had agendas made out ahead of time, including the stated purpose of the meeting, the starting time, and the closing time. If the chairman conducted the meeting improperly, the committee members quickly criticized him for it and thus brought him back on the track. We no longer try to consider everything in these conferences. For instance, no one in the company is wise enough to judge how money taken in through sales should be prorated and expended; this is now a problem for the budget board.

I think we are no longer plagued by too much "meetingitis," as we called it, although we did have trouble for a while controlling our kind of participation management. We used to have dinner meetings once a month from 5:15 to 8:00, but we found we could save several thousand dollars a year by eliminating the dinners, and we now meet for only an hour and a quarter, from 5:00 to 6:15. This gives us plenty of time to present our monthly reports and to inform our executive staff and foremen about important company plans.

The smaller quarterly meetings of our top executives are another matter. They do need to be physically removed from the plant and free from all interference. These meetings, incidentally, provide a wonderful chance for our secondary line of management to run their divisions by themselves for a day or two every quarter. We think it is valuable experience for them to be completely on their own without any of the top-management staff about.

*From the floor:* Mr. Percy has stated that his long-range, five-year planning makes his short-range, one-year, and two-year planning a lot easier. How is this true?

*Mr. Percy:* By becoming familiar with what our cash position is likely to be several years in *advance* of any coming year—barring unforeseeable happenings such as the acquisition of a new business or our competition coming out with a revolutionary new line of product —we find it much easier to estimate our position for any particular year. By the time 1955 came around, we had been planning and working on it for three or more years. Most of my personal time now is going into 1957 and later years—1957, incidentally, will be our fiftieth anniversary, and we have been thinking about it and working on it for many years. We think it will be a fine opportunity for a special drive in several directions. Detailed planning for 1957 should be much easier with all this general, long-range planning in back of us.

*From the floor:* In Mr. Percy's discussion of profit planning, he has mentioned that he looks at the present objectively and the future hopefully. What is the point of this distinction between "objective" and "hopeful"?

*Mr. Percy:* "Hopeful" is one word that almost everyone associated with our company uses extensively. Businessmen have to be optimists; we would get nowhere if we looked with pessimism to the future. We have to figure ways for our company to keep going regardless of the way the economic indicators point and in spite of what our competitors may do. Our theory used to be that when the indicators dropped down, then we buttoned down. Now we try to accelerate our new products ahead faster than originally scheduled and intensify our sales efforts. In other words, we, like other managements, will try to buck any adverse trend—that is our nature. When I said that we look to the future hopefully, I meant we all believe that if any year doesn't turn out the way we thought, at least the approach we took made it better than it might have been.

# 42.

# Planning Principles

## By Harold Koontz [1]

### The Structure of Plans

Four principles, if followed, can go far in tying plans together, in making derivative plans contribute to major plans, and in making sure that planning in one department of an enterprise harmonizes with plans in another part of the business. They may be referred to as the principles of planning premises, timing, policy framework, and planning communication.

1. *Principle of Planning Premises: The understanding of and agreement to utilize consistent planning premises by those who engage in planning is a requisite to coordinated planning.*

Planning premises are assumptions for the future. They may be forecasts of data of a factual nature or basic policies expected to be applicable to the future. They may be matters internal to the firm or external to it. They may be within or beyond a firm's control. They may even be plans of the firm and often are plans of competitive businesses or those firms supplying or buying from a company. In other words, they are the future to which the manager engaging in planning must fit his plans. They are the stage on which he will play his managerial role.

It can be seen readily that the requisite planning premises will not be the same for every manager at every level and in every type of activity in an enterprise. Some of the premises required for most managers will be the same, others will be shaped by the kind of

[1] Reprinted by permission of the author from *A Preliminary Statement of Principles of Planning and Control.*

organizational responsibility he has, and those for managers in lower levels will clearly be shaped by the plans of their superiors.

But, to the extent that it can be done, every manager should have an understanding of the kind of future against which he is to plan. Moreover, these planning premises must be consistent and, in most cases, uniform. For example, despite disagreement among managers as to whether there will be a business recession in the next six months, a given set of plans should proceed upon some uniform premise, even though another set of plans (such as a set held back for use in a given eventuality) may proceed on other premises. While the premises selected may not turn out to be accurate, and a plan may fail for this reason, one can be *sure* that plans will fail, if inconsistent premises are used. For example, failure will surely occur if the sales manager is allowed to plan for a boom year and the production manager for a recession, or if the production department plans for rapid expansion of output, with increasing inventories and capital expenditures, while the treasurer plans cash needs on the basis of a stable output.

2. *Principle of Timing: Effective and efficient planning requires adequate timing horizontally and vertically in the structure of plans.*

Most of the advantages of planning premises lie in proper timing, although the understanding and utilization of uniform planning premises may not assure timing. The importance of timing in planning is nowhere better evidenced than in a complicated assembly line, such as that used for the manufacture of automobiles. The proper blending of chassis, engines, bodies, colors, and accessories in order to achieve the right result of a scheduled car obviously requires timing of the most precise type. While such precise timing is not usually required in other aspects of business planning, I have often thought that, if the mistakes of other managers showed up as readily as the planning mistakes of production managers, the quality of business planning generally would be greatly improved.

What is often overlooked in plans is that timing is a horizontal as well as a vertical matter. It is clearly not enough for the training department to have the right number of operatives trained to utilize a new process or machine, and for the purchasing department to have the machine ordered in time for use when the operatives are ready, while the financial department remains unprepared for necessary accounting techniques and cash resources.

3. *Principle of Policy Framework: Policies establish the framework upon which planning procedures and programs are constructed.*

Policies are guides to decision-making. Policies derive from enterprise objectives, which are the most basic of all policies. As such, they are the guides to thinking which lead to operational plans. In doing so, one policy may beget derivative policies as well as procedures, budgets, tactics, and the other constituents of a program.

Policies, it seems clear to me, are a kind of plan. Involving as they do the choice of an alternative for future action, they are an integral part of plans, the guiding rules under which increasingly detailed plans are made as enterprise goals are transformed into action. If it were not for the complexity of most enterprise operations, or if it were possible for detailed action plans to flow immediately and readily from the architect of the enterprise's objectives without going through a hierarchy of managers, policy formulation could conceivably be limited to the task of stating enterprise objectives.

But complexity in the definition of tasks to accomplish objectives and in the management structure normally required, and the fact that managers often wish to delay given decisions until faced with concrete situations, require a framework of derived policies which must necessarily be consistent and coordinated if resultant programs are to be effective in terms of accomplishing basic objectives.

Policies may be as major as that of a company to finance all growth from profits and as minor as the policy of requiring workers in a machine shop to wear safety glasses. They exist in every aspect of enterprise function and few, indeed, are the managers so low in the organization structure that do not at some time make policy to guide the decision-making of their subordinates. That these various policies must be consistent is often not fully appreciated in practice, as some firms have found to their sorrow when, for example, their policy of promotion from within conflicted with another policy to develop the most competent possible group of managers.

4. *Principle of Planning Communication: The best planning occurs when everyone responsible for it has access to complete information affecting his area of planning.*

It is difficult to expect a manager at any level to do an effective job of planning unless he has available to him an understanding of enterprise objectives, policies affecting his area of planning authority, plans of others—whether superiors or colleagues—which affect his plans, and other information. One of the best means of obtaining communication of planning information is to have as many managers as possible actually participate in making plans affecting their areas of operation.

Because the practical difficulties of furnishing adequate information have been so great, because many managers do not understand the true import of this principle, and because in business, at least, internal security is regarded as necessary to avoid loss of information to a competitor, the typical enterprise tends to develop what might be called a "planning gap." The executives at the top of the enterprise may understand the company's basic goals and policies, and the workmen at the operating level may understand what is expected of them to turn out a day's work, but there tends to exist a gap between the top and bottom where managers do not understand how their departmental goals and policies tie in with the goals and policies of the enterprise as a whole. Even in a well-managed company with which I am familiar, a survey indicated that the most pressing need of the top fifty executives immediately under the vice-presidential level was for knowledge of top-management plans. If this gap existed in the second level of command, one cannot help but wonder how severe the gap was at lower levels.

## The Process of Planning

Within the process of planning itself, I find six significant principles, the understanding of which can do much to furnish a basis for the development of a science of planning. These are the principles of alternatives, the limiting factor, navigational change, flexibility, commitment, and strategic planning.

1. *Principle of Alternatives: In every course of action alternatives exist and planning involves the selection of the alternative course of action which will best enable the enterprise to realize its goals.*

There are almost invariably alternatives to any course of action, and planning seldom involves a Hobson's choice. In fact the problem normally faced by the manager is that he has so many alternatives open to him as to make the selection of the best alternative an extremely complex task.

It is exactly in the area of the principle of alternatives that the methods of operations analysis, the utilization of higher mathematics, and the use of electronic computing machines play their major roles. By exposing to the manager's view a much wider range of alternatives than heretofore possible and by forcing the manager to construct models so that these alternatives are weighed in the light of carefully perceived goals, these tools of management open the way for a new day in planning.

2. *The Principle of the Limiting Factor: In choosing from among alternatives, primary attention must be given to those factors which are limiting or strategic to the solution of the problem involved.*

In every problem area there are certain factors which are of strategic importance to determining whether goals will be attained. These may be few or many and they may change over time in a certain problem area, but, at a given time, there are almost invariably a few which will be most strategic to the solution. While an error in choice of a course of action can be made in concentrating only on limiting factors, the complexity of many decisions facing a manager makes it impracticable for him to consider every facet of a problem, and the risk involved in overlooking the less important aspects of a problem is usually less than the risk of delayed decisions.

Chester Barnard recognized the importance of this principle when he pointed out that:

The analysis required for decision is in effect a search for the "strategic factors"—the theory of the strategic factor is necessary to an appreciation of the process of decision. . . . The limiting (strategic) factor is the one whose control, in the right form, at the right place and time, will establish a new system or set of conditions which meets the purpose.[2]

That this is an eminently practical business planning principle is immediately evident when one approaches a typical business problem. While the horizons of alternatives and the reflection of variables have been considerably broadened by mathematical techniques, models which yield to mathematical solutions in any but the relatively simple business problems can only pick fairly few of the more strategic variables. And, when a manager is faced with a problem for decision-making where either certain significant variables are not quantifiable, or where time or resources do not permit the use of operations analy-

[2] Chester Barnard, *The Functions of the Executive* (Cambridge, Harvard University Press, 1947), pp. 202–3.

sis, he finds his best approach to think through the problem in terms of the limiting factors involved, and solve it in terms of these. As an astute business manager once remarked to me, "all business problems are simple if you can break them down into their most significant parts."

3. *Principle of Navigational Change: Effective planning requires continual checking on events and the redrawing of plans to maintain a course toward a desired goal.*

It is sometimes erroneously believed that planning freezes action for the future. However, the future is uncertain and unforeseen events, whether changes in operating environment or in goals, may obsolete even the best plans. Thus, effective planning requires that the manager, like the navigator, continually check his course and revise plans to meet the goals desired. While it is true that the commitment of funds or effort may bring elements of inflexibility into planning and plans cannot always be modified with changes of the tides or winds of the future, it is likewise true that no effective manager makes *a* plan and then proceeds to put it into effect no matter what events occur. Naturally, to the extent that a manager has been able to forecast the future, make premises which are accurate, establish long-range goals, and arrive at planning decisions which are correct in the light of these, plans may need very little change.

4. *Principle of Flexibility: Effective planning requires that the need for flexibility be a major consideration in the selection of plans, although the costs and dangers of flexibility must be weighed against its advantages.*

To many planners, the principle of flexibility is the most important principle of planning. The need for flexibility arises from the uncertainty of the future and from the fact that many plans require commitment of funds, policy, or effort for varying periods in the future. Since uncertainty tends to increase as a function of time, the greatest flexibility is required where the commitment for the future is large and cannot be discharged (e.g., in returning outlays of capital plus a return) in a short period of time.

Flexibility involves the ability to change a plan without undue cost or friction, an ability to detour, an ability to keep moving toward a goal despite changes in environment or even failure of plans. It thus applies to the adaptability of plans themselves, while the principle of navigational change applies to the planning process and the need for redrawing plans. While it often happens that the redrawing of plans requires the junking of an inflexible plan, sometimes at heavy loss of sunk costs, it is clear that navigational change is easier and less costly if plans have built-in flexibility.

Although flexibility is usually related in business to the ability to change plans without serious financial loss, it cannot be overlooked that inflexibilities in matters other than financial costs are often encountered. Inflexibilities of policies and procedures, psychological inflexibilities of workers and managers, and social and political rigidities often occur to plague the manager who would change his plans.

Flexibility is possible only within limits. In the first place, a manager cannot always put off making a planning decision long enough to make sure of the rightness of his course of action in the light of future events. Decisions must often be made well in advance of the environment for which they are required. For example, the decision of an oil company to build a refinery in the Pacific Northwest had to be taken some five years before it was operated and the financial point of no return was reached several years before the management of the company could be certain that this would be an economic venture.

In the second place, built-in flexibility of plans may be so costly that the benefits of hedging may not be worth the cost. Whether a company spends extra money to make a special-purpose plant so that it might be used for other purposes if the original program failed to meet expectations will depend on the costs of doing so and the importance of the risks to be avoided. Moreover, some companies have felt that they could buy flexibility by keeping their resources in that most flexible of all assets—cash—only to find that their competitor has stepped forth with aggressive expenditures and captured the market.

5. *The Commitment Principle: Planning should encompass a period of time in the future necessary to foresee the fulfillment of commitments made.*

This principle would appear to answer the oft-raised question as to how long to plan. Perhaps the most striking aspect of the principle is the planning ahead for a period far enough to anticipate the recovery of costs sunk in a course of action. In fact, I have previously referred to this principle as the recovery of cost principle.[3] But since other things than costs can be committed for various lengths of time and because a commitment to spend often precedes expenditure and may be as unchangeable as sunk costs, it seems appropriate to refer to this guide for the length of the planning period as the commitment principle.

The application of this principle indicates readily that there is no uniform or arbitrary length of time in the future that a given company should plan or for which a given program or any of its parts should be planned. An airplane company embarking on a new jet aircraft should probably plan this program some twelve years ahead, with five or six years for conception, engineering, and development, and as many more years for production and sale in order to recoup costs and make a reasonable profit. An instrument manufacturer might need only plan its instrument revenues and expenses some six months ahead, since this represents the cycle of raw material acquisition, production, inventories, sales, and collection of accounts. But the same company might wish to see much longer into the future before assuming a lease for specialized manufacturing facilities, undertaking a program of management training, or developing and promoting a new product line.

The planning period will be longer or shorter depending not only upon the length of time it may take to recover costs from an investment or for discharging an obligation under a commitment, but the period will be influenced by the extent to which flexibility has been built into a plan. Thus, a company might be willing to lease a factory for ten years, even though it is impracticable to plan for longer than three, because of the possibilities of subleasing the facilities on a year of two's notice. But where the possibilities of flexibility are not great, it is desirable to plan for the entire period of commitment. This almost surely explains why the major oil companies have led the nation's managements in the excellence and length of their long-range planning, for there is probably no investment quite so fully committed as that made in the development of an oil field, the building of pipelines, and the construction of refinery facilities.

[3] Harold Koontz and Cyril O'Donnell, *Principles of Management* (New York, McGraw-Hill Book Company, Inc., 1955), pp. 441–42.

6. *Principle of Strategic Planning: Effective planning under competitive conditions (i.e., where others are striving for the same goals) requires that the course of action selected be chosen in the light of what a competitor will or will probably do.*

This principle has long been followed in competitive industry, although most of the strategic planning so done has been based on hunch or judgment. But, in recent years particularly, many managers have come to find out that their planning efforts are inadequate unless, in addition to planning their own courses of action, they, in effect, plan what their competitors will probably do. Then, having done this, and to the extent they foresee what their competitors will do, they may modify their plans in this light and thereby take advantage of competitors' plans.

While some form of industrial espionage may help in strategic planning, mere close watch of a competitor's actions may be enough. However, in an increasing number of instances managers are trying to work out in some detail exactly what the competitor will probably do. The policy of a business firm may be clear and its plan well developed, but strategy may require the shading of plans and policies to meet those of others.

# 43.

# Strategies for Diversification

## By H. Igor Ansoff [1]

The Red Queen said, "Now, *here,* it takes all the running *you* can do to keep in the same place. If you want to get somewhere else, you must run at least twice as fast as that!" [2]

So it is in the American economy. Just to retain its relative position, a business firm must go through continuous growth and change. To improve its position, it must grow and change at least "twice as fast as that."

According to a recent survey of the 100 largest United States corporations from 1909 to 1948, few companies that have stuck to their traditional products and methods have grown in stature. The report concludes: "There is no reason to believe that those now at the top will stay there except as they keep abreast in the race of innovation and competition." [3]

There are four basic growth alternatives open to a business. It can grow through increased market penetration, through market development, through product development, or through diversification.

A company which accepts diversification as a part of its planned approach to growth undertakes the task of continually weighing and comparing the advantages of these four alternatives, selecting first one combination and then another, depending on the particular circumstances in long-range development planning.

[1] From H. Igor Ansoff, "Strategies for Diversification," *Harvard Business Review,* September–October 1957, p. 113. Reprinted by permission.

[2] Lewis J. Carroll, *Through the Looking-Glass* (New York, The Heritage Press, 1941), p. 41.

[3] A. D. H. Kaplan, *Big Enterprise in a Competitive System* (Washington, The Brookings Institution, 1954), p. 142.

While they are an integral part of the over-all growth pattern, diversification decisions present certain unique problems. Much more than other growth alternatives, they require a break with past patterns and traditions of a company and an entry on new and uncharted paths.

Accordingly, one of the aims of this article is to relate diversification to the over-all growth perspectives of management, establish reasons which may lead a company to prefer diversification to other growth alternatives, and trace a relationship between over-all growth objectives and special diversification objectives. This will provide us with a partly qualitative, partly quantitative method for selecting diversification strategies which are best suited to long-term growth of a company. We can use qualitative criteria to reduce the total number of possible strategies to the most promising few, and then apply a return on investment measure to narrow the choice of plans still further.

## PRODUCT-MARKET ALTERNATIVES

The term "diversification" is usually associated with a change in the characteristics of the company's product line and/or market, in contrast to market penetration, market development, and product development, which represent other types of change in product-market structure. Since these terms are frequently used interchangeably, we can avoid later confusion by defining each as a special kind of product-market strategy. To begin with the basic concepts:

The *product line* of a manufacturing company refers both to (a) the physical characteristics of the individual products (for example, size, weight, materials, tolerances) and (b) the performance characteristics of the products (for example, an airplane's speed, range, altitude, payload).

In thinking of the market for a product we can borrow a concept commonly used by the military—the concept of a mission. A *product mission* is a description of the job which the product is intended to perform. For instance, one of the missions of the Lockheed Aircraft Corporation is commercial air transportation of passengers; another is provision of airborne early warning for the Air Defense Command; a third is performance of air-to-air combat.

For our purposes, the concept of a mission is more useful in describing market alternatives than would be the concept of a "customer," since a customer usually has many different missions, each requiring a different product. The Air Defense Command, for example, needs different kinds of warning systems. Also, the product mission concept helps management to set up the problems in such a way that it can better evaluate the performance of competing products.

A *product-market strategy,* therefore, is a joint statement of a product line and the corresponding set of missions which the products are designed to fulfill. In shorthand form (see Exhibit XI), if we let $\pi$ represent the product line and $\mu$ the corresponding set of missions, then the pair of $\pi$ and $\mu$ is a product-market strategy.

With these concepts in mind let us turn now to the four different types of product-market strategy shown in Exhibit XI:

*Market penetration* is an effort to increase company sales without departing from an original product-market strategy. The company seeks to improve business performance either by increasing the volume of sales to its present customers or by finding new customers for present products.

*Market development* is a strategy in which the company attempts to adapt its present product line (generally with some modification in the product characteristics) to new missions. An airplane company which adapts and sells its passenger transport for the mission of cargo transportation is an example of this strategy.

A *product development* strategy, on the other hand, retains the present mission and develops products with new and different characteristics that will improve the performance of the mission.

*Diversification* is the final alternative. It calls for a simultaneous departure from the present product line and the present market structure.

Each of the above strategies describes a distinct path which a business can take toward future growth. However, it must be emphasized that in most actual situations a business would follow several of these paths at the same time. As a matter of fact, a simultaneous pursuit of market penetration, market development, and product development is usually a sign of a progressive, well-run business and may be essential to survival in the face of economic competition.

The diversification strategy stands apart from the other three. While the latter are usually followed with the same technical, finan-

Exhibit XI.  Product-Market Strategies for Business Growth Alternatives

| MARKETS / PRODUCT LINE | $\mu_0$ | $\mu_1$ | $\mu_2$ | $\cdots$ | $\mu_m$ |
|---|---|---|---|---|---|
| $\pi_0$ | MARKET Penetration | MARKET DEVELOPMENT | | | |
| $\pi_1$ | | | | | |
| $\pi_2$ | PRODUCT DEVELOPMENT | DIVERSIFICATION | | | |
| $\vdots$ | | | | | |
| $\pi_n$ | | | | | |

cial, and merchandising resources which are used for the original product line, diversification generally requires new skills, new techniques, and new facilities. As a result, it almost invariably leads to physical and organizational changes in the structure of the business which represent a distinct break with past business experience.

## FORECASTING GROWTH

A study of business literature and of company histories reveals many different reasons for diversification. Companies diversify to compensate for technological obsolescence, to distribute risk, to utilize excess productive capacity, to reinvest earnings, to obtain top management, and so forth. In deciding whether to diversify, management should carefully analyze its future growth prospects. It should think of market penetration, market development, and product development as parts of its over-all product strategy and ask whether this strategy should be broadened to include diversification.

### Long-Term Trends

A standard method of analyzing future company growth prospects is to use long-range sales forecasts. Preparing the forecasts involves simultaneous consideration of several major factors:

- General economic trends.
- Political and international trends.
- Trends peculiar to the industry. (For example, forecasts prepared in the airplane industry must take account of such possibilities as a change-over from manned aircraft to missiles, changes in the government "mobilization base" concept with all that would mean for the aircraft industry, and rising expenditures required for research and development.)
- Estimates of the company's competitive strength as compared to other members of the industry.
- Estimates of improvements in company performance which can be achieved through market penetration, market development, and product development.
- Trends in manufacturing costs.

Such forecasts usually assume that company management will be aggressive and that management policies will take full advantage of the opportunities offered by the different trends. They are, in other words, estimates of the best possible results the business can hope to achieve *short* of diversification.

Different patterns of forecasted growth are shown in Exhibit XII, with hypothetical growth curves for the national economy (GNP) and the company's industry added for purposes of comparison. One of the curves illustrates a sales curve which declines with time. This may be the result of an expected contraction of demand, the obsolescence of manufacturing techniques, emergence of new products better suited to the mission to which the company caters, or other changes. Another typical pattern, frequently caused by seasonal variations in demand, is one of cyclic sales activity. Less apparent, but more important, are slower cyclic changes, such as trends in construction or the peace-war variation in demand in the aircraft industry.

If the most optimistic sales estimates which can be attained short of diversification fall in either of the preceding cases, diversification is strongly indicated. However, a company may choose to diversify even if its prospects may, on the whole, appear favorable. This is illustrated by the "slow growth curve." As drawn in Exhibit XII, the curve indicates rising sales which in fact grow faster than the economy as a whole. Nevertheless, the particular company may belong to one of the so-called "growth industries" which as a whole are surging ahead. Such a company may diversify because it feels that its prospective growth rate is unsatisfactory in comparison to the industry growth rate.

Making trend forecasts is far from a precise science. The characteristics of the basic environmental trends, as well as the effect of these trends on the industry, are always uncertain. Furthermore, the ability of a particular business organization to perform in the new environment is very difficult to assess. Consequently, any realistic company forecast should include several different trend forecasts, each with an explicitly or implicitly assigned probability. As an alternative, the company's growth trend forecast may be represented by a widening spread between two extremes, similar to that shown for GNP in Exhibit XII.

## Contingencies

In addition to trends, another class of events may make diversification desirable. These are certain environmental conditions which, if

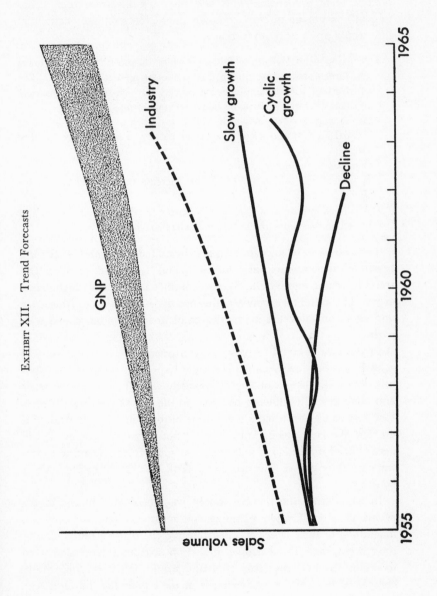

Exhibit XII. Trend Forecasts

GNP

Industry

Slow growth

Cyclic growth

Decline

Sales volume

1955

1960

1965

they occur, will have a great effect on sales; however, we cannot predict their occurrence with certainty. To illustrate such "contingent" events, an aircraft company might foresee these possibilities that would upset its trend forecasts:

- A major technological breakthrough whose characteristics the planners can foresee, but whose timing they cannot at present determine. (The discovery of a new manufacturing process for high-strength, thermally resistant aircraft bodies would be an example of this.)
- An economic recession which would lead to loss of orders for commercial aircraft and would change the pattern of spending for military aircraft.
- A major economic depression.
- A limited war which would sharply increase the demand for air industry products.
- A sudden cessation of cold war, a currently popular hope which has waxed and waned with changes in Soviet behavior.

The two types of sales forecast are illustrated in Exhibit XIII for a hypothetical company. Sales curves $S_1$ and $S_2$ represent a spread of trend forecasts, and $S_3$ and $S_4$, two contingent forecasts for the same event. The difference between the two types, both in starting time and effect on sales, lies in the degree of uncertainty associated with each.

In the case of trend forecasts we can trace a crude time history of sales based on events which we fully expect to happen. Any uncertainty arises from not knowing exactly when they will take place and how they will influence business. In the case of contingency forecasts, we can again trace a crude time history, but our uncertainty is greater. We lack precise knowledge of not only *when* the event will occur but also *whether* it will occur. In going from a trend to a contingency forecast, we advance, so to speak, one notch up the scale of ignorance.

In considering the relative weight we should give to contingent events in diversification planning, we must consider not only the magnitude of their effect on sales, but also the relative probability of their occurrence. For example, if a deep economic depression were to occur, its effect on many industries would be devastating. Many companies feel safe in neglecting it in their planning, however, be-

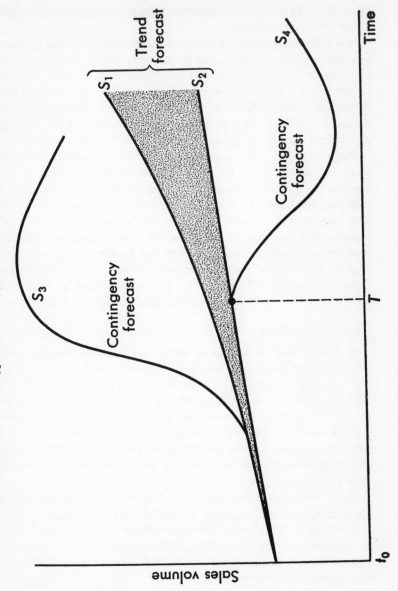

EXHIBIT XIII. A Hypothetical Company Forecast—*No Diversification*

cause they feel that the likelihood of a deep depression is very small, at least for the near future.

It is a common business practice to put primary emphasis on trend forecasts; in fact, in many cases businessmen devote their long-range planning exclusively to these forecasts. They usually view a possible catastrophe as "something one cannot plan for" or as a second-order correction to be applied only after the trends have been taken into account. The emphasis is on planning for growth, and planning for contingencies is viewed as an "insurance policy" against reversals.

People familiar with planning problems in the military establishment will note here an interesting difference between military and business atitudes. While business planning emphasizes trends, military planning emphasizes contingencies. To use a crude analogy, a business planner is concerned with planning for continuous, successful, day-after-day operation of a supermarket. If he is progressive, he also buys an insurance policy against fire, but he spends relatively little time in planning for fires. The military is more like the fire engine company; the fire is the thing. Day-to-day operations are of interest only as they serve to improve readiness and fire-fighting techniques.

*Unforeseeable Events*

So far we have dealt with diversification forecasts based on what may be called *foreseeable* market conditions—conditions which we can interpret in terms of time-phased sales curves. Planners have a tendency to stop here, to disregard the fact that, in addition to the events for which we can draw time histories, there is a recognizable class of events to which we can assign a probability of occurrence but which we cannot otherwise describe in our present state of knowledge. One must move another notch up the scale of ignorance to consider these possibilities.

Many businessmen feel that the effort is not worthwhile. They argue that since no information is available about these unforeseeable circumstances, one might as well devote the available time and energy to planning for the foreseeable circumstances, or that, in a very general sense, planning for the foreseeable also prepares one for the unforeseeable contingencies.

In contrast, more experienced military and business people have a very different attitude. Well aware of the importance and relative probability of unforeseeable events, they ask why one should plan specific steps for the foreseeable events while neglecting the really important possibilities. They may substitute for such planning practical maxims for conducting one's business—"be solvent," "be light on your feet," "be flexible." Unfortunately, it is not always clear (even to the people who preach it) what this flexibility means.

An interesting study by The Brookings Institution [3] provides an example of the importance of the unforeseeable events to business. Exhibit XIV shows the changing make-up of the list of the one hundred largest corporations over the last fifty years. Of the one hundred largest on the 1909 list (represented by the heavy marble texture) only thirty-six were among the one hundred largest in 1948; only about half of the new entries to the list in 1919 (represented by white) were left in 1948; less than half of the new entries in 1929 (represented by the zigzag design) were left in 1948; and so on. Clearly, a majority of the giants of yesteryear have dropped behind in a relatively short span of time.

Many of the events that hurt these corporations could not be specifically foreseen in 1909. If the companies which dropped from the original list had made forecasts of the foreseeable kind at that time—and some of them must have—they would very likely have found the future growth prospects to be excellent. Since then, however, railroads, which loomed as the primary means of transportation, have given way to the automobile and the airplane; the textile industry, which appeared to have a built-in demand in an expanding world population, has been challenged and dominated by synthetics; radio, radar, and television have created means of communication unforeseeable in significance and scope; and many other sweeping changes have occurred.

## Planning for the Unknown

The lessons of the past fifty years are fully applicable today. The pace of economic and technological change is so rapid that it is virtually certain that major breakthroughs comparable to those of the last fifty years, but not yet foreseeable in scope and character, will profoundly change the structure of the national economy. All of this

[3] A. D. H. Kaplan, *op. cit.*

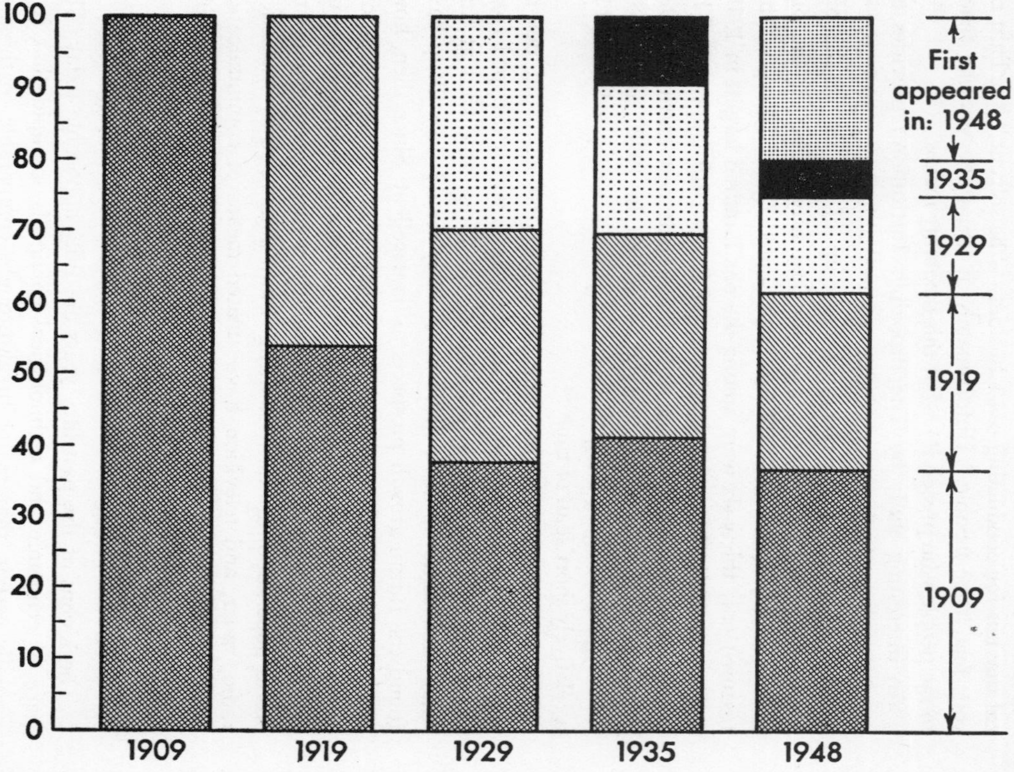

EXHIBIT XIV.  Changes in List of the 100 Largest Industrial Corporations

has important implications for diversification, as suggested by the Brookings Study:

The majority of the companies included among the one hundred largest of our day have attained their positions within the last two decades. They are companies that have started new industries or have transformed old ones to create or meet consumer preferences. The companies that have not only grown in absolute terms but have gained an improved position in their own industry may be identified as companies that are notable for drastic changes made in their product mix and methods, generating or responding to new competition.

There are two outstanding cases in which the industry leader of 1909 had by 1948 risen in position relative to its own industry group and also in rank among the one hundred largest—one in chemicals and the other in electrical equipment. These two (General Electric and DuPont) are hardly recognizable as the same companies they were in 1909 except for retention of the name; for in each case the product mix of 1948 is vastly different from what it was in the earlier year, and the markets in which the companies meet competition are. incomparably broader than those that accounted for their earlier place at the top of their industries. They exemplify the flux in the market positions of the most successful industrial giants during the past four decades and a general growth rather than a consolidation of supremacy in a circumscribed line.[4]

This suggests that the existence of specific undesirable trends is not the only reason for diversification. A broader product line may be called for even with optimistic forecasts for present products. An examination of the foreseeable alternatives should be accompanied by an analysis of how well the over-all company product-market strategy covers the so-called growth areas of technology—areas of many potential discoveries. If such analysis shows that, because of its product lines, a company's chances of taking advantage of important discoveries are limited, management should broaden its technological and economic base by entering a number of so-called "growth industries." Even if the definable horizons look bright, a need for flexibility, in the widest sense of the word, may provide potent reasons for diversification.

## DIVERSIFICATION OBJECTIVES

If an analysis of trends and contingencies indicates that a company

[4] *Ibid.*, p. 142.

should diversify, where should it look for diversification opportunities?

Generally speaking, there are three types of opportunities:

1. Each product manufactured by a company is made up of functional components, parts, and basic materials which go into the final assembly. A manufacturing concern usually buys a large fraction of these from outside suppliers. One way to diversify, commonly known as *vertical diversification,* is to branch out into production of components, parts, and materials. Perhaps the most outstanding example of vertical diversification is the Ford empire in the days of Henry Ford, Sr.

At first glance, vertical diversification seems inconsistent with our definition of a diversification strategy. However, the respective missions which components, parts, and materials are designed to perform are distinct from the mission of the over-all product. Furthermore, the technology in fabrication and manufacture of these parts and materials is likely to be very different from the technology of manufacturing the final product. Thus, vertical diversification does imply both catering to new missions and introduction of new products.

2. Another possible way to go is *horizontal diversification.* This can be described as the introduction of new products which, while they do not contribute to the present product line in any way, cater to missions which lie within the company's know-how and experience in technology, finance, and marketing.

3. It is also possible, by *lateral diversification,* to move beyond the confines of the industry to which a company belongs. This obviously opens a great many possibilities, from operating banana boats to building atomic reactors. While vertical and horizontal diversification are restrictive, in the sense that they delimit the field of interest, lateral diversification is "wide open." It is an announcement of the company's intent to range far afield from its present market structure.

## Choice of Direction

How does a company choose among these diversification directions? In part the answer depends on the reasons which prompt diversification. For example, in the light of the trends described for the aircraft industry, an aircraft company may make the following moves to meet long-range sales objectives through diversification:

1. A vertical diversification move to contribute to the technological progress of the present product line.

2. A horizontal move to improve the coverage of the military market.

3. A horizontal move to increase the percentage of commercial sales in the over-all sales program.

4. A lateral move to stabilize sales in case of a recession.

5. A lateral move to broaden the company's technological base.

Some of these diversification objectives apply to characteristics of the product, some to those of the product missions. Each objective is designed to improve some aspect of the balance between the over-all product-market strategy and the expected environment. The specific objectives derived for any given case can be grouped into three general categories: *growth objectives,* such as objectives (1), (2), and (3) above, which are designed to improve the balance under favorable trend conditions; *stability objectives,* such as (3) and (4), designed as protection against unfavorable trends and foreseeable contingencies; and *flexibility objectives,* such as (5), to strengthen the company against unforeseeable contingencies.

A diversification direction which is highly desirable for one of the objectives is likely to be less desirable for others. For example:

If a company is diversifying because its sales trend shows a declining volume of demand, it would be unwise to consider vertical diversification, since this would be at best a temporary device to stave off an eventual decline of business.

If the company's industry shows every sign of healthy growth, then vertical and, in particular, horizontal diversification would be a desirable device for strengthening the position of the company in a field in which its knowledge and experience are concentrated.

If the major concern is stability under a contingent forecast, chances are that both horizontal and vertical diversification could not provide a sufficient stabilizing influence and that lateral action is indicated.

If management's concern is with the narrowness of the technological base in the face of what we have called unforeseeable contingencies, then lateral diversification into new areas of technology would be clearly called for.

*Measured Sales Goals*

Management can and should state the objectives of growth and stability in quantitative terms as *long-range sales objectives*. This is illustrated in Exhibit XV. The solid lines describe a hypothetical company's forecasted performance without diversification under a general trend, represented by the sales curve marked $S_1$, and in a contingency, represented by $S_2$. The dashed lines show the improved performance as a result of diversification, with $S_3$ representing the curve with a continuation of normal trends and $S_4$ representing the curve in case of a major reverse.

*Growth.* Management's first aim in diversifying is to improve the growth pattern of the company. We can state the growth objective as follows:

Under trend conditions the growth rate of sales after diversification should exceed the growth rate of sales of the original product line by a minimum specified margin. Or to illustrate in shorthand, the objective for the company in Exhibit XV would be:

$$S_3 - S_1 \geqslant \rho$$

where the value of the margin $\rho$ is specified for each year after diversification.

Some companies (particularly in the growth industries) fix an annual rate of growth which they wish to attain. Every year this rate of growth is compared to the actual growth during the past year. A decision on diversification action for the coming year is then based on the disparity between the objective and the actual rate of growth.

*Stability.* The second effect desired of diversification is improvement in company stability under contingent conditions. Not only should diversification prevent sales from dropping as low as they might have before diversification, but the percentage drop should also be lower. The second sales objective is thus a stability objective. It can be stated as follows:

Under contingent conditions the percentage drop in sales which may occur without diversification should exceed the percentage drop in sales with diversification by an adequate margin, or algebraically:

$$\frac{S_1 - S_2}{S_1} - \frac{S_3 - S_4}{S_3} \geqslant \delta$$

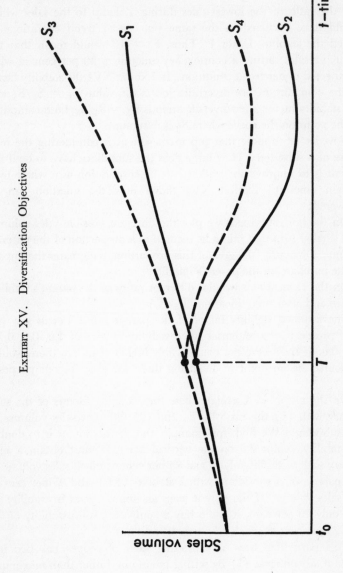

EXHIBIT XV. Diversification Objectives

Using this equation, it is possible to relate the sales volumes before and after diversification to a rough measure of the resulting stability. Let the ratio of the lowest sales during a slump to the sales which would have occurred in the same year under trend conditions be called the stability factor F. Thus, $F = 0.3$ would mean that the company sales during a contingency amount to 30 per cent of what is expected under trend conditions. In Exhibit XVI the stability factor of the company before diversification is the value $F_1 = S_2/S_1$ and the stability factor after diversification is $F_3 = S_4/S_3$, both computed at the point on the curve where $S_2$ is minimum.

Now let us suppose that top management is considering the purchase of a subsidiary. How large does the subsidiary have to be if the parent is to improve the stability of the corporation as a whole by a certain amount? Exhibit XVI shows how the question can be answered:

On the horizontal axis we plot the different possible sales volumes of a smaller firm that might be secured as a proportion of the parent's volume. Obviously, the greater this proportion, the greater the impact of the purchase on the parent's stability.

On the vertical axis we plot different ratios of the parent's stability before and after diversification $(F_3/F_1)$.

The assumed stability factor of the parent is 0.3. Let us say that four prospective subsidiaries have stability factors of 1.0, 0.9, 0.75, and 0.6. If they were not considerably higher than 0.3, there would, of course, be no point in acquiring them (at least for our purposes here).

On the graph we correlate these four stability factors of the subsidiary with (1) the ratio $F_3/F_1$ and (2) different sales volumes of the subsidiary. We find, for example, that if the parent is to double its stability (point 2.0 on the vertical axis), it must obtain a subsidiary with a stability of 1.0 and 75 per cent as much sales volume as the parent, or a subsidiary with a stability of 0.9 and 95 per cent of the sales volume. If the parent seeks an improvement in stability of, say, only 40 per cent, it could buy a company with a stability of 0.9 and 25 per cent as much sales volume as it has.

This particular way of expressing sales objectives has two important advantages: (1) By setting minimum, rather than maximum, limits on growth, it leaves room for the company to take advantage

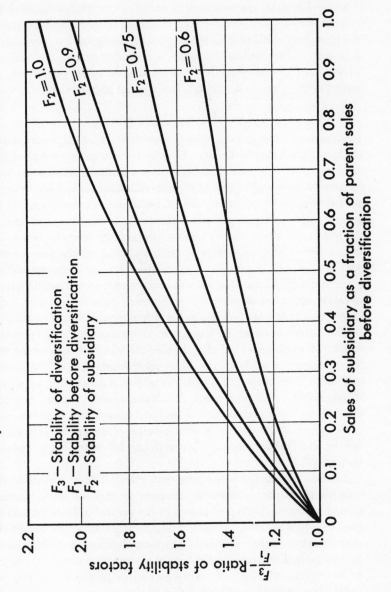

EXHIBIT XVI. Improvement in Stability Factor as a Result of Diversification for $F_1 = 0.3$

of unusual growth opportunities in order to exceed these goals, and thus provides definite goals without inhibiting initiative and incentive. (2) It takes account of the time-phasing of diversification moves; and since these moves invariably require a transition period, the numerical values of growth objectives can be allowed to vary from year to year so as to allow for a gradual development of operations.

## LONG-RANGE OBJECTIVES

Diversification objectives specify directions in which a company's product-market should change. Usually there will be several objectives indicating different and sometimes conflicting directions. If a company attempts to follow all of them simultaneously, it is in danger of spreading itself too thin and of becoming a conglomeration of incompatible, although perhaps individually profitable enterprises.

There are cases of diversification which have followed this path. In a majority of cases, however, there are valid reasons why a company should seek to preserve certain basic unifying characteristics as it goes through a process of growth and change. Consequently, diversification objectives should be supplemented by a statement of long-range product-market objectives. For instance:

One consistent course of action is to adopt a product-market policy which will preserve a kind of technological coherence among the different manufactures with the focus on the products of the parent company. Thus, a company which is mainly distinguished for a type of engineering and production excellence would continue to select product-market entries which would strengthen and maintain this excellence. Perhaps the best known example of such policy is exemplified by the DuPont slogan, "Better things for better living through chemistry."

Another approach is to set long-term growth policy in terms of the breadth of market which the company intends to cover. It may choose to confine its diversifications to the vertical or horizontal direction, or it may select a type of lateral diversification controlled by the characteristics of the missions to which the company intends to cater. For example, a company in the field of air transportation may expand its interest to all forms of transportation of people and cargo. To paraphrase DuPont, some slogan like "Better transportation for better living through advanced engineering," would be descriptive of such a long-range policy.

A greatly different policy is to emphasize primarily the financial characteristics of the corporation. This method of diversification generally places no limits on engineering and manufacturing characteristics of new products, although in practice the competence and interests of management will usually provide some orientation for diversification moves. The company makes the decisions regarding the distribution of new acquisitions exclusively on the basis of financial considerations. Rather than a manufacturing entity, the corporate character is now one of a "holding company." Top management delegates a large share of its product-planning and administrative functions to the divisions and concerns itself largely with coordination, financial problems, and building up a balanced "portfolio of products" within the corporate structure.

## Successful Alternatives

These alternative long-range policies demonstrate the extremes. No one course is necessarily better than the others. Management's choice rests in large part on its preferences, objectives, skills, and training. The aircraft industry illustrates the fact that there is more than one successful path to diversification:

Among the major successful airframe manufacturers, Douglas Aircraft Company, Inc., and Boeing Airplane Company, have to date limited their growth to horizontal diversification into missiles and new markets for new types of aircraft. Lockheed has carried horizontal diversification further to include aircraft maintenance, aircraft service, and production of ground-handling equipment.

North American Aviation, Incorporated, on the other hand, appears to have chosen vertical diversification by establishing its subsidiaries in Atomics International, Autonetics, and Rocketdyne, thus providing a basis for manufacture of complete air vehicles of the future.

Bell Aircraft Corporation has adopted a policy of technological consistency among the members of its product line. It has diversified laterally but primarily into types of products for which it had previous know-how and experience.

General Dynamics Corporation provides a further interesting contrast. It has gone far into lateral diversification. Among major manufacturers of air vehicles, it comes closest to the "holding company" extreme. Its airplanes and missile manufacturing operations in Convair are paralleled by production of submarines in the Electric Boat Division; military, industrial, and consumer electronic products in the Stromberg-Carlson Division; and electric motors in the Electro Dynamic Division.

## SELECTING A STRATEGY

In the preceding sections qualitative criteria for diversification have been discussed. How should management apply these criteria to individual opportunities? Two steps should be taken: (1) apply the qualitative standards in order to narrow the field of diversification opportunities; (2) apply the numerical criteria to select the preferred strategy or strategies.

### Qualitative Evaluation

The long-range product-market policy is used as a criterion for the first rough cut in the qualitative evaluation. It can be used to divide a large field of opportunities into classes of diversification moves consistent with the company's basic character. For example, a company whose policy is to compete on the basis of the technical excellence of its products would eliminate as inconsistent classes of consumer products which are sold on the strength of advertising appeal rather than superior quality.

Next, the company can compare each individual diversification opportunity, which is consistent with the long-range objectives, with individual diversification objectives. This process tends to eliminate opportunities which, while consistent with the desired product-market make-up, are nevertheless likely to lead to an imbalance between the company product line and the probable environment. For example, a company which wishes to preserve and expand its technical excellence in design of large, highly stressed machines controlled by feedback techniques may find consistent product opportunities both inside and outside the industry to which it caters. If a major diversification objective of this company is to correct cyclic variations in demand that are characteristic of the industry, it would choose opportunities which lie outside.

Each diversification opportunity which has gone through the two screening steps satisfies at least one diversification objective, but probably it will not satisfy all of them. Therefore, before subjecting them to the quantitative evaluation, it is necessary to group them into several alternative over-all company product-market strategies, composed of the original strategy and one or more of the remaining diversification strategies. These alternative over-all strategies should be roughly equivalent in meeting all of the diversification objectives.

At this stage it is particularly important to allow for the unforeseeable contingencies. Since the techniques of numerical evaluation are applicable only to trends and foreseeable contingencies, it is important to make sure that the different alternatives chosen give the company a broad enough technological base. In practice this process is less formidable than it may appear. For example, a company in the aircraft industry has to consider the areas of technology in which major discoveries are likely to affect the future of the industry. This would include atomic propulsion, certain areas of electronics, automation of complex processes, and so forth. In designing alternative over-all strategies the company would then make sure that each contains product entries which will give the company a desirable and comparable degree of participation in these future growth areas.

Exhibit XVII summarizes the foregoing steps.

EXHIBIT XVII. STEPS IN QUALITATIVE EVALUATION

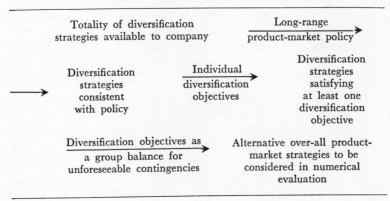

## Quantitative Evaluation

Will the company's product-market strategies make money? Will the profit structure improve as a result of their adoption? The purpose of quantitative evaluation is to compare the profit potential of the alternatives.

Unfortunately, there is no single yardstick among those commonly used in business that gives an accurate measurement of performance. The techniques currently used for measurement of business performance constitute, at best, an imprecise art. It is common to measure different aspects of performance by applying different tests. Thus, tests of income adequacy measure the earning ability of the business; tests of debt coverage and liquidity measure preparedness for contingencies; the shareholders' position measures attractiveness to investors; tests of sales efficiency and personnel productivity measure efficiency in the use of money, physical assets, and personnel. These tests employ a variety of different performance ratios, such as return on sales, return on net worth, return on assets, turnover of net worth, and ratio of assets to liabilities. The total number of ratios may run as high as twenty in a single case.

In the final evaluation which immediately precedes a diversification decision management would normally apply all of these tests, tempered with business judgment. However, for the purpose of preliminary elimination of alternatives, a single test is frequently used—return on investment, a ratio between earnings and the capital invested in producing these earnings. While the usefulness of return on investment is commonly accepted, there is considerable room for argument regarding its limitations and its practical application.[5] Fundamentally, the difficulty with the concept is that it fails to provide an absolute measure of business performance applicable to a range of very different industries; also, the term "investment" is subject to a variety of interpretations.

But, since our aim is to use the concept as a measure of relative performance of different diversification strategies, we need not be concerned with its failure to measure absolute values. And as long as we are consistent in our definition of investment in alternative courses of action, the question of terminology is not so troublesome. We cannot define profit-producing capital in general terms, but we

[5] See Charles R. Schwarz, *The Return-on-Investment Concept as a Tool for Decision Making*, General Management Series No. 183 (New York, American Management Association, 1956), pp. 42–61; Peter F. Drucker, *The Practice of Management* (New York, Harper & Brothers, 1954); and Edward M. Barnet, "Showdown in the Market Place," HBR July–August 1956, p. 85.

can define it in each case in the light of particular business characteristics and practices (such as the extent of government-owned assets, depreciation practices, inflationary trends).

For the numerator of our return on investment, we can use net earnings after taxes. A going business concern has standard techniques for estimating its future earnings. These depend on the projected sales volume, tax structure, trends in material and labor costs, productivity, and so forth. If the diversification opportunity being considered is itself a going concern, its profit projections can be used for estimates of combined future earnings. If the opportunity is a new venture, its profit estimates should be made on the basis of the average performance for the industry.

## Changes in Investment Structure

A change in the investment structure of the diversifying company accompanies a diversification move. The source of investment for the new venture may be: (1) excess capital, (2) capital borrowed at an attractive rate, (3) an exchange of the company's equity for an equity in another company, or (4) capital withdrawn from present business operations.

If we let $i_1$, $i_2$, $i_3$, and $i_4$, respectively, represent investments made in the new product in the preceding four categories during the first year of diversified operations, we can derive a simple expression for the *improvement* in return on investment which will result from diversification:

$$\triangle R = \frac{(p_2 - p_1)(i_2 + i_3 + i_4) + (p_2 - r)i_1 - i_2 r + (p_1 - r)(i_2 + i_3)i_1/I}{I + i_2 + i_3},$$

where $p_1$ and $p_2$ represent the average return on capital invested in the original product and in the new product, respectively, and quantity $I$ is the total capital in the business before diversification.

We can easily check this expression by assuming that only one type of new investment will be made at a time. We can then use the formula to compute the conditions under which it pays to diversify (that is, conditions where $\triangle R$ is greater than zero):

1. If excess capital is the only source of new investment ($i_2 = i_3 = i_4 = 0$), this condition is $p_2 - r > 0$. That is, return on diversi-

fied operations should be more attractive than current rates for capital on the open market.

2. If only borrowed capital is used ($i_1 = i_3 = i_4 = 0$), it pays to diversify if $p_2 - p_1 > r$. That is, the difference between return from diversification and return from the original product should be greater than the interest rate on the money.

3. If the diversified operation is to be acquired through an exchange of equity or through internal reallocation of capital, then $p_2 - p_1 > 0$ is the condition under which diversification will pay off.

## A Comprehensive Yardstick

The formula for $\triangle R$ just stated is not sufficiently general to serve as a measure of profit potential. It gives improvement in return for the first year only and for a particular sales trend. In order to provide a reasonably comprehensive comparison between alternative over-all company strategies, the yardstick for profit potential should possess the following properties:

1. Since changes in the investment structure of the business invariably accompany diversification, the yardstick should reflect these changes. It should also take explicit account of new capital brought into the business and changes in the rate of capital formation resulting from diversification, as well as costs of borrowed capital.

2. Usually the combined performance of the new and the old product-market lines is not a simple sum of their separate performances; it should be greater. The profit potential yardstick should take account of this nonlinear characteristic.

3. Each diversification move is characterized by a transition period during which readjustment of the company structure to new operating conditions takes place. The benefits of a diversification move may not be realized fully for some time, so the measurement of profit potential should span a sufficient length of time to allow for effects of the transition.

4. Since both profits and investments will be spread over time, the yardstick should use their present value.

5. Business performance will differ depending on the particular economic-political environment. The profit potential yardstick must somehow average out the probable effect of alternative environments.

6. The statement of sales objectives, as pointed out previously,

should specify 'the general characteristics of growth and stability which are desired. Profit potential functions should be compatible with these characteristics.

We can generalize our formula in a way which will meet most of the preceding requirements. The procedure is to write an expression for the present value of $\triangle R$ for an arbitrary year, t, allowing for possible yearly diversification investments up to the year t, interest rates, and the rate of capital formation. Then this present value is averaged over time as well as over the alternative sales forecasts. The procedure is straightforward (although the algebra involved is too cumbersome to be worth reproducing here [6]). The result, which is the "average expected present value of $\triangle R$," takes account of conditions (1) through (5), above. Let us call it $(\triangle R)_e$. It can be computed using data normally found in business and financial forecasts.

## Final Evaluation

This brings us to the final step in the evaluation. We have discussed a qualitative method for constructing several over-all product-market strategies which meet the diversification and the long-range objectives. We can now compute $(\triangle R)_e$ for each of the over-all strategies and, at the same time, make sure that the strategies satisfy the sales objectives previously stated, thus fulfilling condition (6), above.

If product-market characteristics, which we have used to narrow the field of choice and to compute $(\triangle R)_e$, were the sole criteria, then the strategy with the highest $(\triangle R)_e$ would be the "preferred" path to diversification. However, the advantages of a particular product-market opportunity must be balanced against the chances of business success.

## CONCLUSION

A study of diversification histories shows that a company usually arrives at a decision to make a particular move through a multistep process. The planners' first step is to determine the preferred areas for search; the second is to select a number of diversification opportunities within these areas and to subject them to a preliminary

[6] See H. Igor Ansoff, *A Model for Diversification* (Burbank, Lockheed Aircraft Corporation, 1957); and John Burr Williams, *The Theory of Investment Value* (Amsterdam, The North-Holland Publishing Co., 1938).

evaluation. They then make a final evaluation, conducted by the top management, leading to selection of a specific step; finally, they work out details and complete the move.

Throughout this process, the company seeks to answer two basic questions: How well will a particular move, if it is successful, meet the company objectives? What are the company's chances of making it a success? In the early stages of the program, the major concern is with business strategy. Hence, the first question plays a dominant role. But as the choice narrows, considerations of business ability, of the particular strengths and weaknesses which a company brings to diversification, shift attention to the second question.

This discussion has been devoted primarily to selection of a diversification strategy. We have dealt with what may be called *external* aspects of diversification—the relation between a company and its environment. To put it another way, we have derived a method for measuring the profit potential of a diversification strategy, but we have not inquired into the *internal* factors which determine the ability of a diversifying company to make good this potential. A company planning diversification must consider such questions as how the company should organize to conduct the search for and evaluation of diversification opportunities; what method of business expansion it should employ; and how it should mesh its operations with those of a subsidiary. These considerations give rise to a new set of criteria for the *business fit* of the prospective venture. These must be used in conjunction with $(\triangle R)_e$ computed in the preceding section to determine which of the over-all product-market strategies should be chosen for implementation.

Thus, the steps outlined in this article are the first, though an important, preliminary to a diversification move. Only through further careful consideration of probable business success can a company develop a long-range strategy that will enable it to "run twice as fast as that" (using the Red Queen's words again) in the ever-changing world of today.

# 44.

# Guideposts for Forward Planning

## By Weldon B. Gibson [1]

Successful long-range business planning, and attainment of these plans, rests finally on business judgment, initiative, enthusiasm, and drive no matter what else is done or occurs. Naturally, a good product, process, or service must be offered. But the spirit of an organization springs from the very top; and the spirit must be right if an organization is to plan and grow successfully.

A prophecy of doom and gloom flowing down through a business soon stifles even the best of companies. On the other hand, an air of confidence in the future coming from the top soon infects an organization with drive and enthusiasm. The differences in spirit among companies often are subtle and hard to detect, but nevertheless they do exist. I am convinced that many companies have opportunities to succeed largely because they give the impression of being successful, on the move, dynamic, imaginative, and willing to invest patient money. Similarly, many companies decline in time because they somehow give an impression of being negative, self-satisfied, self-sufficient, hesitant, and seekers of the status quo. We might even say that a prerequisite for effective business planning in any company is an enthusiasm for growth and development.

We can take it as a heartening sign when leading businessmen of this country publicly express confidence in the future of their companies, their industry, and the country as a whole. Consider the im-

[1] Reprinted by permission of the author from *Proceedings, Industrial Economics Conference* (Menlo Park, California, Stanford Research Institute, 1956).

pact of Robert E. Wood's faith in the country in 1945 and 1946 when Sears, Roebuck launched a growth plan just when many people expected a major business decline. The important point in all of this, as a guidepost for business planning, is that today, more than ever before, industry is making ambitious plans for the future. Optimism is the keynote even in spite of troublesome international problems.

This so-called spirit of the times is a significant economic reality. Many economists, Dr. Sumner Slichter among them, maintain that the very fact of business planning on a grand scale works as a balance wheel on the business cycle and on long-term trends. In other words, planning for the future, and making business decisions on this basis, affects the economy of our nation in a profound way.

The entire idea of long-range planning is based in many ways upon concepts of the future as they arise in the collective minds of business leaders. There are indications that mere faith in the future is one force working to bring about conditions making up this future. Is it possible that this force may be stronger than it at first appears? At least one eminent social scientist believes this to be the case.

## "IMAGES OF THE FUTURE"

In a book selected for the 1954 Council of Europe Award, Dr. Fred Polak, a Dutch economist, businessman, and social scientist, develops a theory that the future of a civilization, a country, or a people is determined in large measure by their "images of the future," their dreams, doubts, aspirations, and fears. He contends that it is possible to measure these "images of the future," that it may be possible to alter or adjust them, and thus to guide a nation's or people's future. His two-volume work, *The Future Is Past Tense,* is now being translated for English publication.

According to Polak, if a society has optimistic ideas, dynamic aspirations, and cohesive ambitions, the civilization will grow and prosper. If it exhibits negative trends, uncertain ideals, and hesitant faith, then the society is in danger of disintegrating. The idea again is that by *thinking* about the future, man creates that same future according to his image.

It is easy to see that an "image of the future" has a bearing on long-range thinking in government, international affairs, and in broad social studies. But, does it have a place in business thinking?

Polak thinks the answer is yes. All of our great industrial enterprises grow on the strength of a leading image of the future whether these images be conscious or unconscious. Industrial expansion, consumer habits, and the world of advertising and public relations all depend upon an image created or stimulated both among producers and consumers.

In one sense, every long-range plan by an industrial organization is its image of the future. Certainly, the General Motors management in its billion-dollar expansion announcements is reflecting a collective image of the future. One of the surest ways to tear down some of the guideposts erected would be for American business in general to perceive gloomy and negative images of the future. One of the best ways to benefit from our guideposts is to see them as images of the future and to believe in their attainment.

But we know that mere believing, no matter how significant, is not enough in the business world. We must have action, we must have practical guidelines. There are problems to be sure, though the general outlook may be good.

Business and industry must have money in great quantities if they are to plan and grow for the future. The final source of this money is business profits. Our thinking, our governing, our economic philosophy must recognize this fact. For if industry is unable to make the advances upon which our proposition is based—then we are in for trouble. It is encouraging that our country seems to be moving in the right direction on business policy. We must keep up the momentum. Our wealth is created in industry; it has a big job to do between now and 1975; industry must keep up with our expanding needs.

In keeping with the long view, we have given the spotlight to several guideposts for planning. Not the least of them is faith in the years to come, a faith bolstered by the onrush of applied science. One day in early 1945 Robert E. Wood illustrated the point when he spoke to me along these lines: "My picture of the future is a country ten years hence with double our economic activity spurred on by an exploding technology. I lay my business plans on this picture."

Maybe we are too conservative. He missed the mark by only about 10 per cent.